SECOND CAREERS

S E C O N D

CAREERS

New Ways to Work After 50

Caroline Bird

LITTLE, BROWN AND COMPANY

BOSTON   TORONTO   LONDON

First Edition

Library of Congress Cataloging-in-Publication Data

Bird, Caroline.
    Second careers : new ways to work after 50 / Caroline
Bird — 1st ed.
        p.   cm.
    ISBN 0-316-09598-2 (hc)
    ISBN 0-316-09599-0 (pb)
    1. Retirees — Employment — United States. 2. Ca-
reer   changes — United States. 3. Aged — Employment — United States.   I. Title.
HD6280.B57   1992
650.14'084'6 — dc20   91-20604

        HC: 10   9   8   7   6   5   4   3   2   1
        PB: 10   9   8   7   6   5   4   3   2   1
                        MV-NY

Published simultaneously in Canada by Little, Brown
& Company (Canada) Limited

Printed in the United States of America

For
Carol and John

CONTENTS

ACKNOWLEDGMENTS

Second Careers started as a reader-participation questionnaire in *Modern Maturity* magazine. As the unexpectedly high volume of responses rolled in, the project became a cottage industry involving computer specialists, coders, inputters, interviewers, occupational classifiers, a vocational psychologist, and a reference librarian.

The project would never have become a book without the support of Linda Hubbard, then managing editor of *Modern Maturity,* and Rob Wood, then publications director of the American Association of Retired People; Patricia Haskell, a longtime friend and veteran book editor, who helped design the book proposal; Marjorie Godfrey, another longtime friend and colleague, who lent her expertise to the design of the questionnaire, and her husband, Dick Godfrey, who advised me on the hardware and software required to cope with what Marge and I were dreaming up.

Although the book is my responsibility alone, AARP generously supported the research behind it with a one-time grant outside any of their regular research programs. For this support I am indebted to Martha Ramsey, now deputy director of the Communications Division at AARP; David Gamse, former director of the Worker Equity Department; as well as Richard Kriner, director of Survey Design and Analysis.

For help in resolving the many policy issues raised by this unique project, I am indebted to Ken Norwick, my lawyer of many years, and Peter Greenwald of Miller, Singer, Raives and Brandes. Both of them proved that lawyers can be creative in seeing how to do something new while protecting their clients.

Dr. Donald G. Zytowski, a counseling psychologist specializing in career assessment, the creator of the quiz, and Roberta Walsh, the creator of the Resource section, contributed to the general concept of the book as well as to the sections of text carrying their bylines.

In addition to Dick Godfrey, Ann Formica, Chris Perkins, and Chuck Ferguson were innovative in getting anything we wanted out of our computer and faithful in keeping it running.

Processing the responses involved a long list of people who found the program interesting enough to sell us a little of their time. Leslie Koempel, Emeritus Professor of Sociology at Vassar, and Sheila Newman of TRQ Enterprises advised us on the fine points of questionnaire wording and tabulation.

Paul Goldschmidt coordinated the coding and inputting by Vassar College students. Marjorie Godfrey coordinated a crew in Raleigh, N.C., which included Carol Collier, Linda Graybeal, Lorna Henderson, and Priscilla Westberg. Catherine Chambers, Susan Dorler, and Anna Feldweg were other people who coded in Poughkeepsie.

Interviewing for us were Sue Amkraut, Carol Barach, Mary Bodel, Susan Dorler, William Draves, Robert Finegan, Nancy Holtzman, Brian O'Connor, Lyn and Greg Priest-Dorman, Jean Theobald, and Virginia Roth.

Government authorities were generous in helping us cope with the anomalies of occupational titles. At the U.S. Department of Labor we are indebted especially to Paul Hadlock, supervisory economist, and John C. Thompson, labor economist for the Bureau of Labor Statistics, for advising us to use the Occupational Employment Statistics (OES) Survey Occupations and providing us with enough of the thick indexes and manuals to go around for all the coders. Mike Pilot, manager of the Occupational Outlook Program, and Donald Zytowski critiqued the rather arbitrary way we finally clustered the 750 occupation titles in the OES.

At the state level, we are indebted to David Gillette, executive director of the Job Training Partnership Council, New York State Department of Education, and Jeremy Schrauf, Director, Research and Statistics, New York State Department of Labor, for advice on careers. Thanks are due also to the New York State Job Service Center in Poughkeepsie for advice and materials on coding.

Jan Davidson, senior research specialist in the AARP Research Information Center in Washington, DC, and Deborah Horowitz of the Adriance Library in Poughkeepsie were helpful in tracking down information for us.

Thanks go to editors and editorial workers at both *Modern Maturity* and Little, Brown, who were patient in dealing with an intricate product. At *Modern Maturity,* Alice Medina, then chief of Editorial Services, and Jackie Johnson Brown, who was then an editorial assistant, dealt with the thousands of questionnaires returned by mail. At Little, Brown, Ellen Denison was the editor who got the book off the ground, and after she left to take care of her baby, Colleen Mohyde was the editor who finished it.

SECOND CAREERS

I. THE WORK-MINDED SENIORS

L ooking for a second career you can start after you're 50?

Don't let anyone tell you that there's something wrong with you or your luck. On the contrary. The evidence shows that you are apt to be healthier, wealthier, and better educated than the general run of your agemates. Instead of a career failure, relegated to an occupational backwater, you are a pioneer of the new, flexible work-styles that go with our postindustrial economy.

If it doesn't feel that way, it's because the ideas in your head aren't keeping up with what's happening. Without fanfare or special advice, thousands of your agemates are finding second careers that fit the way they want to live their later years. They've done it, and as you read about the second careers of people with your experience, you'll think of new ways that you can do it too.

We haven't heard much about these work-minded seniors. When you get into your 50s, you're supposed to start looking forward to a life of leisure, yet all of us know seniors who are supplementing their retirement income with some kind of work, often in a field far removed from their main career. How are they making out? It sounded like a nice little magazine feature, so we put a questionnaire entitled "What's Your Second Career?" in the April–May 1988 issue of *Modern Maturity,* the magazine that then went to 27 million members of the American Association of Retired Persons (AARP) and their families. Members are all over 50, but the membership includes almost half the U.S. population over 55. In 1991 it was 33 million.

We expected a modest response — maybe 2,000 readers, 3,000 at most. But we had badly underestimated the interest of older people in working. As we coped with the mail, we couldn't help telling each other about the people who were writing us:

An executive who didn't like his company's new mangement quit to work for $9 an hour gauging tanks for oil wells.

A lawyer retired early to become a commercial salmon fisher in the Northwest.

A former "girl Friday" said her nerves broke under office pressures and is now happy grooming dogs for a living.

A shop superintendent with thirty-eight years of seniority who was caught in the restructure of his company is working for $4.20 an hour as a funeral attendant.

A sister of Saint Joseph left the order for a second career keeping house for her widowed brother's seven children.

A navy officer disturbed by what he saw in Vietnam went to divinity school and thinks he's a better Methodist minister for what he went through on the battlefield.

A travel escort likes her present work better than her longest job running the office for a plumbing and heating firm, but she's tired of cruises to Hawaii!

Replies kept pouring in until we had 36,000 of the little pink pages readers had torn out of the magazine, most of them crammed with handwritten personal explanations. We had stumbled into a big, fat cross section of detailed information about the second careers of older people unavailable anywhere else — data that deserved more than a magazine article.

With generous help from the AARP we braced to cope with twenty-two file boxes of questionnaires. The first problem was finding a way to classify them by the jobs the respondents were doing. When we went to the experts, we discovered that none of the systems put every worker into one and only one pigeonhole. Jobs and their titles change too fast for that. Specialists at the U.S. Department of Labor advised us to adopt their Occupational Employment Statistics (OES) system as the least troublesome.

Coding the jobs of real-life seniors was a workout. We know in a general way that older people are more various than youngsters: the yearbook pictures of high school seniors look much more alike than the pictures of the class at its fiftieth reunion. But we simply weren't prepared for the broad range of jobs seniors had found for themselves. The distribution of our seniors was different from that of the whole work force, but we eventually had someone in more than half of the 750 job titles in the OES dictionary.

We had too many different jobs to discuss each one individually, so we looked for a way to group them into clusters or families of jobs about which we could generalize. Labor-force analysts can get by with big, general groups such as "managerial and administrative occupations" and "professional, paraprofessional, and technical occupations," but that's not the way people actually doing these jobs think of themselves. All the groupings or job families we could find were designed for the convenience of employers, labor-force analysts, or vocational psychologists rather than job seekers attempting to make sense out of the help-wanted ads. The big popular labels aren't much help. There's no longer much difference between "white collar" and "blue collar": mechanics run health-care machines in hospitals, and the factory floor is awash with clerks. It's not even clear what's "professional." Tax preparers sound like accountants and accountants are professionals, but H&R Block has trained thousands of "tax preparers" who belong in the category "administrative support."

With the job seeker in mind, we set up twenty-eight job clusters (see Contents), but getting every job title into one or another of the clusters was as dicey as herding a fleet of eels through a revolving door. However we classified, somebody or something was always left behind, but after coding 6,347 records, we decided we had a reasonable sample of what seniors were doing.

Some jobs were so special that we created some dummy codes of our own for them. For instance, so many women were happy doing all the office work for a small enterprise, sometimes part time, that we coded them "one-person office" so that we could talk about an opportunity that is made to order for some older people (see Business Services).

The next job was to get them all into the computer. The write-ins were too revealing to pass by. How, for instance, could we afford to lose the former librarian who plans to retire "when I can afford opera and caviar weekly"? We ended by inputting every word written on the questionnaires.

We used DBaseIII$^+$, a program designed to find needles in haystacks. We could, for instance, call up all the people who had been involuntarily retired and find out not only how many were making more money than ever before, but where, and at what.

The open-ended questions led to important generalizations. We could get a good idea of what attracts older women to nursing by listing on a single printout the comments nurses made when asked to tell us what they liked about their jobs.

The possibilities were unnerving. To keep my sanity, I had to tear myself away from the computer and think hard about what a senior looking for a second career really wanted to know, which categories of people would have the answers, which individuals in each of those categories to call up, and what exactly to ask each one of them.

There was no problem getting people to talk. All but a few hundred gave us their phone numbers and freely shared their feelings, incomes, and strategies. Needless to say, we have concealed identities when we have reported facts that might cause embarrassment, even when we weren't asked to do so.

How representative were the 36,000 who took the trouble to fill out the questionnaire, find an envelope, and pay for their own stamp to tell us how they were doing? People who volunteer to return a questionnaire in a magazine may be a special breed. You would have to feel quite strongly about your second career to answer, so the questionnaire was a magnet to draw out of the population older people who were unusually interested in continuing to work.

What, if anything, was special about those who responded? To find out, we created what is known as a "purposive sample." We looked up census statistics on the work force over age 55 (the census age break) and deliberately made up a group of 2,102 respondents who matched the census in the proportion of people of each age, sex, and occupation. By comparing the sample that matched the census with the respondents in general we were able to get a rough idea of what kinds of seniors we had specially attracted.

FACTS ABOUT WORKERS OVER 50

Lower absenteeism
Higher work ethic
Higher productivity
Less alcoholism, drug use
Steadier, more patient
Stay with a job longer
As willing to learn

It's not the age, it's the condition!

There were important differences in age and sex. We seemed to have had a special attraction for older seniors: the average age of all our respondents over 55 was higher than that of the population of workers over 55 the census had reported. We had more women, more college graduates, and more executives and professionals. We were especially long on educated women with first careers in teaching, nursing, or office work.

As a group, our respondents were generally more fortunate than those who matched the census of workers over 55. They were more likely to say they loved their second careers; to have retired from their longest job voluntarily, usually on a pension; and to be working part time by choice. But we heard from the underprivileged, too, eloquent testimony to the pull of work for people who fall through the cracks of our public and private welfare systems.

Women had special problems. Older women were worse off than older men any way you take it. More of them said they were working primarily for money at jobs they didn't like. Those in the census match group were earning an average of only $6,650 a year compared with an average of $9,100 for men.

Women were less likely to have a public or private pension. Of those working past 62 years of age, 68 percent of the men but only 46 percent of the women had a private pension in addition to Social Security. And women who did have private pensions got lower benefits because their wages had been lower to begin with.

Seniors without pensions were pinched in unexpected ways. In California, a 68-year-old widow complained that she has to work twenty-four hours a week in a plastics factory to pay her $275 rent, but when she learned that her apartment house was to be torn down to make way for a flashy development, the only one-bedroom apartment she could find cost $500. And there was a catch-22: with Social Security her income is too high for any help with rent and utilities, so she expects to stare at the walls of the plastics plant for the rest of her life.

A man in upstate New York told us that he has to work two days a week at the city dump to get by and doesn't know what he'll do if they close it. A self-styled "working man" who isn't quite disabled enough to qualify for a benefit survives by binding books at home while his wife takes in sewing. The 66-year-old divorced mother of two handicapped children works a few hours a week in a school cafeteria so she'll have something put by in case she herself falls ill.

What about the involuntarily retired? About a fifth of our work-minded seniors were fired, laid off, "reorganized," or "downsized" out of a job they had held for years. A few of those who took the golden handshake of an early retirement package went on to more money or fun in a second career, but most of them settled — and often with amazing good cheer — for something much less rewarding. In West Virginia, for instance, a coal-mine examiner ("fire boss") responsible for safety lost his $50,000-a-year job when the company closed the mine in which he had worked for thirty-seven years, but he was able to beat out one hundred other applicants in his depressed town for a part-time job as a school custodian.

These sad stories hurt so much that they stick in memory, and rightly so. But they are the exceptions. Most of our respondents wanted to tell us how happy they were with the work they had found. Only 13 percent reported a problem with age discrimination, and two thirds said they had had no problems at all.

Most said they loved their present job, and while managers and professionals were more apt to love their jobs than store clerks, the enthusiasm didn't have as much to do with the pay as you might imagine. Two thirds of those who were earning $5 an hour or less in 1988 loved their jobs, and so did the volunteers who were earning no money at all.

Older workers were the most enthusiastic. The percentage who said they loved their jobs rose with age to 79 percent of those still working past 70. As one 80-year-old explained, "If I didn't love it, I'd stop doing it." Over a fifth of all our respondents planned to work until the day they died or at least as long as they could, and the percentage was even higher for lawyers, accountants, tax preparers, and people running their own business.

What are they doing? Most had made fairly radical changes. They had either moved out of the job cluster of their longest job, or were doing different tasks on a different schedule. Two thirds had to learn something new for their second career, and sometimes it was using a computer. Many took formal training or qualified for a license in school bus driving, cosmetology, home health care, nursing, lock-smithing, real estate, dress design, truck driving, psychotherapy, and library work, among other occupations.

Some learned new vocabularies: "computerese," "legalese," "trade lingo," scientific or artistic terms, even whole new languages, like the Southwesterners who learned Spanish. Many told us of surviving the culture shock of working with immigrants, volunteers, the retarded, "adolescent thought processes," and for one retired serviceman, "the civilian mentality." Quite a few reported learning to be "second banana," to be an "Indian instead of a chief," "to take orders instead of giving them," and "to keep my fat mouth shut."

It was not that their jobs were so wonderful. Most were working less than full time all year long, often on contract or commission, or in dead-end jobs without benefits. A surprising number of our seniors were happy doing the overlooked, incidental chores that are always falling out of the organization charts, the chores that are easy to forget but have to be done. These chores include inspecting property for the bank that holds the mortgage, making public address announcements at a ball game, making up flower arrangements for a florist, caring for the children of welfare mothers while they are being taught job skills, shuttling rental cars from site to site, starting golfers at the first tee, helping people fill out income tax forms.

Why do they love jobs that are supposed to be "bad"? Because they fit the kind of life they want to live in their later years. A few words come up again and again in the thousands of explanations they wrote us: *people, freedom, my own boss, variety, challenge, helping, flexible schedule*. Some liked the task itself because they wanted to work outdoors, with their hands, with animals or children, or because they enjoyed carpentry or the law. While money was the single most important reason for continuing to work, it did not motivate the majority, and very few were reaching for the status that money confers.

Our respondents wrote in because they were surprised — and happily for some — to find themselves still working in their later years. They thought of themselves as exceptions to the general rule of work life laid down by the New Deal in the Depression of the 1930s. Then and now, we think of the work force as a pyramid, like the military: lots of foot soldiers at the bottom, with a few generals at the top. If you were "labor," at the bottom, the idea was to get a good, steady job leading to retirement on a public and/or private pension. If you were "management" or exceptionally gifted or ambitious, the idea was to get your foot on the bottom rung of a career ladder and climb as far as your talents, industry, and luck could carry you until you were eligible for a pension. Either way, you were supposed to get out of the way of the rising generation in your later years.

But something happened to this picture during the 1980s. More people kept retiring earlier: with every passing year, there were fewer people over 55 left working, but when these new retirees found that they couldn't make out on their retirement incomes, they looked around for ways to earn extra money.

The jobs they found were dead-end, small-scale, new, specialized, self-contained, out of the office, off the organizational chart and promotional ladder — exactly the work that bureaucracies ignore. They found these jobs because these were the kinds of jobs that were growing.

From the point of view of policymakers and labor economists, these occasional jobs are bad. They are available because organizations are cutting out permanent jobs and getting the work done by people who aren't going to cost them benefits. By the old Depression rule, that's the very definition of recession and labor exploitation.

But supposing the shape of work to come is a wheel instead of a pyramid or a ladder? Supposing we're going to have a hub or core of permanent managers with benefits and lifelong employment, while most people are temporary contract workers on the spokes? In the traditional view, this means more "bad" jobs and fewer of the good, steady jobs that everybody is supposed to want.

And it's right there that we all need to think again. Our older people don't think of these jobs as bad. Part-time, occasional jobs are exactly what they want at this time of their lives. As you can see when you browse through our clusters, some of our respondents were extremely ingenious in finding ways to do exactly what they wanted on their own schedule.

People over 50 aren't alone in preferring occasional, part-time, contract work. The spoke jobs are ideal for students, young parents, and people who for one reason or another don't want a good, steady job for the rest of their lives. Instead of economic disaster, the rise of these jobs can mean new freedom, an increase in the number of people choosing a personal balance between the demands of work and the other things they want to do with their lives.

Is it good for people to continue working into their 60s, 70s, and beyond? It would be easier to decide if workers over 50 were all alike. Those who think it's bad are thinking about the older women who are cleaning office floors on arthritic knees because they worked as domestic servants for employers who didn't contribute to their Social Security.

Which raises an important question: How many seniors are work-minded? There's no statistical answer to such a question. Surveys find that more than a third of those retired would like to be back in the work force, but a lot depends on how the question is worded. Even if only one in four of all the people over 55 would like to go on working, it's safe to say that many more would like to continue to work if they were lucky enough to get part-time, flexible work they enjoyed.

Those who actually find these jobs are apt to be privileged. In many ways our work-minded seniors are like the working mothers so many of them were in the 1960s. They are the overqualified of their group and the most enterprising rather than those in direst need of an immediate paycheck.

They are similar in another way, too. In the workplace they have voluntarily chosen, they suffer from stereotypes that discriminate against them on the basis of age, just as women were stereotyped on the basis of gender. And if old women of the 1990s are quicker than old men to recognize age discrimination and more willing to complain about it, it is not only because it is more unforgivable for a woman to be old, but also because these particular women were young at a time when women learned to recognize stereotyping and fight it.

Like the working mothers of the 1960s, the work-minded seniors of the 1990s are testing out new workstyles for the rest of us. They are poking into the corners of a job market so vast, so diverse, and, in spite of the best efforts of our hard-working, overworked, underpaid head counters, so uncharted that the simple truth of the 1990s is that we can't spell out with any precision what a lot of people actually do to earn a living.

Our work-minded seniors find and sometimes create jobs that may fall outside the traditional census definitions. They are retiring the factory whistle that used to blow for all, in favor of flexible jobs that give individuals of every age and sex new ways to fit work into their changing lives.

2. WHY WORK NOW?

Why do you continue to work? Or, why are you thinking of going back to work? If you aren't sure, you are going to miss some of the opportunities to get what you really want out of a second career.

Most of us haven't had much experience thinking about the question. When you were 25, you didn't even ask. You just fell into the job with the best pay you could get, and hoped that the other things you wanted would come along with it. Now that you're over 50 you may still be working primarily for money, but you have a different set of priorities and a clear idea of those "other things."

One way to get started thinking about what you want from a second career is to look at the reasons older people give for continuing to work. Money, lifestyle, helping others, the work ethic, and the work itself account for most of what they say.

Money is the most frequent reason, but it tends to cover a multitude of values. To begin with, saying that you are working primarily for money doesn't seem to have anything to do with the number of dollars you earn. Some people work for money because they can earn so much that they "can't afford" to retire. What does this money mean to them?

If you want to continue working primarily for money, you might give some thought to the meaning it has for you. Here are some reasons older people are working for money. Do they make sense to you?

- A retired insurance manager earns $4,000 a month selling from his home "to preserve my capital investments."

- A housewife works "so I can travel and buy things I want without asking anyone whether I can have them."

- A former editor works as director of international marketing for her state because "I like feeling successful."

- A retired sales manager of an oil company sells advertising specialties for "the thrill of the sale."

- A retired construction superintendent finds occasional work as an estimator because "our children need more help than we can afford on my retirement pay."

Money has a more straightforward meaning to older people who have fallen through the cracks in the social safety net and expect to have to work to eat for the rest of their lives. Money is a defense against disaster for the 71-year-old who is working for "money enough to live on without welfare." Or the displaced engineer who works as a security guard because "I still owe a big mortgage." Or the 68-year-old widow who works as a data-entry keyer to pay off the bills left behind by a con artist who departed nine months after she retired from her bookkeeping job to marry him.

You may need money for somebody else in your family. You may have children still in college or graduate school. A 65-year-old married woman cleans a store in order to contribute to the financial support of her 90-year-old mother.

Illness in the family is another reason for staying in the labor force. A retired husband went back to work when his wife came down with a chronic disease that forced her to quit her job. A widow with no private pension works as a home health care aide to support herself and her 36-year-old neurologically handicapped daughter.

Some of the older people who say they are working primarily for money feel they have to explain why they need it. They ought to be retired and they would be retired if it weren't for some extraordinary circumstance that keeps them in the labor force against their will. They may need money to plug a gap in their health insurance coverage. A retired husband on Medicare works to get coverage for a wife who is six years younger. A wife works to have her own health insurance "if something happened to my husband's job or to him." It's easy to lose your health insurance coverage. A 61-year-old management consultant does factory work through a temporary service to pay for health insurance while he's looking for a job in his own field.

Gaps in the pension system keep others working. Many older people, especially women, worked for employers who had no pension systems, or worked so briefly that they were left with a $92 monthly check to supplement Social Security that may cover only the rent. A 72-year-old homemaker divorced after forty-two years of marriage makes both ends meet by stemming flowers at the minimum wage for a local florist. Others lost out on benefits when their companies cut back, like the former phone company manager who wasn't financially ready for early retirement when the system was restructured.

You may continue to work to improve your future Social Security benefits ("I'm 63.5 years old. Don't want reduced Social Security"), to earn enough quarters to get into the system, or to add to your nest egg of personal savings. A former shop supervisor who has his health insurance paid for is working toward "a targeted income for retirement."

The most common reason for continuing to work is that you can't live on Social Security. If the check goes for the rent, then you have to work in order to eat, let alone any of the other things you need. If you can just get by, you may work for a specific goal toward which you bank all or part of a second career paycheck.

You may work to build up a fund for travel. A retired teacher finances her travel by working two or three months a year as a word processor. Or you may want to accumulate money to get yourself settled in another community, "to buy a little house soon — cheap, not around here."

You may earmark part-time or occasional earnings for a hobby, like the man who lays aside the money he earns to buy new woodworking tools. If you're working for "extras" you will be particularly interested in finding a part-time or occasional job that fits your experience or your current lifestyle.

Money is also a reason for *not* working. Some older people deliberately choose work that pays so little that they won't "lose" Social Security because of the income limitation. A church secretary went to part-time work when she turned 65 because she "did not want to give the government" any of her salary.

There's another way to look at the Social Security income limitation. If you think you will beat your life expectancy, you can ultimately get more out of the Social Security system by continuing to work full-time until you are 70 and can keep all the money you make. Every additional year you work increases the benefit you begin to get when you are 70, and if you work beyond, your earnings increase that benefit every year.

It's a nice question to consider. Would you retire early or late if these were the only two options?

If you're working a second career primarily for money, do you think of the money as a symbol of your status, a defense against a rainy day present or future, or a source of some of the nicer things of life you couldn't otherwise afford? Your answer will help you decide how much you are willing to put up with to earn it.

By this time you are probably protesting that money isn't the main reason you want a second career. For while money is the single most popular reason, most older people say that the most important reason is either that they "like working," "like to be with people," or want to "keep busy." They are working because in some way or other the job enhances their lives.

Some older people find second careers that fit exquisitely into the lifestyle they have chosen for their later years. A retired serviceman in Kentucky pays for his stay in Florida every year by watching the crowd as a security guard at a racetrack. In Iowa, an accountant who had no intention of working when he retired has become the relief manager of his retirement community. When he agreed to take the job, he was moved from 150th place to the top of the waiting list for an apartment.

You may work because you think that retirement is downright dangerous ("don't want to die"; "to stay alive"; "retiring is debilitating"). A retired furniture dealer raises beef cattle because "if I had no responsibility to get up and go I would sit and die." A 63-year-old widow went to work for an optometrist at the minimum wage when she lost her factory job because "I'll rust out if I sit down."

Working keeps you young ("I shall never grow old working"). It wards off senility and mental degeneration, keeps your blood flowing, your joints working and freed up, and your mind active. A Texas farmer took on insurance sales for his county farm board when he had to cut back his acreage because "as long as you keep growing you don't get ripe. As long as you aren't ripe you won't rot and die."

Work is good for your health. It keeps you away from food. A nurse's aide works for $2.50 an hour because "I get bored staying home and eat too much." It also forces you to exercise. "I never sit down," says a bookstore clerk, "so my metabolism keeps cooking." When his doctor ordered him to get more physical exercise, a former television writer became a professional handyman. The yard work a retired correctional officer does "sure beats useless jogging or pedaling

---

BARTER YOUR SERVICES

For travel:
with a travel agency, airline, courier service, or invalid traveler.

For housing:
with a property owner or manager, apartment building, hotel, resort, sorority or college dormitory, mobile park, condominium, miniwarehouse, ranch, retirement community, resort, individual homeowner, or invalid. See Real Estate and Insurance; Hospitality; and Personal Caregiving.

For recreation:
with a sports club, golf course, or community recreation program.

For almost any desired good or service:
through a barter membership group, for a fee. To locate a barter exchange in your area, call the International Reciprocal Trade Association at 1-703-931-0105.

---

go-nowhere exercycles." He's only in his 50's, but he doesn't think he would last long if he quit working.

You may work to organize your daily life. A job gets you up in the morning and out of the house on a regular basis. "Get up early, shave, and shower every day" is the reason an involuntarily retired Frigidaire manager works as a minimum-wage sales clerk. Working protects against boredom, breaks up the week, and provides something to look forward to. "After you make a path from front door to kitchen, then what?" asks a woman who took a job in a music store after selling her ceramics business.

You may work to safeguard your mental health. "I go to hell if I don't work," a farmer confesses. Working keeps you away from television, gossip, drugs, brooding over your physical ailments, or wallowing in grief. It's "therapeutic." A widow who manages a miniwarehouse says, "After I lost my husband, working was a godsend." A retired farmer works at minimum-wage groundskeeping in a state park "to keep my mind off the loss of my wife."

Working is good for family life because it gives spouses regular relief from each other's company. A railroad conductor who retired at 50 sells shoes in the winter and manages an RV camp in the summer because his wife wants him out of the house. Early retirement was a domestic disaster for a sales engineer. He now works forty to seventy hours a week to get time away from a wife whom he describes as "the camp director type. She wants to boss everyone and plan all details." A retired industrial engineer works as a shipping clerk to get away from the "honey dos" — as in "honey do this, honey do that," — of a wife who is still working.

Both husbands and wives ward off trouble by going to work. A retired police detective works forty hours a week as a security guard to "give my wife a break!" A wife who took early retirement from a factory job clerks twelve hours a week in a yarn store "to get out of my husband's hair." One woman works "to keep a better relationship with my husband by not being together twenty-four hours a day." A woman whose husband is retired believes that "our time together is enhanced by our being apart."

But when it gets too thick around the house, the wife is the one who is most apt to take refuge in a job ("One retired person at home is enough. Husband retired"). If she hasn't worked outside the home before, she may feel that she deserves a change of working conditions. And a job is the perfect defense against a "camp director" husband who takes over all household duties when he retires.

Husbands aren't the only threat to a woman's control over her time. Some grandmothers go back to work to avoid becoming full-time babysitters for their working daughters. One woman works because "my niece moved into town with two babies." If you're a homemaker who has been in and out of the labor force, you may choose to work part time in your later years to get "time to myself away from the demands of other family members."

But your reason for continuing to work could be just the opposite. Some older people choose work that brings them closer to their life-long mates. A 68-year-old former medical secretary likes working part time at the McDonald's where her 72-year-old husband makes the hotcakes and sausages. A retired architect wrote a book because it involved "pleasant travel and coauthoring with my wife." The bed-and-breakfast business is one of many that couples start in order to work together in their later years.

You may want to work to be with people. You may be a people-watcher who likes the traffic in an airport or store. You may be a born salesperson who loves relating to a constant stream of new prospects. Meeting new people is one of the reasons why women go into selling

WORK WITH YOUR SPOUSE

Here are some of the occupations couples are doing together:

antique dealer	photographer
appraiser	property manager
auctioneer	real estate broker
beekeeper	restaurateur
caretaker	sports coach
farmer	storekeeper
handicrafter	tour leader
innkeeper	weather observer
miniwarehouse manager	writer
mobile-home park manager	

to people in their homes for Amway, Avon, and other direct sales distributors. A retired teacher likes working in her daughter's deli because she is constantly meeting new and interesting people.

If you are new in town, a job is a wonderful way to get acquainted. If you are a widow, the people at work may be your only regular human contacts. A widowed teacher lives alone in a three-bedroom home. One son lives two hundred miles away, the other three thousand. In order to be with people she works eleven hours a week keeping fundraising records for a local historic site. After her husband died, a homemaker learned word processing so that she could work full time in a utility office. When she retired, a high school librarian volunteered to sub at the public library to make new friends with the public and other librarians.

"Being with people" means more than relationships with coworkers you see every day. You may continue to work to maintain your contacts with an organization or occupation or merely to find out what your former colleagues are doing. A retired assistant secretary of the American Hereford Association works part time with the U.S. Beef Breeds Council to keep in touch with the beef cattle industry.

Even more broadly, you may think of a job as the best way to be "part of the world, not alone," to "stay in the real world," "to keep in touch with the outside world," "maintain youthful contacts" or "a contemporary outlook," know "what's going on," or "stay involved." In California, a former timekeeper went to work for the lottery because she likes the idea of being part of a billion-dollar business, "meeting people and having something worthwhile to get up and go to every day and being an active person. I like to dress up and have a reason to dress up."

You may continue to work to help individuals, groups, your community, the rising generation, a cause, God, or the world at large. A great many people do jobs they would never do for personal gain if they did not believe they were benefiting someone else.

For older people, that someone else is often a familiar face. You may come back to work, at least temporarily, to help a friend or colleague out of a bind. When Pan American College lost two full-time political science professors, a 73-year-old professor emeritus came back to take over two required courses. A fundraiser for a private school helped a friend organize the marketing plan for a retirement community. A financial manager came out of retirement long enough to set up the business side of a friend's engineering firm.

You may be working to help a child run a business. In Utah, a retired secretary who would like to spend more time painting pictures is doing the payroll, taxes, and office work for a small business her son is launching. If you have a farm, a veterinary practice, or a small business you are handing over to a child, you may stay on to help on a part-time basis.

Older professionals work to further the interests of a disadvantaged group, such as children with Down's syndrome, minorities, the homeless, or pregnant teenagers. You may use your experience and leisure to advance your profession. In Oregon, a retired official of the teachers' association works part time, at nominal pay, to continue a program of overseas travel and education for teachers that he originated.

You may take satisfaction in work that helps your community, or passes your skills on to the next generation, or helps the world. A pastor quit at 54 to work for world peace as an organizer of the United Nations association. A "dedicated environmentalist" who had enough money to "do what I thought more urgent" retired as an editor to work for zero population growth, animal rights, and the environment of southern California.

You may continue to work to do God's will, not only in church work but in helping fellow humans in any way. A retired customer service representative believes that "we are in this world to help others. Every time you help someone you feel better than the person you helped. That is God's way of repaying you." A Roman Catholic, she helps as the part-time paid secretary of a rabbi.

You may continue to work because you think that productive work is a good in inself above and beyond the pay, personal satisfactions, or help to others that go with it. This work ethic is alive and well among people born before World War II. Many of them continue to work simply because they are "too young to sit around doing nothing." And even those who say they are working primarily for money may add that they would continue to work even if they didn't need it. One man continues to work only for what he calls "self-fulfillment. I didn't need the money, I needed the work."

You may continue to work simply because you "need to be needed, or for "the satisfaction of a job well done," or because you have a useful skill, need to be productive, can't resist a challenge, or need to feel that you are still a useful member of society. Work is the right thing, and you feel better inside doing it. "I've worked all my life," said a conservation scientist, "and when I work I'm happy."

Finally, you may continue to work because you enjoy the work itself. Writing, art, and handicrafts are overrepresented among the people who say they don't want ever to retire, and they cheerfully continue whether they're paid or not. Some of the happiest are people who have found a way to make a little money out of a lifelong hobby. There are opportunities in baking, calligraphy, ceramics, coins, dolls, sewing, geneaology, hiking and biking, pets, quilting, recreation, stamps, sports, and travel. For details, check your hobby in the index.

You may never want to retire from work over which you have complete control because you own the business or work for yourself. You can have a ball starting a program or business you've thought up yourself and can run the way you want. A physicist retired from Union Carbide enjoys the opportunity to exercise all his technical and financial knowledge in developing optical devices for clients. A retired chemist loves solving problems as a troubleshooter for a water consultant.

But you don't have to be a Ph.D. to enjoy creating. A sewing-machine operator loves working at $4 an hour arranging flowers for a floral supply house. A retired mail carrier likes creating, repairing, and designing things from steel and aluminum in a machine shop. If you are going to putter and tinker anyway, you might as well get paid a little for repairing, yard work, or locksmithing.

The work of helping is intrinsically rewarding if you have control of the setting and circumstances. Pastors, counselors, psychologists, and college teachers find ways to continue, but social workers who counsel subject to rigid controls are usually eager to quit.

You can love a job that fulfills a youthful dream. She doesn't get overseas at it, but in Porter, Texas, a secretary who had always wanted to be a missionary loves her volunteer job with the home mission board of her church.

If you've worked indoors all your life, you may be idyllic about an outdoor occupation. A retired teacher feels ten years younger since she's been running a small farm. She's a widow in her 60s without the strength and carpentry skills she needs, and losses are cutting into her savings, but she's lyrical about the "freedom to be outdoors, walk in the woods, watch things grow, be close to nature, and care for animals." Coaching a sport you love may not seem like work, but a way of continuing to participate in it (see page 223).

You figure out what you know you want and then what you're willing to give up to get it. Some people in every one of our occupational groups have discovered, by trial and error, tradeoffs that work for them. A college professor who likes relaxed outdoor work traded off his status and pay to work outdoors as a groundskeeper. A middle manager in a big bureaucracy traded off security for challenge by retiring early to go into business for himself. A housewife traded control over her schedule for the money, prestige, and excitement of the real estate business.

Tradeoffs are what older people are good at. If you think through exactly what it is that you want and don't want, you won't be so apt to miss seeing a tradeoff that will work for you. If you look at the second careers of people who have done your work, or what newcomers are doing in the work you'd like to enter, you'll have to admit that everyone's options are broader than they think.

3. DO YOU KNOW WHAT YOU'D LIKE?

SECOND CAREER QUIZ

by Donald G. Zytowski, Ed.D.

Everyone's fantasy is to unexpectedly receive a sum of money — to win a lottery, receive a bonus, an inheritance, a gift. Not so much that you want to sock it away; not so little that you can just spend it and forget it. What would you do with it? Buy something? How about a vacation trip? Yes, that's it; take a trip. But where do you want to go? You could visit a travel agent and answer a few questions: Ocean or mountains? City or country? Easy or adventurous? History or entertainment? All right, a cruise through Alaska's fjords, the agent says, ought to suit your needs. Or two weeks in the best hotel in Las Vegas, or Vienna in the fall, or a trip to Mauritius, Hawaii, or the Indian Ocean.

A second career can be like an unexpected chance to travel — a happy time, an unpressured choice of work; maybe taken on to supplement your income, or just to keep in touch with people. Of course, you can continue what you've been doing all your life with just a change in format; part time, part year, teaching or consulting. But you may not be the same person you were when you were 20. You may have developed new skills and interests outside your work. Your second career may be a chance to try something you've always dreamed of doing!

But what will it be? The first quiz divides the world of activities into two groups — working with people and working with data, things, or ideas, which for shorthand can be called not-people. This is a handy place to start figuring out where you might want to apply your talents and skills.

Then, what kinds of talents relating to people or data, ideas, or things have you developed in your lifetime that you might turn to your advantage?

Lots of people know, or think they know, the answers to questions like these. But maybe you don't know, or believe it would be wise to answer them more systematically. The quizzes that follow are designed to give you scores that can give you a start on figuring out where you might want to go in your second career.

☑ QUIZ ONE: People or Data/Things/Ideas?

Directions: Each statement below has two endings, P and N. Read each one and decide which is more true of you. Indicate your choice by circling the letter of the statement that best describes you.

1. I tend to make new friends
   P. easily
   N. with care

2. People tend to come to me with their problems
   P. often
   N. rarely

3. I probably impress others as
   P. adventurous
   N. cautious

4. People seem to be able to read how I'm feeling
   P. easily
   N. with difficulty

5. In a restaurant or store, I'm likely to
   P. strike up a conversation with the server or clerk
   N. keep to myself

6. If I had the time, I would
   P. join another organization
   N. take private music or art lessons

7. In an organization, I'd rather be
   P. president or program chair
   N. secretary or treasurer

8. When I travel, I usually
   P. start a conversation with my seatmate
   N. take a book to read

9. I most often
   P. talk
   N. listen

10. When a friend is not well, I prefer to
    P. visit him or her
    N. send a card

11. I like
    P. teaching someone something that I know
    N. learning something I didn't know

To score Quiz One: Add up the number of Ps and the number of Ns you circled.

Number of Ps _____   Number of Ns_____

If you circled more Ps than Ns, you are more people-oriented, and should proceed by filling out the Quiz Two (People) that's next. If you circled more Ns than Ps, you lean toward data, things, or ideas (not-people); go on and take Quiz Three (Data/Things/Ideas) next. If your score is a near tie — say, 6 to 5 — your preferences are not clearcut, and you should take both quizzes.

There are several distinct ways to deal with or relate to people as well as data, things, and ideas, and these will be important in deciding where you want to go in your second career. Let's find out what kinds of skills or talents with people or data/things/ideas you have developed.

☑ QUIZ TWO: The People Quiz

Directions: This quiz consists of a number of statements that people may say about themselves. Indicate for each one the degree that it is true for you by circling the number opposite it according to the following key.

0 Not true at all
1 Rarely or slightly true
2 Somewhat true
3 Generally true
4 Almost certainly true

Here is an example:
I always carry enough cash to buy lunch   0 1 2 3 4

I've circled 3 because I generally have enough cash with me to buy lunch if I want to.

Now mark the following statements to show how true they are for you.

SERVING

1. I think a person's best contribution is help-   0 1 2 3 4
    ing others with their problems.
2. To help others is what is important in life.   0 1 2 3 4
3. I never saw a volunteer job I didn't like.   0 1 2 3 4
4. Helping others keeps me young and active.   0 1 2 3 4
5. I believe that I'm especially sensitive to the   0 1 2 3 4
    needs of others.

COMMUNICATING

1. I am often asked to be on panel discussions.   0 1 2 3 4
2. I can guide others to good experiences.   0 1 2 3 4
3. People ask me what I think about things.   0 1 2 3 4

4. I can give constructive criticism when it is   0   1   2   3   4
needed.
5. I like people who are well-informed.   0   1   2   3   4

SELLING

1. I have recruited new members for an organi-   0   1   2   3   4
zation.
2. I like to meet new people.   0   1   2   3   4
3. I often am asked to get a group of people   0   1   2   3   4
together to do some job.
4. I consider myself a good judge of people.   0   1   2   3   4
5. People tell me that I have good ideas.   0   1   2   3   4

To score Quiz Two: Add up the numbers that you circled in each of
the three parts of the quiz and place the totals below (scores should
range between 0 and 20).

Serving _____   Communicating _____   Selling _____

Here's what your scores mean, and a list of jobs they might suggest.

Serving: You know people who would score high on the Serving
section of the quiz. They're in offices and at reception desks, in schools
and hospitals. They're smiling at you and making you feel that your
need is the most important thing in the world to them at that moment.
If you scored highest on the Serving part of the quiz, you could be
employed by a human service agency or the court system as a social
worker, one of the most popular second career choices.

     Alcohol Counselor
     Church Secretary
     Hairdresser/Barber
     Home Health Aide
     Nanny
     Nurse
     Preschool/Kindergarten Teacher
     Restaurant Host/Hostess
     School Bus Driver
     Social Worker
     Veterinary Assistant

Communicating: If you scored highest on Communicating, you could play a valuable role in this information age. You probably are a skilled listener and can put things into written or spoken words with great ease. That's you speaking out at a public hearing, writing a brochure, or putting on a program for a group. Maybe you should be looking at jobs in public relations, editing, or acting, all popular options in later life.

Actor
Book Author
Book/Music/Restaurant Reviewer
Choral Director
Comedian
Copy Editor
Model
Musician
Newspaper Reporter
Public Relations Specialist
Speech Writer
Toast Master
Santa Claus
Translator/Interpreter
Waiter/Waitress

Selling: All the way from "How may I serve you?" to telephone sales work. That's Selling! Real things, services, things that people really need, things for which you must create a need. Another kind of sales work is leadership, fundraising, or helping in a political compaign. If Selling is your top score, you ought to give a careful look at insurance or real estate, or volunteer leadership positions. Maybe you ought to consider getting elected to public office yourself!

Antique Dealer
Campaign Manager
Door to Door Salesperson
Fundraiser
Insurance Salesperson
Magazine Circulation Manager
Mayor
Newcomers Hostess
Public Board Member

Radio Broadcaster
Real Estate Broker
Sales/Rental Clerk
Telemarketer
Travel Agent

Tied Scores: If you have tied scores in Serving, Communicating, or Selling, or scores within two or three points of each other, that's OK. That will give you the opportunity to consider unique combinations. Tied or near-tied scores simply double the possibilities! For instance, a tie between Serving and Selling might suggest starting your own business as a tour organizer, selling a tour to a group and then escorting the group on their trip. Here are some other examples of jobs for people with a combination of skills in Serving, Communicating, and Selling:

Actor in Commercials
Advertising Copywriter
Bartender
Clergyman
Cosmetic Demonstrator
Cruise Director
Customer Service Representative
Grant Proposal Writer
Lobbyist
Manager of a Bed-and-Breakfast Inn
Manager of Hospital Volunteers
Psychologist
Public Relations Manager
Sales Trainer
Taxi Driver
Tour Organizer

☑ QUIZ THREE: The Data/Things/Ideas Quiz

Directions: This quiz consists of a number of statements that you might make about yourself. Indicate for each one the degree that it is true for you by circling the number opposite it according to the following key.

0   Not true at all
1   Rarely or slightly true
2   Somewhat true
3   Generally true
4   Almost certainly true

Here is an example:
I always carry enough cash to buy lunch   0   1   2   3   4

I've circled 3 because I generally have enough cash with me to buy lunch if I want to.

Now mark the following statements to show how true they are for you.

MANAGING

1.	Deadlines are never a problem for me.	0	1	2	3	4
2.	I keep my checkbook stubs up to date.	0	1	2	3	4
3.	I function better than most people in emergencies.	0	1	2	3	4
4.	I get what I want by setting goals.	0	1	2	3	4
5.	I always have ideas about how to get things done.	0	1	2	3	4

UNDERSTANDING

1.	I know things that I could teach others.	0	1	2	3	4
2.	I go at a problem logically.	0	1	2	3	4
3.	"Discoverer" is a description that fits me.	0	1	2	3	4

4. I get a kick out of learning something new.	0	1	2	3	4
5. I subscribe to magazines in order to learn.	0	1	2	3	4

DOING

1. I learn by watching how others do it.	0	1	2	3	4
2. I like to run things so I know they're done right.	0	1	2	3	4
3. It's a pleasure to use a well-made kitchen or shop tool.	0	1	2	3	4
4. I keep my house in tip-top shape.	0	1	2	3	4
5. I like to be able to see the results of my work.	0	1	2	3	4

To score Quiz Three: Add up the numbers that you circled in each of the three parts of the quiz and place the totals below (scores should range between 0 and 20).

Managing _____   Understanding _____   Doing _____

Here's what your scores mean, and a list of jobs they might suggest.

Managing: Bottom line! Government regs! These are words that you're apt to hear from high scorers on the Managing section of the quiz. If you scored high, you'd be good at understanding financial reports, inventories, or tax rules. Your work would be valued in business, but the nonprofits need you too. You could consider hiring yourself by starting a small business, or advising new businesses. Or you could look for a spot in the growing financial services industry.

Appraiser
Bank Teller
Bookkeeper
Credit Manager
Data Processor
Inspector
Insurance Claims Worker

Lumberyard Worker
Payroll Clerk
Postmaster
Purchasing Manager
Franchisee
Your Own Business
Tax Preparer

Understanding: If your highest score is on Understanding, your talent is associated with ideas — with knowing, finding out, or discovering. Like others who lean in the not-people direction, you work comfortably by yourself; libraries and laboratories are your environment. Work that suits you might include the increasing special applications in science — the environment or safety, computer security, research services, and museum work. With some interest in people, you could look into the whole list of medical technicians: medical lab assistant, emergency medical technician.

Archivist
Biologist
Computer Security Manager
Emergency Medical Technician
Genealogist
Library Technician
Medical/Clinical Lab Assistant
Museum Curator
Paralegal
Private Investigator
Radiology Technician
Solid Waste Resource Recovery Technician
Technical Writer
Weather Observer

Doing: If you score high on the Doing scale, you like work to result in things that you can put your hands on. If this is your top score, you like active work, often outdoors, working on, making, or fixing things, or raising plants or animals. Tools are your best friends. If you scored high on this section of the quiz, you may be happiest in craftwork or hobby farming. But you could also entertain a popular second career choice in contracting — that is, fix-up services, repair and remodeling, and related work. Or consider fine arts or photography. There are a lot of possibilities in this group!

Baker
Bookbinder
Carpenter
Christmas Tree Farmer
Classic Car Restorer
Doll Doctor
Fish Farmer
Groundskeeper
Musical Instrument Tuner/Repairer
Painter or Sculptor
Photographer
Plumber
Silversmith
Window Trimmer

Tied Scores: If you have tied scores in Managing, Understanding, or Doing, or scores that fall within two or three points of each other, you should think of possibilities that fit under both headings. For instance, one popular option for older people is apartment, property, or real estate management. It needs a high score on Managing, but depending on how the job is made up, it might also need your talents in Doing, to cover maintenance work. Here are some other examples of jobs for people who have a combination of skills in Managing, Understanding, or Doing:

Arbitrator
Assessor
Building Inspector
Financial Counselor
Fire/Police/Ambulance Dispatcher
Information Scientist
IRS Taxpayer Service Representative
Property Manager
Quality Control Supervisor
Secretary/Receptionist
Security Guard
Ship's Captain/First Mate
Urban Planner

Vocational Education Teacher
Warehouse Manager

Your quiz scores aren't a ticket to a job, but they may give you a direction in which to go in your search for a second career — maybe even a destination. Now it's up to you to start your trip.

4. SECOND CAREERS TO CONSIDER

Someone your age or older is doing just about every job you can name and some that are sure to surprise you. The following advice on where to hunt for a job is based on 6,347 seniors who volunteered information on their second careers.

The jobs older people actually do can't be easily placed under any system of nonoverlapping headings. The attempt is a humbling encounter with reality. Still, every worker has to be put somewhere. You may quarrel with where we've put you, but we think you'll find yourself in one of the twenty-eight job clusters into which we've grouped the more than four hundred occupations people said they had done or were doing.

Here's how to use our system. If you're wondering what kind of work you want to do, there are two places to look. First find out about the second careers of people who have done your work in the past, then about what happens to newcomers in the work you would like to do if it's different.

For example, if you've been a bookkeeper but are thinking of going into commercial art, you can learn about the second careers of other bookkeepers by turning to the section "Second Careers for Experienced Money People" in The Money Business job cluster.

But what are your chances of breaking into commercial art if you've had no experience in it? To find out, look into the section "Niches for Newcomers to the Arts" in the Visual and Performing Arts cluster.

If you want books, organizations, phone numbers, and addresses of people who can give you more information or help you find a job, turn to Appendix C which lists resources for the job cluster that you are interested in.

☑ THE MONEY BUSINESS

Just as the washing machine created more washing, computers have created more records. Analyzing them calls for the judgment of experienced, reliable seniors.

The world of finance is not only big, but diverse. At the top of the field is the management of investment. Investment banking houses help business and government issue stocks and bonds to raise long-term capital. The stock and commodity exchanges register minute-to-minute changes in the value of various kinds of investment. Brokerage firms and financial services advise as well as execute transfers of funds from one investment to another. Watching changes in these markets is the responsibility of investment groups in large-scale enterprises, pension funds, insurance companies, mutual funds, the U.S. Treasury, and financial services providing investors with news and analysis, among many other institutions.

Since the deregulation of the banking industry in the Reagan years, investment advice to individuals is offered by retail banks, insurance agencies, and accounting firms, as well as by stockbrokers. The newest entry to the field are independent financial planning services which advise individuals, for a fee or on a commission of sales, on all their money decisions — from whether to rent or to buy a house to how much insurance to carry and how to buy and sell stocks and bonds.

Retail banks like the one where you have your checking account store and transfer money, lend money to businesses and individuals, and perform many other services such as holding money in trust and providing safe-deposit boxes for guarding valuables. And there are many specialties. Savings and loan institutions and mortgage banks were founded to finance homes and buildings, land banks to make crop loans. Credit unions provide limited banking services to an occupational group, such as the employees of a large organization.

All these functions are monitored by federal and state agencies set up to regulate financial institutions and insure loans to farmers, homeowners, disaster victims, or college students.

Taxation generates services ranging from the Internal Revenue Service and other government agencies to accounting and tax preparation services advising taxpayers.

Some sort of accounting and bookkeeping system is needed by everyone who has to pay bills, collect money, budget funds, and check to see that money is spent as intended. In big companies, these tasks are done by departments devoted to such special areas as the payroll, accounts receivable, accounts payable, or taxes. In small enterprises all these functions may be performed by a single individual. Accounting and bookkeeping firms provide these services to clients big and small.

What does it take to do all these jobs? Financial managers, stockbrokers, bankers, accountants, and tax preparers have to understand accounting, bookkeeping, and computer systems. They have to like detail and be good at math, analyzing problems, planning ahead, and explaining a complicated situation to people who don't see it their way.

Bookkeepers, credit managers, and bank tellers have to be orderly, conscientious, careful about numbers, and willing to follow precise instructions. A high school or community college course in bookkeeping and experience using office machines will help, but computer literacy is now essential.

Pay depends on responsibility, individual aptitude, and luck as much as on education or experience. Stockbrokers and money managers who invest substantial assets on commission may earn fabulous Wall Street–sized incomes, but newcomers to security selling may not do enough business to pay for their groceries. The chief financial officer of a company doing less than $50 million worth of business a year may earn $50,000, but the same title commands twice that much in a company ten times as big, with proportionately lower pay for their financial specialists.

Median pay for accountants employed year-round, full time, was $533 a week in 1990. At the low end are tax preparers, who may earn as little as $2,000 or $3,000 during the six weeks leading to the April 15 deadline every year.

Median pay for bookkeepers was about $8.45 an hour in 1990, with the top 10 percent getting $14 an hour or more, and the bottom 10 percent less than $5. Bank tellers averaged $6.83 an hour, with some earning little more than the minimum wage. People with college degrees or experience in higher-paying work earned more than the average in both occupations. Earnings for all of these occupations were higher than the average in Los Angeles, Boston, and other high-wage cities.

SECOND CAREERS FOR EXPERIENCED MONEY PEOPLE

Experienced bankers and financial managers who are looking for more money have chosen the career most likely to lead to it. If you've been an outstanding leader in your first career, headhunters may bring you even better earnings for your second. Savings and loan officials forced into early retirement when their institutions were being merged in the eighties were sometimes able to earn more in another bank.

Civil servants who have regulated banks or government lending programs can often get the money or terms they want by switching sides to work for the institutions they have been regulating. In Montana, a county supervisor who had made and serviced loans for the Federal Farmers Home Administration was recruited by a local bank to appraise agricultural properties as soon as he retired. He works part time, on his own schedule. A corporation examiner in the regulatory system of the state of California found a better-paying job in the private sector as an auditor for a bank when he decided to move back to the state of Washington.

The more esoteric the red tape you understand, the more valuable you are to the people who have to unwind it. Roy Snell finds an endless market for what he knows about the different kinds of loans insured by federal agencies. When he retired from the Small Business Administration, the bank officers he had trained began sending applicants to him for advice directly. He now charges borrowers $75 an hour to shepherd their proposals through the thicket of paperwork bank officers can't or don't want to handle.

Another way to make more money is to move your financial experience to a related field that pays better, such as selling real estate or insurance. But a great many bankers and financial managers aren't working at a second career for money. They want to stay on because they like the work or the friends they've made in it. An extreme case is the retired branch manager of a bank in Pennsylvania who works as a courier and custodian for another bank in town. He started doing it in his 70s and plans to continue as long as he is able.

There are plenty of opportunities in financial management for professionals who are willing to trade money and prestige for less responsibility, shorter hours, or more freedom. Consultants whose services are in demand can control not only their hours and their clientele, but can also take off for months at a time when they want to. Roy Snell earns $30,000 in nine months of work and spends the rest of the year traveling.

Many retired bankers and business managers take token pay for the privilege of working only when and if they are really needed. The arrangement is ideal for small new enterprises that desperately need more seasoned business judgment than they can afford. And why do these well-heeled retirees do it? Less frequently for money or status than other second careerists, and more often because they like the work, for fun, to help a friend or relative, and as one put it, "to see what's going on in those new high-rise office buildings."

Volunteer work is a tradition for bank presidents and high-level financial managers. Churches, hospitals, and nonprofit organizations often get superb management for free, and so, often, do the small business people served by volunteers through the Service Corps of Older Retired Executives (SCORE).

Accountants are professionals who tend to stay in their field, but they have many opportunities to move up to financial management in their own or a smaller organization. If you aren't a certified public accountant you are sure to make more money by becoming one.

Getting the certificate is a young man's game, but there are always a few gray-haired people taking the tough five-part examinations which allow you to put the letters **CPA** after your name. Dick Hutton got his at 56, after two years of studying at night. Was it worth it? "Just ego," he says, but when he got his certificate he quit working for an auto dealer, went into business as an **accounting** consultant for auto dealers he knew, and made more money his first year in business for himself than he had ever made before.

Accountants who want to take it a little easier can often call their own shots on time, task, and setting. Many become tax preparers during the busy season, help a small business of their choice, or lend a hand when a local accounting firm is overloaded. Watch your local want ads, apply to an accounting firm in your area, or let a temporary employment service look for exactly the terms you want.

Most of the people who call themselves "accountant" or "controller" are not CPAs, but **bookkeepers** who learned how to manage money on the job. After a series of bookkeeping jobs, Lore Lorsch became the controller in charge of all the financial affairs of a small lighting manufacturer. In 1988 she was earning $33,000 for a four-day week.

The best way to get more money, fun, and time for yourself is to freelance your bookkeeping skills in a business of your own. That's what Joseph Dunlay planned to do when he went to work as an accounting technician doing the paperwork of grant money for the state of New York back when he was 22. And it worked. At 55 he retired and now earns $10 to $25 an hour working as many hours as he pleases, doing payrolls, budgets, and taxes for enterprises too small to justify a full-time bookkeeper. He used to answer ads for bookkeepers but now relies on referrals from satisfied customers.

But you don't have to go into business for yourself if all you want is a little money and a lot more freedom. According to the Labor Department, one of every four bookkeepers works less than a full week, so you may be able to get shorter hours with a present or former employer. Frances Schwartz tried to retire from her full-time job when she turned 70, but the doctor whose books she had kept for nineteen years offered her more money per hour for sixteen hours a week of her own choosing. The new freedom is as important to her as the money.

It doesn't have to be dead-end work. Joan Williams got her start replacing a bookkeeper for the school district who didn't survive computerization. While working, Joan took computer courses and earned a college degree in business administration. After becoming city recorder and chief financial officer, she was appointed municipal court judge of Yamhill, Oregon.

NICHES FOR NEWCOMERS TO FINANCIAL MANAGEMENT

There's always room at the top of the money business for newcomers to the capital markets. **Stockbroker** is a natural second career for business leaders who have been managing their own investments. Milton Sussman learned to watch markets in the wholesale grocery business. When he sold his Hartford Sugar Company in 1965 he started following food stocks for a brokerage firm, moved on and up to another firm, and after giving the Hartford city treasurer some good advice on stocks, was asked at the age of 79 to manage that city's employee pension fund.

Really successful second careers in investments grow out of first careers. It's something to consider if you've been in insurance, banking, or real estate or if you've learned about the capital market by managing money of your own or building and selling a business. But you may have a future in financial services even if you haven't.

Investment used to be for the frankly rich, but now banks, insurance companies, brokerage houses, accounting firms, and independent advisers are trying to help the millions of less-than-wealthy Americans make financial decisions.

These financial planning services are fiercely competitive. They compete with each other for clients, segmenting the market on the basis of client goals, such as planning for retirement or the college education of children. And they compete with each other for the army of salespeople needed to attract the volume of small accounts that alone can make these services profitable.

"Client base" is the name of this game, and there are many ways to get one. As his customers aged, a life insurance agent fell into a second career as a financial counselor of the terminally ill and their families. It began when a doctor asked him to help a brain-damaged patient establish a disability claim and then went on to advise him on other financial matters. Other referrals followed from the doctors, lawyers, stockbrokers, and accountants of dying patients. He charges $105 an hour for his services and in 1990 was so busy administering the estates to which he was named executor that he wasn't taking on new clients.

If you've just retired from the armed forces, teaching, selling, or a job where you've met a lot of people, you may hear about the money you can make as a registered representative, investment consultant, financial planner, financial counselor, or retirement planner.

Is there a catch to it? Joseph Slattery is a good example of what often happens. Joe was a high school biology teacher who didn't know beans about money, so the year he retired he was flattered when a New York Life representative called out of the blue to invite him to become one of their registered representatives. They offered to train him to sell a very limited line of products: life insurance, the company's mutual fund, and for customers needing a tax shelter, a fund of limited partnerships in gas and oil wells.

Joe enjoyed the course and passed the examination that entitled him to call himself a registered representative. Selling used some of Joe's skills as a teacher, and for a few years he made more money and had more fun and freedom than ever before. But when he ran out of teachers and former students to approach, he realized that he could maintain that income only by cold calls, direct-mail appeals, or getting satisfied customers to refer their friends to him. His time is his own, of course, but if his production falls too low New York Life could drop him.

What about a job in a bank? Salaried managers in financial institutions are professionals who come up through the ranks. Only in extraordinary circumstances does a newcomer to finance play a management role. When the savings banks got into trouble in the late 1980s, the Federal Savings and Loan Insurance Corporation hired the former chief executive officer of a large aluminum company to train a team of talented young people to work with failing thrifts. As regional manager of sixty-five FSLIC offices he earned $85,000 a year.

But not everyone wants to be a honcho. Credit unions are sometimes managed by newcomers who know more about the customers than the fine points of finance. In Texas, a former secretary was able to learn enough accounting to manage a credit union serving the employees of a small manufacturer of valves. She likes it because she sees a bird's nest from her desk!

For newcomers to banking who'd like something less demanding there are jobs that require mature good sense rather than long years of specific experience, but they aren't on the career ladders or organization charts, so you have to hunt them down. For example, banks contract with outsiders from many different backgrounds to service mortgage accounts by checking the physical status of the premises and calling on those whose payments are past due.

If you'd like to get into a bank, there is plenty of work for newcomers who are willing to be trained to do clerical work. The pay is low, but while the work may be routine, you get to see a lot of people. A woman who used to teach home economics to junior high school students likes her new job in a bank because she enjoys relating to appreciative adults instead of turbulent teenagers. A former telephone operator admits that her job as a safe-deposit box custodian isn't challenging, but the customers are mostly pleasant and it's less stressful than worrying all the time about whether a supervisor is picking up on her calls.

Another niche for newcomers to money is to switch to the financial side of a business you know like the back of your hand, like the former outside salesman for an electronics manufacturer who became a bill collector of past-due accounts for a friend in the business. He says he needed no special training for the switch beyond what he had learned as a salesman about how to ask for money.

There are many specialized financial jobs that are open to anyone with a little business experience. Credit cards have taken over the work of the credit managers merchants used to employ, but they seem to be creating new opportunities for bill collection services that take this unpleasant task out of the office. Part social worker, part detective, but mostly persuader, it's an interesting and potentially rewarding second career for anyone who likes to help people out of a financial bind.

You can find out whether you want to go into the business for yourself by working part time as a **telephone collector** for an existing agency. A surprisingly similar job is counseling people who need help with their debts for a social agency.

If you've been successful in any field, you may know enough about making both ends meet to be a real help to a budding enterprise that can't afford a professional financial manager. A retired postmaster manages the financial affairs of a construction firm specializing in awnings; a former art supply manager, the business side of selling and servicing boats; a former bookkeeper's assistant, the financial side of a small real estate development.

The enterprises most in need of a **business manager** are small firms of professionals who don't have much training in business. Engineers, architects, research organizations, foundations, churches, schools, athletic teams, publications, theater groups, and especially lawyers and doctors are finding that it pays to hire someone with business experience to watch the money.

She doesn't have to be a financial wizard with a graduate degree in finance. A woman who has worked in doctors' offices ever since she got out of high school forty years ago now charges doctors $50 an hour to take care of the business side of the practice. She does everything from recruiting physicians for a medical group and shopping for office space and malpractice insurance to setting up the clerical systems and hiring the staff for coping with medical insurance forms.

Money isn't the main reason why successful people like to work part time as **business consultants.** A former director of university research keeps an eye on the finances of a small laboratory developing diagnostic antigens set up by his physician son, taking a token $500 a month and a 7.5 percent share of any profits they make. He's not only helping his son launch a socially important and interesting enterprise, but he gets a chance to visit with former associates all over the country who fund the research.

As a learned profession, accounting is hard for a newcomer to crack. Bookkeeping is easier. Banks and big organizations provide formal training for tellers and bookkeepers, so newcomers with good education and experience are not at a great disadvantage. Even if you've done similar work before, they are going to have to teach you their procedures: in a bank, how to handle currency or pull keys for opening new safe-deposit boxes; in a hospital, the medical codes for charges; in a factory, the way that particular firm wants its time records kept. And every organization has its own computer system.

Even if you've had no formal training, you probably know enough about the money side of whatever work you've done to keep its books, and if you've had any experience in business you probably know enough about keeping track of money to do some of the record-keeping work that has to be done in small enterprises. Doing the simple paperwork of a business too small for a regular bookkeeper is attractive to older newcomers if the people are friendly, it's at or near home, and the schedule is flexible.

Financial record keeping sounds cold and impersonal, but in a small firm everyone knows the bookkeeper, because she's the one who makes out paychecks and takes in payments. It can be sociable even in a big firm. A bookkeeping clerk likes her job at Sears because it gives her a chance to talk to the "old-time" Sears customers. A retired high school principal likes keeping the books of a restaurant supply house for the opposite reason: it gives him a chance to learn about "a style of person" he's never known.

There's a financial angle to every enterprise, so taking care of the money is a good way to get into a bookstore, library, law firm, veterinary clinic, sheltered workshop, tennis club, retail nursery, travel agency, outpatient surgery clinic, adoption agency, or some other setting you'd like to try. A former volunteer with an arts organization likes keeping its books at modest pay because he feels he is helping to bring opera to Nevada.

Older newcomers may have the problem of unlearning the culture of a previous field. A retired army officer says he had to learn how to understand what he calls "the civilian mind." A retired personnel assistant for a large international company had to learn how entrepreneurs think in order to do the books of a parking consultant. "Furniture isn't contracting" says a woman who made this switch. And computer shock works both ways. A systems analyst who took a part-time job as a bookkeeper for an auto supply jobber complains that he had to learn how to fill out government forms by hand.

Tax preparer is the most popular job for older newcomers to money. There's nothing to stop anyone from charging to prepare someone else's tax return, but the complicated returns of big companies and rich individuals are made out by one of the small community of tax accountants and lawyers who are prepared to argue the Byzantine fine print of the 2,750-page Federal Tax Code.

Most tax returns don't require this fine-tuning, but people hate filling out the forms so much that fifty million Americans annually pay someone else to do what most of them could do for themselves. This simple tax preparing is a second career for most of the people doing it, who come from all walks of life — not just accountants and bookkeepers, but schoolteachers, advertising managers, engineers, chief executive officers, army officers, bankers, social workers, storekeepers, factory workers, and truck drivers. Some haven't even graduated from high school.

Not everyone has the temperament for it. You have not only to be good with both numbers and people, but tolerant enough of other lifestyles to talk with people about their financial affairs, and willing to keep up with changes in the tax code, which send most tax preparers back to some kind of schooling every year. Tax preparers don't have to be licensed, but they need special training and have to be detail-minded enough to fill out forms according to explicit instructions for applying general rules to individual cases.

Tax preparing is one of the new personal services that make ideal second careers for older people — something you can do anywhere on your own schedule to help individual people with an intimate problem, and open to anyone willing to take the readily available training. The drawbacks are low pay and the pressure of the April 15 tax deadline.

Most older people get into tax preparing by taking the low-cost, thirteen-week course offered every August by H & R Block, the national franchiser of more than four hundred storefront tax preparation offices. The best students are hired at the lowest clerical rate being paid in the community or on a beginning commission of 20 percent of the low fee collected from the customer and given free training that helps them earn more.

How much you can earn depends on how hard you are willing to work between January and April 15 and how much studying you are willing to do to qualify for the higher-paying, more complicated returns. Many semiretired people who learned the business from H & R Block run a little tax preparing business from their homes. For Ann Wesp, the transition was easy. She put up a sign on her house, "Ann's Tax Service," and satisfied clients brought others. She and her husband now work long hours ten weeks a year and then head for their summer place with enough money to keep them comfortably for the rest of the year.

Flexible terms make tax preparing an ideal job for older people who need to work at home or in a controlled environment, as many of them have discovered for themselves. A former storekeeper confined to a wheelchair makes $3,000 doing a few simple returns during the season.

But the upside potential is high. Holmes Crouch is a former nuclear engineer who got into the business by accident. A dispute with the IRS drove him to take H & R Block's course and write a book, *How to Fight Taxes*. When he related his experience with the IRS on a local talk show he was deluged with people who wanted his help. In 1989 he was grossing $100,000 a year.

Tax preparers have to learn about new laws and regulations every season, so continuing education on taxes has become an industry in itself. In addition to H & R Block, colleges, professional associations, and private industry offer a world of courses, seminars, and printed material.

If you really like numbers there's something you'll like somewhere in the money business. It's responsible work that keeps you in touch with what's going on, and it can often be done on a flexible schedule.

☑ PUBLIC POLICY

American public policy is made in a three-ring circus, with the audience joining the act. The major players are legislators and elected or appointed administrators, but there are roles for the managers of privately owned communication, transportation, and energy enterprises that are so heavily regulated that they are called "public" utilities. In addition, private citizens — many of them seniors — are active in influencing all of the above.

Our system needs more actors than are ever on stage at any one time. Take federal, state, county, and municipal legislators or the president of the United States himself. They are highly visible, but they get elected with the help of party workers and specialists in managing political campaigns, and are assisted by staff experts on the issues. Power is fractionated into thousands of very specific decisions made by players working outside the spotlight of the news. To take a few examples:

Does our community want a new shopping mall? Should we raise the pay of our teachers? Do we need to make a new assessment of the value of real estate for taxation? Local zoning, school, and tax boards are always grappling with decisions like these.

Laws passed by Congress and ordinances passed by villages have to be interpreted by those who administer and enforce them. Administrators of essential public services such as the police commissioner or public works commissioner of a city or a cabinet member such as the commissioner of agriculture either make policy or have a lot of discretion in applying it. And the same is true of many high-ranking government officials who come under civil service rules designed to remove them from political influence.

In our free enterprise–oriented economy, energy and telephone companies, broadcast stations, airlines, railroads, bus lines, and shippers are expected to pursue profit with a due regard for the public interest, so those who head them must be counted among our public policymakers, too.

Most of these public and private policymakers play in the shadows, but all of them are watched by a motley army of kibitzers waiting to grab the spotlight with searching questions. Lobbyists, advocates, and political party workers research and attract attention to public issues, ranging from groups as specialized as Bikers Against Manslaughter, devoted to protecting cyclists, to causes as broad as those promoted by the American Civil Liberties Union and the AARP. Countering the critics is a defense army of public and private information specialists.

All public policymakers need the political skills of listening, talking, and understanding others, plus a gift for compromise and a high toleration for the essential untidiness of the democratic process. Qualifications for jobs under civil service are explicit (see page 296), and so are those for managers of public utilities who rise through systems designed to promote on the basis of objective merit.

For elected and appointed officials there are no examinations and no formal qualifications, but there is a very simple test of fitness: this work is not for you if you don't like politics.

The compensation of appointed or elected officials rises irregularly with the size of the jurisdiction: the mayor of New York earned $130,000 in 1990, but in some small towns the mayor was a volunteer. Policymaking managers of large public utilities may earn six-figure salaries, bigger than taxpayers are willing to pay their counterparts on the public payroll.

SECOND CAREERS FOR EXPERIENCED PUBLIC POLICYMAKERS

Like professional managers who move to a better job in a bigger organization, career civil servants can sometimes move to more pay and responsibility in a bigger jurisdiction. Every state has someone in charge of telecommunications in the event of a disaster, but in Hawaii the job paid so little that its chief of telecommunications had to work as a private newsman to make both ends meet. He now makes more as assistant chief of telecommunications and disaster consultant for the state of California, coordinating the work of county and city groups that stand ready to augment official systems for such chores as directing people to Red Cross shelters (see page 64).

Public policymakers often retire with esoteric knowledge and an acquaintance with those who are willing to pay for it. A Commerce Department manager who retired as **congressional liaison officer** gets $500 a day advising private business people how to deal with the government. The president of a firm that specialized in computer systems for utilities learned enough about their problems to become a consultant to power companies on nuclear management. He earns $17,000 a month, but is doing it primarily because he thinks his work is important.

How hard is it to get consulting work of this kind? For starters, you need to know something that is valuable, and just as important, be able to identify not only this knowledge but the policymakers in and out of government who need to know it. This may take a bit of research.

A good example is a retired director of mental health programs for a state education department who sets up social assistance programs for large employers, providing therapy for troubled employees on a confidential basis. He helps the employer choose a facility for these services, and monitors how well they are being rendered. He also advises employers how to comply with legislation on equal opportunity for the disabled and avoid lawsuits. After four years in business, he has raised his fees to $500 for half a day, or a minimum of $125 an hour.

He warns that you can't rest on your oars, or go very long on what you used to do. If you want to keep getting business, you have to keep up with new laws, read the literature of your field, attend meetings of the associations in your field, and join new ones. Federal and state government agencies make retiring policymakers wait for a year or two before doing business with the agencies for which they used to work. These rules are growing stricter, so it's best to check out your status. If you're a government worker, call the personnel officer for your agency for more information.

But while some former public policymakers make more money than ever before, others are content to take their pensions and contribute their services to the public policy organization of their choice. A director retired from the Federal Emergency Management Agency serves as president of the senior lobby of his state, a body organized by the AARP to study senior issues, at no dollar pay "but good psychic income." A retired United Parcel Service manager volunteers to do chapter work on civil rights for the American Civil Liberties Union.

NICHES FOR NEWCOMERS TO PUBLIC SERVICE

Elected or appointed office is the royal road to public service, and while it takes big money and a long apprenticeship to run for Congress or the legislature of a major state, the shoe is often on the other foot at the local level. When Louis Donati retired as superintendent of schools, the city council of little Saint James, Missouri, appointed him city engineer although his degree was in education, not engineering.

He didn't ask for the job, but at 81 he was adding $14,000 to his retirement income by assisting the mayor to serve "people with whom I worked fifty-three years in education."

Small communities have a hard time finding trustworthy people to serve as **mayor, alderman** or **alderwoman, city commissioner, county commissioner, board member,** or **township trustee.** One answer is a retired business or professional person who is widely and favorably known and has the time and the money to devote himself to public service.

It can be a good deal on both sides. A retired insurance salesman is happy earning $400 a month as the part-time mayor of Scottsville (population 4,300), Kentucky, where everyone knows him. In one community of rural Oregon, a retired rancher is the county commissioner; a retired dentist serves another as its part-time **state legislator.** Both were newcomers to politics, but not to their communities, and they're both having a ball. If you're an expert, you may be recruited for occasional work in your specialty. A retired newspaper publisher familiar with local government is **administrator of elections** for a county in Oklahoma.

Consider whether there's a public policy aspect to the work you have always done. If you've been in the building or real estate business, for instance, you know something about the very hot issue of local land use. A retired contractor born and bred on the Columbia River is the **port commissioner** for the city of Vancouver, Washington, administering about $1 million from rents in the warehouses and industrial parks that the Vancouver Port Commission developed. Port commissioners in Washington are elected, but in some states they are appointed.

If you're interested, find out from city hall who oversees land development in your area, get their reports, and attend their public meetings. With a little persistence, you may even be able to create for yourself the job you think needs doing. A retired Air Force colonel was so sure that the state of Delaware should have a director of energy conservation that he sought out the official with the power to set up the program and sold not only the idea, but himself as the doer of the job.

And don't overlook opportunities to serve the public interest in the private sector. Former advertising managers sometimes manage local radio stations, and retired people with capital often buy them. Not all public service enterprises are big publicly owned utilities.

Sometimes what's badly needed is a limousine service to the airport or a freight forwarding service. Take the mounting problem of waste disposal. A retired aluminum company manager who hopes to do well by doing good is starting up a business recycling wastes.

There is a world of occasional, part-time jobs for public-spirited citizens willing to serve for nominal pay. If you'd like to serve only now and then, you could become a public member on one of the many oversight boards set up to watch public utilities, the environment, licensed occupations, and many other activities affected with the public interest. In Arizona, for instance, each electric district elects "directors," who review the budget and performance of the electric company. One of these directors is a retired Army colonel who gets $2,000 for fifteen weeks of half-time work.

It isn't always easy to find these opportunities, but some of them go begging. A teacher retired from the New York State system guessed at an opportunity when she read in the paper that every licensed occupation would henceforth have to have a public member, so that there would be someone who isn't a real estate broker on the board that disciplines real estate brokers. It sounded interesting, so she called the Board of Education and eventually got an application form. So few people were willing to go to this trouble that she was able to choose a board that uses her background as a science teacher, the one that hears charges against dentists. She works a few days a month for per-diem and expenses to Albany whenever there are enough cases to convene the board.

In Minnesota, an AARP volunteer is working to recruit people over 60 to serve as public members on similar boards so that the point of view of seniors will be represented. In states that have these boards of oversight the secretary of state publishes a directory so that citizens can apply for the ones that interest them.

Finally, you can serve by helping the public to understand an issue close to your heart. You can work in the educational department of the Society for the Prevention of Cruelty to Animals, or take phone calls from aggrieved consumers for your local television station, or join the many seniors who help the AARP keep Congress informed on issues affecting the elderly.

You can write, speak, organize, research, or direct a nonprofit enterprise devoted to raising the salaries of teachers or keeping utility rates down. You can work for sea lions or world peace or to elect the person you'd like to see governor.

Money is seldom the reason for going into public service. Some do make more, like the office manager in Illinois who got himself elected **highway commissioner** when his company forced him to retire, or the riverboat freight manager in Arkansas who persuaded the municipality of Bethel to hire him to set up and manage port and harbor facilities with the title of **harbormaster.**

Mostly you'll earn less, but there's no rhyme or reason to compensation in local elected office. Among older newcomers serving in 1988, the mayor of a rural town in Delaware was a volunteer, an Illinois county legislator got $35 a meeting, public members of New York State review boards were paid $100 a day, while in Oregon a full-time county commissioner was earning $30,000 and a part-year state legislator $11,000. And while the port commissioner of Vancouver, who spent $6,000 on his election campaign, was getting honoraria of $50 a meeting with an annual cap of $4,800, the harbormaster of Bethel, Arkansas, was drawing down $48,000 a year.

The classic way to work for the public good is to volunteer your services to the political party of your choice and let your like-minded colleagues know what posts would interest you. For good or for bad — and those who do the work think it can be for the good — decisions about the public interest are bound to involve what we deride as politics.

Public policy is a natural second career for caring older people. Changing public opinion or apathy can be agonizingly slow. Government work can bog down in red tape. But it's personally rewarding to play even a minor role in an activity that affects all your fellow citizens.

☑ MILITARY SERVICE

The military is a self-contained work world of its own. At any given moment somebody in uniform is producing television shows, auditing financial records, making false teeth, repairing electronic instruments, cutting hair, investigating crimes, running hotels, making maps, programming computers, driving trucks, and operating power plants — to name only a few of 134 military occupations for which there are civilian counterparts.

But the distribution of occupations is radically different. For example, there aren't enough private security jobs to take care of all the retired military whose training qualifies them for the work, and while a few uniformed officers buy and sell real property owned by the government, the military isn't training people for careers in the private real estate market.

And it's a world of healthy young adults between given ages. To enlist in the army you have to have passed your seventeenth birthday and not yet attained your thirty-fifth, and retirement is generally after twenty years of active service. Most military people retire when they are still young enough to go into almost any kind of second career they choose. Comfortable pensions and educational opportunities offered by the services expand their options.

Retired military are newcomers not to work, but to the way civilian work is defined and managed. In the past, at least, those who have made the most money have been those who have been able to find a civilian job with the military.

Highest-paid of all are the exceptional army and air force officers who get jobs with defense contractors. A retired air force colonel who earned his engineering degree in the service manages technical contracts for an aerospace engineering company which contracts with the military to do very much the same kind of work that he did during his thirty years in uniform.

Noncommissioned technicians can switch sides, too. A retired navy tech works for a defense contractor. A former quality control inspector for government contracts has developed a lucrative second career helping small contractors qualify for government work. He conducts seminars on the quality control standards they will have to meet and alerts them to his services through mailings to government bid lists.

Some service people have been able to use their inside track on the jobs coming up to be filled to compete for one of the civil service jobs that support the military. In 1990 a sergeant major who retired from active duty at Fort Bliss in El Paso was adding nearly $30,000 to his pension running the motor pool of military taxis and officers' sedans. He estimates that about 40 percent of the civil service people who manage housing, maintenance, and routine office work on the post are retired military who got their jobs the same way.

If you've acquired a scarce and critical military skill you may be needed to work along with uniformed teachers in one of the many service training schools. In 1988, three of the teachers at the Naval Air Maintenance Training Group in San Diego were retired military, one of them from the army.

But it is no longer easy to cash in on your service connections. Veterans' preference for civil service jobs applies only to service before 1976. A civil service rule intended to prevent retiring military from creating a highly paid civilian job for themselves required the Fort Bliss sergeant major to wait six months before going back to work on the post as a civilian.

Conflict of interest laws require a waiting period before government retirees can sell anything to their old departments. This does not, of course, prevent a retired officer from supervising the work of contracts let by his former service, or becoming a consultant advising small contractors where to look and how to bid for a military contract. In 1988 a former army colonel was picking up about $5,000 a year for ten hours a week of this consulting. As the services shrink in size, there will, of course, be fewer such opportunities.

Now that no government retiree can "double-dip," or get the full benefit of a second pension earned from work done for the government — which does not, of course, prevent him from earning a second pension from work done for a private company — some military people move from one postretirement career to another. When he was only 59, an avionics officer who retired from repairing electronic equipment for the Marine Corps was earning a second pension from his second career in the same kind of work for a defense contractor and casting around for a third career in order to continue to "feel productive."

At 60, a former navy baker who retired from the service in 1967 and the post office in 1988 went right to work at a job he had done before he was old enough to go into the service. He's baking doughnuts at $4.50 an hour and though he complains about the low pay, he likes to bake so much that he plans to go on working until he's 70.

If you've done a counterpart job you know just where to look for your second career. Military doctors, nurses, butchers, and bakers have many choices. They make out best if they've planned for civilian work while still in the service, like the army cook who wanted to be a meat cutter and hung around the butcher shop when they wouldn't transfer him there. As soon as he retired he got a job cutting meat for a frozen food packer.

Officers often make good civilian use of the education they were given in the service. Many technical people got their engineering degrees while in uniform. A staff psychiatrist at a Veterans Administration hospital was trained in psychiatry when he was an army doctor.

But there's more to the transition than knowing how to do the job. Even if you'll be doing exactly what you did in the service, you'll have to adjust to what a retired air force colonel calls "the civilian mentality," which to him means working with one eye on the clock. He advises a little humility: instead of looking for the kind of authority you exercised in uniform, look for a civilian job where you'll have the chance to prove yourself all over again.

It's no surprise to find that retired servicemen are overrepresented in civilian jobs that match work that occupies a lot of military manpower, such as teaching and training (see Education), purchasing and stock keeping (see Retailing), repairing equipment (see Production), private security (see Law and Enforcement), dispatching, and driving (see Transportation). For some of these skills nothing beats military training. As the Fort Bliss sergeant major puts it, "If you've driven a sixty-ton tank you can drive anything."

Yet in spite of such possibilities, most main career servicemen aren't working at civilian jobs that have anything much to do with their military duties. They do, however, gravitate to bureaucracies such as the public service for which they used to get veteran's preference. They are also favored for jobs in management and supervision, finance, and management services which require teamwork and following rules. Many do well selling real estate or insurance (see page 111).

Manufacturers have learned that people who have been noncommissioned officers are likely to make good managers, foremen, or quality control supervisors (see Production), even if they have no previous experience in the field. Their training in courtesy and following rules recommends them for such jobs as desk clerk in a motel (see page 210). Their reputation for honesty makes them a natural for such jobs as servicing automatic teller machines for banks.

Don't write off your military experience even if it seems irrelevant.

If you think about it, you may find something to tell a prospective employer about how it could help you do his job. It could be something as simple as first aid training, or learning to travel lightly. An air force security officer thinks he's a better psychiatric technician because his military job taught him how to "work with troubled people," and a naval officer who works for the IRS as a taxpayer assistant says the navy taught him how to "interpret obscure directives."

A minor part of your service work may qualify you for a civilian job you had not at first considered. Developing an affirmative action program for the base was an incidental assignment for an air force colonel, but now he's the equal employment opportunity specialist for the Bexar County Mental Health/Mental Retardation Center in San Antonio (see Human Resources). Eugene Wickersham retired from the military to go into a second career as a training supervisor for a nuclear electric utility (see Education).

The career of John Kirchner is a good example of the way that military and civilian jobs can build on each other. In 1990 Kirchner was safety engineer for Rensselaer Polytechnic Institute, a job whose principles he had learned when he was a junior officer in charge of maintenance at an air base. Later the air force sent him to the University of Arizona to get an electrical engineering degree, and on a tour of duty in Germany he acquired a master's degree in education at a branch of the University of Southern California set up in Wiesbaden for American service people. With all this college experience, his logical last tour was teaching ROTC at RPI. While there, the college established the post of safety engineer to cope with the growing number of federal, state, and local safety and environmental regulations, and when the post fell vacant, Kirchner was on the ground and the logical candidate for it.

One skill learned in the military is becoming so valuable in all civilian enterprises that it is worth pointing out to any kind of prospective employer. The services are huge educational enterprises, rivaling in size our civilian postsecondary facilities. Everyone who has spent any time in uniform has experience learning and usually also in teaching and training others.

Teaching and training at every level is a favorite second career for the military, and a wonderful way for them to continue serving their country. More than one-tenth of our newcomers to teaching are retired military people (see Education). It's easy to see how Eugene Wickersham became a training supervisor for a nuclear electric facility when he retired from the military, but military retirees may be even more urgently needed in our beleaguered public schools. A retired gunner's mate spends six hours a week teaching math to freshmen in a vocationally oriented college, and it's hard to think of anyone more likely to command the respect of tough kids from an urban ghetto. Those who have taught sixth grade think that you need to be a master sergeant to handle a class of 11-year-olds, but Leo Moore, a twenty-three-year veteran master sergeant in the air force, is up to the job.

If you want to teach and don't have the right education, investigate "alternative certification" and volunteer opportunities (see page 152).

But when all is said and done, the most valuable preparation for civilian work is the attitudes and work habits learned in the service. Even those who found civilian jobs through a skill or body of knowledge that was scarce at the time when they retired fall back on a list of intangible values and qualities to describe what they learned that helps them most today. They talk about "management," "leadership," and "getting along with all kinds of people."

They also generally agree that the experience improved their character, teaching them self-discipline, self-confidence, patience, pride in their work, doing their best, loyalty, and responsibility. Mentioned, too, is a long list of specific work habits that are important to employers: how to manage time, set priorities, make decisions, and get to work on time.

If your skill is scarce and in great demand, a second career may come looking for you, but you can't expect to get any vocational or career planning help from the military services of the kind that some private companies provide for their retirees. If you want a radical change of occupation, you should look into the educational benefits to which your service may entitle you, and get vocational help from the school or college.

Another handicap is that you have had little occasion to know civilians who do the kind of work in which you are interested. Service people are less apt than other older people to get a job through a friend or relative; more often they find work through an ad or by applying directly. Working for them, on the other hand, is the prestige of military experience with employers and the bearing and good manners learned in the service.

☑ PUBLIC SERVICE

Public policies are no better than the people who carry them out. Every conceivable human skill is needed to deliver the thousands of services provided by federal, state, and local taxpayers, and in spite of efforts to contain it the public sector continues to grow. Public service work is built into the fabric of every aspect of life, so there are professional workers on the public payroll in almost every one of our occupational clusters, especially The Money Business, Social Work, Law and Enforcement, and The Outdoors.

Some public service workers enforce the thousands of laws protecting health, safety, and fairness. Others keep records, issue licenses, collect taxes, fight fire and crime, move the mails, and maintain roads, sewers, and water systems. Most of this work is done under federal, state, or local civil service systems, some by locally elected or appointed officials, some by licensed and regulated private organizations, and some by citizen volunteers.

The variety of work done on public payrolls is staggering. It's one thing to pass a law, but quite another to see that everyone obeys it. Among many others, there are, for instance, federal agencies set up to inspect meat-packing plants and granaries, working conditions in factories, the safety of air and rail travel, illegal immigration, banking and security frauds, tax evasion, the purity and efficacy of drugs, and complaints of discrimination in employment, education, or housing because of race, sex, age, and disability.

State and local agencies reach even further to protect the health and safety of citizens. They inspect new construction for compliance with building codes and restaurants for compliance with sanitary codes, monitor the quality of air and water, and investigate complaints of discrimination in access to jobs and housing. Through their power to license they enforce safety standards for drivers and vehicles and the conduct of professionals from doctors to real estate brokers. Some enforcement chores are as explicit as weighing trucks to insure that they comply with the limitations on access to a highway.

Not all the monitoring is done directly by the taxpayers. Insurance companies help enforce building codes by requiring compliance from policyholders. And citizens' groups such as the Better Business Bureau and the American Civil Liberties Union investigate violations of laws in which they are particularly interested.

Finally, we should not forget all the government services we take for granted: the mails, property records in city hall, fire fighters and police, air traffic safety, and the preservation of historical monuments, to name a few.

Federal, state, county, and often local civil service commissions require explicit education and/or experience for each nonpolitical post, and fill them on the basis of competitive examinations. To get a job in the post office, for instance, you have to be a citizen or permanent resident alien and rank among the top three on a written examination that measures speed and accuracy at checking names and numbers and ability to memorize mail distribution procedures. Five extra points are added to the scores of honorably discharged veterans, and ten extra points to veterans who are disabled. You may also have to pass a machine aptitude test and demonstrate that you can lift a seventy-pound sack.

In addition to an examination, a license is required by some states for some civil service jobs. In Texas, for instance, you have to have a license to be a car inspector.

Pay is often higher in the federal government than in the private sector or in state and local jurisdictions. It's higher in larger states, cities, and towns, but scales are erratic and titles often misleading. And though scales are publicly advertised, the actual paycheck of any individual depends on factors such as grade and seniority. In 1988, for instance, a disabled veteran who couldn't quite keep up the pace expected of a carrier was earning considerably more at the simpler task of sorting incoming mail.

Median weekly pay for full-time work in 1990 was $552 for **postal clerks,** $554 for **mail carriers,** and $582 for **compliance officers.**

SECOND CAREERS FOR PUBLIC SERVANTS

If you are a lucky public service worker you may fall into a second career that uses your experience. A retired **postal inspector** who investigated mail frauds became a private eye. A barge company transporting bulk commodities on inland waterways hired a **battalion chief** away from the fire department to become its **director of safety.** A retired **state unemployment tax auditor** works part time assisting employers at hearings over their tax liability. A **tax assessor** went private as a **property consultant** for a law firm.

It's also possible to switch from a private to a public job in the work you know, although it isn't as common as switching from public to private. A former **loss control engineer** who used to inspect risks covered by an insurance company is now inspecting safety hazards for his state.

But by the nature of public work, relatively few public servants find second careers in exactly the type of work they have done on the public payroll.

NICHES FOR NEWCOMERS TO PUBLIC SERVICE

Civil service systems are designed to protect the career tracks of incumbents, so it is hard for older newcomers to enter at the level for which their past experience in the private sector may have fitted them; but older newcomers can get in if they are (1) skilled in a scarce specialty, such as computer systems, (2) a veteran of the armed forces, or (3) applying for an occasional offbeat job that isn't firmly cemented into the bureaucracy.

All three routes work even in the post office, the biggest and arguably the most militantly unionized of all the public bureaucracies. In a small post office in the Northwest, for instance, an **administrative assistant** coordinating schedules and working the computer is a former **warrant officer** who learned managerial and administrative skills administering an army legal office. Extra points were added to the boost that goes to all retired veterans because he had been retired on 50 percent disability. And competition for the job in Bothell, Washington — population 7,943 — was not as keen as for jobs in bigger places. Like most postal employees, he was earning roughly half again as much as private employers in the area were paying for comparable work.

Specialists with scarce skills may avoid the competition altogether. A detailer who drafts by computer in a Maryland post office doesn't work for the post office, but through a technical help service with which the post office contracts. Mechanization of mail handling is increasing the number of jobs not yet integrated into the personnel system.

Competition for the younger entrants is less keen for the one in every four post office jobs that are part time, helping out with occasional overloads or staffing small offices or contracting to deliver mail on a rural route. A former general manager of a steel company who earns $13 an hour sorting mail and waiting on customers in the post office of a little town in Arkansas thinks he has the best part-time job in the country.

The first route — special experience — is the most neglected. The government needs just about every skill, so there's bound to be one or more government jobs for yours. A quick way to find out what they are is to call the federal job information center number in the blue pages of your phone book and ask them to tell you the jobs for which your special experience is a qualification. Even if they are not currently hiring for any of these jobs, the listing may lead you to state or local counterparts worth exploring.

Did you major in biology in college? If so, you have the educational qualification to be a **health inspector**, and with a little brushing up you may do as well as the youngsters when the next competitive examination is held.

No college, but plenty of know-how? In Pennsylvania, a farm mother of six became an "intermittent" **food inspector** of poultry and red meat for the U.S. Department of Agriculture. She was able to substitute three years of slaughtering on the farm for the degree in biology usually required. In 1988 she was on call for days when they had an overload of meat to be inspected. She gets training at government expense, and the extra money helps keep the farm going.

The **municipal clerk** of a big city or county is a highly paid, highly political elected office, but in smaller towns and counties it can be a pleasant, appointive job. The clerk of rural Lincoln County, Maine, is a retired school superintendent from Ohio who gets $12,572 a year for part-time work. He says that local jurisdictions are glad to make use of talented summer people who have put down roots in the community and come to Maine in their later years to stay.

Community-minded older residents like being municipal clerks because it keeps them in touch with what's going on, and some of them stay on for decades: in 1988, one had held the job for sixty-six years. But in affluent suburbs and rural villages **town clerk** is a part-time job that can sometimes be had for the asking. In 1988, the **deputy town clerk** of a small New Hampshire town was a former seamstress who collected taxes and disbursed emergency aid when her friend, the clerk, was away.

Every level of government has work that seems made to order for older newcomers because it is newly created, occasional, or flexible by its very nature. For instance, cities are beginning to employ someone to concentrate on dealing with complaints about rats, barking dogs, fallen trees, and violations of city laws and building codes that create public hazards. In Alameda, California, it's done by a **community services officer**, who in 1988 was a retired sales manager working twenty hours a week at $9.05 an hour.

Finally, older newcomers are welcome in odd, one-of-a-kind public service jobs that don't require a great deal of special training, such as reading meters for a public utility or inspecting cars for the state division of motor vehicles. In one town the pictures for drivers' licenses are snapped by a former keno writer who had to leave her job in a casino.

Dispatchers of ambulances and police cars have to be tactful people who aren't afraid of emergencies and can learn to use a two-way radio and keep a log. Some of them are former secretaries, housewives, and salesmen. Pay depends on the size of the community and the responsibility the dispatcher has to take. In 1988, a fire dispatcher in Long Beach, California, who could send out equipment was earning $30,000, but a **desk sergeant** was taking messages for a small police department in New England at the minimum wage. The hours are awful and the strain can be high, but it can be exciting and a great way to help people in trouble.

Occasional jobs that attract older people are the extra **assessors** or **data card collectors** who go around measuring and inspecting property whenever a town overhauls its tax valuations. This job involves a lot of walking around outdoors and requires a knowledge of basic math and simple drafting and drawing. In 1988, deputy assessors were earning from $5 an hour to $10 for those with permanent status working on complex buildings.

Child support collector is a another public service job off the main career ladders. It requires no college degree, and is uncertain because it depends on the state voting to match federal funding every year. A policeman who found out about the job when he was retiring from the force was earning $25,000 at it in 1988, but found it depressing to chase after irresponsible fathers.

Some older newcomers are drawn to public service because equal opportunity is more vigorously enforced than in much of the private sector. At 51, Adelina Figueroa felt that her age, sex, and Hispanic name barred her from promotion beyond administrative assistant for an aerospace manufacturer in California, so she quit and went to work for the U.S. Department of Labor. When she retired fifteen years later she was earning $46,000 overseeing the compliance of employers like her former bosses with equal employment opportunity laws for the Office of Federal Contract Compliance Programs.

If you are looking for more freedom and time to yourself, there's a great deal of public service work that isn't strenuous, full time, year-round, or highly competitive. Many agencies have to take on extra help for their busy seasons, and some of it can be fun.

Everybody likes working in national parks. At 74, a retired auditor was doing repairs, making signs, and caring for tools as a minimum-wage helper in the Senior Conservation Program of the U.S. Forest Service in Montana. In Seattle, a retired YMCA director is a volunteer forest technician, supervising campgrounds and trails in a national park. He likes everything about being outdoors but members of the public who don't follow the rules.

If you live in a rural area and like the outdoors, you could work as a substitute mail carrier or help out as a mail clerk or handler during the Christmas rush. For opportunities, watch the bulletin board in your post office.

But there are other possibilities. You could, for instance, get occasional, part-time, or part-year work answering phones for the Internal Revenue Service. The IRS likes to keep its ten service centers

---

SHOPPING FOR A VOLUNTEER JOB
To find a volunteer job matching your interests consult:

VOLUNTEER — The National Center, 1111 North 19th St., Suite 500, Arlington, VA 22209; 1-703-276-0542.
"Volunteer Center" or "Voluntary Action Center" in the white pages of your telephone book.
The AARP Volunteer Talent Bank, 601 E St., NW, Washington, DC 20049.
Helping out in the Outdoors: A Volunteer Directory to American Parks and Forests (American Hiking Society, 1015 31st St., NW, Washington, DC 20007; $3.00).
Volunteer Vacations (Chicago Review Press, 814 N. Franklin St., Chicago, IL 60610; 1-312-337-0747; $11.95).
Volunteer! The Comprehensive Guide to Voluntary Service in the U.S. and Abroad (Council on International Educational Exchange, Campus Services, 205 E. 42nd St., New York, NY 10017; 1-212-661-1414; $5.95 post paid).

staffed so that a taxpayer can always get some kind of answer to any question, and they need more people around tax time. They hire taxpayer service representatives in August, train them through the fall and start them talking to taxpayers in January. To find out more about this and other occasional federal work, call the Federal Job Information number in the blue or government pages of your phone book, or ask at your local state job service office.

Many older people work in their community's emergency disaster service. A retired fire chief or contractor may serve his town or county as **disaster** or **emergency coordinator,** or **director of civil defense,** a job of planning for cooperation among public and private authorities created during World War II. Titles and appointments vary, but every U.S. county has someone in charge of disaster planning. In South Dakota, for instance, a retired veterinarian earns $7 an hour twenty hours a week as the director of his county's emergency disaster service, but many ham radio buffs are glad to volunteer their services.

There are interesting jobs for volunteers in many federal agencies. In the Southwest, retired people work as volunteer **fire inspectors,** checking structures for compliance with fire codes or asking residents to cut back brush near canyons where forest fires are a danger. When arson was suspected, a retired high school principal was asked to patrol an area in her own car and take down license numbers of suspicious vehicles.

All over the country, fair-minded, analytical people are checking misleading ads for the Better Business Bureau. They shop for the products, handle complaints of consumer fraud, mediate disputes between customers and vendors, and even conduct binding arbitration hearings. Some bureaus have extensive training courses. You can find out what's available to you by calling the Better Business Bureau, listed in your local phone book.

The best way to find the volunteer job for you is to think of what you'd like to do and then talk to the agency that is serving the public in the area of your interest. Half the battle for any public service job is finding that it exists. You may learn about volunteer opportunities from a newspaper article, or about a job that is hard to fill from an ad, but the good public service jobs tend to be snapped up by people who get the news of an upcoming opening from somebody who can tell them just when and how to apply. This isn't sinister "pull" but healthy networking: the owner of a mobile home park in rural California knew that the **meter reader** for the project was about to retire, decided he'd like the job, and found out just where he had to go to be first in line to get it.

And if you are interested in local government, make a point of talking to the town or village clerk. She's often an unofficial letterbox for the entire community. A retired bookkeeper who asked the clerk of a small New Jersey town about a library job learned that the town was about to create the new job of **municipal treasurer.** It was right up her alley so she applied and got it.

Finally, don't let the examination put you off. People who are serious about the civil service take the examination for every job for which they qualify. You can take the examination over as many times as you please and every time you are likely to raise your score.

Public service work is slowed by red tape, but the federal government tries to be a model employer and it sets the standard for the state and local civil services. If you can find a second career in some public service you will have the respect of your fellow citizens and the satisfaction of serving them.

☑ SOCIAL WORK

We've all felt the impulse to reach out to another human being in trouble. Social work keeps up the safety net that channels government and private resources to the particular individuals we would all like to help. More people need help as they live longer to encounter more problems, but fewer young people are entering this helping profession.

It's work that takes special training and knowledge as well as an open heart. So many public and private programs have been set up for different circumstances that it takes professional judgement simply to refer a person in trouble to the public and private programs that could help him or her. And since most people in trouble have no idea of what's available, social workers have to be on hand in hospitals, nursing homes, institutions for the disabled or the mentally retarded, schools, churches, prisons, courts, even private organizations — wherever people turn for help or their misfortunes come to light.

In government welfare agencies, the facts of each case have to be collected and evaluated in order to determine eligibility for assistance.

In public and private agencies, individual cases are assigned to counselors trained to help with a specific problem. Some help with family problems, such as desertion, violence, or teenage pregnancy. Those who deal with medical or psychiatric problems arising out of a disability or illness may refer a client to a program that coaches them in skills of everyday living, to jobs that they can do to earn money, to a support group of other people coping with the same problem — such as Alcoholics Anonymous for people with a drinking problem — or for assessment and/or counseling to a clinical psychologist certified by a medical board. (see The Health Business).

Not all of the one-on-one work requires long professional training. Records have to be kept. Clients have to be driven to clinics. Phones have to be answered, appointments set up, offices maintained. Some of this work is done by paraprofessionals or volunteers working closely under the direction of credentialed social workers, but there is a great deal of overlapping.

For the professionals, there's a lot more to do than dealing directly with clients. All these highly emotional, draining, one-on-one services have to be supervised to maintain consistent standards. Programs have to be defended against charges that recipients are defrauding the taxpayers and controversy over how much of society's resources should go to the unfortunate.

For professional posts, civil service usually requires a bachelor's degree in social work or a social science and experience, plus a master's in social work for the better-paying supervisory jobs in major hospitals and state institutions. A bachelor's degree will often be accepted by nursing homes, in state departments dealing with suspected cases of child abuse, in senior centers funded by state offices on the aging, in mental health clinics in inner-city communities, and, with short training, in drug and alcohol counseling centers.

Older people experienced in a related field may qualify for responsible work through one of the hundreds of programs in local colleges and vocational schools across the country that lead to certification or associate degrees in counseling, mental health, special education, rehabilitation, and other social work specialties. For what's available near you, cousult your local community college.

Both public and private employers look for candidates who are good listeners, sensitive but objective, emotionally stable, and genuinely interested in helping others. Some states require a state license for clinical social workers (see page 298).

Median full-time weekly earnings of all professional social workers was $445 in 1990. Hospitals and state institutions are supposed to pay best, but the range is wide. Counselors in private practice charge from $60 to $90 a contact-hour in the Bay Area of California, but most earn considerably less; the net is always lower when preparation and planning time is counted.

SECOND CAREERS FOR EXPERIENCED SOCIAL WORKERS

An exceptionally motivated social worker sometimes makes more money in private practice. When she was forced out, a director of family therapy in a private agency expanded her part-time private practice to $60,000 a year. But most of those who go into private practice make less than they did when they were working on salary, even when they go back to school to qualify as clinical psychologists, (see page 127). The main advantages are fewer hours and freedom from oppressive social work bureaucracies; the problem is finding clients who can pay for the services they need.

But there are other ways to get more control over your work and your time. If you've worked for an agency, a hospital, or a nursing home, ask about the possibility of doing some of what you did on a part-time basis. Keep in touch with your professional grapevine for news of occasional contracts to plan or monitor social programs or conduct workshops. And don't forget that there may be opportunities in the employee assistance programs big companies are setting up, which give confidential counseling to employees struggling with a personal problem such as family dissolution, a disabling illness, or alcohol or drug addiction (see page 186).

NICHES FOR NEWCOMERS TO SOCIAL WORK

"Helping others" is high on the list of what older people want in a second career. Many of them want to "pay back" the help they themselves have personally received while coping with bereavement, alcoholism, cancer care, mental illness, or some other problem they have experienced. And we now know that the very act of giving this help can be a continuing therapy in itself.

The urge to help is so strong that a surprising number of older people are willing to go back to college to qualify. Homemakers are especially good candidates. They have had the life experience to understand emotional needs, and many of them have hands-on experience as volunteer workers in hospitals and social agencies.

A good example is Shirley Cotton. When she was divorced at 50, she took her alimony money and spent $10,000 and two years of time earning her master's degree in social work. Two years later she was earning $34,000 as the head of the social service department of a hospital. Previous experience? "Homemaker, corporate wife, mother, community volunteer, gardener, etc."

Many of the newcomers who undertake the long and arduous training have a little income to help them through the education and the low pay they can expect afterward. A marine who spent twenty-eight years in uniform got a bachelor's degree in the humanities so that he could help straighten out kids as a probation officer. A freelance actress who started college at 50 and received her master's degree in social work five years later earns $27,000 a year as the site coordinator of an Alzheimer's disease respite center.

But you don't have to get a degree to deal directly with troubled people. Older people with little or no specific training, many of them volunteers, work under a wide variety of titles: casework aide, human service asistant, weekend manager, hospice volunteer, food coordinator, outreach worker, crisis center clerk, human services counselor, director of transportation for Meals on Wheels, prison visitor, shelter advisor, facilitator for Child Assault Prevention (CAP), long-term care ombudsman, disaster chairman for Red Cross.

Their tasks are as various as their titles. They may run a meal site or food bank or do the housekeeping, record keeping, and supervision for a residential facility such as a temporary shelter for battered wives, alcoholics, or disaster victims.

They may help welfare clients through the red tape of entitlements such as food stamps; drive people to meal sites, doctor's offices, or adult day-care programs; help organize and sometimes even lead support groups of people coping with a common problem; visit homes to see that clients are actually receiving the services that have been ordered for them; check on the treatment of children in foster care and locate those who ought to be in a Head Start program or are threatened with abuse from a family member.

Older people are drawn to the largely administrative work of managing and sometimes training the volunteers in a hospital. In one, a retired telephone manager supervises the forty volunteers who schedule hearing tests for newborns. A retired librarian is the assistant director of volunteers in another, and a retired factory inspector is a hospice volunteer coordinator in a third institution.

Some bring skills learned on other jobs. One house parent for six troubled teenagers is the former director of company schools for a copper company in Peru, and a retired supervisor of nurses has become a geriatric mental health therapist.

But previous exprience isn't all that necessary. The information and referral counselor for an area Office for the Aging in Missouri is a high school graduate with thirty-three years of business experience. She sets up programs like the one under which mail carriers report seniors living alone whose mail has been piling up. The house manager who teaches the skills of daily living to deprived youngsters in South Chicago is a former choral music director of a high school. And while it undoubtedly helps, you don't have to have twenty-eight years in the Marine Corps to be a good probation officer: a retired insurance agent and a retired line supervisor for Pacific Bell Telephone are among the many older people doing it.

The nonprofessional newcomers bring a valuable enthusiasm to jobs that eventually wear everyone down, such as assisting the victims of crimes. In a small town in New York, a woman whose own children are grown earns $5 an hour working in a child assault prevention program. After extensive training, she visits schools to teach children how to react to potential abuse by parents, strangers, or bullies. They role-play various situations, practicing what to say, how and when to say no. "This program has helped hundreds of children," she says. "We help keep them safe, strong, and free." Another nonprofessional helper, a former foster mother, wants others to join her in helping care for children under the age of 5 who have special needs. She spends ten hours a week visiting these children in the specialized homes where they are being maintained. She earns $5.67 plus mileage from the Illinois State Department of Children and Family Services, but the real reward is "watching failure-to-thrive babies grow to almost no-problem toddlers."

Some nominally paid jobs are routine clerical assistance, but others are fascinating. In New Hampshire, a retired hospital secretary has learned to use a teletypewriter (TTY) machine to comunicate with deaf people. The machine looks like a small typewriter with a screen and allows the deaf person to send and receive written messages. She started as a volunteer, but now earns $6 an hour from a local agency that sponsors the service. She likes the people she works with and feels good about what she is doing.

Social programs serve a wide gamut of needs, and not all are available in every community. If you're interested in the general field, ask the people at your local United Way or agency coordinator what programs in town need help. Or better yet, since many of the more interesting hands-on jobs require short-term training, ask what kind of social work training is offered at your community college.

If you already have a particular kind of need in mind, the quickest way to see whether you are really going to like it is to take a course at your local community college that offers field experience in the problem that interests you, or volunteer with one of the social agencies you will find listed in the community numbers of your local phone book.

There's a lot going against social work as a second career. Red tape abounds. Pay is low. Budgets are constantly under pressure. Burnout limits the number of years anyone can give it full emotional commitment. But the high of making a real difference in someone else's life makes it all worthwhile.

☑ RELIGION

America isn't godless. We have at least ninety different faiths if you count only those with fifty thousand or more adherents. The challenge is that all of them have to be privately funded while attendance, financial support, and the number of young people training for the clergy is generally declining.

However they differ in doctrine, governance, or practice, all faiths support a professional clergy to lead each congregation in prayer, preach the faith, give religious instruction, and render pastoral services to their members. They officiate at marriages, funerals, and rites of initiation into the faith, such as baptism, confirmation, or bar mitzvah. They visit the sick, comfort the bereaved, and render spiritual and often practical help to individuals.

In addition to serving a congregation, clergy of all faiths give spiritual comfort and guidance in hospitals, the armed forces, prisons, and privately funded schools.

Almost all religious groups also support formal religious education of some kind, ranging from early childhood to the education of their clergy. Almost all employ musicians, chorus, or cantors to provide the music required in their worship services. And almost all also regard it as a religious duty to provide practical assistance to those in need, which parallels social services provided by publicly funded and private social agencies.

In theory, religious work is divided between an educated clergy and services provided by lay volunteers or employees. In practice, the line is sometimes hard to draw.

To begin with, faiths differ widely in the qualifications they set up for their clergy. Some evangelical faiths, notably independent Baptist denominations, are served by clergy with little formal training — in some cases not even ordained — while Roman Catholic priests and rabbis go through extensive special training.

Mainstream Protestant denominations usually require four years of college followed by three years of seminary and a probationary period of field service similar to a medical or legal internship. Chaplains in state-supported institutions usually have to be seminary graduates with experience in a congregation, and Protestant denominations have accrediting agencies for military and some institutional chaplaincies.

Then, lay members of many faiths assist the ordained clergy in nonliturgical aspects of worship. A Christian church may have a **prayer**

group leader who arranges time, place, program, music, and speakers for the traditional midweek evening meeting and sometimes for meetings in institutions such as nursing homes as well. In many Protestant churches, church business and education is delegated to lay **elders.** In Anglican and Catholic congregations, the **deacon** is counted clergy, but in other Protestant churches, the deacon is a lay assistant to the clergyman.

The shortage of clergy tends to break down former sharp distinctions between clergy and laity. As far back as 1969, for instance, the Roman Catholic church reinstituted the office of **permanent deacon,** open to older married men. The deacons can administer sacraments such as baptism, but not the Eucharist, and they usually continue to earn a living outside the church.

Nobody goes into religious work for the money. The median pay of all clergy in 1990 was $433 a week, but compensation varied widely with experience, denomination, and the size and wealth of the congregation. Many congregations provide a residence, a car and other fringe benefits for their clergy, and in the major Protestant denominations they expect generous pensions.

In Christian churches, Sunday school teachers are usually volunteers, but directors of religious education and church secretaries are usually paid, though nowhere near as much as they would get for a full-time job doing the same work in a nonreligious organization. In the eighties, most professional Christian educators in the United Methodist Church earned between $10,000 and $15,000 for less-than-full-time work.

In most small congregations, a great deal of the administrative and maintenance work is done by volunteers or members of the congregation at nominal pay.

SECOND CAREERS FOR EXPERIENCED RELIGIOUS WORKERS

Like judges and writers, most clergy continue what they regard as their calling as long as they are physically able. Roman Catholic clergy see their calling as a lifetime status carrying obligations to serve, rather than a job from which they can expect to retire at some given age.

The career of one **Roman Catholic Sister of Mercy** shows how service can change over the years. She started out as a parochial school teacher. Since she had taught Spanish, she was assigned to social services for Spanish migrant workers, served with the Chicgo police force in a post equivalent to a chaplaincy, and after special training was qualifed to look after the spiritual and psychological needs of the dying in a skilled care facility.

If you are a Protestant minister who wants to continue to serve after your nominal retirement, your own church organization will usually have plenty of suggestions. If you feel the time has come to retire from the leadership of a demanding congregation, you may step down to play what one Protestant minister cheerfully calls "second fiddle," assisting a younger successor with administrative work or home visits to parishioners, many of whom are old friends. Or you could assist in another church by conducting midweek services.

Your church may find you a part-time job as a chaplain in a hospital or a prison, or help you undertake a ministry to a specialized group, such as the hearing-impaired. An 80-year-old former broadcast pastor records Christian programs and counsels listeners by mail.

Retired Protestant clergymen are sometimes retained by the headquarters of their church to do occasional or part-time jobs of research, administration, or the supervison of religious education. One retired pastor works full-time training friendly visitors to the aging in all the congregations in his region.

Others minister in humbler ways. One former pastor takes the night shift at a funeral home, answering calls that come in between five o'clock at night and eight in the morning. Another cleans and delivers linen in a hospital.

Those who move out of religious work are well positioned to get the interesting part-time jobs that seniors especially like. They are ideal organizers of volunteers and programs for nonprofit organizations. One works part time producing television shows for the United Nations Association.

An extremely pleasant second career is in travel. Ministers who have led congregations have the temperament and experience for guiding tours (see page 220). Those who have led their own parishioners to the Holy Land make a regular business of it after they retire. A former Methodist minister in Wisconsin now works with a nonprofit agency sponsoring tour groups to areas of the world that have contributed to the Christian faith.

NICHES FOR NEWCOMERS TO RELIGION

Christian churches have an increasingly hard time attracting qualified young people to the clergy at the pay they can offer, so they welcome older newcomers.

Older people are responding. The average age of **seminarians** is rising. Many are now people over 50 who have been teachers, military, engineers, housewives, office workers, salesmen, and blue-collar workers. In 1988 a 77-year-old widowed female Episcopal priest was the **bishop's** liaison to the gay and lesbian communities of the Diocese of Michigan: retired against her will for age from her job as a university professor, she had entered seminary at age 65.

There are many reasons why older people want to become clergy. It may be the career they wanted when they were young. A chemical engineer who had put aside thoughts of the ministry while his children were young went to seminary when he retired on a pension. In 1988 he had become a self-styled "greenhorn minister with white hair" for the Presbyterians of a small town in Louisiana.

Churches are making it easier for older newcomers who have another source of income, like Roman Catholic permanent deacons or Protestant lay preachers. An engineer who served as a lay preacher in the American Baptist Church became uneasy about working on a nuclear plant and took early retirement so that he could earn a master of divinity. In 1988 he was earning $180 a month and expenses as a floating minister serving a new congregation every few months. Now that their children are grown, he and his wife enjoy the travel.

There are even more opportunities for small pay in church work that does not require ordination. The **church secretary** is very frequently a retired office worker or teacher (see page 200). A widowed housewife in Texas is the **wedding coordinator** who arranges for the use of the chapel of her Methodist church: the church pays her $60 a wedding to run the wedding rehearsal and handle the administrative details.

Most Christian churches have a part-time **director of religious education** supervising and training their volunteer Sunday school teachers. Retired teachers are especially welcome. The board of a big Methodist church in Michigan drafted a retired elementary school principal to supervise their 150 volunteer teachers at the high pay of $20,000 a year for three-quarters time.

Each of the major Christian denominations has a central clearinghouse for volunteers. There are even opportunities to work for short periods in underdeveloped countries as missionaries, social workers, and teachers of basic skills such as gardening.

Ordained clergy generally get their jobs through church employment services or other channels set up by their national church organizations. A church considering you will expect you to visit and preach a sermon.

If you are looking for work that does not require ordination, talk to your own pastor. He or she can tell you about the education you will need and clue you in to opportunities in other congregations and to the clearinghouse for volunteer work elsewhere.

Religion is underpaid in money, but it offers sustaining fellowship in working with the better side of human nature.

☑ SCIENCE, ENGINEERING, AND TECHNOLOGY

Science and engineering is the high adventure of exploring the physical world and harnessing it to human uses. Some of it is done by research scientists in universities, whose only equipment is a pencil. A great deal of it is done in offices or factories by people in physical touch with machinery or structures.

There's a lot of work to do. The structure of matter and living organisms has to be studied for principles that work as well for atoms as for galaxies light-years away. These principles have to be applied to human enterprises that range from listening for potential signals from other parts of the universe to combating a pest that threatens the Florida citrus crop.

Bridges, buildings, utility systems, railroads, airports, and every kind of machine, tool, production process, and physical object begin on the drawing board of a designer.

Labor, equipment, and materials for producing the work have to be planned, assembled, managed, and monitored by professional engineers and technicians.

Products, working conditions, and the environment have to be constantly tested to guard against unintended hazards.

Methods and systems, such as computer analyses, have to be developed to do all of the physical work better.

Qualifications for jobs in science and engineeering are a combination of field experience and professional education in a particular field, such as civil engineering. Engineers, architects, and land surveyors who take public responsibility for a piece of work must be licensed by the appropriate state licensing board, but others working in the profession under their supervision need not be licensed.

Licensing practices vary by state. For instance, all states require a license for land surveyors, but an increasing number also require a license for geologists whose work impacts the environment. Some license scientific workers who test for compliance with state standards — for example, milk testers in Minnesota, agricultural consultants in Louisiana, and environmental health specialists in Idaho.

Compensation for engineers and scientists reflects their education and specialized knowledge. Median weekly full-time salaries in 1990 were $695 for architects, $830 for aerospace engineers, $890 for chemical engineers, $790 for civil engineers, $848 for electrical engineers, $764 for industrial engineers, and $805 for mechanical engineers. Natural scientists averaged $661 weekly, including $676 for chemists and $602 for biologists. The median for all engineering technologists and technicians was $509, a little higher for those in electronics ($533), a little lower for surveyors ($446) and drafters ($499) including computer-aided design (CAD) operators.

SECOND CAREERS FOR EXPERIENCED SCIENTISTS AND ENGINEERS

If you've been a scientist, engineer, or technician, you are used to moving from project to project even if you have stayed with the same employer, so the career you begin in your 50s may be your fifth or sixth instead of your second.

Scientists and engineers laid off or pushed into early retirement by technological change can often find a job with another enterprise just beginning a project that uses their skills. An aeronautical engineer who took early retirement at TWA found a job designing aircraft wiring for a company manufacturing helicopters. As so often happens, he got the job through the recommendation of a supplier serving both companies.

Technical people retiring from government jobs can often make more money in private enterprise, especially if they can help them comply with regulatory codes they have administered (see page 59). An architect who had planned the review of health facilities for the state of California got work merely by writing a letter about his retirement to private architects and hospital administrators with whom he had worked. His consulting jobs come by fits and starts, but bring him more dollars at the end of the year for part-time work than he ever earned working for the state full time.

Switching sides is a good way to increase your income, but rules against "double-dipping" into public funds restrict how much you can earn from a second career with the federal government (see page 54).

Another way to make more money is to specialize. Some of the most valuable specialties have had to be developed on the job. Packing and shipping hazardous materials according to government specifications made a technician out of a worker who in any other industry would have been just another foreman in the warehouse. At 72 he was earning $20 an hour for the company from which he had retired as a consultant directing the work he used to do.

Computers have made specialists of people who had to apply them in the course of their work. Henry Kahrmann spent seventeen years as a logistics officer in the army. He then became a data manager for GTE Sylvania, an electronics manufacturer. In his retirement he has become a highly paid configuration consultant, setting up computer systems that produce specifications for new parts to a tank, an engine, or any assembly that will ensure conformity to existing hardware. Configuration specialists cut through the jungle of paper records, plans, test results, procedures, and technical manuals that account for 20 percent of the cost of some military contracts. Kahrmann never went to college, but in 1988 college courses were beginning to be set up in the art that he helped develop.

Computers were virtually unknown when Nolan Sample started keeping the financial records of an oil company on punch cards. In those days, security meant locking the cards up every night. But when the records he kept were computerized into consolidated databases used by all departments of the company, he was charged with finding ways to protect them against tinkering by ambitious managers trying to improve the rate of return for their cost centers, as well as embezzlers and competing oil companies interested in trade secrets.

By the time Nolan retired in 1986, he was a nationally recognized specialist in the art of protecting databases against all sorts of intruders, including teenage hackers. He was immediately hired to protect the data of the local utility company and could double the $50,000 he earns if he were willing to move out of Richardson, Texas. In the 1990s, more than thirty thousand computer specialists wage continual warfare adapting database security packages to the latest technological assault.

Safety engineering is another growing specialty. It used to be an incidental responsibility for engineers doing other work, but it's now so big it's a field in itself. When a merger displaced Joseph Kosh from his job designing the testing of metal products, he answered a newspaper ad for a job as manager of industrial safety at a manufacturer of scientific instruments and was able to pass the examination that certified him for the work.

No longer mere watchdogs over plant safety rules, the safety engineer may now specialize in industrial hygiene or environmental protection. A senior staff nuclear engineer who quit to start a motorboat sales and service firm has sold his business and gone back to professional work as an **air quality specialist** for the county.

Nuclear safety is the best-paid specialty. A Ph.D. in nuclear engineering who learned the business in the navy didn't like his second career supervising the design of nuclear power plants for an engineering company, so he quit to become a consultant with a firm that helps manufacturers assess and solve problems of environmental safety. He now can earn more than $90,000 in a good year at work he likes, but the work comes in spurts and there's no security in it.

Finally, some engineers and scientists make money beyond their wildest dreams as consultants on a technology they learned or developed in a salaried job.

Federal law prohibited Cornelius Mock from patenting the Galveston method of growing baby shrimp he developed on the payroll of the National Marine Fisheries Service, but when he retired at 55, foreign governments gladly paid him for the kind of advice and training he had been giving as part of our foreign aid program. Peru, China, Ecuador, Vietnam — he travels the world with a machine gun and a portable fax, helping poor countries set up a baby-shrimp industry that will bring them the foreign exchange they desperately need.

If you would rather take it little easier, there are many ways to get part-time work. To begin with, you may be called back to your old employer to help out in overloads, or for a technical skill developed on the job that they can't do without. This happens so frequently in the aerospace industry that the big companies often hire back their own retirees through technical help contractors.

Some technical jobs are made to order for retreads from another field of engineering. Dan Daugherty was an electrical engineer who pioneered the first computers, but soon deserted the technical frontier for better-paying work in marketing and management. After his heart attack he retired from the competitive pressures of Silicon Valley to Big Cone, a tiny town in the California desert. When he got there, he discovered that Big Cone is the site of the radio telescope for the California Institute of Technology and spent the next eight years tracking solar flares as an **observer technician.**

It was a big cut in pay and status, but Dan loved working with the friendly, noncompetitive little group of fifteen astronomers and technicians. They quickly taught Dan all he needed to know about astronomy and the many computer programs and machines that keep the two ninety-foot antennae recording radio emissions from all over the universe. His computer skills were obsolete, but his judgment was good when things went wrong and he had the basic background to tackle many different kinds of maintenance problems. When he finally quit he was working part time for $11,000 a year.

For a change of pace, you can use your professional background to write, teach, train, give expert testimony in court, or serve your community. A retired electrical engineer is the western editor for *Design News*. A retired industrial engineer earns $15,000 a year for twenty-five hours a week of pleasant work as the engineer of a small New England town.

If you'd like to teach, you are so badly needed that you may be able to make your own schedule at a local high school or college. A retired senior research manager for Scott Paper finds teaching basic engineering at a community college a challenge because it's "different from solving problems yourself." He plans to go into the business of producing video teaching aids.

Finally, you can volunteer. A retired astronomer promotes his field by operating the telescope open to public stargazers at the University of Arizona at Tucson.

NICHES FOR NEWCOMERS TO SCIENCE AND ENGINEERING

The training required of mainstream scientists, engineers, and architects is designed for the young and hardy, but every year some older people get the training and walk in by the front door.

Audrey Barnes worked in a chemical lab during World War II, but she had never been to college when she quit her secretarial job at the age of 50 and went straight through Southwest Texas State University to a master's degree, the oldest student in her class. At 70 she had no plans for quitting her job as a chemist in the laboratories of Dow Chemical, and she thinks they're glad to have her because her short seniority makes her a talent bargain for the company.

But there are many back doors. With short training, you may learn a specific technique or machine that makes you indispensable to a scientific, engineering, or architectural project. You may learn a new technology on the job; study up to qualify as a professional in a craft you know; or learn enough about a hobby to become a professional at it.

Computer-aided design (CAD) is a craft you can learn in about a year, which will qualify you for a well-paying job wherever technical work is being done. When Helen Gloor was 61 she was earning $420 a week for forty-eight hours of work as a CAD operator, but until she was 57 she had been a music teacher. She took a cram course designed to attract homemakers at the local community college, survived the math, mechanical drawing, and computer programming, and was immediately hired by a local service bureau that does design and drafting work for architectural and engineering firms.

CAD work is so new that it is a second career for most of the people doing it. Some of the newcomers started with no more than a basic high school education, but it's not everyone's dish of tea. You have to be neat, precise, dexterous, sharp-sighted, good at math, and able to visualize how an object looks from different angles.

Another niche is a new technology you may have had to learn because it changed the work you used to do. If you've a bent for science and mechanics you may have learned enough about it to be grandfathered into professional work before credentials were established for it. The best examples are in computers. Older people who learned about them in military or civilian work have become specialists in their use. A medical lab technician who took time out to raise a family manages a computer system which collects data from instruments used in medical research. A retired master sergeant in the air force who spent his second career working in a computerized warehouse has a third career as a consultant computerizing small businesses.

The burgeoning safety field is a different kind of frontier. A new perspective as well as a new technology, it draws people from many different occupations. It's something to consider if you've been a fireman, responsible for safety in construction, manufacturing, or the military (see page 56), or a manager in an industry which has to contend with new regulations on workplace hazards or industrial threats to the environment. When Andrew Askew, Ph.D., retired as district manager of a chemical company, he increased his income by working with firms consulting on environmental science and public health.

Still another back door is a skill you know that can substitute for academic credentials. A supervisor who spent thirty years checking on raw materials in a steel plant learned enough metallurgy to become a **professional mining engineer** evaluating mining properties. An electrician has gone to work for an engineering firm as an **electrical designer,** and a retired power plant supervisor learned enough electrical engineering to become an electrical draftsman.

Some jobs in science and engineering are naturals for people who have learned some of what is required elsewhere. The manager of a milk processing plant has become a self-employed **sanitary engineer,** servicing water wells and wastewater plants in his neighborhood. The

city council of Saint James, Missouri, invited its retired school superintendent to serve as **city engineer** because he knows how to work
with everyone in the community.

Teachers are especially adaptable. A high school math teacher easily
learned how to use dosimeters to measure radiation as a **physical
science technician.** A teacher who tired of bells, parents, and kids is
working in medical research as a **laboratory technologist:** she says
that all she really had to learn new was how to insert a needle into a
blood vessel.

Surveying attracts older people from other outdoor occupations.
Foresters have to learn surveying, and some become surveyors when
they retire. A retired fire fighter is happy working as a **surveyor:** he
likes being outside and the main thing he had to learn was how to be
precise.

Don't overlook the potential of your hobbies. Betty Thurman
dreamed of gardening during the thirty-five years she worked as a
clinical dietitian in Michigan hospitals. After she retired she took a
$90 course offered by Wayne County, which qualified her as a master
gardener, and was so good at it that the Macomb County Extension
Service hired her as an **assistant horticulturalist** to answer questions
on yard care.

"Doc" Jamback sailed and bought boats and books about boats all
the forty years that he practiced dentistry. When he retired to Bidde-
ford, Maine, with his collection, so many other boat people asked his
advice that he began to charge for it. A qualified **marine surveyor,**
he earns $30 an hour checking the safety, seaworthiness, and value of
all kinds of boats for prospective purchasers and insurance claimants.
He has to climb all over and under them, so it's dirty, strenuous, and
sometimes smelly work, but since safety is involved, it's serious.

Neither Betty nor Doc mind that they don't earn as much as mainstream professionals in their fields. Amateurs like the "work" of hobbies so much that they cheerfully do it for nothing — or pay to do it.
Volunteers interested in the environment pay Earthwatch and university researchers (see page 89) for the privilege of collecting water
samples or writing down every two minutes what the orangutans are
doing overhead in a tropical forest.

Are you interested in the weather? The report you reach for first
thing every morning is the result of readings on land and sky conditions
phoned in every hour to the National Weather Service from forty
thousand stations maintained by citizens in their homes. The Weather

Service trains you and, if you pass the examination, installs the instruments in and around your home. You are paid $1.90 for each day call, $2.25 at night.

It's a marvellous job for homebodies. In 1990, Frances Airas of Mullan, Idaho, received a pin for twenty years of service. Her husband is a retired weather reporter for the Federal Aviation Administration, now slightly disabled. Both now in their 70s, they earn almost $800 a month making sixteen calls a day and pay a young man $5 to make two of the night calls for them. The equipment takes up one of their kitchen cabinets and a wall on their porch in addition to the thermometers located outdoors on their property.

The place to start looking for any technical career is your local community college. They'll tell you what technical work is locally in demand, and if you take the training they offer for it they may have employers waiting for you.

Another resource is your former or present employer. They may have or know of the kind of work you want even if it's not what you've done for them, and since they know you and what you can do they are more willing than a stranger to let you try something new. Rather than quit entirely, a contract administrator for a research institute was transferred to less stressful part-time work as a consultant in environmental studies. He had to do some boning up on the subject, but his familiarity with the problems made up for his lack of academic training. He's earning much less money than he made as a top executive, but it's outdoors and he likes being able to see a completed job instead of a pile of paperwork.

Engineering is relatively well paid, but it's feast-or-famine. Though skills can quickly become obsolete, it's exciting work for those who love to keep learning.

☑ LIBRARY AND RESEARCH WORK

Knowledge is power, but only if it is organized so that you can get what you need when you need it. We know so much now that we depend more than ever on data managers and librarians to keep us from drowning in it.

And it's not confined to print. If they can find the money and the staff, public libraries may house and lend art, films, records, cassettes, and computer programs as well as books, periodicals, and newspapers; provide computer searches of hard-to-find data for business patrons, interactive computer programs for career seekers, material designed for the blind and deaf, meeting places for community organizations, bookmobiles to bring material to rural areas, lectures and even courses for adults, and story readings for preschoolers. School libraries have so many services that they are now called "learning resource centers."

Law firms, medical centers, universities, advertising agencies, and big corporations maintain libraries of their own, and there is more demand all the time for the data held in special collections, such as the Family History Library maintained by the Mormons in Salt Lake City. In these specialized services, the librarian may be a computer-literate **information scientist** maintaining database systems for storing and retrieving specific items of information.

Artifacts are data, too. Museums are finding new ways to display and explain their treasures to a widening public audience. Historic houses are being preserved and opened to the public. Archaeological sites all over the world are being explored, and not only by a small circle of experts.

Professional librarians trained to acquire, catalog, and prepare material for use, with a master's degree in library science, were averaging $489 a week in 1990. **School librarians** who had to be certified as teachers generally made more, and so did **college** and **special librarians** working for universities, business and professional firms, or the federal government, and **information scientists** with degrees in computer science. Median weekly earnings for **library assistants** without formal library training were $281 in 1990.

Closely related is the work done by library patrons seeking out information for a professional or personal interest. **Researchers, archivists,** and **genealogists** are sometimes paid, but many of them are delving into the records for the sheer fun of it.

Library and research work requires people who are orderly, patient, good at detail, and able to deal with the public.

SECOND CAREERS FOR EXPERIENCED LIBRARIANS AND RESEARCHERS

A librarian with decades of professional experience has many choices. If she wants to take it a little easier she can almost always find part-time work in a local school, town, college, or special library. The retired head librarian of a high school works fourteen hours a week as a **reference librarian** for a local college. It's just enough to get her away from a twenty-four hour caretaking role at home, and she likes it because she's working with students instead of administrative problems.

But graduate librarians over 50 are likely to have suffered from the historic change in the role of women over the course of their lives. Most of them did not work steadily enough to repay the investment they made in their professional training. One master of library science who worked only three years found her skills so rusty when she was widowed decades later that she was happy to get a job typing and filing catalog cards for a library supply firm.

Some who came back to an automated library were willing to take a deep cut in pay and status rather than learn how to work the computer, and many others simply don't want to work full time in their later years. Some of them become talent bargains. An independent school pays only $6 an hour to the doctor's wife who manages its library. She has a master's degree in library science but "couldn't afford to work for pay" after her husband started practicing. Another master of library science chose to go to work as a caterer's assistant when she was 68. None of the women who stopped out to rear families have private pensions, and since library salaries have always been low, those who do can't always get along on them.

If you're a librarian who needs to make more money, learn more about computers and take your library skills to medicine, law, engineering, business, or a field where pay scales reflect the rising value of access to timely information. **Special librarians** working for law, medical, engineering, or scientific research organizations earn more than reference librarians in public or academic libraries, and the more specialized the field, the higher the pay. If there's something very special you know a great deal about, find out whether there are special libraries for it that may have an opportunity for you.

Or look into the college courses you would have to take to qualify for a job as an information scientist in the computer center of a university, major company, or government agency. Information scientists classify, store, and retrieve data in computers on much the same principles which librarians use to catalog books, but they work under better conditions as well as getting higher pay.

Some of the most exciting information-science jobs are in the new small service enterprises that are packaging and selling computerized data, such as Medline for doctors and Lexis or Westlaw for lawyers. These firms need a lot of people skilled in the library arts of indexing and updating organized information. They sometimes escape notice because they are concentrated in one location — and not necessarily a big city — but new ones are always springing up. Look for them in the want ads of the business, rather than the education, section of the paper.

Librarians who are not highly motivated to make money can use their skill to get work in a setting that interests them. Some volunteer for arduous work in a hobby, like the former government information specialist who is cataloging a handwriting analysis research library in Massachusetts. Others contribute their skill to a field of their choice, like the college librarian who works on auction catalogs for the Boston Museum of Fine Arts or the retired college librarian who is studying the voluminous diary left by the college's nineteenth-century founder.

Some librarians become curators. Managing collections of library materials translates easily into managing collections of museum artifacts, so librarians have an advantage in getting into work that is so popular that a great deal of it is done by volunteers. And training in categorization, order, and detail makes librarians such valuable additons to archaeological expeditions that organizations like the Smithsonian actively recruit them.

NICHES FOR NEWCOMERS TO LIBRARY AND RESEARCH WORK

It's perfectly possible to become a professional librarian after 50. Many gray heads graduated in library science with Julie Melly, an art historian whose husband moved her away from her job at the Boston Museum of Fine Arts. When the family returned, her old job at the museum was being done by volunteer **docents,** so she enrolled in the Library Science School at Simmons College. She's now a reference librarian in the Boston public library system.

But you don't have to have a degree. If you like the idea of working in libraries, you'll find that they have more tasks for paraprofessionals than money to pay them. Some are interesting, like telling stories to kids, running the film machine, or staffing the bookmobile. Others are essential housekeeping chores that any careful person can do under the direction of a professional librarian. Books have to be mended, prepared, shelved, checked in and out. Records have to be typed, filed, and photocopied. Telephones have to be answered, records accessed through computer terminals, overdue notices sent to delinquent patrons.

Pay for this work may be as low as the minimum wage, and some of it may be done by volunteers. A great many people like the quiet atmosphere and the company of the educated patrons a library attracts. Since libraries try to keep open during the hours that people have off from work, support jobs can be part time on flexible schedules. Former elementary teachers, secretaries, housewives, salespeople, postal clerks, waitresses, and even blue-collar workers like to put in a few hours a week helping out at the library. Turnover is high for these **library assistants,** so if you want to work in a nearby library, all you usually have to do is to walk in and ask them if they need any help.

Using the library for research of your own is an absorbing second career in its own right. Almost everyone has a passing interest in his or her family history, but tracing ancestors through public records and family Bibles, wherever they may be, has become a profession.

People get into it through their own family history or by accident. A typical example is Hugh Denney, a retired college professor of area planning who agreed to help a woman trace her ancestors because he knew how to look up local land grants. He and his wife then started looking up theirs, traveling to the libraries of the eastern cities from which they knew their ancestors had come. They met so many people who wanted the kind of help he could give that in self-defense he began charging. Now most of his clients are out-of-towners referred to him when they write for help to the Missouri Historical Society Library. He pursues local records for them at $7.50 an hour, with an initial minimum of $30, but in 1989 many **researchers** were charging $15. The Denneys take a tax deduction for the expense of an annual trip to major genealogical libraries up and down the eastern seaboard, but the real reward is the satisfaction of tracking down a hard-to-find bit of information.

Some amateur genealogists get back some of the money they spend on their hobby by writing a book about their findings and selling it to everyone they can find who bears the family name. A retired registrar of voters in Bellingham, Washington, earns $2,500 a year as the desktop publisher of *The Heard Journal, & Herd, Hird, Hurd, Too.*

Bev Morant is a retired teacher of engineering who has become an industrial archaeologist. He started as a tool engineer, then learned archaeology and taught industrial engineering and research at the California Institute of Technology. At 74 he was leading tourists to visit canals in Britain and promoting the restoration of canals in the United States. In Berlin, Wisconsin, for instance, a boat club has restored a historically accurate canal lock.

Preserving or discovering the past attracts so many people that museums and archaeological digs have developed programs for training amateurs to help the professional curators and **archaeologists.** You'll never get rich at this work, but you may find it the most satisfying thing you have ever done.

Elizabeth McClave began when the Stephentown Historical Society in New York State asked for volunteers to help list the names on the town's gravestones for the bicentennial in 1976. She soon discovered not only that the best history is in the cemetery, but that preserving the inscriptions on gravestones is a desperate race against acid rain. She's now the volunteer curator of the Stephentown Historical Society's Heritage Center and spends seventy to eighty hours a week compiling what she calls a "living gravestone" of everything known about every resident of the town since its founding in the eighteenth century.

The easiest way to become a curator is to start as a volunteer docent or tour guide (see page 213) for a small house museum near your home. Those who learn a lot about the site are often entrusted with managing it. To find out about what's needed near you, browse in the local history department of your public library and join one of the local historical societies they'll tell you about.

Once you prove yourself as a volunteer you can learn more about the work from seminars, short courses, publications, and professional advice available from your state historical museum and large private museums, universities with museology departments such as Eastern Illinois or Hoffstra in New York, and historical associations. If you're a collector, they can tell you where you can take a course in the restoration of books, paintings, or furniture.

Another way in is through something you know or can do that a small museum needs. A retired construction man may be preferred over a museology graduate to manage one of the reconstructed villages which have become tourist attractions in many parts of the country. And there is volunteer work in arboretums and zoos for people who've been interested in plants and animals.

Robert Girvin was a lifelong collector of clocks, so when he was retired from his job in a bank he and his wife became the live-in caretakers and docents of the museum home of a famous colonial clockmaker. When the stairs to their living quarters in an upper story became too rough for his wife, he was able to get a paid job at a clock museum that did not require a live-in caretaker.

Before the seventies, archaeologists worked hard to preserve sites from the damage done by amateur diggers. Now they organize the work so that some of it can be done by closely supervised amateurs, who volunteer for two weeks of service all over the planet. To find them, join Earthwatch and browse through their quarterly catalog of expeditions, which asks for volunteers in archaeology, ecology, en- tomology, herpotology (snakes), icthyology (fish), mammology, marine ecology, ornithology (birds), vulcanology (volcanoes), pri- matology (monkeys), geology, and public health.

There are always more volunteers for an expedition than the dozen or so who are needed. To qualify, you have to be under 80, in good health, and endowed with "enthusiasm, common sense, and good humor." You have to pay your own share of the expedition and your travel, but these expenses are tax deductible.

The possibilities are exciting. Vilna Kohn is a doctor's widow who got tired of practicing law and earned a Ph.D. in zoology after she was 50. At 61 she spent a week diving in the Red Sea to collect reef fish for the New York City Aquarium and another week on Easter Island. She has helped dig into the origins of the city of Buenos Aires and the prehistory of Chile. Some of her roommates on these field trips were women in their 70s.

But you don't have to pay your way to Patagonia to get in on the fun. There may be cheaper places to dig that are closer to home, but don't explore them on your own. To find a local opportunity, inquire at the nearest museum of natural history or the anthropology de- partment of the nearest college.

There may even be a lot to explore and preserve in your own hometown. Houses that seem merely old to you may qualify as historic. In the South and the East, neighborhood groups are preserving these houses, delving into the color they used to be painted, for instance, or collecting and restoring the funiture that used to be in them. Some home crafts people are even reviving obsolete crafts, such as the formulas for making old paints.

Maintaining the growing volume of data in all the forms it is now recorded is not always well paid. Work in libraries and museums may not be done under the best of conditions. But it is fulfilling to help preserve the human record in all its forms and organize it so that it can be used for many different purposes.

☑ THE WORD BUSINESS

Words are everywhere. We hear and see them in books, periodicals, junk mail, instructions, news reports, ads. They come to us over the airways, from podiums, in print on packages, billboards, and T-shirts as well as paper — and someone had to write every one of them.

Qualifications, education, psychological tests, or even experience are of surprisingly little help in predicting success at these occupations. Word people are judged by subjective reactions to their product, and a lot of that is luck.

Median weekly pay reportd by the Bureau of Labor Statistics for 1990 is only $513 for editors and reporters, $581 for public relations specialists, $673 for technical writers. But the median conceals a bewilderingly wide range. A handful of book authors reap hundreds of thousands of dollars in royalties the year they hit the best-seller list, while there may be as many as millions of people writing for little or nothing simply because they enjoy it.

Writers are less secure than other salaried employees because their work is more affected by policy changes, and many are entrepreneurs who write on speculation. For these, pay ranges from a high of $10,000 for a junk-mail sales letter to zero for the lovingly chosen word of a poem.

SECOND CAREERS FOR EXPERIENCED WORDMONGERS

If you've been a writer, you have had so much experience shifting gears that you have a leg up on your agemates in finding a new career in a different field.

Writing is the royal road to cushy jobs in the public service. A writer of historical brochures for the National Park Service now plans exhibits for them. One women's-page editor became director of international marketing for the state of Indiana and another a program officer in the New York City Department for the Aging. All of them make more than they did as writers.

By the same token, writing is a marvelous stepping stone to a business of your own or one of the professions that depend on persuasion. In their later years, successful writers become farmers, teachers, counselors, psychotherapists, and real estate brokers. In Texas, Robert Mays is a good example of what can happen to someone who begins life as a writer. In the fifties he was reporting sports events for radio and televison networks. Later he was able to buy some local radio and television stations. Now in his 70s, he's in the business of providing cogeneration systems that undercut high Texas utility rates.

If you want to move out of writing, you have the advantage of knowing about many word-related fields that may provide exactly the lifestyle you are after. You might consider running a little bookstore or office newsstand, helping out at a library or travel agency, or proof-reading part time.

But most word people don't want to move out of their field. Free-lancing is the dream of freedom for the salaried. It's a risky way to make a living but you can make out if you develop a specialty and cultivate the people who need it.

It pays to plan ahead. While he was still science editor for the U.S. Information Agency, Bill Froehlich joined and became active in thirty organizations of professional scientists. At meetings just before he retired he passed out a business card — "International Science Writers" — and the phone has been ringing off the hook ever since with writing assignments from industrial and scientific organizations.

No specialty? Don't be too sure. Try making a list of everything you know better than the next fellow: cars, guns, cooking, cats, deer hunting, school systems, computer software. Who wants to know these things?

Next make a list of all the word tasks you know *how* to do — proposals, advertising copy, documentary films, the conventions of academic writing, television productions, how to write signs on the sides of blimps. Who needs these skills?

The next stop is the public library to get names, addresses, and phone numbers of organizations that could use your services. Pick out some likely targets, and write to them, listing your credits and cere-dentials, proposing article ideas or asking for work. If you've held a salaried job, you may not have to search further afield than your past employers or their competitors. Newspapers and magazines often buy special articles from former **staff writers.** A retired home furnishings editor continues to do occasional articles on home decoration for the paper.

You may be able to make a regular part-time job out of one of the chores that you did when you were working full time. Think of some-thing time-consuming that a newcomer couldn't do as well. In New-ark, Ohio, a retired sportswriter works fifteen hours a week writing up the reports that legmen phone in from games. On Long Island a former architectural news correspondent for McGraw Hill checks local building permits for his old office.

Public relations departments and firms call back former staffers when they have an event, an anniversary book, or a project for a client with whose needs a retiree is familiar.

Book editing, copyediting, indexing, and **proofreading** are increasingly sent out to retirees who used to do this work for the firm or a competitor. The pay may be low, but the work can be done at home and there is plenty of it. Write to public relations firms and major publishers telling them of your experience, availability, and hourly rate expected. If you're not sure, you might specify a minimum of $15 an hour. Big-city law firms often send out proofreading, so it's worth querying them about their rates.

Technical writers are in such demand that it's easy for them to work on a job basis or part time at home when they retire. In 1989 they were earning upward of $45 an hour. Ordinary journalists can't do the work unless they have a background in science, engineering, or computers, but if you are in a manufacturing center you might qualify and get leads to the work by taking a course in the subject at your local community college.

But there are so many things to do in communications that you don't have to stick to the same old thing. Word people move their skills to a different media, switch sides, or go into the publishing business. Seasoned print writers try their hand at writing for television and newspaper columnists are sometimes asked to host a show on their topic for local radio or television — not much money, perhaps, but always a lot of fun.

Public speaking before large and well-heeled groups is more lucrative. A writer who has attracted national attention on a hot topic may be offered speaking fees of several hundred times more per hour than she can earn at the word processor.

But this is just another jungle. Like literary agents, lecture agents won't help you until you're established, so if you're new at public speaking, start out with talks before local groups for little or nothing and get the paper to cover the speech so that you have something to show a higher-paying platform.

The classic way for journalists to make more money is to switch sides and go to work for the organizations they have been covering. There's nothing shameful about this switch if you're up-front about it. Let it be known that you are interested and you could be recruited.

The U.S. Customs Service offered a magazine staffer more than he was earning to head their public information service. Public relations firms pay writers about two-thirds of what they charge the client for the work, which is usually more than a publication pays.

If your name is known at all you may fall into a second career of serving the burgeoning market of people who want to be writers. When magazine freelancer Frank Thomas retired to Sun City, Arizona, his neighbors drafted him to teach a course that eventually became a book, *How to Write the Story of Your Life — A Family Gift.*" He now flies around the country giving speeches and short courses to seniors. So many people dream of writing a cookbook that Sara Pritzer's *How to Write a Cookbook and Get It Published* did better than hundreds of the cookbooks published every year.

There's room in this market for everyone in the book business. **Book editors** become **book packagers,** helping authors structure and sell a book, sometimes to their successors in a publishing house. Authors pay **packagers** a percentage of the royalty or consulting fees of $50 to $100 an hour.

And don't overlook fundraising. "Development" projects need competent writers for all the letters, brochures, and material they beam at potential contributors. Charles Doering retired early as vice president of human relations for Navistar, the agricultural equipment manufacturer, and went to work at $60,000 as the director of development for a university. He says that the switch to an academic environment was one of the best things he ever did.

Doering got his national job by answering an ad in the paper, but if you are looking for something closer to home, it wouldn't hurt to talk with the people in a local nonprofit agency that interests you.

If you're an experienced writer or editor, it may not be as hard as you think to become a publisher. Don Tabor had only the $4,000 he drew down from his retirement fund when he quit his steady job as the editor of a daily newspaper. With a little help from the local bank, he bought a weekly newspaper that was up for sale and to his great surprise made more money his first month in business than he had ever earned in salary. If this is your dream, Tabor advises pursuing it in a Texas hometown where the bank knows you and your daddy.

It's cheaper to start a newsletter. If you can write persuasive copy about something you know very well that interests a group of people you know how to reach, you can learn enough about selling by mail to start a newsletter at home on a shoestring.

A faster but more expensive way into the newsletter business is to buy one. When the magazine she was editing changed hands, Helene Mandelbaum sold a New York real estate mortgage she had inherited and bought a newsletter for managers of New York City real estate. She now publishes books on the subject for her subscribers.

But money isn't everything. Successful older word people look for second careers that are rich primarily in fun, freedom, challenge, congenial people, or service to the community, and the very nature of their work makes it especially easy for them to find all these good things.

You can't stop writers. An intelligence specialist retired from the air force intends to continue writing commentaries for himself, where he can "tell it like it is" until "they plant me." A public relations director who spent forty-four years on the phone relishes the solitude of writing novels, short stories, and poems for himself.

When they have enough to live on, retired word people have a ball working for little or nothing for specialized publications and local newspapers or broadcasters, speaking up at public meetings, raising money for the United Way, lobbying the legislature, organizing the community behind a civic project, advocating the good cause of their choice, or teaching journalism at the local community college.

NICHES FOR OLDER NEWCOMERS TO THE WORD BUSINESS

Writing or public relations work is the second career that older people are most likely to want — not only teachers, secretaries, librarians, salespeople, managers, and other workers with words, but butchers, bakers, bankers, dentists, storekeepers, nurses, and housewives who have never held a paying job.

Writing a book is what most of them have in mind, and every once in a while an older newcomer brings it off. John Webb was a home builder who drew on his Cherokee heritage to write a successful novel. Myra Rowe was a teacher of English and history who sold her first novel by sending it cold to a New York publisher who specialized in historical romances, and a handful of homemakers have drawn on their own imagination to supply the vast paperback market for steamy love and sex.

But these are exceptions. Even journalists and scholars are hazy about placing a book with a trade publisher. Literary agents aren't much help on a first book. At 10 or 15 percent of a publisher's advance against royalties, which may be no more than $3,000, agents simply can't afford the risk of spending time on someone new to the business.

You can write the book and mail it to a publisher, but thousands of unsolicited manuscripts and proposals arrive at a major publishing house every week, many more than limited staffs can read, let alone consider. It's far better to write asking publishers whether they are interested in the kind of book you have in mind. Try intriguing an editor into asking for more by writing a a one-page letter covering what the book is about, who will buy it, why you are the best author for it, and enough about you to suggest that you are capable of delivering it, with a very few sample pages.

But supposing this doesn't work. Almost half of the older people who say their second career is writing aren't making any money at it. But even when they say they are writing only "for themselves" they want to be read, some of them so much that they are willing to pay to be published.

There are many ways to do this. Mainstream publishers aren't out for this business, but they will give favorable attention to an author with a respectable story to tell who can guarantee to buy a few thousand copies. This is the avenue to explore if you have something to say that will interest a limited audience, such as other people in your industry.

Another way to go is to buy the production of X copies of your book from a book manufacturer who supplies no sales, distribution, or editing. In between are "self" or "subsidy" publishers, a wide assortment of actors irreverently known as the "vanity press." They have to be watched because they are selling to you rather than to the book-buying public.

There's nothing wrong with self-publishing if you know exactly what you are getting for your money. Before you sign anything or hand over any money, ask these questions:

What will my book look like — hardcover, softcover, size?

Will I have the right to approve the physical appearance of the book before it is produced?

What legal rights, including copyright, do I retain, and what rights will go to you?

How many copies will you produce?

What will you do to distribute, sell, and advertise the book?

How will you account for any proceeds you receive from the sale of the book?

If you don't get firm answers, you might get ahead of the game by hiring a lawyer familiar with book publishing to look over the contract. If your own lawyer doesn't practice in this field, he or she can usually find one for you who does.

You may feel it's worthwhile even if you don't get rich at it. Alberta Atkins doesn't regret the $4,000 she eventually spent to get five hundred softcover copies of a 136-page book about her recovery from a hip implantation, although her first publisher went bankrupt before delivering. She sold a few at local autograph parties, but mainly she gives the book away to friends and relatives.

Norman McLeon did better because he developed and serviced a specific market for his stories about the California gold rush. When he couldn't sell them, he spent $1,500 typesetting and printing fifteen hundred copies of his 176-page book and personally sold and delivered them to stores serving the tourist trade in northern California and Nevada.

If you are up to a big challenge, you can write, produce, promote, and sell the whole thing yourself on your own equipment at home. To prepare camera-ready copy on a personal computer that can be run off by any commercial printer, you have to invest between $5,000 and $10,000 in special software and a laser printer.

Desktop publishing is ideal for authors serving a small but very well defined group of readers with such projects as a genealogy of interest to everyone whose name is "Baker," or the two hundred pages of statistical formulas applying genetic rules to specific plants and animals that a retired professor of genetics produces for a thousand specialists.

Beginners are supposed to write about what they know, and here's where older beginners have the edge. There's a word side to almost anything you have done. In Los Angeles, a supervisor of city housing projects who loved to write continued with the agency, writing an in-house newsletter when she retired. She likes it because she makes her own hours and gets to meet all the people who work for the agency.

Think of all the things you've learned on your first career. Among newcomers who are earning money at writing are retired scientists and engineers who become technical writers, a retired psychiatric nurse who writes about Chinese and holistic medicine, and a retired insurance sales manager who programmed telemarketing machines with canned spiels for selling insurance over the phone.

Hobbies are great springboards. A retired trade school teacher has a mail-order business in instructions for constructing crossword puzzles. If you really know something about guns, there are dozens of outdoor magazines on the lookout for new angles and information.

If you don't expect to be paid, try contributing to your local weekly newspaper, shopping paper, or senior paper and remember that your church, club, trade association, or the charity of your choice have publications which rely on volunteer writers.

If English was your own second language, or you are really fluent in another one, you may find an interesting second career as a translator or interpreter for a business or government agency. In many parts of the country courts need Spanish interpreters, and there is a rising market for people with Asiatic languages.

Finally, consider using words on behalf of something dear to your heart — your college, your hospital, your industry, saving the sea lions, or turning the rascals out of the county legislature. As part of her volunteer work for the Office for the Aging, Flo Parrish writes a column for a newspaper checking on the service local stores provide for senior citizens.

Go to work as an educational coordinator informing the school system about your industry, or selling a business on moving a plant to your town, and you may even get paid a little for it. And remember that all good causes need help with the words that raise money. Talk to the people running an organization you like and ask them how you can help.

Making words is deceptively easy. In everyday life, they come as naturally as breathing, yet using them to convey a specific message to someone out of sight is as hard as disciplined thinking. That's the appeal and challenge of working in the word business.

☑ THE VISUAL AND PERFORMING ARTS

The arts are everywhere. Music fills the air. Everyone you see on the screen is an actor. Every picture or photograph in every book and on every screen is the work of some artist or photographer. Clothes, computers, automobiles, kitchen utensils — everything you use, including the package it comes in, owes its looks to the artistic eye of a designer. The furniture in a hotel room and the flowers you order from the florist have been arranged by a professional. Except for the performers and fine artists who create paintings and objects solely for their aesthetic value, the people who do this work are invisible.

Designing is built into the industry which manufactures or sells the product. Fashion design is part of the garment industry, textile design part of the textile industry, package design part of the packaging industry, furniture design part of the furniture manufacturing industry. Designers of store displays and windows are part of the retail business.

While floral and interior designers sometimes work directly for the consumer, most work for florists or retailers or home furnishings. And while some work for large manufacturers, a great deal of design work is done by free-lancers who sell their work rather than their time.

"Commercial art" is similarly split into ever-narrowing specialties. The format of books, magazines, newspapers, and catalogs is designed by specialists attached to each of these publishing fields; the illustrations and ads in them are provided by graphic artists or photographers who may be experts in the subjects they portray. The structure of a plant may be so delicate that it can't be captured by photographs, but must be drawn by an illustrator who is also a trained botanist.

Fashions, catalogs, medical and scientific books all have to be illustrated by knowledgeable experts. Some work on salary for manufacturers, advertising agencies, or design studios, but the great majority of illustrators are self-employed free-lancers.

Photography is the same story. Still pictures of people and events have to be taken for the print media, for commercial use in advertising and promotion, and for legal and scientific records. Portrait photography made for the individuals pictured includes the speciality of recording weddings or children and the quite different business of turning out raw but rapid identification photographs for passports. Motion pictures have to be shot for television news and commercials as well as films for documentation, instruction, and entertainment. Nearly half of all photographers are free-lancers.

Show business is even more specialized and occasional. Changing tastes may relegate even a star to the chorus line or catapult an unknown into instant fame. Competition is fierce. There are never enough jobs to go around. At any one time, less than one-tenth of a percent of the employed population are acting, producing, or directing in film, broadcasting, or theater, but several times that number have done one of these professional jobs at some time in their lives. An actor has to wait for a part that uniquely fits him, and so do **clowns, magicians, dancers, choreographers, standup comics,** and **models.** Some photographer's models contribute only their hands.

Music is performed by **instrumentalists, singers, composers, conductors,** and **choral directors** for recording studios; for operas, musical comedy, or ballet companies; in nightclubs, restaurants, churches, synagogues, and the armed forces. It is also widely taught both to individuals and in public and private schools.

All this work is done by a very few irregularly employed and — with the exception of some musicians — underorganized professionals. Most successful professionals have trained at one of the schools devoted to their particular art and continue to learn and practice all their lives, but there are no objective qualifications and no generally accepted tests of talent. Every artist has to demonstrate his or her fitness for each new job with a portfolio of past work or an audition.

Actors, models, photographers, musicians, and many artists get their work through agents who charge a percentage of any income they secure.

In 1990 the median weekly salary of employed designers was $500; for painters, sculptors, craft artists, and artist-printmakers, $412; for photographers, $410; for actors and directors, $594. But medians mean little because the extremes are so wide apart. In acting, for instance, annual income ranges from millions of dollars for media stars at the height of their popularity to zero for actors in little theaters who are often thrilled to perform for nothing.

SECOND CAREERS FOR EXPERIENCED CAREER ARTISTS

Artists are glad to retire at any age from the jobs they have to take for bread but they continue their real work as long as they are able. Melville Bernstein complains that sculpture is messy, noisy, and full of heavy lifting, but he was still doing it at 77 because it induced in him "dreams of glory."

The most successful move steadily on to more money, more fun, and most important, more freedom. At 78, Maurice Pederson was still playing the organ and directing music in churches and, counting daily practice, still working sixty hours a week, but he was doing it from a music studio in his home in Phoenix. A documentary film maker who quit when he was 57 to form his own company was roaming the world and netting $85,000 a year in his 60s. None of these artists had the slightest intention of ever quitting. In the arts, the winner takes all the goodies.

Some free-lance wherever they can. A cartoonist who once was employed by a comics company earns $10,000 a year drawing portrait sketches at business conventions. An industrial designer retired from IBM does some work every year for private clients. When the opera company which employed him went out of business, a costume designer turned to designing costumes for the Mardi Gras in New Orleans.

Teaching is the most reliable way for a visual or performing artist to stay in the field, and there is a lot of moving back and forth between teaching and doing. Art and music teachers practice their arts when they retire, and successful practitioners can always make a living teaching.

Dancers, singers, and actors who are no longer up to performing become coaches. An actress who went back to college in search of a second career got a chance to use "the gift God gave me" directing the college theatrical productions. There's even work in writing about the arts. A former music director was earning $350 an issue editing a music education magazine for his state.

Most drift into other work in their later years, but artists can be surprisingly adept at applying their talent to new occupations. A retired layout artist runs an inn which houses workshops for artists and an art gallery. A former theater director has created a job for herself as a therapist in a psychiatric hospital. As director of psychodrama she earns more than $50,000 a year for twenty-two hours a week of work helping patients act out their problems.

NICHES FOR NEWCOMERS IN THE ARTS

The appeal of the arts is universal. They are more popular second careers than first ones, attracting older people from a wide variety of trades and professions. For one thing, they are easier to enter than other professions. Most of the work is in irregular jobs that are off the promotional ladders and open to all comers, and formal credentials matter less than being at the right place at the right time. After he was laid off, a lithographer became a professional clown. A fire fighter earns $15,000 a year working as a professional model.

Some of the newcomers are remarkably successful. A retired army colonel who spent his middle years contracting for weapon systems now earns $60,000 a year manufacturing the bronze sculpture he makes. Another successful sculptor used to be a speech pathologist, diagnosing and treating the brain-damaged, and a third was a house-wife.

Some successful newcomers have spent years in an occupation that developed their talents. Teachers can't help but learn something about acting and many of them make it their new profession. After twenty-nine years of elementary school teaching, Marion Doss was retired with a contract to bring her "Mother Goose" show to every school in her district. She's making more money than ever before and de-lighted to be "on stage" all the time.

Other successful newcomers aren't really beginners, but people who have been practicing their art as a hobby over a lifetime of earning a living at something else. An optometrist was a good enough violist to win a chair with a symphony orchestra when he retired from the eye business. A salesmen for the *Encyclopedia Britannica* had become so good a cartoonist that he was able to earn $28,000 a year as a free-lancer when he retired.

Do you take pictures your friends say are as good as those taken by professionals? They may be right, but luck is as important as skill in breaking into professional photography. Publications and ad agencies have their own favorites, but news organizations will always buy the exceptional picture a talented newcomer gets of an event such as a tornado that she was on hand to catch, and if you can write as well as take pictures you may have a better chance to sell illustrated articles to small, specialized publications that pay very little for their material.

Your chances are better taking pictures for the record in a field you know. An example is the before-and-after photographs that insurance companies and policyholders like to have of high-value property such as jewelry and antique furniture. But there's much more out there to photograph. The problem is finding the opportunity and presenting yourself at the time that it is needed.

If you like horses and know your way around racetracks you might get work photographing the finish of races and developing them immediately for the stewards. Allen Hull is a retired postal supervisor who has become a photo-finish operator for a service that provides stewards with an immediate picture of the finish of races. He and his wife Peggy travel from racetrack to racetrack during the season, earning $100 a day. Next time you go to the races, find a steward and ask if they need a photographer.

The same route gets an amateur into filmmaking. Watch for news of a documentary or training film in a field you know and ask if the team needs a technical adviser.

For pure paintings and drawings, art galleries are the classic market, and there are now art galleries in quite small towns all over the country that will display a promising work of art and sell it on commission. If there isn't one in your town, your second career might be to start one.

More accessible than fine arts galleries are the many arts-and-crafts fairs which display all kinds of visual arts. If you don't already belong to your local art association you can find out about these opportunities from the arts council of your state.

Many dedicated artists create not only works of art, but the market for them. When Peggy Steucek went to work for a real estate firm she mentioned to her new boss that she liked to draw, so he asked her to draw a house. He liked what she did so much that he now has her working ten hours a week doing pen-and-ink illustrations for real estate ads in the paper. The firm finds that the drawings attract more attention than the usual photographs.

Vincent Aylward had studied art and "fooled around" for years developing a system for etching portraits from photographs on clear plastic or glass. When he retired from the insurance business he put samples of his work in trophy and gift shops. He now has more commissions to make awards commemorating individuals and events than he can comfortably handle.

The many people who have made calligraphy a hobby can make a little money lettering any documents that need to look nice, from signs and posters to the addresses on wedding invitations. For specialized jobs, the fee can be high: Jewish couples have paid $1,000 or more to have their wedding certificate lettered in Hebrew. You can get this occasional work by advertising in a local shopping paper or on community bulletin boards.

Calligraphers make up their own products. In Tennessee a retired sportscaster who took up calligraphy started hand-lettering his wife's favorite recipes. They've now published a cookbook of special recipes in calligraphy that can be taken out of the book and framed as kitchen decorations. There is so much interest in calligraphy that it's promoted and taught by local schools and organizations. If you have an impressive portfolio you may be able to persuade a local community college to let you teach a course in it, always a good way to get commissions.

Interior decoration is an appealing second career for homemakers, but, as in photography, the professionals fight hard against amateur competition. To succeed, you really need experience in the home furnishings industry, ideally some of it in retailing. As in other consulting businesses, the trick is to find clients who believe in your ability and are willing to trust you. Homemakers who have been active in community affairs have a potential client base.

One of the easiest ways to work in design is to help out at the shop of a local florist. Making up pieces for weddings, funerals, and parties is taught professionally by schools approved by the American Institute of Floral Design, but so many people want to do it that florists can usually get what they need done by hiring amateurs who are willing to work part time at anything from the minimum wage to $8 an hour. You have to have artistic talent and an eye for form and color, but commercial work is much more stressful than arranging flowers for yourself at home. It takes speedy fingers, standing on your feet for hours, and tact in dealing with customers. "Easter is hell," says one florist.

If you've been an amateur musician, a church is the easiest place to begin getting paid for making music. In addition to playing at services, you may get engagements from members of the congregation for playing at weddings, parties, and special events. And there are always opportunities in private teaching.

If you've always wanted to act, produce, or direct, you can often get a chance to show what you can do in your local little theater group and move on from there into the profession. In some work, your age may even be an advantage.

Thanks to the movement against discrimination on the basis of age, attractive older people are now in demand both as actors in television commercials and as photographic models for advertisements aimed at the growing market of seniors. A retired fashion designer who knew the ropes in New York spent her 70s working as an extra in television movies, but former teachers and secretaries get this work by applying to talent agencies which hold auditions in major cities. Another way to go is to ask a modeling school whether they train and place models for this market. If there's a school near you, you'll find it listed in the yellow pages of your telephone book.

How to get started? Photographers, artists, designers, and actors should spend some time assembling a portfolio of their best work to show to a prospective employer or agent. Good agents will take on only those they think they can sell, so your first step is finding and selling to an agent.

Amateur or professional, artists are always learning. They take courses, they go back to college, they learn from each other, they teach themselves. A good example is the newcomer to acting who began by watching the actors in commercials and followed up by taking acting lessons.

About half of the older people who think of themselves as artists don't get paid a cent for it, but they are among the most enthusiastic. One lifelong painter says that her art is like a jealous spouse — demanding, exhausting, but irresistible. She says she'll never stop drawing and painting every waking hour for the rest of her life.

☑ REAL ESTATE AND INSURANCE

Real estate and insurance are exciting fields for people who like big money, big deals, big risks, and big responsibilities. Both fields call to mind salespeople we know because they go out of their way to cultivate a large acquaintance.

These smiling people work hard for their high pay. Buying or selling a home is the biggest financial move most families make. The stakes are even higher when commercial property changes hands, as we learned to our sorrow when so many of these deals unraveled in the 1980s.

Insurance salespeople have to persuade individuals who don't like to think about what they would do if fire, accident, or illness struck, or how their dependents would manage after they died. The protection businesses need is even more complex and often requires the advice of specialists.

In both fields, however, selling isn't the only work to be done. Real estate has to be objectively appraised for the guidance of buyers, sellers, and lenders. Property of all kinds has to be managed by people who find tenants, collect rents, and see that the physical property is maintained.

Some property managers work directly for the big companies or government agencies that need real estate of different kinds or hold it as an investment, but many others work for one of the property management firms that represent many apartment buildings, shopping centers, office buildings, or owners of other property. Even military bases contract with outside services to manage their family housing. In the big property management firms, there is work for people skilled in marketing, law, maintenance, bookkeeping, tenant relations, and the hiring and firing of personnel for the entire enterprise as well as on-site managers of each location.

It's the same in insurance. Behind your friendly insurance agent stands a "home office" of professionals who figure risks, design policies, decide which applicants for insurance will be covered, handle claims made by policyholders, and manage the voluminous records needed to do all these things. Much of this home office work may be done by independent contractors or specialists as well as by people on the company payroll.

Some of these nonselling insurance specialists work for insurance systems run by the Veterans Administration, workmen's compensation, unemployment insurance, civil service and union pension systems, Medicare, Medicaid, or Social Security, the biggest insurance system in the world. A few work for "captive" insurance systems set up by very large enterprises such as oil companies to insure themselves against risks unacceptable on reasonable terms to an insurance company organized for private profit.

Wherever there's insurance, there's a blizzard of data stored in computers that must be kept accessible for processing policies, honoring claims, and studying losses to set premiums. So much paperwork is required to keep track of health insurance that keeping the records is a growth industry not only for insurance companies but for hospitals, doctors, and employers.

Personal qualifications for real estate and insurance selling include an outgoing disposition, tact, honesty, maturity, energy, optimism in the face of turndowns, and a good memory for names, faces, and business details. All states require licenses for real estate brokers, sales agents, and appraisers. Licenses are also required for insurance agents and brokers.

Property managers have to get along easily with all kinds of people and public housing managers may have to be certified by training.

Median weekly pay in 1990 was $507 for full-time real estate brokers and sales agents, $513 for insurance brokers and agents, $592 for underwriters, and $407 for insurance claims agents. Median pay for salaried real estate and property managers was $419 in 1990, but managers of shopping centers and corporate real estate holdings sometimes earn double that amount. On-site managers often get part of their pay in housing.

SECOND CAREERS FOR EXPERIENCED REAL-ESTATE AND INSURANCE WORKERS

There's a sad second career ahead for the real estate developers, brokers, appraisers, and property managers who rode the boom of the eighties. Those who want to continue working in their later years will be needed to deal with the huge inventory of failing commercial and residential properties repossessed by banks, and ultimately by the Federal Deposit Insurance Corporation (FDIC) which underwrote them. Appraising property for insurance companies and banks used to be a quiet berth for retiring real estate brokers, but the profession is being scrutinized and seems headed for more regulation.

People who have been successful in selling insurance or real estate are sometimes able to cut back on their work in their later years. When her health failed, a specialist on employee benefit plans for Alexander & Alexander, the huge international insurance firm, was able to continue consulting with her old clients one day a week.

Insurance brokers like helping other people with financial advice, and some of them find more relaxed ways to continue doing it. Mike Yordon came out of retirement to help a friend start an agency and finds that he still enjoys "the eternal challenge of getting people to start saving money." The manager of a captive insurance company owned by a big oil company for the purpose of insuring its own risks retired with enough investment income to call his own shots as a financial and estate planner. Since he's not grubbing for clients, he can afford to take on only those he thinks he can help.

These are lucky exceptions. Most brokers who want a second career are small business people who can't cut down. They have to be available whenever a client calls in order to stay in business at all, so they tend to look for other ways to use their experience when they want a less stressful second career. Many find what they want in selling, teaching, appraisal, or property management.

Real estate and insurance brokers like to sell, so they often switch to a kind of selling that looks less competitive or more attractive in some other way than the kind of selling they've been doing. Insurance salespeople switch to selling real estate, retirement homes, annuities, advertising, or "business development" for a bank, or even to storekeeping, telemarketing, or demonstrating a food product. Real estate salespeople switch to selling insurance, financial consulting, or whatever looks like a rising business.

If you love real estate but not the stress of heavy selling, consider teaching the many starry-eyed newcomers trying to get licensed, selling repossessed properties for a bank, working for an appraiser, or managing property.

Real estate appraisal is a natural second career for people with experience in real estate, morgage loans, or insurance, and the life experience that comes with age is seen as an advantage. They're needed whenever private property is condemned to build a highway or public building. Most appraisals are made by appraisal services which can offer newcomers the supervised field work they need for licensing, as well as the part-time work that many of them want. A real estate salesman who liked real estate but not selling is happy working toward his appraiser's license with a service which pays him $100 for each appraisal he does while he is in training.

Property management is a favorite second career for insurance as well as real estate salespeople. It's a classic retirement for brokers in a position to pick up income-producing bargains. A broker who moved into a triplex, or three-family house, he bought twenty years ago keeps it and himself in good repair and producing income at the age of 82.

If you don't have the capital to become an owner, you may find a salary and living quarters too as an on-site property manager. A trainer of salespeople thrown out of work when the developer stopped building is happy working for $1,500 a month and free housing as the manager of a mobile-home park. He doesn't mind listening to the minor complaints of older residents. A woman who sold her brokerage business picked up a full-time job for herself as the resident manager of an apartment complex. The only bad part of the job she could think of was being bothered at night by tenants who had lost their keys.

The salespeople are the most visible but not the only professionals in real estate and insurance: some real estate people buy or manage properties, and some insurance people appraise risks, inspect properties, process policies, and handle claims. In both fields there's a certain amount of moving in and out of selling.

Salaried managers of real estate for big companies who retire on a pension can continue meeting people and staying active by working — but on their own schedule — as real estate brokers. A retired manager of land acquisition for a paper company quit to become a broker when he wasn't promoted. A manager of parking facilities for the city of Houston tried selling real estate, but he retired during the slump in values and wound up selling insurance for his son.

At 69, Ken Hubbard quit his job as an insurance adjuster to become an insurance salesman. Within a few months he was making more money than ever before as the president of an insurance agency and kicking himself for not having made the change sooner.

Switching sides can bring you a welcome change of lifestyle. Sometimes a seller switches to the buying side, like the manager of a real estate firm who landed a job acquiring property for the county when he quit and moved to Florida. More often the switch is to selling.

The nonselling work of insurance is so specialized on so many different terms that professionals have many opportunities to move to a job that fits a new lifestyle. Insurance adjusters make more when they quit their salaried jobs and do the same work as independent contractors, but they also quit services to take salaried jobs or move from one company to another. Insurance companies themselves cut back, move in and out of territories, and some of them even go out of business. Even home office managers move. The vice president of an insurance company who retired when the company was sold is a part-time policy analyst at another insurance company doing the same work "but without the responsibility and worry."

Some top insurance professionals become expert witnesses. A retired assistant vice president for claims, called back to testify in the lawsuits that followed a disastrous fire, now works full time at $125 an hour as an expert witness for both plaintiffs and companies. If you want to get into this work, ask a lawyer who handles insurance claims where she gets the local experts in various fields and get yourself on the list of the services who credential them (see page 123).

Switching sides has a future as bright as the growth of bureaucracy. A special agent inspecting property for a casualty company made more money per hour making the same inspections for an insurance agent. A claims adjuster, moved away from her job by her husband, saw an ad for an insurance recovery specialist in the paper of her new hometown and landed a job pursuing health insurance claims for clients of the local welfare department.

Some insurance people stay in their field doing part-time work with one of the many institutes, commissions, and trade associations their industry supports. Companies sometimes call their retirees back for special assignments, so it pays to keep in touch with former bosses. Travelers is one of the insurance companies with a regular program for employing retirees, and executives are among those who come back to do clerical stints.

NICHES FOR NEWCOMERS TO REAL ESTATE AND INSURANCE

There's so much turnover in real estate and insurance that big brokerage firms are always actively recruiting newcomers. If you're interested, talk to people you know in the business or apply to a firm you respect, find out what schooling you'll need to be licensed, and let them sell themselves to you.

In real estate you need enough cash to survive and maybe even lay out expenses in fees and overhead for a year or two after you're licensed *plus* a base of potential prospects. Almost any group of people who know and trust you can become a base. Rather than take a transfer away from the farmers he knew when funds ran out, a county extension agent in Oregon took early retirement and went into the real estate business selling dairies.

People retired with some kind of pension from the military, public service, teaching, or any big bureaucracy are well positioned to sell insurance or real estate, especially if they have had experience counseling and looking out for other people.

Military retirees do especially well. Among many earning more than $50,000 in 1988 were an army colonel who retired because he did not believe in the Vietnam War, a former air force auditor who also works as a paint contractor, and a senior master sergeant who retired from the air force to New Mexico. Other high earners include an air force colonel and Dorothy Fox, the wife of a retired officer, both of whom are real-estate brokers.

Their age is a help. When the air force colonel started job hunting at 58 he discovered that "nobody cares how old you are if you're selling something." Dorothy Fox often wishes she had discovered real estate when she was younger, but consoles herself that "the older real-estate agent *looks* knowledgeable and trustworthy." For the last twenty years she and her husband have "done little but engage in the exciting business that we know so well — moving. Having done so much of this ourselves over a thirty-year stint in the service, we can understand the needs of the military families who come here for a three-year assignment. We can counsel on the basis of our own experiences and smooth the way for our brothers-in-arms."

Teachers and counselors also do well, and so do homemakers. Those with a base in community service sometimes earn high incomes selling residential real estate.

But you don't have to sell. There are niches for newcomers in the nonselling work of both real estate and insurance. Property management for the big service companies is an attractive second career for business owners and managers who have been successful in other fields.

There are many opportunities for real-estate people who know the properties in their area. A printer who sold his share of a business he had inherited bought into a limited partnership in a real estate development firm and heads the management of its commercial properties. In 1990 he was managing two properties for the Resolution Trust Company and earning more than $70,000 a year. If you've made political connections on a first career you may make a big salary managing public housing for a city.

The large number of modest opportunities in managing residential property make ideal second careers for home-loving older people. If you are an owner, you can ensure a high rate of return on the money you have invested while creating a job for yourself managing the rentals, taking care of the repairs, taxes, insurance, and bookkeeping.

You can almost always come out ahead by creating a rental unit in your house when your family shrinks. You don't have to be an expert, but talk to several of the remodelers you'll find in your yellow pages and get their suggestions and advice on financing. You may decide to be your own contractor and let an experienced local carpenter do all the work on hours and steer you through the building code paperwork. Many local ordinances make exceptions in zoning laws to permit senior citizens to add one separate living unit to their homes, but you should check with your insurance agent about a possible change in your coverage.

If you're willing to do the work, you may improve the income you are getting from CDs, mutual funds, bonds, or stocks by investing the money in rental property, even after you pay yourself modest wages for the work of advertising, showing, leasing, collecting, and seeing to the bookkeeping and repairs.

Amateurs do it all the time. A widowed homemaker took the plunge when she discovered that an estate had to sell a cute little run-down house in her small hometown in Michigan. She cashed in an $18,000 CD and, with the help of a local carpenter, rebuilt the interior and rented it first for $250 and later, with the addition of a storeroom, for $300 a month. Best of all, the neighborhood has improved, so her total investment is worth more. The main thing you need, she says, is an "eye for property."

A hospital supervisor in California was more ambitious. When her husband died, his veteran's insurance paid off their house, so she sold it and bought first an eight-unit apartment house and later, after taking a course in apartment management, a share of a twenty-five-unit building. She's a full-time manager, the voice you hear when you call the building.

A mobile-home park or campsite takes less work than an apartment complex. A retired industrial arts teacher, now a widower, spends only ten hours a week managing a trailer park he inherited in Saratoga, New York. His mechanical skills come in handy for the repairs, but he says that school teaching didn't prepare him for dealing with "adults who behave like children." He likes the job because it provides him with "unbelievable sociological stories and behavioral science observations."

But you don't have to own property to get in on this fun. You can earn a salary and free rent too as the on-site manager of an apartment complex, condo, housing project, retirement community, mobile-home park, campsite, or resort. Pay depends on the duties and number of units managed, but you may be able to get a modest rent reduction in exchange for doing odd jobs, and the work can be tailored to individual needs. When her husband died, an 81-year-old widow who lived in a senior citizens' housing project was allowed to keep the rent adjustment her husband had earned by locking up and showing apartments. And there's room in property management for the disabled.

Living where you work attracts older people who are single. If you like to be with people, your instant neighbors will never allow you to be lonely, but the downside is that they won't let you get away from home as much as you might like, either. The prospect appeals to people in special and sometimes temporary life situations. A burned-out musician tired of traveling enjoyed living in a lovely two-bedroom apartment as the resident manager of an apartment house in California. Whenever he felt he was stuck at home he invited his friends to visit him. But a few years later he was gone. People don't stay long at these jobs, so there are always opportunities. Watch the papers for ads, or advertise exactly what you want in the situations-wanted classified section. Some learn of a vacancy from the person leaving or when they apply for an apartment.

An interesting opportunity for retired couples who don't mind staying put is the management of one of the self-service or "mini-warehouse" storage facilities springing up to serve the growing number of people who don't have room for all their possessions. Office skills and the ability to use a computer are helpful, but no special talent is required. Managers get an apartment on the premises and little more than $500 a month (double for a couple) for maintaining the facility, selling the spaces, and keeping the computerized records. Beryl Medberry earns what she thinks is an exceptional $17,000, with a chance for a bonus based on sales, from a small firm in Virginia which kept her on and provided her with a helper after her husband died.

Hours are long and it's hard to get away between opening the gates in the morning and closing them at night, but couples can work together without direct supervision and some of the bigger chains have incentive systems, benefits, and advancement to regional management positions. If you want this work, watch the want ads or apply directly to a company listed in the yellow pages of the community you'd like to serve.

The home offices of big private insurance companies are hierarchies with few opportunities for older newcomers, but there are niches for newcomers to most of the nonselling work of insurance if you look off the beaten track. For instance, there may be a place for you in the insurance end of the work you have always done. A company insuring risks in a field you know might be willing to train you to become an outside claims adjuster. In Yuba City, California, crop insurance claims were being adjusted by a retired crane operator who was using the $75 a day he earned to support his little almond farm. He got the job by approaching the insurance company himself.

Or there may be an opportunity in an insurance system peculiar to your industry. He may be overqualified for the job, but a retired district sales manager of a car manufacturer likes processing automotive factory claims a few hours a week for a dealer. He calls himself a "warranty clerk consultant."

Product warranties are only one of the many kinds of insurance that aren't sold directly to the public. Workmen's compensation, product warranties, service contracts, and pension systems all have to issue policies, accept applications, figure losses, handle claims, and cope with the kinds of data kept by the commercial insurance industry.

Health insurance claims have become such a burden for doctors, hospitals, employers, unions, and other insurance groups that they welcome anyone with the patience to read the fine print and help their claimants follow the zigs and zags of the health insurance system. It's a nice job for an older woman who knows the claimant group. In 1988, a retired secretary was earning $11.43 an hour as the insurance adjuster in charge of paying medical claims for the Michigan Conference of Teamster's Welfare Fund, while in Texas the retired credit union manager for the *San Antonio Light* was back working part time handling all the insurance claims for the paper's employees and their dependents.

There's room in real estate and insurance for everyone who likes numbers and helping people deal with the important financial decisions of their lives.

☑ LAW AND ENFORCEMENT

Law, order, and the rights of individuals are maintained by a patchwork of institutions high and low, and they all need help. Laws and lawsuits multiply, especially in new areas such as the environment, consumer protection, and employee benefits. Police, jails, courts, and prisons can't keep up with the rise in crime.

Courts range from the United States Supreme Court, which hears only suits disputing conflicts of law and the interpretation of the Constitution, to justices of the peace employed by rural villages to deal in the first instance with minor disputes such as neighborhood squabbles.

More than judging is involved. All courts need some system for keeping a calendar of the issues to be heard, recording proceedings and decisions, maintaining order in the courtroom, and executing orders for the appearance of witnesses or the disposal of property. And at every level courts are saddled by legislatures with extrajudicial responsibilities such as supervising parole officers or educating drunk drivers.

Legal advice and representation is needed by every organization and individual from the federal government to a tenant on welfare threatened with eviction. In governments it's provided by departments of justice, attorneys general, and district attorneys. In private organizations it's provided by a salaried legal department, often in consultation with an independent law firm paid by fee. Individuals and organizations too poor to pay may be represented by lawyers in legal aid societies, social agencies, or firms which permit their partners and associates to contribute some of their time for the public good. All this legal work requires paraprofessional specialists in researching, investigating, recording, and preparing legal documents.

Violators of law are apprehended by institutions ranging from the Federal Bureau of Investigation and specialized federal agencies to state, city, and local police departments and auxiliary forces recruited for specific purposes, such as rounding up stray animals and directing traffic at streets children have to cross when they get out of school. Technological advances have shifted more of the work of law enforcement to specialists in such diverse fields as accident prevention, firearm and fingerprint identification, canine patrols, mobile rescue teams, and arson, fraud, and terrorism details, and a great deal of the work involves computerized record keeping.

Detention facilities range from federal and state penitentiaries for criminals serving sentences of more than a year to jails housing criminals serving sentences of less than a year or persons charged with crimes and held for arraignment or trial.

All legal professionals must be good listeners, good communicators, respectful of opposing points of view, sensitive to ethical implications, honorable as well as honest, and able to inspire confidence and respect.

In order to practice in a state, a lawyer must be licensed under rules of that state's supreme court, almost always by passing a bar examination, admission to which is limited to graduates of a law school approved by the American Bar Association. Admission to law schools is highly competitive and usually requires at least three years of college, adding up to seven years of schooling after high school.

Whether appointed or elected, all states require their judges to be members of the bar, who are in practice recommended by screening panels set up by the state for the purpose. Local judges and magistrates, arbitrators, and mediators need not be lawyers.

Judges generally earn less than the lawyers appearing before them. In 1990 the eight associate justices of the U.S. Supreme Court earned $118,600. Chief Justice William Rehnquist earned $124,000. In New York State, pay ranged from $120,000 for the chief judge of the New York State Court of Appeals to $18,000 for the city court of the small town of Watervliet. Retired judges serving as referees earn several hundred dollars a day. Arbitrators and referees are paid sometimes by the courts and sometimes by the disputing parties. Mediators work for modest fees and are often volunteers.

Pay for lawyers reflects their long and expensive education, but it's more erratic than the pay of doctors or college professors who have comparable education. Median weekly pay reported by the Bureau of Labor Statistics was $1,045 in 1990 for the minority on salary.

Federal court clerks earned from $49,000 to $70,000 in 1990; salaried paralegals a median of $24,700; title searchers, $17,000 to $19,000. Some paralegals were volunteers for nonprofit organizations. In many states, escrow officers and notaries public are middle managers for whom these duties are part of their regular salaried work. Notaries public are not allowed to charge more for their services than a set fee, which may be as low as twenty-five cents per transaction.

All law-support people have to be physically fit, responsible, and without a police record, and some need to be able to use firearms. Federal agents may have to be lawyers or accountants. Entry to federal, state, and local law-support jobs is usually by civil service examination. Most states require private detectives to be licensed and to qualify on a range before a testing officer if their duties include carrying a gun, and a few require a state certificate for security guards.

Law-support pay is modest. According to the Department of Labor, in 1990 median weekly salary for full-time police and detectives in the public service was $559, for supervisors $645, for sheriffs and bailiffs $445, and for correction officers $449. All of these workers, however, enjoy good benefits and retirement pensions.

SECOND CAREERS FOR EXPERIENCED LAW AND ENFORCEMENT WORKERS

The law holds its professionals. Nothing can be more stressful than serving as a judge, yet Supreme Court justices who have lifetime tenure stay with their strenuous work into their 70s and 80s.

Some states require elected **judges** to retire at a given age, usually 70, but they are so badly needed that ways are being found to use them. They may serve as a referee appointed by a court to take testimony and determine issues of fact, such as the assets of a bankrupt, or take the load off the courts by serving as private mediators, arbitrators, or volunteers in social agencies with conflict resolution services.

An **arbitrator** is an impartial person, not necessarily a lawyer, chosen by the parties to a dispute, who agree in advance to abide by his decision. A mediator merely tries to get the parties to come to their own agreement. Mediators of labor disputes may work for federal or state departments of labor, but mediators for matrimonial, landlord–tenant, and everyday neighborhood disagreements may work as volunteers in a city- or county-funded mediation center.

Private judges are one answer to overloaded courts. In California, you can hire a judge and get an immediate hearing for a suit that would otherwise wait five years to be heard. Your case will be heard by a retired judge who works only when or as much as he wishes but may earn more for his time than he did on the public payroll. The trials are arranged through a private association.

Some states have created a system for employing retired judges to work in various judicial capacities, such as domestic disputes, when and where they are needed to move a clogged calendar. New York State has created the post of **judicial hearing officer** for retired judges who are willing to serve as referees by the day when and as they are needed. California, Colorado, Pennsylvania, and other states have similar systems.

These retired judges don't mind that they're saving the taxpayers money. A Pennsylvania senior judge continued at the modest $250 per diem "because I'm better at the law now at 71 than I was at 50." A survey of retired New York State judges found that a fifth of them would serve without any per diem at all.

Lawyers have more options. There are so many different ways to practice law that you don't have to retire completely when your interests change in later life. In one Wisconsin community of thirty-six thousand there are five lawyers in their 80s who go to their offices every day. If you're a partner in a large law firm, you can maintain your income while working fewer hours and choosing exactly what you want to do in them.

There's a lot of work to choose from. A few lawyers are **litigators** who spend most of their time bringing actions before courts or administrative agencies, but most negotiate contracts and counsel individuals, corporations, nonprofit organizations, or government agencies about the legal implications of their work. Senior lawyers may limit their practice not only to old clients, but to a specialty in which they have become expert, such as intellectual property, the environment, real estate, taxes, estates, or product liability.

There's a legal side to any activity, so you're an especially welcome volunteer in any cause that interests you. There's important legal work to be done for nonprofit organizations such as the Sierra Club or the American Civil Liberties Union, which file briefs as friends of the court on cases setting precedents of interest to them. And the goal of equal justice for rich and poor depends on lawyers working for little pay through legal aid societies.

For lawyers and judges, it's the work itself that matters most. Lawyers "retire" to become judges, often at the sacrifice of some income ("you have to be able to afford being a judge. You have to have your children through school"). A judge may "retire" to the practice of the law where he can make more money. But money isn't usually the main reason for these switches.

When judges and lawyers quit, it's usually because they feel that they aren't living up to their idea of what the law should be. A lawyer left private practice to become an arbitrator of labor disputes because he was fed up with the commercialism of private legal practice; a judge, to go back to practicing law because he was tired of the parade of drunken drivers through his court.

Court clerks are highly specialized administrators who have more in common with executives than with clerical workers. The clerk of superior court who planned and ran the court system for a county in New Hampshire chose to work occasionally as a title examiner after his retirement.

Legal secretaries and assistants stay with the law, too. Some of them go on working into their 70s, not because they need the money but because they like the excitement. Others become so interested in the dramas they see unfolding that they go to law school on the side. Maria Walp didn't like being a legal secretary after her old boss retired, so she went to law school and started practicing at 63.

Virginia Talmage started studying law after-hours and summers while she was working as a court reporter, and continued five years after she had been admitted to the bar. She didn't start practicing until arthritis in her left thumb prevented her from using the shorthand machine. At 65, she was working eighty hours a week and enjoying it so much that she intends to continue as long as her health permits.

Those who do quit the law say that the training has helped them in business, teaching, counseling, property management, writing — even photography and acting.

Second careers are important to people who work in law enforcement. Career police and correction officers who supervise the inmates of jails and prisons retire young enough to have mortgage payments and college bills. But like the lawyers and judges, most of them like what they have done, and some of them find ways to stay in it. One retired detective was hired back as a court prosecutor preparing cases.

It's hard to enforce laws all your life without thinking about being a lawyer, and some achieve that dream. Forced to retire because of an injury, a New York State corrections officer went to law school and now works as a town justice. When he retired from raiding stills more than twenty years ago, a T-Man, or special agent for the Treasury Department, went back to school and got his law degree at the age of 63. Now in his late 70s, he earns more than $50,000 a year while enjoying the leisurely life of a part-time country lawyer.

If you want fewer hours you may find them in special assignments in your own or another law enforcement agency. The governor of

Arizona recruited a retired native of that state who had worked all over the country as a federal drug enforcement agent to work part time as drug enforcement director. He's now the full-time executive director of the Arizona Criminal Justice Commission. In Chicago, a retired homocide investigator has switched sides, so to speak, to work part time as an investigator for the Cook County public defender. A deputy sheriff beefs up his Social Security quarters by working part time as a state trooper.

It's even easier to get part-time work and the lifestyle you want in your later years by going private with your skills. There's private **security** work to be done in the setting of your choice: stores, offices, hotels, gambling casinos, banks, museums, factories, airports, hospitals, schools, and colleges (see page 201).

Retired policemen can usually get security work by letting it be known that they are available, but most of this work is low-key, for long hours and low pay. One retired policeman earns $20,000 a year securing doors, screening visitors, and where necessary reporting crimes as the full-time security officer for a children's hospital. Most of this work is low-paying because it doesn't require police experience, but it's a way of getting the hours and setting you want. One retired policeman works part time at less than $8 an hour as a **guard** in a bank.

Private detectives do more than shadow erring husbands. A detective with the Connecticut state police who specialized in suspicious fires went right to work doing the same thing for the Insurance Investigations Bureau when he retired. A casino pays a retired FBI man $20 an hour to investigate suspicious incidents.

If what you want is everything — fun, prestige, and freedom from the schedules, discipline, and red tape you've been enduring on your regular job — consider going into business for yourself as a consultant in the part of the work you know best. A Utah highway patrolman earns $15,000 a year reconstructing automobile accidents. A polygraph examiner who was forced to retire because of a heart attack continued for more than ten years to administer the tests for private clients.

Getting a second career may be easier than you think. Some jobs come looking for law enforcement people. Private security jobs may be posted on the bulletin board where you work, and an unsuspected opportunity may come your way through the grapevine. A retired New York City police officer fell into an almost perfect second career as the part-time manager of a resort maintained by the Patrolman's Benevolent Association. He didn't even know about the job until he was approached by the officer who had to fill it.

Law-support people who move out of their own or a related field gravitate to manual, outdoor, or service jobs or work that uses what they've learned about getting along with the public, such as property manager, tour guide, real estate salesman, or storekeeper. And law-support experience is helpful in getting many of the jobs that older people like to do: park ranger; school bus driver; child support collector; bill collector; assessor; dispatcher; bank courier; lifeguard; manager of a halfway house for parolees. Some even become teachers: a California deputy sheriff who retired early teaches criminal justice at the local community college.

Networking comes naturally to law enforcement people. They get to know a lot of people both in and out of the field, and they like to help each other. If you talk about your talents, hobbies, and interests, the chances are good that someone will pass the word along to a potential employer.

NICHES FOR NEWCOMERS TO LAW AND ENFORCEMENT

Even if you've never had anything to do with the law you can become a lawyer later in life. Many older people go to law school at night while working at other jobs, or take early retirement and use a pension to finance a legal education. Late starters don't become senior partners in fast-track, metropolitan law firms, but there are many niches for them. One, of course, is volunteering to do pro bono ("for the public good") legal work for a cause, or work at nominal pay for the nonprofit Legal Aid Society, serving the poor.

The most successful late-starting lawyers find a way to hitchhike on their first careers. Previous experience in law support or the military is good preparation for the somewhat similar work of lawyers employed in government. An air force colonel went to law school after he retired and now is a staff attorney with the Louisiana State Department of Public Safety.

Another niche is serving the community of people you have worked with in the past. Dolores Preston Cooper had always wanted to be a lawyer, but like many ambitious black women of her generation she became a teacher instead. As she rose in the Detroit system, she studied law at night, passed the bar, and began doing wills, divorces, and

Social Security claims for the many people who knew her through the Board of Education. Now that she has her pension, she is building a general practice in family law, probate, employment law, and Social Security claims against the government.

Still another niche is a leisurely general practice in a small community where you are personally known. After thirty-one years as an administrator with Exxon, William McAllister became a lawyer and set up a general practice in Billings, Montana, getting his first clients from a lawyer friend who was overloaded. He's not earning as much as Exxon used to pay him, but he's enjoying himself. Like most small-town lawyers, he takes on anything that comes in the door.

But if you live in a small town it may be easier to get into law as a judge. Municipal judges and justices of the peace are elected or appointed by mayors. They need not be lawyers, but are required to take short training after they take office. In rural communities it's a part-time job paying less than $1,000 a month, which may be held by people with no more than a high school education.

In 1988, municipal judges in small towns in Texas included a retired Gulf Oil manager, a retired civil service supervisor, and a retired railroad telegrapher. In another Texas town, the justice of the peace was a waitress whose friends persuaded her to run when the cafe where she had worked for twenty years went broke. If she isn't reelected, she'll just go back to waitressing.

You have to be a lawyer to sit on a bench of general jurisdiction, but your work in business or another profession may qualify you for one of the many administrative, investigative, or regulatory chores that courts have to do. In Marysville, California, a retired clothing merchant was appointed by the judge as a part-time juvenile traffic hearing officer to counsel kids and teach the classes to which drunk drivers are sentenced.

Some of these judicial jobs can be both important and interesting. A special agent working in security for the army and air force became the chief investigator of violations of attorney ethics for the New Jersey Supreme Court; a newspaper editor, chairman of the state parole board.

There may be a job for you in the legal side of your first career. A school tax collector switched sides to work for a law firm as a property consultant, handling the collection of delinquent taxes. A former manager of a steel reinforcing manufacturer now directs technical support for a law firm serving the construction industry. If you're a registered nurse, you may be able to get a job helping lawyers prosecute malpractice suits.

If you can qualify as an **expert** in any field involving litigation, you may fall into interesting occasional work as an expert witness. **Appraisers** of real estate, art, antiques, books, or jewelry are needed by lawyers in settling divorces and estates. People with impressive experience in the normal or expected practice of any trade or profession may testify in lawsuits to clarify issues of liability or damage. Pay depends on the stakes in the case and the rarity of your knowledge. Some historians have been paid $250 an hour for testimony on boundary disputes, land claims, and water rights.

The way to get this work is to ask a local trial lawyer for the name of a service that supplies her with lists of experts in various fields available in the area and ask them to add you to their roster. Older experts have an edge because they have more years of experience.

Arbitrator or mediator is a natural second career for older people, and you don't have to be a lawyer. You may be ideally qualified to settle disputes that arise in the work of your first career. When Donald Kokjer retired as general manager of a West Coast shipping company, the governor of Washington appointed him as a commissioner to hear grievances of unfair labor practices under maritime law. He works a week a month, sometimes at home, and for modest pay, but it keeps his hand in the work he has always done.

If you have been a leader in a heavily litigated technical field such as engineering or software rights, you may be eligible to serve as one of the volunteer arbitrators supplied by the American Arbitration Association (AAA). The AAA was founded early in this century, but alternative (to the courts) dispute resolution (ADR) has become a movement with many players, some of them funded by municipalities or social agencies. Your local United Way can tell you about opportunities in your community if a dispute resolution center isn't listed in the blue or government pages of your phone book.

It's hard for an older newcomer to land a job as a full-fledged **court clerk** of a court of general jurisdiction, but they are sometimes hired to do work that is really clerical in a local court of limited jurisdiction. A former flight attendant with only a secretarial school education leads a glamorous life as the court recording monitor in the criminal arraignment court of a Connecticut suburb of New York City.

The most popular way to get into the law is to become a **legal assistant** or **paralegal,** helping a lawyer investigate facts, research past legal decisions, prepare briefs, obtain affidavits of witnesses, and keep the voluminous paperwork in order — work that used to be done by experienced legal secretaries. If you've never worked in a law office you may be able to find a training course for paralegals accredited by the American Bar Association.

Some older newcomers go into the work for the money, like the divorced housewife from Grosse Pointe who took a short legal assistant course and landed a job doing legal research for a lawyer at $12.64 an hour. Others go into it to do good, like the health association executive who qualified as a certified legal assistant when he retired and now serves the elderly poor in his county Legal Aid Society.

If you like the law, you may qualify in your later years for the legal odd jobs that don't require special training but have to be done by a responsible citizen, such as an **escrow officer** in a real-estate or law office, who holds the money paid down on a contract until its provisions are fulfilled, a **title searcher,** who checks the public records to establish the validity of a deed, or a **notary public** commissioned by the state to attest signatures.

Did you want to become a **policeman** when you were a kid? Regular police officers are hired under civil service rules but are exempt from the Age Discrimination in Employment Act (ADEA), so a maximum age can be a legal requirement. Even when there is no age limit, educational, physical, and other requirements which are bona fide qualifications for the work discourage older applicants, but in small towns desperate for help older people who can meet them may be recruited to serve as part-time policemen or deputy sheriffs.

But you don't have to bulge with muscles to hang around the police and help them with their work; they need plenty of clerical and other support staff. You may become an all-purpose recordkeeper and helper to the sheriff — especially if you're a woman who can double as a police matron. Fingerprinting and record keeping are clerical jobs you can get without previous law-support experience by applying to the police station where you would like to work. Even if they aren't civil service, these jobs will be posted in libraries, state job services, and other places where civil service jobs are listed.

Most fun is helping schoolchildren across the street. It's a minimum-wage job older people like because it gets them outdoors near their homes for fifteen to eighteen hours a week on a regular basis. At 76, **school crossing guard** Dorcas Laa of Dallas was still enjoying the "happiness and vitality" of the children in spite of "crazy drivers."

Some communities enlist citizen patrolmen who volunteer as extra eyes and ears for the local sheriff. The quickest way to find out whether there is anything you are qualified to do for the police is to call the local station that serves you.

The least-liked opportunity for newcomers is **jailer, correction officer,** or **prison guard,** a job often done by retired servicemen.

Law and enforcement involves the seamy side of human nature in our society, but it's never boring. If you're fascinated by people and the tangles they can get themselves into, you'll enjoy playing a part in the legal system.

☑ THE HEALTH BUSINESS

Health care is a national challenge. The bureaucracy created by health insurance and new technologies cuts both ways. Medicine is less attractive to established professionals like doctors and nurses, but it has created new jobs and opportunities in a bigger and more technologically advanced industry.

There's much more that can be done for patients, many new kinds of hospitals and health care organizations, many new medical specialities, and many new jobs to fill.

The bureaucracy itself is a growth industry. There are many more institutions where health care is provided, and all of them have to be managed and their services monitored and recorded for insurance reimbursement. There are not only general and specialized hospitals and private practitioners, many of them practicing in groups so large that they require an internal bureaucracy, but institutions devoted to a specific kind of medical service, such as urgent care centers for people who need immediate medical attention, health maintenance organizations providing primary care for their members, nursing homes for long-term care, hospices for the care of the dying, and home health agencies for homebound patients. These institutions require top and middle managers with titles like **hospital administrator, quality assurance director, medical director, director of blood service, nursing home administrator, director of medical records, administrator of home care, and chief of nursing services.**

In addition, every community is served by free-standing centers for specialized treatment. There's usually a rehabilitation center for counseling and treating the disabled, mental health clinics for treating the emotionally troubled, centers for diagnostic tests such as X-rays and imaging devices that permit a specialist to "see" what's going on inside your body.

Complete or partial medical services have to be provided or made available to people in schools, colleges, prisons, the armed forces, and in many workplaces.

Most health service administrators are women, many of them trained in business rather than in medicine. In 1990, women health managers earned a median of $592 a week compared with $788 for men, but the pay of the chief administrator of a hospital varied from six figures for those with one thousand beds to under $50,000 for those with fewer than one hundred.

Inside these institutions, patients may be diagnosed and treated by one or more of hundreds of practitioners. At the top of the list are those qualified to deal directly with the complaints of patients by licenses which require some combination of postbaccalaureate professional training and supervised internship in the work itself.

All medical schools and some nursing schools require a college degree for admission; some dental schools, three years of college; veterinarian and chiropractic schools, two years; pharmacy schools, at least one year. Nurses may train in a hospital, community college associate nursing program, or a four-year nursing school.

Earnings of licensed health care practitioners vary by specialty, type of practice, and gender. Physicians in private practice take home more than six figures of income after all expenses, with board-certified specialists earning more and chiropractors less than primary-care MDs, but these earnings are less spectacular when viewed as a return on their investment in medical training and the rising costs of maintaining a medical practice.

For *salaried* physicians, median weekly earnings in 1990 were $978 for males and $802 for females; registered nurses (RNs), $616 for males, $608 for females; pharmacists, $794; psychologists, $605 for males, $514 for females. Among practitioners whose earnings were not reported by the Department of Labor, professional associations estimated that dentists earned $70,000, optometrists $65,000, and veterinarians $40,000 to $60,000 per year.

Next comes the growing list of specialists skilled in new ways to help patients with such problems as difficult breathing, stiff joints, impaired speech or hearing, or special diet requirements. These special treatments are provided by practitioners qualified by at least a bachelor's degree and supervised field work. Most of the specialized therapists are required to have a license at least in some states, and all can be certified by taking an examination given by their professional association. Starting salaries are in the low $20,000s. Median weekly salaries in 1990 for those numerous enough to be reported by the Department of Labor were $525 for physical therapists, $454 for dietitians.

The equipment available to diagnose and treat patients has become so complicated that it has to be run by technologists trained to run each kind of machine. New technology is lifesaving for victims of accidents who need first aid before or while they are being brought to the appropriate treatment center. The technologists who run these and other machines learn their work in courses offered by vocational schools, community colleges, hospitals, or on the job, and some may be certified by examination. They usually earn in the middle $20,000s but may work up to higher incomes with experience. They may be assisted by lower-paid technicians with less training.

Finally, basic human needs have to be met for patients in all these settings as well as those confined to their homes. Medical care depends on subprofessional but caring aides who are always on hand to feed, bathe, transport, and very often comfort people in pain who feel helpless and fearful.

Median pay for salaried health aides was $287 a week in 1990; for orderlies and attendants, $251. Much of the nonmedical work of hospitals, such as running errands for patients, is done by volunteers.

Some personal characteristics are essential to health care workers at every level. To work with the ill, you have to be mentally and physically healthy and able to maintain a caring attitude to human suffering while enduring stress, bureaucracy, and the constant introduction of new technologies.

SECOND CAREERS FOR EXPERIENCED HEALTH CARE PEOPLE

Health care managers are very much like managers in any other industry. Those who retire on pensions may continue to work part time in the public service at a job like fundraiser for the United Way or mayor of a small town; for fun like the chief executive of a county hospital who clerks part time at a resort hotel; or at a combination of the two, like the retired administrator of mental health services for the state of California who spends part of his working time as a tour director and part of it as a social worker.

Those who want to stay in the field may move to a similar job in another organization. Hospital administrators leave to work for another hospital where the management or the money promises to be better. A nurse gives up running her own nursing home to take a salaried job in another. Others consult. Health services are under such scrutiny that there are many opportunities. When the chief nurse for the Connecticut State Department of Mental Health was forced out by a young new commission, the federal authorities retained her at $250 a day to review psychiatric hospitals against federal standards.

A medical chief may have many reasons for dropping back to become one of the workers she once directed. The retired head of physical therapy at a big California hospital likes filling in five hours a week as a physical therapist in a small hospital where she knows and likes the people. But sometimes the demotion is involuntary. A 50-year-old director of patient care replaced by a 31-year-old male for what she was told were "economic reasons" is working at $20,000 less a year as a supervisor of nurses in another hospital.

Health care management is growing so fast that there's plenty of opportunity for ambitious medical secretaries and clerical workers to advance in the business side of medicine, like the daughter of a doctor who charges $50 an hour as a consultant advising physicians on managing their offices (see page 43).

Hands-on practitioners have ambivalent feelings about their profession. Doctors and nurses feel stressed, overworked, underpaid, and underappreciated for their investment in training. They talk a lot about quitting. Some of them actually do it. An obstetrician fed up with malpractice suits and paperwork packed it in and bought a cattle ranch. A radiologist retired at 56 to work half of the time as a flight instructor and the other half writing fiction. A nurse quit her job in a hospital, went back to school to learn real estate, and made $125,000 in 1987 while "dressing up and being with all kinds of people."

But most doctors and almost half of the nurses who change careers in later life find something else to do in their own profession. Doctors who retire from practice may be invited to lecture at a medical school. A retired chief of the pulmonary disease service of a hospital works part time at $20 an hour on a fellowship training and research program in another hospital.

Former practitioners may find work in hospital management. A doctor who gave up practicing at 69 has no plans ever to retire from his part-time job as quality assurance director of the hospital with which he has long been affiliated. A surgeon monitors the health bureaucracy for a hospital as its director of government affairs.

Even those who take on less prestigious medical chores don't seem to miss caring for patients of their own or even the money they used to earn. There's always part-time work for a doctor reviewing charts in a clinic, examining patients or counseling case workers in a drug treatment or rehabilitation service, serving as a plant physician, or doing routine physical examinations. One retired doctor earns $100 an hour supervising stress tests of candidates for exercise programs, a job with stress of its own. If he lets them push too hard he could be sued for malpractice.

A few even volunteer. Dr. W. Sterling Edwards was always concerned about the emotional cracks in the health care system. When he retired as head of surgery at the University of New Mexico he took courses in psychology and started a one-man volunteer service he described as "health counseling one-on-one small groups." His new role is as "listener to patients with life-threatening illness."

More often than doctors, nurses look for a second career that will pay more money. Some move on to better jobs; those who retire from the armed forces seem to have no trouble earning more than $30,000 in civilian hospitals.

But there are other ways to do it. You may be able to make more money by moving from bedside nursing to public health, first aid in a factory, managing a doctor's office, or insurance work. Dorothy Milton had filled out health insurance forms when she worked for a physician, but although the computer scared her at first, she was able to find a better-paying job reviewing insurance claims for Blue Cross when her family relocated to Maine.

You can always make more money by taking more training. A delivery room nurse in Arizona went back to college and qualified as a clinical psychologist so that she could work as a therapist for abused and neglected children.

The highest-paid nurses are certified registered nurse anesthetists (CRNAs), who now can do everything that MD anesthetists do, but at less than half the cost to the patient. They're in such demand that the pay of one who specializes in caesarian sections was increased from $18 to $28 an hour between 1988 and 1990 to keep her from leaving. To qualify, an RN has to spend two years getting the equivalent of a master's degree at one of the two hundred schools of anesthesia in hospitals around the country.

But more training doesn't always mean more pay: a nurse in an explosives factory who went back to school to become a chiropractor loves the work, but can't get enough patients to earn what she made in nursing. A nurse who became a nurse practitioner on a federal grant had to go back to regular nursing because she couldn't afford the continuing education her state requires to renew her license.

If you love nursing but want to get out of the stress of hospital work, you may be able to find just what you're looking for drawing blood at the local blood bank, teaching nurse's aides, or doing physical exams for insurance, in schools, or in family planning clinics. Just write a short note to let these potential employers in your community know what you want. And watch the ads. When a nurse practitioner retired from her job in a large jail she found a job as a writer explaining her state's organ donor program.

A nurse who is willing to volunteer can write her own ticket. After an automobile accident, Marie Lake devised a rehabilitation program for herself that utilized her experience as a teacher of nurses: free preventive health and exercise lessons for seniors in a studio her husband built especially for her. A 75-year-old nurse contributes thirty-six hours a week to the blood bank, Alzheimer's victims, and the mentally retarded. She says she couldn't have made it after her husband died if she hadn't had something to do every day.

Dentists seem happy to get away from the chair, sometimes to paying work in hobbies that grow out of their work. A dentist forced to retire because he developed a tremor in his hand says he will never retire from the second career he has created for himself. Using small, specialized tools, he repairs department-store mannequins which are shipped to his home. He solicits the work from corporate headquarters of chain stores.

Clinical psychologists, speech pathologists, nutritionists, rehabilitation therapists, and other medical professionals may teach, go into private practice, or move to a different setting. When funding ran out for the work he had been doing with children in the public schools, a speech pathologist switched to treating people with head injuries in a hospital.

Veterinarians find ways to cut down on the physical effort required by their strenuous profession. One confines himself to the small-animal part of the practice he sold to his son. Another supervises meat inspection for the Department of Agriculture, while a vet retired from the Department of Agriculture consults on animal diseases.

If you're a pharmacist who misses the daily contact with patients you may be able to take a shift filling prescriptions at the nearest drugstore, wherever you are; most states honor licenses issued by other states. After he sold his pharmacy and moved to Leisure World in Laguna Hills, California, Bertram Newman was invited to teach a course in contemporary health to retirees at Saddleback Community College. Another retired pharmacist is a volunteer teacher of biology to seventh- and eighth-graders in a private Christian school.

Health technologists and patient aides are usually newcomers to medicine recruited from other fields, but licensed practical nurses (LPNs) have been around for several generations with steadily improving status and training. RNs are now so scarce that LPNs are replacing them wherever possible. During her nineteen years as an LPN at the Wichita Falls, Texas, hospital, Catherine Cox took every training course offered by the Red Cross and cancer and heart associations. Her years of experience and training qualified her for a job as an industrial nurse where she gets benefits and can work with patients on her own.

Sometimes a very specific skill can be transferred to a job in a pleasanter setting. A hospital lab technician who learned to be dexterous and careful preparing tissues and slides for diagnosis now uses these skills as a plant mounter in the St. Louis botanical garden. She affixes dried plants, many of them collected from South American rain forests, to special acid-free paper that botanists hope will keep them intact for centuries. The pay isn't great, but she loves it because it's easy, her coworkers are friendly, and it's a beautiful place to work.

NICHES FOR NEWCOMERS TO HEALTH CARE

Health management is a growth industry. If you're a good manager you can manage a health service without knowing much about medicine. One homemaker moved from running her own home to running a nursing home as a salaried administrator. A widow who used to work in a bank is now the **nursing home administrator** of the fifty-six-bed institution of a rural county in Arkansas. The hours are long and the pay is low, but she likes the contact with people. She has a job she got by answering an ad, but if you have funds to invest and faith in yourself you can start your own facility (see Your Own Business).

Some homemakers get into high-salaried health care jobs through volunteer work. Dorothy Britton broke into paid employment directing volunteers and organizing fundraising drives, and moved from one hospital job to another. At 67 she was earning a respectable salary directing leisure activities and public relations for a private retirement community in posh Westchester County.

You'd have a hard time becoming a doctor after you're thirty because medical schools don't think you'd have enough years left to practice to be worth the years of schooling, although one woman practicing now on Park Avenue managed it by starting out as a Ph.D. candidate in anatomy, but there are disciplines out of the mainstream of medicine for which you can qualify to treat patients with shorter training.

Four years of advanced training is usually all you need to practice independently as a **chiropractor** or **podiatrist**. It's easier to get into these professional schools, some of which require less than a college degree for admission, and chiropractors don't have to serve the internships required of medical doctors.

Both are possible careers for late starters. After twenty-four years in accounting at Chrysler, Ed Duncan took early retirement, went back to school, and at 61 opened his own chiropractic clinic in Allen Park, Michigan. He doesn't take home as much as he did at Chrysler, but he enjoys the helping role of the old-fashioned family doctor.

An alternative discipline that attracts many older people is **hypnotherapy**. It's easy to get into because some states don't even bother to license it. An assistant manager who left Pitney Bowes has a hypnotism center which brings in $800 a month in fees for helping smokers to stop or witnesses to remember details of a crime the police want to know.

Nurses are in such short supply that money is being spent on recruiting them to the profession. There's a big turnover. Burned-out older RNs dream of getting out, while older newcomers take the two to five years of college training after high school for an associate degree in nursing (ADN), or a hospital diploma, or a bachelor of science degree in nursing (BSN) and find the work more interesting than homemaking, schoolteaching, hairdressing, or the office or factory work they have been doing. It's especially attractive to homemakers and retiring office workers who need health insurance for themselves.

Some make the career change when they are moved to a new community. A homemaker who quit as a foster mother to go back to school at 50 likes working as an RN because it "makes me feel good about myself." A widow started going to nursing school before she retired from her office job as deputy sheriff and likes the people and the earnings she can add to her pension, although she admits that some days she would rather be working in her yard.

For older women, nursing extends the nurturing role they enjoyed when they were raising their families. At 58, a mother of four grown children who had decided she needed a radical change in her life decided she wanted to work in a hospital with newborn babies. Before going back to nursing school, she took courses in golf and tennis to test her physical ability for a profession that would keep her on her feet for long hours, and courses in English, psychology, and public speaking to test her ability to get through nursing school. It was the right choice. Now in her 70s, she continues to work part time in a hospital because "nothing in this world compares with the feel of a newborn baby."

For men, a second career in nursing can be a natural extension of a first career in a protective service — like the retired fire fighter who continues to serve his community as a visiting nurse — or a way to go back to a youthful dream of becoming a doctor. Charles Ballard was 58 when the Bank of America restructured him out of his job as a bank manager. Too old for medical school, he enrolled in nursing school and was hired on graduation in the pediatric department of Pasadena's Huntington Hospital. Not only does he like it better than banking, but the night differential he gets on the night shift makes the pay per hour almost the same.

Sex and age discrimination can be problems that are especially hard for men because they have no experience in coping with it. In hospitals, it sometimes comes from older women patients, who are prepared to be nude in the presence of a male doctor but not a male nurse, and sometimes from female charge nurses who may stick the male RNs with especially hard or unpleasant duties.

The one-year LPN course is quicker than the two-year RN course, and there's not much difference in the way older newcomers feel about the jobs its gets them. Pay is lower, of course, but LPN rates vary all over the map. In high-wage areas they may be as much as RNs are getting where wages are low.

Psychologist is the dream job of older people who have had to cope with emotional problems as housewives, teachers, clergy, lawyers, or social workers. Many of them are so good at it, and the need is so great, that with a little training available at community colleges members of these helping professions can be qualified to work as a correctional counselor in a prison, a child custody mediation officer for a county court, or a family counselor in a health organization (see Social Work).

But it's harder for a newcomer to practice as an independent clinical psychologist. There's no law against charging for advice of any kind, but health insurance won't pay your fees unless you have a license to practice psychology, and that license is as hard to get as a license to practice medicine.

One of the few newcomers who have made it is a former actor

who started his training at 42 with no more education than a high school equivalency diploma. When casting agents stopped calling he went back to college, got his Ph.D. in psychology, and did the fifteen hundred hours of supervised field work required by California law. At 60 his schedule is filled with patients paying $90 an hour, but he has to hustle for them. He lists himself in the yellow pages, visits physicians for referrals, and gives courses, seminars, talks, and adult education courses that keep his profile high in the community. He sees nothing strange about this transition: "Acting helps you get into the skins of other people."

But you don't have to hang out your shingle to practice as a psychologist. If you really want to help, you can qualify to counsel, as a volunteer or at modest pay, for a long list of public and private social agencies and churches (see page 68).

Less demanding than clinical psychology are medical therapies that require only two years of study beyond college. The **expressive therapies — art, music, dance —** are fascinating second careers for people who have practiced these arts. Art therapy is mandated in California for patients with severe emotional disturbances; for instance, a therapist might loosen up an obsessive-compulsive patient by interesting him in the imprecise medium of watercolor painting. **Recreation therapy** isn't licensed, but it is not to be confused with recreation in general and several associations certify it. Mary Gamson is now paid $7 an hour to organize bingo, discussions, arts, crafts, and music for wheelchair patients in a recuperative center attached to a hospital in Massachusetts. She did it at first as a volunteer.

Less training is required for specialized work in new medical technologies. If you want the thrill of saving lives without the stress of doing it all the time, you can work as a **paramedic** on call. You could join the ski patrol and earn a nominal $5 an hour providing emergency care to skiers who are injured on the slope, or get into the deeper stuff; a retired professor of biology went back to school for six months to become a practicing paramedic and chief of the voluntary rescue unit of the fire department in Mayer, Arizona. He's paid $10 every time he's called.

Massage therapy is attractive to seniors. Healthy older people have the strength to do it: one professional did several massages on her 90th birthday. Fees are high, and if you are licensed to practice independently out of your own home you can do only as much of it as you enjoy. But you have to run ads, post notices on gym bulletin boards, and get referrals from doctors in order to build a therapeutic clientele who will keep you comfortably loaded.

If you have office skills and have always been interested in medicine you might enjoy a second career as a **medical secretary** in a hospital or doctor's office, where you get a chance to deal directly with patients. And if your shorthand skills are exceptionally good and you are a quick study on new and difficult terms, you might qualify for well-paid work as a **medical transcriptionist**, typing doctors' reports and correspondence from dictation recorded on tapes. If you haven't done it you'll need special training, available at community colleges and private vocational schools. Once you qualify, this is work you can do at home, through temporary help agencies or medical transcription service bureaus.

Finally, if you have no health experience and need a job right now, you can always find work at a hospital or nursing home. A few weeks training, if any, is all you need to start earning as a **nurse's aide, attendant, orderly, ambulance driver, or transporter,** wheeling patients within the facility, among many other unskilled hospital chores. If you'd rather help people stay in their own homes, watch the ads for **home health aide** jobs with a social agency, senior citizens center, or private home care service. You may be asked to clean, cook, shop, or bank for a housebound person or frail senior, and sometimes to bathe, take the vital signs, help in and out of bed, and generally provide some cheerful companionship for people who can't get about on their own.

Pay for these caretaking jobs is low, sometimes little more than the minimum wage, but there are a lot of advantages. You can work from three hours a week to full time, with some choice of schedule. Sex, race, or age is no bar, and older newcomers get a warm welcome from geriatric patients who prefer an older caregiver. If you want more money, the hospital or home health service will help you train for it while you're on their payroll. Most important, you have the satisfaction of doing the essential physical work of dealing with patients that keeps the health system running.

Finally you can join the sterling citizens in every community who **volunteer**. In hospitals, volunteers shop for patients, write letters for them, deliver the newspaper, run gift shops, staff receptionist desks, show slide shows, and drive outpatients to the doctor. Ask your favorite local hospital how you can help. Especially rewarding is the role of **ombudsman** or **patient advocate** for inmates of nursing homes. Your local United Way or social service clearinghouse will tell you about the training available and the commitment you will have to make. A former pastor devotes six hours a week to these visits.

Whatever the pay — and not all of it is high — health care work is physically and emotionally demanding, but it is one of the most direct ways to involve yourself in helping people in need.

☑ HOUSING AND CONSTRUCTION

Building things is fun. Houses, bridges, roads, dams, airports, shopping centers, skyscrapers, multipurpose structures without a name. Big construction work is done by national firms that have become brokers, contracting everything out to specialists, but there are still general contractors who do almost all the work of building a house themselves, sometimes on spec, a house at a time. There are also still carpenters who will build a shed for your garden tools for hourly wages.

But big or small, construction is competitive, risky, active, outdoor work, a feast-or-famine that gets in the blood of those who do it. And big or small, there's a lot of work to be done. The hardest and riskiest part of the job is figuring out how much to bid for it. Construction companies have to study blueprints and specifications provided by architects and engineers (see Science, Engineering, and Technology), plan how to achieve them, figure the cost of all the labor, equipment, materials and other costs they'll incur, and add a profit that is neither too high to lose the bid nor too low to cover unforeseen expenses.

Once the contract is signed, the building permits have to be secured, superintendents, foremen, and crew chiefs hired for the dates on which they'll be needed, subcontracts let, equipment and materials ordered, and arrangements made to have labor on hand for each step of the schedule.

The first people on the job are the surveyors, who lay out exactly where the ground must be broken. Then the foundations have to be excavated, the structure built, and utility systems, heating and air-conditioning, walls, doors, and windows installed and finished.

At every stage, the work has to be inspected by the contractor and the owner or his agent — often the architect or designer — for compliance with the specifications, as well as by building inspectors employed by government agencies for compliance with the applicable codes or regulations.

Even a modest-sized building requires the skills of craftsmen in carpentry, plumbing, pipe fitting, electrical work, cement finishing, glass installation, and painting, to name only a few.

Construction managers have to be able to enlist cooperation from a temporary team, solve problems quickly, relish stress, and be experienced at construction work, often at one of the crafts such as carpentry. Pay runs from little more than craft wages for self-employed

local contractors — and then only when they are actually working —
to six-figure salaries with liberal perks for those employed by a big
construction or construction management company. In 1990, median
pay for full-time salaried construction supervisors was $590 a week.

Construction cost estimators need an aptitude for numbers and an
ability to interpret poorly defined requirements as well as hands-on
experience in construction. Their pay is as wide-ranging and almost
as high as that of construction managers.

Building inspectors need craft experience, and many are trained as
engineers. They're paid less than construction cost estimators but their
work is steadier.

Construction foremen need a thorough knowledge of their craft
and leadership ability and, according to government statistics, earn at
least 20 percent more than the workers they supervise.

Construction craftsmen work for hourly wages, and sometimes
through unions. Highly paid construction workers may have no more
than a high school education, but they may have acquired highly
specialized skills on the job and through apprenticeship programs
sponsored by state labor departments, employers, and unions. They
all need good health and quick physical reflexes.

On union jobs construction workers are paid at least the minimum
rates agreed upon through collective bargaining. There are lower rates
for work done by apprentices and higher rates for work done on
evenings, weekends, and holidays. In 1990, median weekly earnings
for wage and salary construction workers who usually work full time
were $457. Carpenters made $412, electricians $524, plumbers and
pipefitters $508, and painters $382.

SECOND CAREERS FOR EXPERIENCED CONSTRUCTION WORKERS

Construction is a way of life, so those who do it like to stay in it as
long as they can, but it's essentially a young person's game. Construction managers carry the heavy responsibility for bringing a job in on
schedule and budget and without loss of life, and the time comes when
the hardiest are ready for something a little easier.

One way to stay on the job without the stress of running it is to
work as a consultant to those who are taking the bottom line responsibility. So much paperwork is now required for big publicly-funded
projects that more and more of it is contracted out. The career of Bill
Macabe is a good example. Working up from a common laborer, he

retired at 63 from supervising rehabilitation projects for the Department of Housing and Urban Development. But he likes work, so he found it first with U.S. Escrow, a licensed private service that holds and disburses federal and state housing grant monies according to all the regulations the law requires, and then with another service that supplements U.S. Escrow by providing the necessary field inspections.

Cost estimators are responsible for making a bid that will land the job without bankrupting the contractor. Those old enough to retire learned how to do it on the job, moving up from one job to another. But here, too, the new specialization creates easier slots. Edward Mueller liked figuring concrete when he worked for a general contractor and did it so well that he was offered more money by a contractor specializing in concrete. After three heart attacks, he worked for them half time doing nonbinding budget estimates of the cost of the concrete work on a building not yet let out for bid. It's less stressful because his firm isn't held to his numbers, but he's one of a few dozen concrete estimators who do it so fast that he's called in by architects all over the country.

Another way to cut down on the physical wear and tear of running a construction job is to become a building inspector: you may sometimes have to stay on your feet all day, but you won't have quite as much worry. If you've been a local contractor and everyone knows you, the town may waive the examination you are supposed to take, and because it's steady, salaried work, you might even make more in a year than you did when you were in business for yourself.

There's more money inspecting for an engineering firm, particularly if you have a track record in a hot specialty. Douglas Chesshir started as a telephone company lineman and retired as construction supervisor laying fiber-optic cables. He now makes more than $50,000 a year, inspecting the work of contractors who lay fiber-optic cables for a national engineering firm.

If you've been a foreman, you could take it easier on the job as a dispatcher of the heavy equipment that has to arrive at exactly the right moment in the schedule. If you are a construction foreman or craftsman you may have to drop back to hourly craft work. A retired foreman of road maintenance crews works at his father's trade of housepainting and loves it in spite of having to climb up on roofs at the age of 67. A pipe-laying foreman retired from the gas company turns to fitting pipes on ships. A carpenter foreman does small remodeling jobs "more or less" as his own boss, but he misses the health insurance that went with his old job.

Some foremen and craftsmen find easier work in their skill, like the disabled shipyard welder who earns $60 a week estimating jobs for a firm that makes ornamental railings to order, or the former owner of a heating and air-conditioning business who now limits his work to consulting on finding the right equipment to correct plumbing problems. An electrician whose health forced him to retire from troubleshooting for the power company works a few hours a week checking out the wiring systems of residences for prospective purchasers at $100 an inspection. A self-employed roofer has become more choosy about the jobs he takes, and a retired inspector of mechanical installations enjoys working part time inspecting mechanical work done for the Brooklyn Museum.

Some who have been self-employed give up and go to work for wages, and some wage workers go into business for themselves. Salaried electricians and plumbers continue by serving the public, on their own terms, when they retire. But skilled craftsmen and construction supervisors think of the office as the enemy and very few make the natural move into less physically demanding white-collar work in the "paper mill."

Older construction managers have often risen from blue-collar jobs themselves and when they move to other work they seek out physically active pursuits regardless of status. Those who have held management jobs may go into property management, real estate sales, operating heavy equipment, driving cars across country for an auto rental company, or even unskilled farm labor. One home builder turned his hand to managing a car wash when he sold his business. Another construction manager helps a woodshop teacher of special education, and still another volunteers with the park service.

Foremen and hourly workers move into similar second careers in maintenance, security, property management, and driving any kind of vehicle on any kind of errand — backhoe operator, school bus driver, courier, parts driver, volunteer driver of the infirm to the doctor, citizen patrolman, RV rental gofer.

NICHES FOR NEWCOMERS TO CONSTRUCTION

Home building and remodeling attract older newcomers to construction and there's something in it for everybody who has ever hankered to knock down a wall.

The riskiest and most rewarding entry is to build a house before you've sold it and hope for a rise in real-estate values. A "spec house" is for you if you have accumulated some money you are willing to gamble with and can persuade a bank to lend you some more. But you'd better know something about the business. Thomas McDonald acquired his little pile working for a construction company in Saudi Arabia after he retired from the army and shot it building on land being developed as a posh suburb of Houston. After selling it, he took his money and built another. In 1990 he was trying to custom-build contract houses designed for particular families, sketching possibilities with them by a computer-aided design (CAD) technology newly available for personal computers. His advice: If you can't sell one or two spec houses, get out and bet your money on the horses.

Remodeling an existing old house usually takes less capital, and you can stretch it even further by doing some of the work or directing the workmen yourself. Jean Hasch was a technical editor who impulsively bought an abandoned house from the city for $2,000, fixed the windows, moved in, put $15,000 in cash and her own labor into renovations and sold it at a profit. At one time she had eight homes, which improved the neighborhood so much that they eventually sold for a handsome profit. Jean got to be better at Sheetrocking than any of the people she could hire and enjoyed working with things because they "don't talk back."

Both McDonald and Hasch knew something about what they were getting into. McDonald had been responsible for construction in the army and worked at it overseas; Hasch had been married to a real estate agent. Most people who make a go of it have a similar former connection, if only as one of the many people who have worked briefly in some capacity on a construction job.

But you don't have to invest a lot of money or shoot so high to get in on the fun. Older people often add to their retirement income doing simple remodeling work that is too small for established builders. There's room for you if you have always liked carpentry and enjoyed maintaining your own property, or worked in construction on occasion, as teachers have often done in the summer.

A good example is Dick Poiner. When he was retired from his job as a textbook salesman he was offered a job by a local contractor who happened to see him helping a neighbor work on his cellar. After brushing up with a course offered through the adult education department of his local high school he passed the examination and was issued the builder's license needed in his state to be a self-employed construction contractor. Then, looking to the day when he wouldn't be physically able to continue rough framing, he started selling contractors a computer software program that simplifies the laborious calculations required for making estimates.

Poiner's advice to retirees who have their own tools and can cut their overhead by working out of their homes: go for the unfilled market of unhandy older people who can't find anyone to paint, rewire, plumb, replace a window or a roof, do interior trim, add a deck, or make other simple alterations. Find a condo, ideally a retirement community with a lot of elderly women that leaves alterations to the owners, and offer your services through a stuffer in their mailboxes. You can also find work by listing yourself in the services columns of the local shopping newspaper.

There's even work in remodeling for those who can't hammer a nail. When Carroll Huffner retired from his federal work overseeing court facilities he answered the ad of a local builder for a remodeling salesman. He loves visiting the customers who call, and though he gets paid full time, he waits at home until he's alerted to a call by a beeper. The boss showed him how to measure and calculate.

Are you an amateur who is pretty good, if you say it yourself, at painting, paperhanging, taping Sheetrock, hanging doors, or one of the little finishing jobs that are a nuisance to a busy home builder? See if you can get the subcontract to do this work on new construction. One of these pesky jobs is laying out the drainage pipes that carry the water from the gutters away from the house. Marjorie Tolson learned enough about how to do it from her husband to manage subcontracting it after he retired.

Construction can be physically hard, dirty, and dangerous, and it comes by fits and starts, but the pay is good and it's exciting to see a building go up and feel that you had a hand in it.

✔ EDUCATION

There's so much more to learn that schools now have to teach what was formerly learned in life. Formal schooling now reaches down to ages we still call "preschool" and up to programs we still call "adult" education.

We've added grades and what we teach in them. Schools now hold classes in driving a car and in diapering a baby. In addition to teaching, they provide students with the services of specialists to watch over their health, assess their abilities, detect and remedy handicaps, and counsel on personal problems, careers, and further schooling.

High school graduates go on to immediate vocational training in a nonacademic vocational high school, a private trade school, a two-year community college offering both vocational training and liberal arts, or an academic four-year college. Those who pursue a profession such as law, medicine, or science may spend years in postgraduate institutions and reach the age of 30 before they are ready to earn a living.

All these schools are self-contained little worlds administered by their own professional managers. Even a small college or a secondary school system may employ specialists in finance, public relations, health care, librarianship, fundraising, student affairs, grounds and buildings, food service, transportation, audiovisual, and record keeping.

But, impressive as they are, traditional schools and colleges aren't doing half the job of educating people. Classroom training and education provided by employers cost more money and instruct more students than all the colleges and universities put together, yet economists keep telling us that we are going to have to do more of this training to compete with German and Japanese workers.

Employers provide the lion's share of specific job training. Schooling of some kind or another is the first assignment of almost every new hire and the amount of payroll time spent in formal schooling increases with the importance of the job. For many self-employed professionals, continuing "job training" is mandated by laws that require them to go back to school for additional courses every few years in order to renew their licenses.

Consumers have to be taught how to use new products by salespeople, and sometimes which products to avoid by consumer advocates. All of us want to learn more about the arts, crafts, sports, and hobbies we like to pursue, and some of us desperately need instruction in simple techniques of daily living.

The real demand for teachers is greater than the supply of those fitted to do it. You need personal qualities in addition to the detailed qualifications set up for teachers in the public schools and academic postsecondary institutions. You have to be patient and a good listener as well as a good talker to get through to people who don't understand you, and if you can't maintain your own enthusiasm for your subject you'll never be able to impart it to reluctant learners.

Teachers have traditionally taken home less in dollars for their short year than their education commands in other professions, but they are catching up. In 1990, median weekly earnings were $344 for pre-kindergarten and kindergarten teachers, $519 for elementary school teachers, $589 for secondary school teachers, $510 for special education teachers, $595 for educational and vocational counselors, and $747 for college and university teachers.

Among nontraditional teachers and trainers, pay was highest for self-employed management consultants offering seminars in sales and management skills to business organizations. But a great deal of such urgently needed adult education as teaching illiterates to read or the defensive driving courses offered to seniors by the AARP is done by volunteers.

SECOND CAREERS FOR EXPERIENCED EDUCATORS

If you've retired from a college or public school your pension is good enough so that money won't be the main object of your second career. Public school teachers are often so disenchanted with the system that they are ready for almost anything else, like the high school teacher who loved a job in a bank because it allowed her to associate with adults.

Education holds only a small minority of educators who choose to continue to work after retirement. Some of those who find second careers in the field move ahead to more money and responsibility, often in administration, but most who stay find educational work with less responsibility and shorter hours or move to teaching another subject or another kind of student.

If you have been a **public school administrator** you have many interesting options. You could work in education consulting, either as an individual or through one of the organizations that exist to provide it. In Missouri, a retired school administrator works for the school board association advising school districts on alternative financial programs for getting the money they need for plant improvements.

You could teach in a college of education. In California, an assistant superintendent of a school district responsible for curriculum and instruction took early retirement to teach students who were training to become school administrators in a private college. He's only earning $12,000 a year for half-time work, but with his pension it adds up to more income than he had before he retired.

In Michigan, the retired administrator of the social workers, psychologists, nurses, and other support staff in the Ann Arbor schools spends ten hours a week counseling and observing senior students doing practice teaching at Eastern Michigan University. She enjoys working with young people just entering the profession. In Maryland, a retired elementary school teacher got a similar part-time job supervising student teachers at Towson State University simply by applying to the school of education directly.

College professors who want to continue working when they retire can teach as adjunct or hourly professors and may be importuned to do so when their old department is shorthanded. Some retired professors get part-time work doing odd academic chores, usually at very low pay. One retired professor of education comes back to his old department to grade papers and correspond with graduate students doing independent study.

When she retired to another state, an English and speech department chair got part-time work as an instructor in reading effectiveness and study skills for a technical college.

Some college teachers have specialties that are made to order for consulting assignments. An economist retired from the faculty of Texas A&M gets $100 an hour for consulting with the boards of directors of agricultural cooperatives all over the country. The main drawback he sees is the travel required.

A retired professor of pharmacy is domesticating medicinal herbs for an agricultural research firm in Germany. He works about forty hours a week in the growing season, much of it traveling. He learned about the job from a university colleague.

If you've been a **schoolteacher**, you might get a job in a college. Schoolteachers who know their way around college faculties are often hired as adjuncts or graduate assistants. Although he's earning only $8.58 an hour for part-time work, a retired teacher who resented being a "babysitter and policeman" works happily as an academic advisor to Youngstown State University students because he's "treated like a professional for a change." He got the job on his own, just by applying.

In a small town in Virginia, a teacher retired from the New Jersey public school system is coordinating services for graduate students at the Institute of Manufacturing Technology. The pay is not high, but the hours are flexible and he likes the director.

One way to get these special jobs is to be around when they are being created. That's how a retired English and social studies teacher got the part-time post of director of continuing education at the University of the Ozarks in Arkansas. The job gives her a chance to use her administrative talents and to help working people complete a college degree.

Some college jobs are best done by high school teachers familiar with the problems of entering students. At the University of Dearborn in Michigan, a retired high school English teacher works about a month a year interviewing minority scholarship students.

You might find a job you like better in your own or another school system. A science and math teacher in the Missouri school system became the superintendent of schools in a small town in the neighboring state of Arkansas simply by applying when he heard that the job was vacant.

If you've risen above the classroom, you may be more interested in moving back to working more closely with actual students. In Texas an elementary principal who retired early rather than cope with new paperwork requirements directs individualized instruction in a private Christian school where he has an opportunity to include morals in the curriculum. The only drawback he sees is the lack of a staff lounge and restroom.

There are personally rewarding opportunities to work part time with students outside the regular public school classrooms. After forty years of teaching and running the sports program in a Fort Lauderdale high school, Harold Cox works eight hours a week teaching dropouts the subjects they have to make up to get a diploma. He earns $16.42 an hour and thinks being with young people keeps him young both in mind and body.

In Eastchester, New York, a retired assistant to a New York City elementary school principal earns $17 an hour tutoring housebound students. She enjoys the opportunity for working one-on-one without normal classroom distractions. A former administrator of educational services in California has taken on the exacting responsibility of tutoring a blind child who attends a regular preschool. She works sixteen hours a week and earns $6.75 an hour.

In Iowa, a public school music teacher loves to teach so much that she hasn't been able to keep away from it. At 72 she returned after her second retirement to teach piano, voice, and organ twelve hours a week to children at a special school for the severely handicapped. At the minimum wage, it's like the volunteer work in music she does in her church and the local chorale and little theater.

After retiring, the headmistress of a private school went back to school herself to learn how to tutor dyslexic children who have trouble learning to read. Some of these special jobs are so hard to fill that they may be advertised in the paper, but if you are interested in working with handicapped school-age children, make yourself known to your local board of cooperative educational services.

If you're really desperate to make money, you can, of course, always work as a substitute. At 69, a retired primary teacher earns $105 a day in the Los Angeles system. In addition to the money, she likes the feeling that she is competent and needed, but she is only too keenly aware of the drawbacks. "Some classes are very poorly organized," she complains. "No standards. No plans. No supplies. No respect for the substitute."

But if you're tired of the red tape of traditional education, there's a whole new world of teaching adults in nonacademic settings. After seventeen years in the school system, an elementary school principal quit out of what he calls "sheer boredom" and answered a newspaper ad for director of training for a franchiser of miniwarehouses. He loves the variety, the pace, and particularly the boost in pay to $56,000 a year. If you are interested in more money, look into the schooling offered by franchisers who have no direct tie to any vocational training (see page 182).

In Raleigh, Malcolm Knowles not only writes books about adult education since his retirement from North Carolina State University's school of education, but continues to teach it for profit to the private sector. He travels all over the country putting on workshops to teach middle managers of corporations how to train adults.

Adult education in the nonprofit sector is likely to be lower-paid than work in the regular school system, but less strenuous and more inviting. Most attractive are one-of-a-kind, part-time jobs where you have a lot of freedom and a chance to do it your way. A teacher who went back to college and got a degree in adult education was able to add workshops in art, acting, and handicrafts to a city recreation program for seniors which began as a card club in an abandoned schoolhouse.

If you want to volunteer, teachers are always needed not only in literacy programs at home, but all over the world. Pat Murphy taught high school English and history for twenty-three years. When she retired she joined the Peace Corps and developed a school counseling program in Grenada.

If you've been a nontraditional teacher or trainer in industry you may be in the catbird seat to locate a second career in management, sales promotion, or something that may impress you as "better" than what you've been doing. Training managers know the work that they teach, and their former students are seeded throughout the company or industry.

Some former trainers make a great deal of money. Jo Ann Paulin began as a telephone operator, was lucky enough to be involved in training the people who had to computerize the yellow pages, and ended her career with the phone company as a manager of the people who developed company courses. She's now a management consultant who charges $500 a day advising corporate clients on their personnel and training policies. A sales trainer for another phone company is now a consultant for telemarketers (see page 240), and a man who trained automobile dealers for General Motors makes a good living training salesmen for dealers.

Teachers have some built-in advantages when they go into other occupations. They may be able to do the work that they taught. Nursing instructors can always practice nursing, and some of them become consultants to health care organizations or expert witnesses in malpractice suits.

Teachers of art, music, and drama move easily into their arts. English and math teachers have less trouble than other newcomers learning how to do the highly paid and exacting work of technical writing. Vocational arts teachers find jobs in woodworking and machine shops.

For any second career they choose, educators have the head start of skills in reading, writing, speaking, and listening. These skills are especially valuable in sales and politics. If you've motivated reluctant students you may be able to persuade reluctant prospects or voters and start these careers with a constituency of former students.

NICHES FOR NEWCOMERS TO EDUCATION

If you want to work in a school or college, you may be able to transfer your first career to a school or college setting. Educational institutions need investment specialists, accountants, fundraisers, recreation and human resource specialists, secretaries, librarians, audiovisual specialists, drivers, mechanics, groundskeepers, and guards, among others. The pay may not be the highest, but the benefits are usually good and it's a nice place to work.

There's a niche for newcomers to education in **administration** and **professional services**. If you've had administrative responsibility in any large bureaucracy, such as the military, you can manage the money, people, and facilities of a big school system. At the University of Missouri, a retired naval officer who served both as a flyer and in personnel directs county extension programs and counsels on business. At 60, the managing partner of a big law firm in Boston decided to withdraw from active work with the firm to devote himself to work for peace and international development. He arranged to meet the heads of organizations doing this work and signed on as a senior advisor to the Experiment in International Living, a private voluntary organization with intercultural exchange programs and a school for international training. To his new work he brings a lifetime of experience with "people, problem-solving, compromise, cultural differences, negotiation."

If you've been a social worker or psychologist in a public or private agency you can transfer your practice to the school system.

Would you rather teach? You'll find it hard to qualify for a mainstream job in a traditional school or college. You'd have to take rigid teacher training and graduate school courses that may put you off because they are frankly designed to mold the attitudes of young beginners. But if you decide to go back to school to get these credentials you won't be the only one in the class your age. About one-third of teachers in training are older than traditional college students. Some of them are military officers, many of whom have been to service schools and acquired skills that fit them for hard-to-fill jobs teaching science, math, and technical subjects.

Others are homemakers who find teaching a natural extension of what they've been doing at home. Wanda Johnson got her degree at the age of 54 and is now an enthusiastic fourth-grade teacher.

Older people are so eager to counsel that some of them are willing to go back to college to get the equivalent of a master's degree in counseling. In San Antonio, a displaced housewife who had never held a paying job got her degree at the age of 47 and became a diagnostician evaluating deaf children in the San Antonio school system.

But there are ways around the credentialing system that will get you into classrooms from kindergarten to college. To start at the top, if you've had a distinguished career in business, a profession, or in the public service you may be invited to teach what you know in a **college**. Former presidents, governors, and legislators often end their careers as professors of political science. But you don't have to be that exalted if you have unique firsthand experience about a field that young people want to enter.

One of these hot, uncharted fields is international business. The marketing manager of an apparel manufacturer that went broke because of foreign competition is teaching what he learned about international marketing at the Philadelphia College of Textile Science. Back in 1981, the manager of the export-import department of a petrochemical company thought it would be fun to teach, so when he retired he volunteered his services to the American Graduate School of International Management, a private institution set up on an old air force base in Arizona to train business people in foreign trade. They hired him on the spot and he's been happily teaching full time ever since, earning almost as much as he made the year he retired.

If you've been a manager you may be able to teach management. Not only do you understand the subject, but as a manager you've had hands-on experience in teaching and motivating others. A sales operations manager chairs a college department of business administration. A retired Internal Revenue Service tax auditor and postal service manager are among the former middle managers who are teaching business, accounting, and management courses in community colleges.

Military officers have a double advantage. They have usually had enough management experience to teach many business courses but they've counseled, coached, and motivated subordinates and spent so much time in service schools themselves that they are comfortable in classrooms, too. They make splendid advisers to adult students.

It's no surprise to find a former drug research director teaching research methods, a former journalist teaching journalism, a former dentist teaching dentists, a clinical psychologist supervising the doctoral dissertations of psychologists, or a deputy sheriff teaching criminal justice. Nurses retire to teach nursing, civil engineers become professors of engineering. Artists and musicians whose work is their credential teach in colleges as well as the primary and secondary school systems.

What about you? You might spend an instructive hour or so at the library looking in catalogs of nearby colleges for courses you could teach. The exercise is good for morale even if you don't want to become a teacher.

But can you get such a job? It's easier, of course, to become an adjunct or hourly professor teaching your specialty part time without academic tenure, but that may be exactly what you want. The truth is that sheer accident has a lot to do with the way these jobs are handed out. You might get hired simply by walking in and presenting yourself. In Hagerstown, Maryland, a retired diplomat called up the local junior college to see if they needed someone to teach and wound up teaching American history and international relations. He likes working with young people better than with "some academics who view the world from the tower of the campus."

Don't be shy about your abilities. When he sold his company, a marketer of grass seed moved to Reno because of the climate, introduced himself to the president of the University of Nevada, and said he wanted to share his lifetime of business experience with students. A persuasive salesman, he wound up teaching journalism and likes everything about it except the low pay, which he thinks "keeps people from appreciating what you do."

But there are other, gentler ways. Quite often you can network an introduction to the dean. If you hanker to teach at your own alma mater, get active in the alumni association and lend a hand with fundraising. Both are good introductions to the people who could hire you.

In **school systems** the standard credentials are being challenged. When the shortage is desperate, the system gives a little. In some states, including Texas and New Jersey, college-educated older newcomers who have not had all the education courses required may be able to get "alternative certification."

A system desperate for qualified math and science teachers may waive or postpone the usual courses in education for retired scientists and engineers. In Tucson, a mine manager with an engineering degree went to work teaching math and science to students in danger of dropping out. He eventually acquired the master's degree in education required for the job.

If you have something to contribute, you may be asked to donate the time it takes to share it with a class or at an assembly, and there are career programs at which local people are invited to talk about their occupations. At 76, one of these speakers was earning $8.50 an hour recruiting others for the School Volunteers of Boston.

Occasionally specially qualified outsiders can be integrated into an ongoing school program. In a New Mexico high school, an administrative assistant who directed the flow of communications in a federal safety program is a team teacher of journalism. She works ten hours a week at $10 an hour and heard about the job through a friend.

One way to get paid is to work with an organization that is contributing to the curriculum. In Placerville, California, a research chemist retired from Aerojet lectures five hours a week in local schools as "Dr. Rocket." He's part of an Aerojet program to turn kids on to science. In Huntsville, the University of Alabama pays one of its retired research associates a modest stipend to help junior high school teachers prepare active science projects. If your organization has an educational service, ask them whether they have a role for you.

Another niche for newcomers is working in one of the remedial or **special services** that schools provide for students who need more individual attention than the regular teachers can give them. There's no regular state certification for tutoring students having trouble keeping up with the class or in danger of dropping out. In Monroe, Louisiana, a 60-year-old mother of four grown children tutors kindergarten children in math and reading readiness. She took a test at the school media center, and was put right to work full time at $6,000 for the school year.

Teacher's aides work under the professional direction of the teacher, but they get just as close to the children, especially those who are having trouble with the work. Teacher's aides get to help with the special education of children with handicaps, get kids on and off the bus, and do paperwork and typing. The varied duties and the children themselves attract people like a retired contractor, an aerospace engineering manager, and a firefighter, as well as secretaries, letter carriers, retail store clerks, and homemakers.

There are also second careers to be had in high school extension classes for adults teaching English as a second language, high school equivalency subjects, text processing, or almost any subject for which there is a demand in the local community. The possibilities are intriguing. One California school district has a program for teaching music to older adults, both those living independently and those in nursing homes. In 1988 it was being taught by a social worker disabled by osteoporosis, who was trained for the work by a state vocational rehabilitation program. Under the terms of the grant, she was restricted to working only twelve hours a week.

Some of these special teachers contribute their services. A nurse who had always wanted to be a teacher volunteers to help students muddled by algebra. In New Jersey, a munitions engineer who quit designing warheads for the army rather than accept a transfer teaches twenty high school dropouts at an adult and community education center. He got the job through the Voluntary Action Center of Morris County.

For opportunities, pay, and training required, consult your local school district. If you are credentialed in a related field, such as social work, or hold a degree in math or science, you may be put right to work even if the job requires training or certification.

Substituting is the most popular second career in teaching for newcomers who don't have credentials in education. Subs are so urgently needed that all you may have to do is to appear at a school and say here I am. In Idaho, a soil scientist retired from the Department of Agriculture was hired over the telephone.

If you have a college education you may be put in charge of a classroom with no more than an orientation session on when school begins and how to take attendance, but you will be encouraged to take courses in education. In New York City, a sewing plant owner who lost his shop was able to qualify for subbing by taking several college courses in education. During the school year he works half-time at $80 a day, twice as much as subs in most other places.

There are good reasons why it's so easy to get. You may have no more than an hour's notice to appear in a strange school before a class of unruly kids out to "sink the sub." If you are doing it for money, the income is uncertain and there are no fringe benefits. It's not the most beloved second career, yet most older newcomers love it. They like the challenge of working with kids, the feeling of helping, and as one former army officer exulted, "no administrative responsibilities!"

Private schools are usually hospitable to newcomers without former credentials, if only because they pay less and can't afford to be as picky. A widow who had been turned down by the public schools in her area was hired by a parochial school to fill a vacancy that occurred the day before school opened. Religiously oriented Protestant schools recruit teachers from among their congregations, some of whom work part time without pay.

But the overqualified are attracted to private schools, too. Seniors in a parochial high school are taught Christian justice by a retired telephone manager who went back to college to get a master's degree in religious education after retiring. And Montessori schools require a year's academic work and a year of internship training.

Private institutions for educating adults with special problems have more leeway in hiring people with informal qualifications. In Roseville, California, the retired director of an air force recreation center is an instructor in a day-care center for developmentally disabled senior citizens run by the Placer Association for Retarded Citizens. If you want to teach young people, consider volunteering to be a den mother or teacher of a craft you know in a youth organization. A former foreman in a steel plant teaches his knowledge on nature and conservation to the Scouts.

Whatever you've done, someone teaches it somewhere. Where, for instance, did you learn how to do it? If your own best teacher wasn't credentialed, the job he or she was doing at the time may give you your chance to pass on what you've learned, too. Good first-line supervisors often think of themselves as teachers.

If you'd like to teach your trade, consider working in a **vocational technical** school or a program run by the federally funded but state-run Bureau of Cooperative Educational Services (BOCES). Even when you have to take further schooling, your practical experience may warrant a temporary credential that will put you right on the payroll until you take the courses and pass the examinations for a permanent certification later on.

In New Mexico, a retired navy warrant officer in electronics teaches electronics in a vocational high school. He chose teaching because of the vacations, the hours, and the nice environment. A 74-year-old vocational teacher of offset presswork in New York hopes to encourage teenagers to choose a career in the graphic arts. He has no degree but keeps his license by getting more college credits every year. In a vocational technical school in Alaska, a former master of oceanographic research vessels at Woods Hole in Martha's Vineyard teaches seamanship.

Vocational schools are no longer confined to "blue-collar" trade schools. There's somewhere you can teach any occupation for which you are licensed. Real estate, therapeutic massage, and many other occupations that have to be licensed are taught in special schools or community colleges.

But the second careers that are made to order for older newcomers are in **nontraditional adult education**. The sponsor may be an employer, a marketer, an advocate, a public or private social agency, or a government agency. The subject and student body may be as specific as AIDS education for teenagers or as broad as environmental threats to the planet affecting all of us. Meetings, seminars, short courses, closed-circuit television, audiovisual tapes, correspondence courses, computer information databases, and filmed and live demonstrations are only a few of the innovative ways of delivering material pioneered by nontraditional educators. And all of it depends on people old enough to be experienced in the subject.

Nontraditional classrooms spring up to solve immediate problems. There's a marvelous new machine for making ice cream in a store while the customers watch, but to sell it, the manufacturer finds he has to run a short course for his franchisees in how to run the machine. A new machine in a Tennessee factory stands idle for lack of workers who know enough about fractions and decimals to read the dials, so the plant manager hires remedial math teachers and sends new hires to school on the payroll.

The military maintains a vast school system that teaches every skill in the book, including such social skills as the way to behave at a formal banquet. There are also etiquette classes for civilians. Teenagers can learn how to behave at charm schools run by department stores, and older folks can learn the fine points of ballroom dancing at a senior citizens' center.

Many courses are started by nonteachers who see some group that needs more information. Take health. If you are an insurance claims adjuster you may develop a lecture telling doctors and nurses how not to get sued for malpractice and arrange to deliver it in hospitals. If you manufacture hospital equipment, you may set up a short course showing hospital technicians how it works. If you know massage, you can teach it to nurses as a private enterpriser. And if you're enjoying a ripe old age you may find yourself lecturing to doctors and nurses on a positive approach to death and dying.

Think about your own field. Are there special groups who need to know something you can teach them? What's the best way to reach them? Who has an interest in seeing them instructed? If all else fails, you can commit your message to a book and get yourself invited to speak wherever the people who need to know it gather (see page 94). In Ogden, Utah, a former medical claims adjuster lectures to women on her book of advice to prospective widows, *Are You Prepared to be Alone?*

Training employees is a huge industry in its own right. It supports its own movie industry of training films, its own publishing industry of training manuals. Managers and highly paid salespeople are almost always trained by outside specialists who come in to put on seminars, short courses, sometimes even briefings with a very few top managers. The people who teach the boss are paid top dollar, but these plums go to nationally known authorities in the big national management consulting or accounting firms, or to retired top managers in the industry. Newcomers need not apply.

For salespeople, there are traveling workshops on leadership which go to businesses, colleges, clubs, and other organizations. Part instruction, part pep talk, and part entertainment, these "motivational seminars" are well-paid, standard numbers on the programs of company meetings and business conventions.

Most professional and technical industries are constantly retraining their people. A maintenance man for GE teaches soldiers how to repair tanks. More often, military officers train employees in a private company. Teaching what you used to do is a second career in everything from piloting airplanes to painting pictures (see page 101).

Training customers is a big business. Take just the job of training distributors. Oil companies train gas station managers, car companies train automobile dealers, insurance companies train their agents. A retired manager of the Washington State Department of Natural Resources earns $10.50 an hour training for the city and county road department.

Even the trainers have to be trained. A public information officer for the California Department of Corrections earns $22 an hour writing lesson plans and setting up the program to train corrections officers in the system.

Training customers is the only way to sell a technical innovation. IBM can afford to teach the customers for big-ticket mainframe computers how to use them, but small-business purchasers of inexpensive personal computers are on their own. They could learn how to run the machine at a school, but a dentist or a video store may need help in setting it up to solve their own particular problems. Helping them out, at $20 to $50 an hour, has become a second career for retired computer engineers, designers, and salespeople.

Students are waiting somewhere for anyone who knows anything about an **art, craft, sport,** or **hobby** that anyone wants to learn (see pages 223 and 253). If you're a specialist in Chinese cooking, you may be drafted to teach it by the adult education program of the nearest public school. If you're a calligrapher, bridge player, chess player, or furniture refinisher, your local community college may let you teach a course in it. You won't earn much money, but you are sure to make new friends and have a lot of fun.

Finally, you can be of real service teaching the **skills of daily living**. When "education" is prescribed as the solution to a social problem, specialists in the field organize short courses wherever they can reach the targets. Short courses and seminars may be offered by a high school or state agricultural extension service, a service organization such as the YMCA or the AARP, the armed forces, recreation centers, social agencies, and even department stores, hospitals, and courts.

The most basic life skill for those who lack it is the English language itself. It's needed so urgently by newcomers to the country that English as a Second Language (ESL) is taught everywhere, at pay reflecting the different auspices: $31,000 a year for a former clinical psychologist teaching English to prisoners; $22 an hour in the public school for a former child-welfare worker; $6.42 an hour at a community college for a former legal secretary; nothing at the local public library for the former owner of a day-care center who is doing it because "the job is fun!" Your local community college can tell you where you can get the short training usually required.

But not everyone who grew up speaking English can read and write it. If you are a high school graduate, you can volunteer to teach the first two Rs to adults at an adult literacy center. Joe Donnan, a retired technical editor for GE, has switched from teaching immigrants at night school to volunteering twenty hours a week in the adult literacy program.

Another basic life skill is driving. If you have ever gotten a speeding ticket, the chances are that you were sent to traffic school by the judge. In California, a retired cab driver and driving instructor earns $270 for a three-day week of lecturing traffic violators on safe driving. The school is a private enterprise licensed and run by the state but financed by fees from the violators, which are lower than the fines they would have to pay if they did not attend. A former sales manager teaches "alcohol awareness" classes to second offenders of driving under the influence (DUI). If you are interested in teaching good driving, get in touch with your local traffic safety department.

Good driving instruction is not only for lawbreakers. Many retired professionals volunteer to teach "55 Alive," the short course in defensive driving sponsored in every community at regular intervals by the AARP. One is a former Pan American flight engineer who uses his training in safety. Another is a former pastor who says he uses what he learned in the ministry about "helping people feel good about themselves."

Maintaining your health is a life skill that is being taught in programs set up as needed in schools, colleges, workplaces, hospitals, and senior citizen centers. This can be a personally rewarding second career, not only for a doctor or nurse but for social workers and caregivers.

In spite of the bad press and poor pay of school systems, the actual work of teaching is attractive and expanding. If you're a natural-born teacher, there are plenty of opportunities to do it.

☑ PERSONAL CAREGIVING

Caregiving is the cement that keeps a society together, but it is rapidly becoming an occupational frontier. Within the memory of seniors of the nineties, all but the very rich took care of their own homes, yards, clothes, hair, animals, children, and old folks. Now we do without these personal services or have them done by outsiders for pay. Many of these jobs are new and their number, variety, level of skill, and pay are rising.

Home is where a lot of this work has to be done, and neither men nor women spend enough time at home to do it all. At least once in a while, the house has to be cleaned, if only to get rid of the trash. It takes labor to run the labor-saving machines that do household tasks in a jiffy, and skilled labor to repair them. Electrical, plumbing, heating, and air-conditioning systems have to be maintained in working order. Grounds and yards have to be kept.

Caring for people is moving steadily out of the home to places where it is economic for professionals to give this care. Hair is cut and groomed in beauty and barber shops. Counsel on diet and exercise is no longer left to motherly advice but dispensed in weight loss, fitness, and health clubs. The sick and the fragile old who need custodial attention are cared for in health care institutions or by home health aides organized by a publicly or privately funded agency (see page 136).

The care of preschool children is a good example of important work that is becoming professionalized and transferred to new, increasingly regulated institutions. Day-care centers serving many little children may be run for profit by a big publicly owned chain like Kinder-Care or not-for-profit by a social agency or a parent's employer. Family care providers take care of a limited number of children in their own homes. Both kinds of care are licensed and subject to federal, state, county, and local regulations on the physical premises, zoning, local traffic, equipment, program, ratio of caregivers to children, and many other details. Families also have the option of bringing in a nanny or babysitter to take care of the child at home.

Finally, a miscellany of personal services is provided by specialized caregivers. Among those reported by older people are the care of plants, pets, children, and house when the householder is temporarily away from home; the care of animals in kennels, stables, shelters, pet stores, veterinary facilities, laboratories, and zoological parks; and assistance in funeral services.

Liking the work is the main qualification for caregivers who learn the work in their own homes or on the job. Child caregivers should be patient, energetic, and physically up to meeting the demands of active small children. Hairdressers, barbers, cosmetologists, embalmers, and those who care for children or pets outside their homes must usually be licensed or work under the supervision of a licensee.

Pay for caregivers is low and many of them are part time. For full-time salaried workers, median weekly pay in 1990 was $247 for hairdressers, $203 for child care workers outside the child's home, and $132 for those who worked in the child's home.

SECOND CAREERS FOR EXPERIENCED CAREGIVERS

Women caregivers duck in and out of the labor force. They tend to think of their jobs as episodes in their lives during which they are free to make money doing for other families what they do for their own when they're needed. An 80-year-old who had cared for one child for nine years quit her job to take care of her grandchildren while her daughter was having back surgery, but when that crisis was over she went back to earning $20 a day taking care of a 2-year-old.

Even trained beauticians who own their shops give them up for family reasons: "I married and sold my beauty shop," "got pregnant," "moved to California for my husband's health." No matter that they may have to go back to working as an operator the next time they have to make money ("doing the same thing but am not responsible for the bills"). And if not back to hairdressing, then to work in a shop or factory or a job with a caregiving orientation such as practical nurse, mobile-home park manager, hotel valet, or shelter adviser in a housing project for elderly.

Social service work is the natural second career for caregivers. It's less strenuous, more structured, and you enjoy more prestige. If you've worked for a private family, you may find it more rewarding — though probably not in money — to work as a home health aide for a social agency helping older people stay in their homes. "I know I'm appreciated," says a former private houseworker who can't do heavy cleaning any more, "and I can help these people so much!" When foot surgery kept her from cooking and cleaning, the housekeeper for a pastor became a half-time pastoral associate, visiting the ill and elderly of the parish.

NICHES FOR NEWCOMERS TO CAREGIVING

Caregiving is chronically underpaid, so you have your choice of jobs if you are willing to take part of your pay in the pleasure of helping people. And that's exactly the way a lot of older people feel about it.

Even highly paid managers and professionals work as handymen, helping neighbors with routine repair and maintenance chores, after they retire. Few are doing it for the modest hourly wages they charge. They like it, and they think it's good for their health. A great many think this physical work can prolong their lives.

A biology teacher retired after thirty-two years in Chicago schools travels around in a small pickup truck fixing things because he says his wife insists that he get out of the house from 8:00 A.M. to 5:00 P.M. every weekday. Though he has only a master's degree, his card reads "Quentin 'Doc' Talbot, Director of General Information."

These all-purpose older newcomers to home maintenance stay away from work requiring specialized training and equipment, such as large-scale groundskeeping, pest control, knife sharpening, or repairing locks and home appliances, although more and more of the traditional work of the man of the house is going to such specialists.

If you really like fixing things in a house you'll have no trouble finding work. Run an ad in the local shopping paper or stick a notice on the supermarket bulletin board, and your first customers are likely to tell their friends about you. Handymen who charge less than the going craft wages — and most of them do — complain that they soon have more work than they bargained for. What "Doc" likes is the freedom to turn down work whenever he pleases.

Older women caregivers seldom have such choices. They may enjoy child care and even housework, but most of them do it for pay because it's the easiest and sometimes the only job they can get. A credit supervisor who quit because the boss harrassed her had to go to work cleaning houses at $15 a day without any benefits. The "stigma" of housecleaning bothered a bookkeeper who dropped out of white-collar work because of pregnancy, but she likes it now because her people are nice, and "it's honest work, nothing to be ashamed of."

Elderly cleaning ladies complain of more than their public image: driving long distances in shaky cars, getting tired and sick, employers who expect too much, even misplaced pity. "It's hard work," says a former food service manager; "people don't understand why I like it." What housekeepers like is appreciative employers, working at their own pace, and making a house "sparkle."

Caregiving doesn't have to be depressed slave labor. Status and sometimes pay go up whenever a specific caregiving task can be specialized into a recognized profession, or organized so that it can be done by an institution. Chimney cleaning is a good example. A dirty job once done by exploited little boys is now as modern as running a special vacuum cleaner. It has become a profitable small business that you can start with an investment of $5,000 and the explicit instructions that come from the manufacturers of the equipment.

Do you have a caregiving talent or interest that you can professionalize? If there's some household task you are known for doing especially well, start charging for it. A doctor's wife who had raised five children and run her husband's office developed so good a system for keeping track of her family's far-flung possessions that lawyers and appraisers tried to hire her to help them inventory estates. After her divorce, she developed a business helping busy young couples organize moves and retiring couples to move to smaller quarters.

If you like cleaning cars, explore the possibility of working as a "detailer" who puts $100 worth of spit and polish into painstakingly cleaning every nook and cranny.

If you're a skier with a reputation for keeping your gear in tip-top condition, let other skiers know that you are available to tune up their skis for $35 a pair.

There's even an unfilled demand for old-fashioned mending. A retired teacher who put up a sign reading "The Village Mender" on her porch donates all the money she charges to a church charity.

Local ads and bulletin board notices should get you started as a handyman or in any of the special services that have a local market. The quickest way to tap the market for an unusual service such as organizing moves is to get a newspaper reporter to write a feature article about you and your specialty.

Has the caregiving you like to do been organized so that you can do it through a program or institution? If you've lost weight or trimmed up through a health club, spa, or diet or exercise center, you may have a caregiving career encouraging others to do likewise. Weight Watchers trains its successes and pays them a fee, plus a commission based on attendance, for each meeting they run. Women like this arrangement because they can work as much or as little as they want. Estelle Swilling does ten hours of Weight Watcher meetings a week and would never go back to working full time as an officer in a bank. She says you either love it or know right away that it's not for you.

If you love animals and have bred and cared for them all your life, you may want to "go to the dogs," as one chief telephone operator described her retirement. She now devotes herself full time to feeding, cleaning, grooming, showing, and breeding dogs in a kennel she had run on the side for twenty-three years. But you don't have to make a big investment to spend your time with dogs or cats. You can work, at very low wages but often part time, as a groomer or attendant. Watch the ads or apply directly to kennels, stables, and vets.

The office manager and medical assistant to a podiatrist loved cats. When she retired she walked into the office of a vet who specialized in cats and asked if he needed help. He did. She loves seeing all the different kinds of cats so much that she signed on to assist him full time at a nominal $5 an hour. A retired secretary who applied to the local humane society was hired to work part time coordinating the many people who volunteer to care for the animals, keeping the records, and receiving visitors.

If you like to comfort the distressed, you don't have to become a psychologist. You can work as a home health aide (see Medicine and Health), or as a friendly visitor for your church (see page 73), or relieving the family of a victim of Alzheimer's disease through the agency that offers respite care in your community, or helping others a little older and weaker than yourself. Minimum-wage pay boosted the morale of a 72-year-old who works at a senior citizens' center: "Instead of being the ol' lady with the cane, I'm the one lending an arm to somebody else."

Have you ever thought how much help you could be to the bereaved in a funeral home? Old people do not shrink from it. One funeral home pays a 70-year-old retired fashion manager $15 for visiting a family two or three weeks after the funeral. Her title is "social caller" and she says it's the most satisfying work she has ever done. Another memorial chapel pays a 74-year-old retired school bus driver $5.15 an hour to work as a "widowhood counselor." She heard about the job while taking courses in health and psychology after she was widowed herself.

Retired pastors help with everything from answering the phone for death calls after-hours to what one termed "the details of funerals I had always taken for granted"; but there's work in funerals for people from all walks of life. A retired fire chief drives hearses and helps at the cemetery.

If you like being with children, you can have more of the fun and less of the responsibility through Foster Grandparents. This is a locally operated, federally sponsored program that pays low-income people over 60 a small stipend, carfare, and a meal for spending part of a day with children who need special attention in hospitals, foster homes, or day-care centers.

Family day-care sounds like a logical second career for a woman left alone with a big house, but it's not a bonanza. Caring for large numbers of very small children is physically strenuous and presents new problems to women who have been accustomed to caring for children on an individual basis. Those who do well at it are apt to be women with professional business experience.

One who likes it was a medical assistant who wanted to provide better service to working mothers than she herself had been able to get when her own children were small. However, she nets little more than $150 a week for full-time work, from before her children arrive in the morning until after they leave at night. In addition, she must contend with social workers from Florida review agencies who inspect to see whether she has the specific toys and is following the rigid schedule the regulations prescribe for each age group. In 1990 she was trying to keep the cost down to $65 a week per child. Her advice: "Don't go into this business unless you truly love children. Let money be your last thought."

In California, Katherine Allison went into family day-care when she lost her job as a drill press operator. She got her license for caring for up to six children in her home, but only after making some alterations, such as installing safety clasps on her kitchen cabinets and building a guard around her wood-burning stove. She makes little more than $250 a week for full-time responsibility, but she likes it because she can do it at home.

Before going into this business, find out what regulations will apply to you. Every municipality, county, and state has its own regulations, and when they conflict the strictest one applies. Even the federal government gets into the act with recommendations. And before embarking on taking care of other people's children, you would do well to see whether there's a course in early childhood education you can take at your local community college.

Fewer and fewer children are cared for by a professional nurse or governess who lives in the household. Those who seem to be the happiest doing it are older women without business experience who have raised a family and no longer want to maintain a home of their own. Some move in to care for grandchildren at nominal pay plus room and board. The best paid are the certified professional nannies and the nurses who help a new mother when she brings the baby home from the hospital.

Pat Hall worked for a few years as a purchasing agent after her children were grown, but she was lonely after her divorce and her grown children scattered, so she sold her house and enrolled in the National Academy of Nannies in Denver. After being certified, she worked first caring for the children of a widower and then for the two children of a lawyer couple in Connecticut. She earns $375 a week plus hospitalization, car allowance, workmen's compensation, and all her living expenses, with all holidays and weekends off and a month's paid vacation in the summer. Drawbacks? "Think before you speak. Stay in the background. Parents are sometimes jealous when children put you first."

Nanny courses are given as one or two semester programs in regular colleges at whatever the college charges per point. The National Academy of Nannies in Denver charges $3,300 for a course including academic instruction in child development, which can be completed in less than six months of full-time attendance or part time for a year. Those who have completed the schooling can command higher wages.

Newborns are a pleasant and profitable specialty. Ruth Esposito is an LPN who moves into a home when the mother and baby come home from the hospital and stays from two weeks to a month, sleeping in the baby's room. She had worked only with geriatric patients until one of them asked her to take care of his new grandchild. Now she takes care of a baby a month, earning about $1,000, and finds it much more fascinating than the office work she used to do before becoming a licensed practical nurse. She says that so many people need help with their new babies that she has considered training others to do the same work, but this would take time away from her babies.

Most older women work at plain old babysitting by the hour, or relieve the pinch on a working couple by covering for them. Some help out during the hectic mornings when everyone is getting out of the house and in the afternoon when the children return. Pay is low, but the women who do this work become attached to the children.

House sitting is less strenuous than babysitting. If you are unattached and like an occasional change of scene, you may enjoy caring for the plants, animals, children, and security of a household when the family or the adults are away on a trip. Pay can be as much as $50 a day. Householders prefer to leave their property in charge of some-one with references, so put a notice on the bulletin board of your church or get on the grapevine of a big company which has people going away on vacation.

Caring for hair, houses, children, or cats is a bore if you're forced to do it for money, but a pleasure if you like what you're tending.

☑ HOMEMAKING

If you're one of the many women who proudly give their first career as "housewife," "homemaker," "farm wife," "pastor's wife," or "wife and mother," you know that you've been doing real work. At various times you've done a staggering variety of jobs that command a range of wages from high to low: housekeeper, cook, seamstress, interior decorator, gardener, hostess, travel agent, social director, accountant, counselor, chauffeur, tutor, adviser, social worker, secretary, and animal tender, to name a few.

But homemaking is a "career" with age and sex qualifications that make it like no other in the labor market. It's entered almost exclusively by young women as an incidental adjunct to an emotional relationship. And while you can't get fired or quit without disrupting the family relationship that got you into it, as an all-consuming, full-time career it usually lasts no longer than the career of a professional dancer or athlete.

When this first career ends happily, with children grown and gone, many mothers are ready for a second career to establish an identity of their own in the wider world. When it ends unhappily in the dissolution of the family, a displaced homemaker needs a job to support herself and sometimes her children.

Either way, it's a hard transition. If you've been out of the job market raising children for ten or fifteen years you have a hard time getting back in. For starters, your experience is very likely to have been as an office worker, telephone operator, teacher, nurse, librarian, or one of the other low-paying, limited "women's jobs" you might not want to go back to.

Or couldn't, even if you wanted to. In libraries, banks, hospitals, and offices, a lot of the work women used to do is now done by a few computer operators. And even if you had a relatively good job (or "man's job," as it used to be called) you may find that your education and experience has aged more than you have.

Returning homemakers experience a new version of the old double bind. You don't have the experience to get a job that pays you enough to maintain your lifestyle and you can't get that experience because employers don't want to hire an older beginner. Even worse, you may be *expecting* less than a fair shake because you assume that employers prefer younger women, as they used to do when "women's jobs" were especially structured for them.

So the first job you have to do is to psyche yourself out of the double whammy of prejudices on the basis of age and sex (see page 283, "Avoiding Age Discrimination"). Don't fall back on the excuse that older women aren't serious about working. Most of them are working for survival, and their families don't hold them back because their children are grown. And don't accept the howler that you are a bigger expense to employers because of sickness. In the vast majority of companies medical costs for older workers are not a penny greater than for younger workers. And they're out sick less, too. The fact is that older female workers have fewer sick days and fewer on-the-job accidents than younger workers of both sexes.

Once you've swept the cobwebs out of your head, you have some real obstacles to face. You may have been out of the work world so long that you don't know what kind of job you can or want to do, or how to go about getting it if you did know what it was. Formidable hurdles, indeed, but a surprising number of former homemakers have ignored or found ways around them. Self-described homemakers have second careers doing almost all the jobs that anybody else does: writer, secretary, real estate broker, house mother, nurse, salesperson, pastor, bed-and-breakfast owner, lecturer, talk show host, computer operator, electronics assembler, yarn shop owner, rental manager, sports director, used car dealer, and more. Health care administration is a natural.

Those who have made the most money have ignored their lack of experience in standard jobs and struck out into new territory. After raising nine children, Emma Strebe went back to school, got her real estate license, and earned $40,000 the year she was 71. Catherine Kidwell started writing novels in her 50s and now earns $50,000 a year at it. Others have started a successful small business or service. And in spite of a late start, a few go back to school and land responsible, high-salaried jobs.

As always, the successful are cockeyed optimists who look at the doughnut instead of the hole. Some of them have been ingenious in identifying what they learned at home and how they can use it in the workplace. Catherine Kidwell confesses that her novels are based on her experiences as the full-time caretaker of her family. Emma Strebe thinks she knows what women are looking for in a house because she raised nine children, and another late bloomer in real estate ascribes her success to the knack of meeting strangers she acquired as the wife of a politician.

Even the downers of homemaking can be an advantage later on. A nursing home administrator says that homemaking taught her "how to buy groceries, settle feuds, and survive on a pittance."

It's frustrating. There may be all sorts of cushy jobs you know you could do, but you need more than your current skills to land them. You need an employment record, workplace smarts, computer skills, credentials, a diploma.

The best advice is what you've been giving to your kids. Go to school. If you have the money and the time, it's the best investment you could make. The skills you learn will allow you to leapfrog over younger workers whose training is older than yours. And though tuition can seem a barrier, you may be able to get some aid.

Jacquelyn Holt was always a good amateur pianist and organist, but when her husband retired and took over most of the housework she looked into music courses available at her local college and discovered that she was eligible for financial aid. At the age of 50 she took demanding courses in music theory, piano, organ, and the synthesizers unknown in her youth. She's now a full-fledged professional teacher and musician.

Formal training comes in all sizes, shapes, and packages. It doesn't have to be a big deal. If your typing is rusty and you don't want to admit that you can't use a word processor, the adult extension service of the high school your kids attended will either have a short course you may take for nothing or tell you where you can get one at low cost.

If you know the career you'd like, your local community college can tell you how you can qualify, and if you don't know what you want, it's the best place to find what you would like to do. The median age of community college students goes up every year. You'll find gray-haired fellow students as eager as kids and a warm welcome from teachers who like the contribution older students make to a classroom. Talk to the career planning office about your interests and shop around in the catalog for courses you'd enjoy taking.

One interest opens up others. Vivian Picker went back to school to study survey research. A survey the class made on air pollution got her thinking about pollution of other kinds, so she took a course in water pollution for which she had to do field work at a wastewater plant. There she fell in love with the blue-collar world and became a wastewater treatment plant operator, earning $15 an hour. At 60 she was climbing up and down ladders, liquefying oxygen, and keeping up with men in work and pay. What has she had to learn to do it? "Pumps, motors, hydraulic chemistry, union strategy, and how to hold my tongue."

There are community college courses, vocational technical schools, proprietary training schools, even correspondence courses (see page 271). A regular four-year baccalaureate degree takes longer, of course, but it will get you more money, even on jobs such as respiratory therapist that you can get without it.

And don't let computers drive you away. When you try them, you may even like them. A 70-year-old who had never had a regular job in her life was so fascinated by the computer in her son's law office that she taught herself how to use it and went to work for the firm.

Conventional career planning advice and job finding techniques weren't designed for older beginners male or female, so you're going to have to find your own way. For starters, you're working for different reasons. Unless you're a displaced homemaker who needs to make enough money to support yourself in a hurry, the work itself and the experience of playing a role in the wider world is as important to you as the actual dollars, and that's going to color the occupations you choose.

Older homemakers have discovered a number of routes to the job market. You may develop a dormant talent, go back to a career you laid aside to have babies, or find a spot where you are needed as much as they used to need you. One homemaker got her degree in divinity so that she could fill the need her church had for a minister to children. If you hit it right, you're in for a whole new ball game. "For me the tape runs backward," said a woman who began working at 48. "I feel as if I had been retired the first half of my life."

Unlike the youngsters, you may have to hunt around in your life to identify your marketable skills. Take stock of what you have learned from the working members of your family, your volunteer work, hobbies, and interests. Can you hitchhike on the skills of a father, mother, or husband? One widow without any job experience remembered what she had learned about car and truck repair by hanging around her father when she was a girl. She found she was good enough at it to repair all kinds of vehicles for dealers and owners. Soon she was buying old cars that looked shabby but were basically sound ("runs good"), fixing them up to look pretty as well as run "like new," and selling them for a handsome profit. She now owns a prosperous business. Working with machinery usually pays more than a nice, old-fashioned "woman's job" in an office, so pay especial attention to skills you may have for a "man's job."

Remember all your volunteer work, however trivial it seemed to you at the time. Hospitals, museums, and social agencies with big volunteer programs sometimes hire a former volunteer to run the program. Even if all you did was a little filing or typing, it counts as the office experience that employers are looking for. And don't underestimate the market value of the skills and visibility you may have acquired working to better your community. After managing several community projects Doris Whitten walked into a local bank and told the president just why he needed a public relations office. He agreed and she walked out with the job.

Consider your hobbies. The best yarn shops are run by women who are knitters themselves. The best pet shops and dog boarding kennels are run by people who were interested in the animals before they thought of making money out of them. If you're interested in antiques, you don't have to tie yourself down to running a shop. By studying up you could earn a little extra money appraising antiques for estates (see page 232).

And don't think you're too old for sports. At 53 a former volleyball star was hired to run the adult volleyball program for her town. Follow your enthusiasms, no matter how outlandish: if you're enthusiastic, you may inspire others. To keep the thrill of skiing through the summer, a 50-year-old took up Windsurfing, the cross between sailing and surfing in which you stand on a board while managing a sail. So many friends wanted to do it too that she became a certified instructor and now sells and rents the equipment as well as teaching it.

There's no telling where a hobby will lead you. A professional math teacher whose hobby was flying became a flight instructor and eventually went into the charter flying and pilot service.

Finally, it's never too late to go back to preparing for the career you laid aside. All that life experience and volunteer work counts for you as soon as you get those educational credentials, and you'll be more up-to-date than younger competitors who haven't been to school as recently. Forty years after completing her undergraduate work, a mother of six got her master's degree in public health and landed a job administering the feeding program for women and children in six Michigan counties.

Ann Kane had studied interior design in college before her marriage, so when she was left a widow after thirty-seven years of homemaking she took a course in interior design at the local college and went into business with another widow in her class. Interior decoration is a very competitive business, but they were able to succeed by pooling their contacts. They joined a homebuilders' organization, where they met contractors who retained them to decorate model units for new buildings. They're not only making money, but having as much fun "as a couple of kids."

Once you have set your sights on an occupation or two that you'd like, you're ready to hunt for it. Start by making a list of everything you know you can do. You may think that the duties you performed as a homemaker are too numerous to list, but list them anyway.

You may be surprised at all the skills you really have. If you have managed the family finances, you know something about budgeting and keeping books. If you have bought and/or sold a home, you know something about real estate. Did you pitch in when working family members needed help with their jobs? Did you keep books for a family business, type letters or reports for a family member, do library research, take phone messages or more? What particular tasks are you skilled at? Party planning? Tutoring? Remember, anyone who has raised a child has experience in training novices.

What have you done as a volunteer? List not only the organizations — church, school, charity, community programs, political campaigns you served — but exactly what you did for each. For example, were you involved in fundraising? If so, what specifically did you do — write press releases, solicit by phone, collect pledged contributions? If the organization had to hire someone to do the tasks you did as a volunteer, what kind of worker would they have needed?

After listing your accomplishments and skills, put each into a business setting. Give your skills a title. For example, if you took competitive bids for repair jobs in your home you were a **purchasing agent**; if you had lobbied for the installation of a traffic light at a dangerous intersection, you were an **advocate**.

Now that you know what you can do, look in the newspaper and find what jobs are available in your community. Match your skills with each of the jobs listed. Even if you don't *want* to be a purchasing agent, it will do you good to realize what one of your skills is called in the world of paid employment.

When you've made these connections, you're ready to write a resume of your experience and credentials. Start with your education, degrees, diplomas, and certificates, as well as a summary of what you studied, and put down any job you had, no matter how brief or long ago. If your employment history looks skimpy, you'll simply have to be creative. Go back to your list of skills and accomplishments and see if you can define them in the functional terms that personnel people in business use when they define the qualifications they expect in a candidate for a particular job. You'll see some of these qualities listed in the want ads.

A frequent quality is skill in "communications." It sounds formidable, but it means nothing more than the ability to speak, write, read, and listen. Looking over what you've done, list any speech you made, articles you wrote, or correspondence you managed as experience in communications. "Administration" is another skill employers are after. It means nothing more than organizing and managing some activity. Under "administration" you could list offices you held in organizations and their duties, such as chairing meetings or organizing events.

If possible, get written documentation of your accomplishments outside the home. This documentation should have dates and times as well as a description of your activities. Ideally you would have written evaluation of your work, or at least the name, address, and phone number of someone who could give that evaluation.

Now that you have a resume, you are ready to approach an employer. Even people with job experience usually get jobs through friends or relatives, followed by ads in the paper, or employment agencies. Begin your hunt right at home. Make a list of everyone you know and let them know not only that you're looking for a job, but the particular kind of job that you want. If they don't know of anything themselves, ask them to pass the word to their own circle of friends and relations. And don't be bashful. People usually like to help this way. Word-of-mouth is not only the most frequent way jobs are actually found, but it is often the route to the best jobs.

Watch the help-wanted ads every day in the newspaper. Even if you don't find anything you want, they'll tell you what employers in your area are looking for and what they are paying. And don't forget to check the help-wanted notices on the bulletin boards of schools, churches, public offices, your town hall, even your supermarket.

An amazing number of people simply walk in to a company and apply. Often jobs with the state or city start by going to the personnel office and filling out an application. If you are entering a field with a chronic labor shortage such as hospital work, you might find that there is a job for you if you go in and apply.

After preparing your resume, finding the job, and filling out the application, the next step is often the most daunting — the interview (see page 280). Successful survivors of the interview offer some suggestions beforehand. Research the company or organization as thoroughly as you can. Think about what you have to offer the firm. Remember the skills you listed and try to relate them to the specific needs of the job you are applying for. Prepare the questions you have about the organization, not only for your own information, but to project your interest and concern to the interviewer. Anticipate the tricky questions and prepare answers. One difficult question is "Why is there such a gap in your work history?" Your answer should be truthful — that you stayed home to care for your family — but be sure to accentuate the experience that will help you on the job that you gained while you were at home.

Translate the skills of homemaking into the vocational language of paid employment. You have valuable assets. You've had to manage time and money, keep records, remain cool in crises, and understand other people. Don't be ashamed to talk openly to prospective employers about the patience, steadiness, and understanding of human nature you've learned at home, because these are often just the qualities they are looking for.

Another stumper is "What are your weaknesses?" The spin on your answer should be that a seeming weakness really turns out to be a virtue. This is not the time to bare your soul with searching self-analysis such as "I take things very personally and get overwrought emotionally too easily," even if it's true. It's better to say "I am too much a perfectionist. I stick to a task until it is performed just right. I have little tolerance for hasty, slipshod work." What boss wouldn't love such a "weakness"!

You may want to work up a number of answers to expected questions. One basic interview question is "Tell me about yourself." Now is the time to tell all the things that you have accomplished that show workplace skills. Would your experience running the fundraising campaign for the local zoo help prepare you for this job? Tell your interviewer about it.

Talking about money is sticky for some people, but it is bound to come up in a serious job interview, with a question such as "What do you think your skills would be worth to this organization?" Since you have done your research on this job, you should know the range of pay. You could name a salary somewhere in the middle; you could put the salary question back in the interviewer's court, saying "I am willing to consider whatever you think my services would be worth to your organization"; or you could postpone salary considerations: "I would like to know more about the position before discussing salary." You may be in a stronger salary-negotiating position after the job offer has been made.

One of the best ways to prepare for the interview is to rehearse it, with a friend playing the part of the interviewer. Ask your friend to be a real Scrooge of an interviewer, even throwing you some sexist and ageist questions so that you can practice dealing with them tactfully yet firmly. For example, "At your age are you going to have the stamina to keep this job?" You might say, "My health is excellent." Period. Or "Why did you get divorced?" Your answer: "My private life has nothing to do with this position." After considering hot potatoes like that, the real interview should be a breeze.

Finally, get your hair done and wear up-to-date clothes. You don't need to be high-fashion or trendy; rather, project a modern businesslike image. Do not try to hide your age (see page 283, "Avoiding Age Discrimination"). It won't work and it isn't necessary. Remember the interviewer has a problem — a job that is going undone. You are the solution to that problem. Look your prospective boss straight in the eye. And don't smoke or chew gum, no matter how nervous you feel.

If you're worried about competition from younger applicants, emphasize the strengths that go with your age. You have the patience to get the job done right. You're reliable. You are settled and unlikely to move. Your children are older and you do not need to worry about child care. Your employment history has yet to be written and, like the entry-level workers, you are offering potential. But your experience in all the various things you have accomplished shows that you are capable of learning new skills.

Your prospective boss cannot properly ask personal questions about your family arrangements, but that does not mean that you can't offer information on your own if you feel it would help you. You can say, for instance, "Now that the children are grown and have families of their own, I am free from everyday family responsibilities, but do intend to stay in this town permanently to be near them."

Don't forget to follow up the interview with a brief thank-you letter. Apart from demonstrating your skill at business etiquette, you give the employer a reminder of the interview as well as another demonstration of those highly priced communication skills.

Even if you don't want to work but have to in order to survive, you may find that there are other rewards besides money to your new life as a career woman. You may enjoy playing a grown-up role in a world wider than your own home. One woman looks back on her life before she started to work outside the home; "I was a shadow in the real world. . . . It [work] gives me an identity other than my family." Some women need to be needed. A nurse's aide says she enjoys "making someone's life a little better."

Homemakers returning to the labor force or entering it "without skills" can do very well indeed, thank you. The demographics favor you. There are fewer young people for entry-level jobs, so employers have to consider you. And a job can work wonders for your morale. There is something truly wonderful about being paid after working for years without money.

☑ YOUR OWN BUSINESS

Small business is the backbone of America. The high profile of companies making nationally advertised products blinds us to the fact that most people work in stores, shops, restaurants, motels, farms, law firms, doctor's offices, and service enterprises that are run by their owners, with fewer than fifty employees. And though most people work for salaries or wages, a great many dream of getting out from under the boss and starting a business of their own.

Those started by older newcomers, often with salaried experience in the field, are usually small. Some are one-person enterprises providing services that resemble self-employment in a trade such as plumbing or a profession such as law or medicine. Some are run from home (see box "Work from Home" later in this section).

No matter how small the business, no matter what else the owner does (and some do empty the trash baskets), she is the general manager who sets the goals of the enterprise and mobilizes human and capital resources to meet them. And as anyone who has tried to do it can attest, defining these goals and translating them into policies is the hardest part of any business.

There have been many attempts to define the qualifications of a general manager. Intelligence is required, of course, but successful managers are seldom intellectuals and brilliant students don't always wind up running a business. Understanding people and communicating with them is required. Street smarts are a help. A drive to succeed is essential. But none of these qualities, nor all of them together, reliably identifies a successful manager before she's had a go at it. Why some qualified candidates succeed and others fail is either a mystery or a matter of luck and timing.

And the same can be said of compensation. If you get into the right business at the right time you can wind up a multimillionaire. More often, and just as unaccountably, you lose your shirt, or bump along making a reasonably good living for a great deal of effort.

SECOND CAREERS FOR EXPERIENCED SMALL BUSINESS OWNERS

Small business owners tend to retire when they can sell their business for an attractive price. If they can't find a buyer they may have to keep running a business that bores or tires them or lose the money they have invested in it. If you're trying to sell, there's a world of advice and a little industry of appraisers and business brokers specializing in small newspapers, radio stations, stores, and insurance agencies, among other fields with many individual owners (see page 232).

Owners who sell usually come away with a little wad of cash they may invest in another business. Those who want to be active have no trouble finding work in public service, real estate, executive search, volunteer work, or a nonmanagement job in their own industy. When he sold out, the president of a company manufacturing floor machines became a salesman for another maintenance equipment factory.

But running the show is a habit hard to break. Before he was 35, William Brooks made several million dollars inventing and promoting new kinds of bread products. At 100 he was putting in sixty to seventy hours a week as manager of a chain of stores he had founded and complaining that he couldn't find the time for "all that I want to do."

William Markle sold the family aluminum recycling business and bought a retirement home in Vermont to pursue "other agendas," but an executive at Dow Chemical persuaded him to start a joint venture in recycling. At 70, he runs the new company and the processes it has pioneered from Vermont. He's planning to turn more of the management over to colleagues, but he hopes always to keep his hand in a business for which his grandfather started preparing him when he was 5 years old.

If you're a born enterpriser, one business leads to another. A retired plumbing contractor who had made some solar energy installations in the seventies joined with some engineers to form a privately funded solar energy association and wound up setting up a solar desalinization plant in Saudi Arabia.

A common and comfortable but usually temporary second career is staying on to help the people who bought your business. A widow who sold her husband's insurance and real-estate business stayed on as the secretary to the new owner. Staying on is such a good deal for both sides that a contract for consulting services often accompanies the sale of a company or a manager's retirement, but after a few years the weaning process is usually complete.

Consulting for other companies is harder. To attract clients, a consultant has to identify exactly what he knows better than anybody else and then find people willing to pay for it who know that he knows it. Clark McDonald was in such a spot when he retired as president of the Hardwood Plywood Manufacturers Association. His high visibility brought him opportunities for jaunts to Asian manufacturers at $250 a day and expenses.

Of course, if you're known in your industry for a unique

achievement clients may recruit you. Arthur Lewis had pioneered manufacturing in the West Indies. When a politically motivated strike shut down his plastic garment plant in Antigua, others trying to fulfill offshore contracts came to him for advice and he was soon managing the Barbardos operation of an electronics manufacturer.

You may be tempted to help a floundering business that needs what seems to you like very simple general advice, but those who have tried to enter the general consulting business late in life are glad that they don't have to make a living out of it. In general consulting you are up against formidable competition.

Clients who can afford to pay for advice on a management function such as finance, marketing, planning, or product development retain one of the big management consulting or accounting firms who maintain staffs of specialists in every conceivable business problem. You're better off joining them than trying to beat them. You don't have much to lose by offering your services on an occasional basis to a local management consulting or accounting firm, or doing it on a volunteer basis with the Service Corps of Older Retired Executives (SCORE) (see page 39).

NICHES FOR NEWCOMERS TO BUSINESS OWNERSHIP

Salaried chief executives usually work their way up from sales, production, or finance in their own or a similar organization. The production manager of a dress manufacturer takes what he has learned about the bottom line to the presidency of another firm whose owners give him more leeway. Occasionally a military officer is hired to run an enterprise that isn't directly related to the military. But if you are really a newcomer, you are going to have to buy or start a business in order to get the job of managing it.

It's easier to make that dream come true if you retire early in good health with a good pension from civil service, the military, or the police. A retired highway patrol chief in Nevada made more money in the construction business than he ever made on the force (see Housing and Construction). A police captain in Wisconsin runs a campground, and a retired New York City corrections officer owns a bed-and-breakfast place in Massachusetts for which he and his wife do all the work (see page 208).

Some are forced into it. Delores Lintel was out of a job when Metromail sold the direct mail advertising division where she had been an executive secretary. So she went back to her kitchen and applied what she had learned about organizing a job to what she had learned from her grandmother and started making and selling "Grama's Jellies" by mail and at local craft fairs. She's long since outgrown her kitchen and has a going business to sell to her children.

James Murphy was a business trainer of gas station owners for oil companies and never realized how much he hated it until he was forced to retire at 51 to make room for young blood. So he took his own advice and $23,000 of his severance pay and started an ice-cream store that he decorated in green for Murphy. Why ice cream? Because the five Murphy kids had so much fun making ice cream at home that he figured others would like to eat it while watching it made, too. Ten years later, he's taking home a little more than his old salary for seven months work and enjoying every minute of it. His advice to small businessmen now? Be sure you know why you are going into business — and it's not money. "Money is the result," he says, "not the purpose."

Many try, but most fail for lack of capital and management. So before making plans, study the "Checklist for Going into Business" compiled by the Small Business Administration. If you have the temperament and the capital, you don't have to worry about your age or sex.

What to go into? There's a wealth of minibusinesses you can start at home with your own labor and a few thousand dollars of savings. Here are a few general places to look:

1. You may have a new idea that grows out of your first career. A biology teacher patented a simple, hand-held microscope with which his students could explore living things in the field and sold it to school systems after he retired. A retired service representative for Scandinavian Airlines has set up a reservation system for bed-and-breakfast accommodations in Alaska.

2. You may have a product or service you can make or sell economically from your home. There are opportunities in almost all of our occupational clusters: lawn care; repairing clocks and lamps; locksmithing; transporting kids to school; picking up and delivering laundry, dry cleaning, or small parcels; preparing income tax returns; keeping the books of small neighborhood stores; and, if not personally typing, cleaning houses, trimming trees, or caring for children or invalids, finding those who will perform those services for people in desperate need of them. If your state allows

it, you may even be interested in answering a help-wanted ad in a local newspaper for industrial homework, like knitting ski caps or embroidering pillowcases.

3. You may have a skill or a hobby you can make into a business: making and selling dolls or dollhouses; serving as a hunting or fishing guide; repairing old clocks; cabinetmaking; or handicrafts. An air force captain who has been stuffing animals all his life has a thriving business in taxidermy. When she was 88, a Pennsylvania Dutch lady living in a retirement community was buying scraps from a coat factory and braiding them into rugs that she was able to sell at a handsome profit.

4. Finally, you may make a business out of the space in your house: bed-and-breakfast, catering, ranching, massage, growing rare flowers, an after-school program for kids, or weather watching (see box "Work from Home").

What do you need to get started? Now's the time for sharp pencils. Do market research by interviewing prospective customers and suppliers. Write out a business plan describing your product, your customers, your prices and costs, the records you'll have to keep, and the money you'll need. Ask your accountant whether in your particular case the business could cut your taxes.

Get all the free help that's available at the library and through the Small Business Administration, which keeps a list not only of government but of volunteer advisers such as SCORE. Get some of these advisers to look at your business plan and suggest where you might get funding.

Franchising is a quicker, less risky, but more expensive way to get started. A franchiser sells you a license to do business under its trade name and charges you a percentage of sales for advice and help with everything from choosing a site to training the staff and buying supplies and equipment. Some will even lend you money.

Burton Finger spent $30,000 starting up a Mailbox store in Amherst, Massachusetts — $17,500 for the franchise fee, the rest for mailboxes, copiers, and other equipment. It's a convenience business, so he and his wife put in long hours, but they like it better than the traveling he used to do when he was selling auto parts. He advises checking out the competition and visiting franchisees in other areas before signing up.

WORK FROM HOME

accounting, bookkeeping
appraisal
art
breeding kennel
bed and breakfast
bookbinding
calligraphy
consulting, any occupation
caregiving, child or adult
desktop publishing
field interviewing
gardening, plant breeding
genealogy
handicrafts
interior decoration

photography
piano teaching, tuning
private investigation
repairing, locksmithing
sales
sewing
tax preparing
telephone answering
therapy or counseling
transcription, medical or
    legal
translation, interpretation
weather observing
writing, lobbying, or
    public relations
yard maintenance

There's a franchising opportunity for every taste and pocketbook. For a total outlay of $8,400 a Chem-Dry franchise will put you into carpet cleaning from your home, but you have to have a minimum of $600,000 in cash to start a motel that can carry the Red Carpet name. Fast foods, launderettes, car rentals, real estate brokerages, computer centers, eyecare, cleaning, lawn care, fitness, auto painting, temporary help services, convenience stores, travel agencies, and the ubiquitous H & R Block tax services are only a few of the possibilities.

There's a downside to franchising. As with any small business, you're going to have to put sixty or seventy hours a week of your own sweat capital into it. Remember that the initial franchise fee is only a small part of the capital you'll need, and you can't hold the franchise company to the estimates that they give you of what else you'll need. Check on the company with its suppliers, its banks, and other franchisees, and never sign anything without consulting your own lawyer and accountant.

Small business is so attractive to older people that it supports a thriving industry of enterprises purporting to help you get started. In addition to schemes for selling virtually everything in sight, there are firms that undertake to supply you with everything you need to go into the mail-order business with your telephone, teach you some lucrative skill in a jiffy, or promise you big pay for knitting bootees, assembling costume jewelry, or stuffing envelopes at home.

Many "be your own boss" advertisers are con artists who manage to stay just within the law. The suspicious words are "easy," "no experience necessary," "big profits," "top pay," and dollar estimates of earnings too good to be true. A woman who had assembled computer boards in a factory sent $29.95 for a kit that was advertised as enabling anyone to assemble PC boards at home, only to discover, when it came, that she didn't know enough about electronics to figure it out.

A librarian who sent $30 in response to an ad that offered a way to "Read Books for Pay" discovered that she was being solicited to *buy* a book listing names and addresses — available at any public library — of publishers to whom to apply for work as a reader of unsolicited manuscripts. And to gild the lily, these con artists also told you how to make money conning other would-be readers by placing a similar ad ("900 TELEPHONE LINES! NEW! EASY! GUARANTEED! Learn how you can make a fortune!"), which enlists the phone company in collecting so that the suckers don't realize what's hit them until the phone bill comes.

If you've been bilked out of money you've sent through the mail, you can get prompt attention from the postal inspectors. Just ask at your post office. In 1990 the office of the regional chief inspector of the U.S. Postal Service was answering inquiries about "multilevel marketing" programs that were really chain letter schemes — in violation of postal lottery and fraud laws — rather than opportunities to make money selling products.

Of course, there are less risky ways to be your own boss. The simplest is to get off the payroll and negotiate to do your old work by the job or the hour. Freelancing this way can be a good deal on both sides: you get rid of the alarm clock; your erstwhile boss gets out of paying fringe benefits and carrying you on the payroll over slack times.

If you know things other people need to know, you may be able to go into business for yourself as a consultant. According to the dictionary, a "consultant" gives expert or professional advice. In plain words, he doesn't make or do anything immediately useful, he just talks. One half-facetious consultant described his work advising individuals on the management of their money as the "opposite of the Peter Principle: instead of working up to beyond the level of your competence, I'm working below the level of mine."

Many older people find easy work that answers this description. An architect reviews the house plan drawn by a builder who needs his signature to get a building permit. A contractor is retained as an expert witness when customary practices in his field are disputed in a lawsuit. A former military officer advises a defense contractor on what the air force needs. A SCORE counselor advises a small business owner how to apply for a loan. A medical researcher advises a hospital on its methods of controlling infections.

But the term is being stretched to fit all the many new kinds of knowledge work, from advice on starting up a small business to what the stars say about the date for your wedding. Some consultants are really small business people serving a regular clientele. Others are occasional workers called in for a specific purpose. And the fees can range from hundreds of dollars an hour — one Manhattan lady charges $100 an hour to help career women clean out their closets — to zero for SCORE volunteers.

☑ HUMAN RESOURCES

Big challenges are ahead in the art of matching work and worker. How fast and how well can private industry make use of the superb training of the hundreds of thousands of military people who won't be needed in uniform? How well can we mobilize the skills we already have to a labor market that never stands still and reaches across national boundaries?

Especially in technical fields, locating the right skill is critically important. The change of name from "personnel" to "human resources" signals a rise in the status of the work. The matching can be seen from the point of view of the employer or the job seeker.

There's a lot that any employer has to do. Fair and consistent policies have to be made and enforced on the hiring, promotion, training, and firing of thousands of different workers with different skills in different parts of the country or the world. When there are jobs to fill, candidates have to be attracted, evaluated, and the best-qualified induced to join the organization. A small business may have a single person wearing all these hats as the need arises.

In a big company, problems have to be anticipated. Pay scales have to be set so that they are perceived as fair, or they have to be negotiated with unions. Disputes may have to be settled by calling in outside mediators or conciliators. Benefits programs such as health insurance, pension plans, and stock options have to be administered and explained to those eligible for them.

The bigger the employer, the more specialized the work of looking after its human resources. The education and training of employees can involve a system of company classrooms rivaling a college, but specialists of many kinds are needed to provide for their health, safety, and welfare. Some big companies have departments for first aid and medical care, food services, recreational activities, family and retirement counseling, and employee publications.

There's much less opportunity for human resources specialists who work exclusively on behalf of job seekers. Private employment agencies fill very few of the job openings, but some of them are paid by both the employer and the employee, and a growing proportion of placement work is handled by labor contractors, such as temporary help services, that work for both sides.

A few private career counselors and aptitude testers are paid by job seekers themselves, but most of this help is provided at no cost to the individual through educational institutions, public employment services, nonprofit social service agencies of various kinds, and out-placement services maintained by employers to help laid-off employees search for another job.

There are no hard-and-fast qualifications for most of these jobs. Big organizations may hire beginners who have a college degree in personnel and labor relations, but most senior officers are simply lev-elheaded individuals who have demonstrated the ability to work with diverse individuals toward organization goals.

According to the U.S. Department of Labor, median weekly pay in 1990 for full-time personnel managers and trainers was $881 for men and $604 for women, but the median conceals variations from modest hourly rates in small organizations to more than $50,000 a year for top managers in major corporations or the specialists they retain as consultants. A **director of labor relations** who negotiates important union contracts may earn $100,000.

SECOND CAREERS FOR EXPERIENCED HUMAN RESOURCES PROFESSIONALS

Human relations managers can usually make more money by going into business for themselves as an **executive searcher**. One way to get started is to look for a specialty that supplies a need you've dis-covered in the course of the work you've been doing all along. Robert Martin became interested in the special problem of recruiting board members, so he made a deal with the search firm for which he worked to handle all such requests and give them any other business that came his way. Within five years he was earning $80,000 a year and hob-nobbing with the world's most interesting people.

Another way to specialize is to search for hard-to-find professionals in a field you know. Honey Yates had experience in banking as well as in interviewing for an employment agency. She knew what banks needed, so she and a partner started Associated Bankers Search, Inc., in Los Angeles.

Outplacement counselor is a challenging second career when big companies are cutting back upper and middle managers. It's demand-ing, but the price is right. Win, lose, or draw, the former employer pays the outplacer 15 percent of the fired executive's last year's salary — less for junior people and more for senior executives, who have a harder time landing a comparable job. Clyde Meredith quit his job as human resources manager of Jostens, Inc., the school jewelry and yearbook company, to go into the business in 1981, when the out-placement field was new. He retains professionals in law, communications, adult learning, chemical dependency, social service, and advertising and marketing.

Another option is to go into business as an independent **career counselor** suported by fees from job seekers. The American Association for Counseling and Development can tell you about the opportunities and license requirements.

What if you don't want to go into a feast-or-famine business? You may have experience or knowledge of a particular organization that you can sell on a part-time, temporary, contract, or consulting basis. When health forced her to retire, the personnel director of a book publisher continued to hunt for the most appropriate editors, writers, and photographers for each publishing project as a consultant at home. The retired manager of a group of regional health and human services personnel programs earns $25 an hour classifying jobs for the Indian Health Service. Both work part time at home.

If you've worked for the government, you might become a consultant investigating violations of Equal Employment Opportunity laws in your old agency. The Office of Personnel Management in Washington usually investigates violations in federal agencies, but there's so much to do that they run courses for investigators. Not everyone can do it. You have to be analytical, put people at their ease, write clear decisions, and be willing to travel. Ask your former employer whether he or she would recommend you and let your local state Job Service know of your interest. If you've worked for a state or local government service, you may find out which of them use consultants by calling the state information number in your state capitol.

Most personnel people don't even try to stay in the field. Some find second careers in a related field, like the manager of benefits who went into insurance or the vice president of personnel who became a business speech consultant, but many of them find a helping role in teaching, real estate, insurance, travel, fundraising, or recreational therapy.

NICHES FOR NEWCOMERS TO HUMAN RESOURCES WORK

Human services attract people from many different occupations, and the work is so hospitable to newcomers that most of the older people doing it have come from first careers in some other field. A good example is the woman who quit a dead-end job in state government to become one of the newest employment specialties: nanny recruiter.

Executive recruiting and **outplacement** are open to anyone willing to take the risk. Miles Jordan became an outplacement counselor after he retained one — at his own expense — to help him locate a suitable second career in Dallas, where his wife had a job. He liked the process so much that he asked his outplacer to coach him while he networked his way into his present job with another outplacement firm. He now earns more than he made as an IBM salesman. An easy way to try your hand at it is to persuade an outplacement firm to let you help out when they're overloaded. The business is so erratic that they keep the permanent staff to a minimum.

The easiest niche for a newcomer is a human resource job in the industry of your first career. A former employer might be glad to have you interview applicants for jobs you yourself have done. If you're an active union member, you may find a second career as a full-time **union steward**, dealing with the grievances of the people you used to work with.

Some teachers just beef about their hard lot. Others count the months to retirement. Not Sammy Ruetenik; after twenty-four years in the Bloomfield Hills system, she got herself elected president of the union and embarked on a new career of advocacy, public speaking, political action, and negotiations that pays her more than she could ever have hoped to make in the classroom.

There may be an opportunity for you in the services a former employer may provide for retirees. Liz O'Donnell is the **retiree volunteers coordinator** for the First Bank of Saint Paul, Minnesota. She matches retirees of the bank who want to do volunteer work to tasks such as wrapping Christmas presents for the Salvation Army. The bank pays her $300 a month for what always turns out to be more than 30 hours a month, but she has a bank pension and loves what she's doing.

If your company doesn't have a retiree program, maybe you can get them to start one. When Don McClenahan was involuntarily retired from Waste Management, Inc., he persuaded the company that it needed the goodwill of its retirees to counter the unfavorable publicity the industry was getting. As **retiree counselor** he now helps individual retirees with finances, health, or any other problems of adjustment and runs preretirement seminars which bring them doctors, nutritionists, and experts in sports and finance to talk about the problems ahead. His contract pays him $2,500 a month for half time.

If you'd like to help younger people get ahead in the work you have always done, you may be able to create a job for yourself in the career planning service of your alma mater. Jack Shingleton, the father of college career planning, says that veteran managers are better counselors for younger people in their fields than Ph.D.s in counseling without any business experience. When he was building the model career planning and placement service at Michigan State he tapped alumni in every professional field to work part time advising younger alumni. If your college doesn't have a system like this, you might volunteer to start one.

Finally, if you are looking for the thrill of helping other people, your experience in business may be accepted in lieu of education and training in social work for the civil service position of job developer, or you may be able to do the same thing as a volunteer with a private social agency. And don't forget that volunteers are needed to recruit other volunteers. You can find out about opportunities through your area Office for the Aging.

Human service work is a satisfying way to help people, productivity, and the quality of life on the job.

☑ PURCHASING

Purchasing is a management function that is increasingly delegated to specialists who keep abreast of the market for the changing mix of goods and services a major organization has to buy. It's one of the best seats in the house for watching the drama of what's ahead for the economy as a whole as well as a particular industry.

It's a different ball game from the buying for resale that is done for stores and distributors (see Retailing, page 233). Schools, hospitals, the military, and government agencies use huge quantities of the products, from computers to pencils, that they need for their work, and they contract for them with vendors to detailed specifications tailored to their particular needs. These institutions also contract with providers of services such as scientific research, cleaning, security, or temporary office help.

It can be a fast game. Computers instantaneously record the changes in the volumes of data on vendors, specifications, prices, and delivery dates, among other factors purchasers have to consider. To keep up with the standards and clout of the biggest and most expert buyers, smaller institutions increasingly buy through services that represent a number of purchasers of a category of goods, such as medical equipment.

Purchasing requires not only a knowledge of markets and how they work, but experience in the needs of the industries served. There's no special training for this profession; it's learned on the job, and those who learn a great deal about a specialized market may earn high pay without a college education. They need to be able to work independently, remember details, and handle large sums of money responsibly.

The median weekly salary for purchasing managers was $738 in 1990. Purchasing agents earned $517.

SECOND CAREERS FOR EXPERIENCED PURCHASING PEOPLE

Good purchasing agents can make more money by moving from one employer to another, often by switching to a competitor who knows their work. Increasingly, they work for services specializing in the needs of a single industry, such as hospitals, though opportunities for advancement may be better in a good small company where the purchasing manager is part of the management team. The purchasing agent for a hospital furniture manufacturer is earning close to six figures.

Purchasing agents who have worked for the government or the military make good use of this experience when they retire. Some transitions are straightforward. A contract administrator for the air force found a job buying spare parts for a commuter airline. A purchasing agent for an army base went to work for the private firm that had the contract to test items like the ones he had bought.

A purchasing agent may switch to selling. One of the best ways to become a merchandiser in charge of both buying and selling an item like hardware is to learn about the merchandise by buying it. There are also opportunities to use what you know about the procurement system to work for one of the vendors whose rules and systems you know. A purchasing agent of hardware who had to quit his full-time traveling job because of his health was able to get a congenial part-time job tracking orders for a manufacturer's representative with whom he used to do business.

Selling often pays better than buying. A purchasing agent who spent seventeen years buying supplies and products for a manufacturer of modular homes is making more money and having more fun selling vinyl replacement windows.

NICHES FOR NEWCOMERS TO PURCHASING

Don't forget that there may be a purchasing job in a field you know from your first career. An engineer designing highways for the federal government in Alaska went to work letting road building contracts for the city of Juneau. A nurse headed central supply for a hospital.

Whatever the economy, there's always something to be bought. A displaced geologist got a job acquiring repair material for the water and sewer system of Houston. When he was fired, the divisional controller of a food processing firm bought parts for a local processor.

Buying can move you from manual work into the office. A construction worker who got a job doing maintenance for a bank wound up purchasing its supplies. When his company folded, a tool maker used his knowledge of machinery manufacture to become a purchasing analyst for a company assembling fifty-ton off-road trucks.

And remember that you can switch from sales to purchasing as well as the other way around. A branch manager for an office machine company landed a better job as purchasing manager for a multibillion-dollar financial service that bought for the hundreds of offices maintained by its independent agents.

☑ BUSINESS SERVICES

An organization has to do a lot of work just to keep its doors open. Big or small, it needs business services and housekeeping to keep the environment clean, safe, and in working order.

Outsiders have to be directed to the appropriate party, whether they address the organization by letter, phone, or in person, and their inquiries must be considered and answered. Information on markets, government policies, customers, and technological advances affecting the business has to be collected, analyzed, and distributed to those concerned. Insiders have to be kept in touch through regular channels. Someone has to allocate tasks and provide the information needed to do them.

To handle these external and internal communications, telephones, teletypes, radios, computer networks, photocopy machines, and facsimile transmission systems may have to be staffed, and spoken words reduced to writing. Records have to be kept not only of the flow of money resources but of production operations, sales, inventories, and the transfer of property from one location to another. Data may be recorded or manipulated on business machines and kept on computer databases, film, audio or video devices, or on paper in filing cabinets.

In addition to office services, every organization is responsible for its physical environment. The property of a school, hospital, business, or government agency has to be protected against theft, vandalism, illegal entry, and fire. The places where the work is done have to be cleaned, and trash removed. Buildings have to be lighted, heated, air-conditioned, kept in repair, and their grounds and parking lots maintained.

Most office jobs do not require college and many are open to people who have not worked before in offices or anywhere else. Familiarity with computers is desirable, but routine data-entry procedures are often learned on the job.

Employers look for people who are willing and able to learn new skills and specific systems, and they prefer candidates good at spelling, grammar, business arithmetic, and such widely needed office skills as typing and word processing. To be employed in the federal government, a stenographer must be able to take dictation at a minimum of eighty words a minute and type at least forty words a minute. Receptionists should have an outgoing personality, telephone operators a pleasant voice and good eye-hand coordination.

Environmental service jobs in maintenance and repair may require specific craft skills. Police or military experience is preferred for private detectives and investigators, and security guards need a clean police record, but there are no specific qualifications for janitors, grounds-keepers, and parking lot attendants.

Pay for office workers is generally higher in big organizations, in the North and West, in metropolitan areas, and for males. Utilities, transportation, and manufacturing usually pay better than finance, retailing, insurance, and real estate. Median full-time salaries in 1990 were $448 weekly for women office supervisors and $595 for the minority who were men; $446 for male computer equipment operators, $348 for women.

In occupations more than 85 percent female, medians were $327 for typists, $367 for payroll and timekeeping clerks, $343 for secretaries, $312 for billing clerks, $319 for telephone operators, $288 for information clerks, $304 for interviewers, and $273 for receptionists. Supposedly "male" skills involving machines and numbers were consistently rated higher than the supposedly "female" skills of personal communication, regardless of the actual gender of the worker.

In occupations less then 50 percent female, medians of both sexes were $494 for production coordinators; $346 for stock clerks; $323 for traffic, shipping, and receiving clerks; $300 for private mail clerks; and $315 for messengers.

Among environmental services, the median for private security officers was only $307, with many earning little more than the minimum wage. Supervisors of cleaning and janitorial services, most of them male, earned a median of $385 a week. The janitors and cleaners they supervised earned $294 if male, $248 if female.

SECOND CAREERS FOR EXPERIENCED BUSINESS OFFICE WORKERS

If you worked years ago in an office, you'll find that radical new information technologies have made the place over. The steno pool is gone, the files have been computerized, and there's an elaborate security system. There are fewer secretaries, but those who remain are now called administrative assistants, with new decision-making responsibilities, and everyone seems to be operating some kind of computer terminal.

Office systems are changing so fast and they differ so much from one place to another that typing is one of the few specific skills you can carry with you. If you've been a very good typist, by all means transfer your skill to the keyboard of a computer. You can learn how at a community college or even for free at an adult education class at your local high school or from a temporary help agency.

But don't underestimate your job experience, even if it was long ago. It's harder for employers to find people with good work habits than it is to teach them simple office systems and skills. Think of what you bring to the job: attention to accuracy and detail; setting priorities and managing time; dealing with the public; getting along with colleagues even when you don't like them. Before you go job-hunting, make a list of these personal assets so that you can talk about them to a prospective employer.

Rather than look for a job exactly like the one you have done before, look for one that fits your particular situation. Supposing, for instance, that you are an old hand who has stayed long enough in one place to work up to a decent salary, perhaps as a supervisor. You're due to retire on a pension, but you're going to need a lot more money and you're willing to work full time for it — at least until you qualify for Social Security or a second pension.

The best time to look for this second job is while you're still working in your first one. A stenographer working in the Wayne County recorder's office found a similar job in the more interesting setting of the Detroit Civic Center by watching the personnel-wanted lists for the city before she retired.

If you keep your eyes open you may find exactly what you want coming up in your own or a related office. A California secretary to an elementary school principal was promoted to the school's district office. When she discovered she needed college she got a bachelor's degree through the University of the Redlands Life Experience Program, and her own employer helped her to find a well-paying second career as the executive assistant and office manager for the city.

But there's a quick cap on how much money anyone can make in office services. Only supervisors and executive secretaries to highly placed managers can expect to make more than $50,000 a year. If you're bent on making this kind of money, consider starting an office service business of your own. When Jane Angel lost her hearing, she retired as executive assistant to the city manager of Costa Mesa, learned high-tech computers, and opened a word-processing center. She works full time, but counting her pension, she's making more money than ever before (see Your Own Business).

Supposing you're an old hand with a good job behind you and a pension but you aren't quite so ambitious. You want to go on working, but part time, and at work that has more than money to recommend it. You may not have to look further afield than your longest employer. There may be a more interesting job you can do better than an outsider. A specification clerk keeping track of engine parts for a diesel manufacturer moved to a job dispatching them.

Many large corporations have organized special programs to bring retirees back on a temporary or part-time basis. Personnel directors like them because they come fully trained, arrive on time, can spell, and literally know their way around the company. When Ruth Gilbert retired from twenty years as a school secretary she put her name on the substitute list to fill in for absent secretaries.

It doesn't hurt to let your longest employer know of your interest in doing self-contained odd jobs that don't fit into the schedule of any regular worker. Marion Hill enjoyed coming back to Weber State College to type a handbook because she knew how their computer worked and could choose her own hours.

But if you're sick and tired of the old place you'll find that a part-time job is a wonderful way to get a change of scenery. If you've been working in a bank, you may find a different atmosphere and a whole new set of friends doing work you know in another bank. If you've been a secretary, you may have the communications skill and ability to size up a situation that qualifies you to be a dispatcher of an organization's vehicles. One former secretary works for a motor club, dispatching road services to people stranded in disabled cars.

Or you can use a part-time job to try something radically different. A manager of order clerks in a big national firm enjoys the challenge of a job with the county getting information from inmates of the jail. A supervisor of telephone operators started helping a friend work a typesetting machine and found it so much fun that she won't take more than the minimum wage for it.

Old hands on pension like part-time work because it is less stressful ("don't take any work home") and more flexible ("can work at my own pace," "perform duties independently") than the jobs they had when they were cogs in a big machine. Some of them like feeling needed ("provide service to teachers"), or the variety and challenge of some of the work that goes to part-timers ("always learning something new," "invigorating because I work with young people").

But what's challenge to some can be culture shock to others. One part-time retiree misses associating with coworkers her own age. A former administrator may have to learn how to follow instead of lead or adjust to the folkways of a different industry ("furniture is not insurance!"). A retired administrator of personnel policies in an insurance company loves her job assisting the bookkeeper of a parking consultant, but she has had to learn the difference "between working for a large international company and an entrepreneur."

Part-time work usually comes without holidays, sick leave, health insurance, benefits, or permanence, drawbacks of less importance to retired old hands than interference with travel plans, uneven workloads, and the awkwardness of schedules that are flexible on both sides. Even if you already have your health insurance, you ought to ask about it when you take a part-time job. Employers need to be reminded that health benefits are critical to some displaced homemakers.

Part-time office work is relatively easy to get. Pass the word through your personal networks of friends, relatives, and former employers, watch the classified ads, visit your local job service center. But the royal road to a good part-time job is through one of the many temporary help services you will find listed under "Employment Contractors — Temporary Help" in your yellow pages, which supply workers of every kind to employers (see page 278).

Supposing you are in a third situation. You aren't an old hand at office work. Maybe you've worked a few years here and there whenever your family could spare you from home, but never long enough in one place to earn pension credits. What are your chances of getting a decent office job with benefits now?

Not very good. That yellowing old college diploma isn't worth much extra money in an office. If you are really serious about a second career, you'll do better going into sales or training for professional work. If you stick with office work, your best bet for good pay and benefits is in public service, where rules against age and sex discrimination are taken more seriously, but you may have to wait for an opening. Patricia Maxwell had been a secretary before her children came, so when she heard the school needed secretaries, she went down and applied and was told she would have to take a civil service examination. The examination for an entry-level clerk typist wasn't very hard — they waived the typing test that year — but the opening came years after she had forgotten she had taken it.

If what you need is money now, your best bet is to find a good temporary help service — one that will help you brush up on your typing and office skills and if necessary introduce you to computers.

If, on the other hand, you aren't in desperate need of cash and all you want is a pleasant part-time office job, look for it in a small business or nonprofit organization off the beaten track of office employment. Back before she had children, Mary Loyden worked for the Society for the Prevention of Cruelty to Animals. When they no longer needed her at home, she answered an ad for a part-time job keeping the records of a gun dealer. The hours are flexible, the work is interesting, and she likes the boss.

If you're not quite willing to volunteer, you may find a happy alternative in working at nominal wages for parks or museums that train citizens to help with their extra work. A woman who quit the Chicago social service office because of bad vibes is happy "volunteering" part time at the minimum wage in the boat department of the New Mexico Parks Department.

Friends, relatives, and ads, especially in local shopping papers, are the way to find these low-key, flexible jobs, but many of them are supplied by nonprofit senior employment services you can find by calling the area Office for the Aging listed in your phone book.

If you've been a supervisor of buildings and grounds for a big installation such as a college, or a skilled repair craftsman, you'll find similar work with another employer who can give you the schedule and pay you want, or less strenuous work managing rental property.

Nothing sounds more dead-end than staying with janitorial work or building cleaning. Actually these essential services are one of the most attractive opportunities for people with little education and capital beyond their own labor to build a substantial business. A good example is Doran Rose. In the early fifties he was a young demolition worker who moonlighted supervising janitorial work at night, then quit to go full time with the cleaning service. When Sara Lee bought it out, he built it into a $50 million division with forty-five branches in thirteen states. Now retired, he's a management consultant advising the thousands of small enterprisers who hope to follow in his footsteps.

Custodial work is a rough business. Easy to get into, easy to go belly up. Rose warns against "franchisers" who advertise in the business-opportunity section of the classified ads that they'll set you up in the business. Many of them simply supply you with accounts, do the billing, and leave you working for little more than your wages. Better go into the business yourself — but not before you get the schooling or help you'll need to set up a business plan and follow it (see page 182).

But supposing you've worked for a cleaning service and want no part of managing one. With luck and a little training you may find lighter, pleasanter work in a number of semiskilled occupations such as managing a small property, driving a school bus, working as a nurse's aide or crossing guard, or babysitting. If you've been cleaning for an institution, you may be the first to learn about one of these opportunities.

NICHES FOR NEWCOMERS TO BUSINESS SERVICES

Newcomers are welcome in business services. Most people doing office work have come from other fields, and older newcomers like it because it can be part time. You may be interested primarily in money, or primarily in the lifestyle aspects of the job.

If you have no special skills or you can't or don't want to go back to the physically strenuous or mentally stressful work you used to do, an office job can be a quick and undemanding way to support yourself for a few years. You may be a former homemaker who suddenly needs health insurance or income until you are old enough to qualify for Social Security or a private pension, or you may need a temporary infusion of cash for any number of reasons.

It can happen to anyone. Sonia Sandstrom majored in zoology in college but married and raised a family and was widowed in her 50s. Through a newspaper ad she landed a full-time job doing clerical work. She's bored. It's not biology. But she plans to stay with it until she is 62.

If you are disadvantaged in some way, you may get help in finding work with Operation Greenthumb, or one of the other job programs for seniors with limited incomes. Many of the jobs they have may be part-time, temporary work at the minimum wage with employers who can't afford advertising or temporary service fees. For information about senior job programs in your area contact your local Office for the Aging.

But an office job may also be the best way to get rewards that may be more important at this stage of your life than the paycheck. You may be ready to take it a little easier, but you don't want your mind to go to seed, you want to continue to be a productive member of society, you want some structure to your days.

Receptionist jobs appeal to outgoing women of every age who enjoy getting dressed to meet the public. Messenger jobs help people living alone get around to see lots of people. And you may have reasons of your own for getting out of the house on a regular basis. Take Margaret Dewar. Divorced for thirty-two years, she was relieved to retire from the decisions on welfare eligibility and community charges of welfare fraud that went with her full-time job for the state, but she wasn't ready to retire from the human race. Through an ad in the paper she found a part-time job as a church secretary. It pays much less per hour than she used to earn, but it gives her life structure. "It keeps my mind active and alert. I meet both young and older people."

Interviewing for a survey research firm is a wonderful way to get out and about with people. You are trained to ask designated people specific questions about a product or topic of interest to the client. Some of this work is done by phone, some of it visiting people in their homes or collaring them in a store or outside a movie theater. An assignment may last no longer than a week, but you can sign up with more than one survey firm. Watch your local newspaper for help-wanted ads that survey firms run when they have an assignment in the area. The pay isn't great, but it's fun and it's flexible.

Don't dismiss the possibility that there's a job for you in business housekeeping services. Newcomers are badly needed to repair, clean, and protect the environment of public places from the White House to your local parking lot. It can pay well, especially if you go into business as a specialist, repairing windows and doors or cleaning carpets, boats, or chimneys. A former drilling and blasting foreman has built himself a very nice little business cleaning the grease exhaust systems of restaurants. A Florida woman who went bankrupt in the business of cleaning the auto train continued to do it for the railroad on wages because she loves the trains and driving the cars on and off of them.

You might even do it primarily for love. A former air traffic controller earns an unskilled hourly pay rate as a maintenance man for a small airport. A professor who thinks he'll miss the campus when he retires is planning a second career repairing college buildings. The buildings of small churches are usually maintained by volunteers.

It's worth finding out who does maintenance for the environment of your first career. A platform man who used to unload trailers works part time for a trucking company, keeping up its terminal. A retired school cook earns $10 an hour cleaning the lunchroom tables and classrooms. A retired pilot of boats in San Francisco waters earns $13.50 an hour taking care of a small island in the harbor.

Security jobs rely on newcomers. They're needed by every office, store, mall, school, college, hospital, hotel, restaurant, airport, and parking lot. Most of the work is easy: the most taxing duty may be walking some distance every day to check doors, being outside in bad weather, and working alone through the night. The pay, of course, is correspondingly low.

Light work, low pay, no previous experience required — but there's a lot of security work to be done and it's easy to get. Watch the ads. Register with your local state employment service. If you walk into the personnel department of a place you'd like to work they may hire you on the spot. Big organizations may get their security people through a security service, so it pays to check in with one whose name you can get in your local phone book. Some jobs carry no benefits, so be sure to ask when you apply.

And don't think the job is beneath you. You'd never guess what your friendly nightwatchman used to do. Among security workers of 1988 were a former newspaper bureau chief, carpenter, dairy company president, air force communications specialist, cattle buyer, postal worker, auto parts salesman, and an 81-year-old who once headed his own milk products company.

Why do they like it? Some because it can be part time, an untaxing way to make only enough money to supplement other income and, when it goes with the job, health insurance benefits. Some for the exercise they get walking, some to be generally useful. Security guards are the first to spot trouble, so there's even a potential for excitement.

Business services are not always the most thrilling occupations, but it's work you can always get when you want it.

☑ HOSPITALITY

We don't stay put, but we expect to eat wherever we get hungry and sleep wherever we get tired. More of us spend more of our nights in hospitals, nursing homes, residential care facilities, ski lodges, bunk-houses, camps, trailers, boats, and even in bed-and-breakfast rooms we rent in other private homes.

Less food is being eaten at home or in traditional, sit-down restaurants and more at work, at sports events, in schools, hospitals, nutrition sites, senior citizen centers, camps, colleges, stores, national parks, and out of paper boxes handed to us while we sit in our cars. As a result, more food is prepared in factories and stores for consumption elsewhere.

But the basic tasks remain the same. In every food service someone has to plan, order, prepare, serve, and clean up. Safety, sanitation, and health department rules have to be enforced. Money has to be collected. Workers have to be hired, trained, scheduled, and paid.

In every kind of lodging, someone has to keep track of reservations, check guests in and out, assign rooms, give keys, make beds, clean rooms, collect rents, make repairs, hear complaints, and keep people and property safe.

Within the memory of people over 50, hospitality has been transformed. Less of it is grunt work: we tote our own food and bags instead of expecting waitresses and bellhops to do it for us. More of it is sophisticated administration, training, and labor-saving shortcuts. There are fewer independent operations owned by the people who do the work. More food and lodging is supplied by national chains, by contract with food services, or by small owners using the central resources of a lengthening list of outside services.

So is there less opportunity to own your own hospitality business? Not necessarily. The new specialization means more opportunity to identify and serve a specific need. And for imaginative older newcomers, that means more niches off the beaten track for a job or a business that suits you.

Food service people have to be healthy, neat, clean, and able to work with others as a team. Lodging managers and clerks have to be able to get along with all kinds of people, watch details, and keep their cool under stress.

Median weekly earnings of full-time, salaried food service supervisors in 1990 were $285. Bartenders earned $248. Waiters and waitresses earned $208, cooks $226, bakers $304, kitchen workers $215, and hotel clerks $234.

SECOND CAREERS FOR EXPERIENCED HOSPITALITY WORKERS

If you've managed a hotel for a big chain or worked in the food service of a school, hospital, office, or factory, you can expect to retire on a pension. Retired cooks who want to work are always in demand. One who retired from a hospital was cooking suppers for her church at the age of 80 in addition to volunteering for Meals on Wheels.

But what happens if you've been tied down running a little inn or a bar and grill where you and your family do all the work and manage to make little more than a modest living? There are fewer of these owner-operated businesses now, so if you can't sell your location to a chain your only way out may be to sell into a buyer's market and find another way to earn a living.

You can always drop back to cooking in somebody else's kitchen if that makes sense in your life. One owner wanted to keep busy after the divorce that forced him to sell his bar and grill ("my wife thought I was having too much fun"), so he cooked part time, at $8 an hour, for the owner of another small cafe. He likes everything about it in spite of the fact that his new boss "doesn't know his ass from a horse." But if you're a former owner in your 60s, working in somebody else's kitchen is low-paying, hard on the feet, and may force you to learn your way around the bureaucracy of a large corporation.

The ideal second career is a regular job with benefits that uses what you've learned. You may find it in a bigger company that you know because you've done business with them. After her husband died, Nada Elliott took a job as bookkeeper for the produce company that supplied the bar and grill they had run. She hoped to rise in the firm because she understands firsthand the small restaurants to which they sell.

If you've run a successful restaurant, you may do well selling to the restaurant trade. When Harry Heiz lost the lease on his restaurant in Arizona he went to work selling for Con Agra, a big full-service food company that offers restaurants everything they need down to paper goods. He earns more than he netted from his last restaurant and enjoys giving his customers the benefit of his decades of experience. It's commission selling, so it's flexible and relatively easy to get.

There has always been a lot of moving around in the hospitality field. People change jobs, and jobs themselves are always being created and discontinued. The manager of a restaurant that went out of business got an unskilled food service job in a hospital. The head of a hospital dietary service quit to go into the catering business, where she can be her own boss.

Catering special events or private parties is an attractive second career for quantity cooks who want to get out of the long hours and physical demands of an institutional kitchen, and demand for these services has been growing. A YMCA camp cook who has built a catering business in Carsonville, Michigan, loves working with different recipes and people, but hates hauling and loading food and equipment.

But there's more to catering than cooking. Martha Rowlands had been preparing meals, planning diets, ordering supplies, and scheduling staffs as the head of the dietary service in a convalescent hospital. When she quit to go into the catering business for herself, she had to learn how to get business, keep records, and analyze costs. She earns about a thousand dollars a month working part time, and gets help in setting her fees from a volunteer adviser at the local Service Corps of Older Retired Executives (SCORE) office. Her advice: before taking the plunge, take some courses in food service at the local community college and then do a little work cooking or serving for a local caterer.

The growth of the luxury market has created opportunities for caterers and highly trained graduates of the new culinary institutes, but the skills of ordinary cooks and bakers in everyday restaurants and food services are being replaced by fast-food techniques that can be taught as quickly as assembly jobs in a factory. Cooks who stay in fast foods may go up, like the bread company baker who went into researching new products and quality control. Or down, like the retired navy cook who likes doughnuts so much that he enjoys turning them out on a fast-food machine at low pay.

But most hospitality workers don't stay in the field. They find a second career doing something else. Gregarious both by temperament and training, hospitality workers gravitate to serving people in stores, health care, real estate, customer service, property management, or recreation. When waitresses quit, they seek out work that involves them one-on-one with people as receptionists, telemarketers, beauty consultants, Avon ladies, store clerks, or community aides helping older people continue to live in their homes.

The switch to a profitable new career is easiest if you can use your first career as a stepping stone. The catering manager of a restaurant who moved to a similar job in Las Vegas wound up as a "marketing executive" who earns $130,000 a year, bringing in new customers for a casino hotel by promoting low-cost chartered flights.

NICHES FOR NEWCOMERS TO HOSPITALITY WORK

Mainstream jobs in the new, large-scale food and lodging chains are subject to rigorous training, restrictive rules, long hours, bureaucracy, and stress — just what people over 50 want to avoid. But in this big, diverse industry there are jobs that older newcomers love to do. One of them, oddly enough, is working at McDonald's, the fast-food chain. This chain has set up an elaborate nationwide program to recruit older people, give them special training, and put them in jobs that take advantage of their interpersonal skills. But McDonald's is an exception. Most of the niches for older people are off the beaten track.

Love entertaining and cooking? You won't get rich, but you can have a lot of fun providing a personal or homelike service on a scale too small to interest one of the big outfits. If you're a newcomer thinking of starting an eatery of your own you'd be out of your mind to compete with a fast-food store or ordinary restaurant. Just to get started, you'd need several hundred thousand dollars and enough money to live on for a year, and the odds on being still in business at the end of that year are heavily against you.

But you have a fighting chance if you go into business with someone who does have experience, or buy the experience from a franchiser, if you avoid competition by picking your location and a narrow specialty, and if you like the idea so much that you are willing to work long hours and don't expect to make a lot of money. A few newcomers have everything — including the luck — it takes to succeed. A college professor and a food public relations executive who wanted to get out of New York City started and sold two restaurants at a profit and are now on their third. If you are a tourist interested in the ghost towns of Arizona, you'll find these two women at Maud's Downstairs Cafe, the best of the three restaurants in Jerome, Arizona, population 450. (Maud is their cat.) Theirs is the only restaurant they know where all the bread, pies, soups — even the mayonnaise — are made from scratch on the premises, the handiwork of the food PR executive, who used to run a test kitchen.

Between them they started with money, savvy, and experience.

They used the capital from the sale of one partner's suburban house and the income from the professor's sabbatical salary to see themselves through the first year. They had experience in quantity cooking and promotion. They had researched the site on a series of trips. They had the distinctive specialty of offering nothing that was not homemade, and they carefully chose a tourist location that attracted just the kind of customer who would appreciate that specialty. They like what they do so much they are willing to work long hours for a net of about $10,000 a year apiece. Finally, they are small enough so that they can afford to combat the inevitable burnout of long hours by simply closing the place for a couple of weeks and going away on a cruise.

Another way to get started is to find a specialty too narrow for a big operation. A refugee from the oil fields who sells nothing but yogurt dishes got his financing from the bank and his experience from a franchiser. He and his wife learned how to make the shakes and yogurt products in five days of training. Each of them ran a store in Longview, a market town in Texas, and did so well that four years later another franchisee bought them out at a profit. Their advice: pick a good franchisor and talk to their franchisees before you lay out your money.

Unless you've done it before, resist the temptation to go into the catering of private parties unless you have had experience in business and quantity cooking. An office manager who had planned company parties continued after her retirement to plan private events for the executives who knew her. She did the menus, budgeting, decorations, and invitations, learning calligraphy at the local high school to write them prettily, but she was smart enough to hire a caterer for the actual cooking and serving. Lugging around food and pots is heavy work.

Small, local, special, or occasional food services are the places to look if you really want to get into this work in your later years. Older newcomers are providing food in depots, posts of the Veterans of Foreign Wars, or concession stands at sports events. If you really want to cook, consider doing it on a volunteer basis for a senior citizen center, a meal site, or a hospitality shop set up to raise funds by serving hospital visitors.

People who like to bake should think small and specialized, too. You could, for instance, sell the homemade cookies you like to bake to people and organizations who know you, or even donate your work to the local bake sale of your choice. But you should think twice before trying to compete with a big commercial bakery. If you have the talent, you'll have a happier life and make more money becoming a professional cake decorator. Cheri Dickson had to sell a small bakery she had bought because it didn't return enough profit to cover the benefits her five employees expected, but by 1990 she was earning $10 an hour custom-decorating birthday and wedding cakes for a big industrial company with five cafeterias. She advises taking a basic course in cake decorating at a local community college or bakery supply house to see whether you have the talent. If you do well, you should have no trouble getting work because big grocery chains are always short of cake decorators.

What about the lodging business? How about running a sweet little inn in a place you'd like to be yourself? Just a few bedrooms in an old house you can buy in an out-of-the-way place for a song and run with a minimum of service; just bed-and-breakfast you can manage with a little local help or maybe none at all. It's a seductive dream for anyone tired of life in a big city or a big bureaucracy, and every year thousands of newcomers pursue it. A bed-and-breakfast business fits many late lifestyles. It's a social adventure for motherly widows who like having people around. It has a big-family, old-time flavor for career women who have never been able to spend enough time at home and for couples who like the idea of working together.

What you do about the dream depends on what you expect to put into it and what you expect to get out of it. If you have a little chunk of capital — say a retirement benefit, the proceeds from the sale of a suburban house, or an inheritance — you could buy an existing inn and run it as a business that would return interest on your investment and wages for your labor.

If you are willing to invest money, time, and energy it can be a very good business. The Nelsons are a retired couple who do well at it. They bought an existing business in a part of North Carolina that isn't heavily traveled, but they have their prices and expenses set to earn a reasonable living and return on their investment at 50 percent occupancy of their seven units.

You can promote a bed-and-breakfast by registering with reservation services that take a commission on the business they send you. A slower but cheaper way is to pay a small fee for a listing in one of the regional bed-and-breakfast guidebooks. The Nelsons began by advertising in many different places. When they discovered that their guests were mainly people from nearby cities, they concentrated on ads in Chapel Hill and Raleigh papers. They find it pays to offer a "sailing package" to tie in with a local attraction. Their advice: Don't go into the business unless your health is good, you really like people (they'll know if you're pretending), and you have a little income from another source, such as a pension.

"Mo" Faulkner couldn't afford to be that prudent. At 60, he had gone broke in the import business and was "overqualified" — i.e., too old — to go back to the marketing executive jobs he had quit. All he knew about the lodging business was what he didn't like about the hotels and motels he had been spending a lot of his life in, but it looked like a business that he and his wife could run. After looking through several states, they found a run-down motel in Prescott, Arizona, that they could buy with the $30,000 they had realized from the sale of their California home and borrowed $10,000 from a business associate to get it going.

Sue Faulkner made curtains, cooked breakfasts, cleaned rooms. Mo discovered he could do a lot of the physical work the place needed. And, to their surprise, they loved it. Mo applied his marketing talents to advertising and networking to get the place known and to developing sales points, such as delivery of breakfast direct to each cottage. Less than four years later the business was appraised at $500,000, and the Faulkners were borrowing on it to build another place. His advice: If you don't like the servant role, stay away from innkeeping.

But you don't have to work as hard at it as the Nelsons and Faulkners. Many older newcomers get into the business to earn a little money out of the extra space in a house they already own or want to buy. In South Dakota, for instance, a retired teacher fell in love with a nineteenth-century house in her hometown and decided to make it income-producing in order to get a tax deduction for the expense of restoring it. She gets $4,000 a year out of it and the satisfaction of using "a creative talent I never knew I had." Many seniors turn down paying guests when they want to go away or use the house for a family gathering.

The Ellings weren't intending to be innkeepers when they moved to Great Barrington, Massachusetts, after Ray retired from his job as a correction officer, but when the family grew smaller, Mrs. Elling inquired at the chamber of commerce about letting her rooms and began to get referrals from them. They wrote to all their friends in the city and were listed in some New England bed-and-breakfast guides, but never spent the money to advertise or employ a reservation service because they have as many guests in their six units as they can handle themselves without any hired help. Financially, they're better off than they have ever been.

Not everyone wants the responsibility of owning a business. There are regular jobs in the hospitality business for older newcomers who like to provide some of the intangible comforts of home. If you're a homemaker presently without a home, and like working with young people, you may enjoy the role of "house mother" for students in a sorority or college dormitory. You may be paid less than $1,000 in cash per month during the school year for being on tap long hours, but it's not hard work and you get your own apartment. Talk to people you know on college campuses and watch the ads for openings.

You might like to be the dining room host or hostess who greets and seats guests, sees that they're properly served, and runs the cash register. In an expensive restaurant, it's a nice job for a woman who takes pride in her appearance, but a lobby hostess or dining room hostess may be hired to greet and direct guests in fast-food places that don't offer full table service. One that invites children's birthday parties has a 74-year-old lobby hostess who comes in six or eight hours a week to supervise them. It's a job you could create for yourself by suggesting it to a restaurant with a family clientele.

You might like to be the friendly bartender who dishes out sympathy with every drink. There are bartenders' schools that are accredited by the National Association of Trade and Technical Schools, but many newcomers get their jobs through friends or an ad in the paper and learn how to do it after they're hired. You can work in a lodge or country club, but the most fun seems to be in occasional work as banquet bartender for special events in a hotel.

Some retired people like to watch the world go by from a part-time job at the front desk of a motel or hotel. You can get these low-paid jobs through ads and employment agencies, but if you want to help finance a stay in a resort area you might write ahead of the season to lodgings in the area, asking if they need a part-time relief manager or desk clerk. They are looking for stable, personable people with clerical experience who can deal with the public, so you might enclose a snapshot.

If you have experience in accounting or inventory control, you might supplement your retirement income working in a hotel as the night auditor who computes accounts, prepares bills, and counts up the day's cash flow while tending the front desk during the quiet night hours. An auto parts inventory control executive displaced by a plant closing likes the independence of being in charge during the graveyard shift.

Instead of going to work for wages or salary, think whether you can offer the industry a service they need that you can do better and cheaper then they can do it for themselves. One of these services is handling the clerical work of reservations for hotels. Short training is all you need to become a reservationist. In Seattle, a displaced home-maker who spent thirty-eight years raising ten children is earning $1,000 a month with a service handling reservations for independent hotels and resorts in the West. She was placed by the travel school she attended after her divorce. Jean Parsons runs a reservation service for bed-and-breakfast owners scattered all over Alaska. She founded "Accommodations Alaska Style Stay with a Friend" after working as a customer service representative pioneering the polar route for Scandinavian Airlines.

Did you know that you can work for a shopping service checking the quality of a restaurant, hotel, or store? The curator of a clock museum and his wife were recruited by an ad in the paper to dine, free of charge, in local restaurants in exchange for filling out a questionnaire on such items as the time it took to be served, whether the food was hot, and the condition of the rest rooms, carpets, and telephones.

These national services keep a low profile, but they hire local people all over the country through classified ads or tiny offices in large shopping malls. To find out what's available, ask the national association for the industry you want to inspect to give you the names of services active in your locality.

Finally, not all feeding and lodging is done in big, stressful settings. After her heart attack, a nurse's aide had to quit her physically demanding job in a big hospital, but she's happy cooking in the relaxed setting of a small nursing home. She got the job after taking a low-cost, six-week course in food service at the local Board of Cooperative Educational Services (BOCES). "It's best to keep going as long as you can," she says. "My motto is, if you can't do one thing, try something else."

But even without special training in quantity cooking, you can probably learn enough on the job to do plain cooking for church suppers, breakfasts for the guests of a bed-and-breakfast, lunches for the children in a day-care center, or even food that will satisfy the crew on a big farm or ranch.

Most of these jobs are filled informally by word of mouth, but watch help-wanted ads. For work cooking in senior citizens' centers, apply directly or through a senior citizens' employment service. Hospitals and state institutions always seem to be in desperate need of kitchen help, so it pays to apply cold in person. One machine operator who found it hard to get work in her own trade at 59 kept applying for a job as a cook at a facility for the mentally retarded and calling them on the phone until they hired her.

Waiting tables is a physically strenuous job, but a surprising number of older people do it. A widow who had no private pension because she had been self-employed in selling took to waitressing at racetracks as her business dwindled and joined the AFL Waiters and Waitresses Union. Although she liked nothing about it, she was still doing it part time during the season when she was 80. But at 64, the divorced wife of a doctor was making $30,000 a year for part-time work as a banquet waitress for a yacht club and liking every minute of it. "Each day is different, each party a surprise."

Waitresses have to like people. "People are amusing," says one. "I've learned a lot by eavesdropping." But they all complain about their feet, being stuck with a colleague's chores, working weekends, and the income tax levied on tips as well as on salary. Earnings can be respectable where the tips are good, as in serving banquets and hotel room service, but hourly pay from the management can be less than the minimum wage, and when trade is slow that's all there is to take home. There are always jobs in the ads, but it pays to apply directly to the place you think you'd like.

Some hospitality work is glamorous. All of it takes teamwork and hard, physical labor over long, unpredictable hours. But if you enjoy watching all sorts of people at close quarters, you'll find it endlessly fascinating.

✓ TRAVEL AND RECREATION

The demand for travel and play grows to fill up the time and money available to spend on them. Not just to Europe, but to Easter Island, too. Not just the beach, but Windsurfing. The horizons are endless.

Dreams are free and easy, but a lot of people earn their livelihood making them come true. It takes air traffic controllers and bus drivers to get you out of town, and a baseball game wouldn't be as much fun if you couldn't buy a hot dog while you watched it. Travel and recreation is a big and growing industry but it's fractionated into thousands of small, diverse enterprises, both public and private.

Instructors and facilities for sports, crafts, arts, games, and hobbies are provided as public services by cities, counties, parks, employers, the armed forces, colleges, retirement communities, nursing homes, and nonprofit service organizations such as the Scouts and the Ys. Some of the same resources are offered for profit by the organizers of sports events, ski resorts, bowling alleys, skating rinks, gambling casinos, amusement parks, riding academies, and the commercial theater.

Overseas travel has been brought within the reach of people of modest means through tours organized by large-scale operators who contract for transportation, accommodations, on-site documentation of the sights to be seen, and tour guides to see that the schedule goes smoothly.

Finally, the attractions worth traveling to see have to be maintained and explained to visitors. Museums, historic sites such as battlefields, natural wonders such as limestone caves and redwood forests, historic houses, public buildings, and industrial establishments such as wineries have to be restored by specialists, run by curatorial staffs, and protected by security guards.

Qualifications for work in travel and recreation are personal enthusiasm and the ability to motivate others. Travel agents should enjoy working in sales and with computers. Tour guides should like people and be good organizers and leaders, with lots of physical stamina. Recreation and entertainment managers need to understand the motivations of the people around them as well as the recreational activity they are managing.

College courses leading to a bachelor's degree in park and recreation management and shorter training leading to certification is available for travel agents and recreation leaders, but most people learn the work on the job.

Travel agents are paid in ways that depend on the commissions the agency earns from carriers and services; usually 10 percent, but ranging from as little as 7 percent on some air tickets to as much as 40 percent of travel insurance policies. They are also paid in opportunities to travel at bargain rates that depend on the volume of bookings. Tour guides are paid by the day for their services or by a fee per head or commission when they also sell the tour.

Pay is low for seasonal, part-time work in recreation, and much of it is done by volunteers or in exchange for participation. The median weekly pay of full-time ticket agents was $394, and recreation attendants earned $228.

Whether owners or employees, travel agents are paid by commission on the fares they sell. Regular salaries with benefits are paid to employees of airlines, many of whom belong to unions, and to those who work in travel and recreation for large organizations such as universities, industrial companies, and the armed forces, most of which serve young adults.

SECOND CAREERS FOR EXPERIENCED TRAVEL AND RECREATION WORKERS

Travel agents compete so fiercely on personal service that it's hard to stay in the business if you want to cut back. The owner of an agency who had to sell it during the oil slump in Texas continued selling to faithful customers on commission with another agency, but she isn't saying how much she is earning. Another who was fired from one agency when the owner's son took over was taking home $190 for a forty-hour week, no lunch, no breaks, and no travel privileges.

Is there anything you can do in the travel business after retiring from the demanding work of dealing with the public for an airline? Travel agents are always glad to have former **flight attendants** or **ticket salesmen** sell for them on commission. You can work near the planes by driving an airport limousine or selling in an airport shop. But in all these jobs you may find yourself working longer hours for much less pay than you've been accustomed to earning.

If you've retired as a salaried **recreation manager** for a big, stable organization such as the Ys, the Scouts, the armed forces, or a college, you may be attracted to public service or volunteer work in helping others that can be done part time. One retired recreation manager manages a campground for the Forest Service, another works as a foster grandparent, and a third spends some time teaching retarded children.

The commercial entertainment business is less stable and more subject to unpredictable changes of public taste. One **movie theater owner** whose business was ruined by videos landed a full-time job maintaining and scheduling the auditoriums of the local school system. Another became a self-employed handyman after selling one of his last theaters to a church.

For an older entertainment pro, the ideal solution to obsolescence is to ride the growing interest in nostalgia. Dale Higgins was a bandleader in love with the big-band music of the thirties and forties. When he sold his music store he bought a rundown old ethnic club, assembled a thirteen-piece orchestra, and started holding weekly dances and dancing lessons. Some of his customers are young, but the old music and dancing is popular with senior citizens. His advice: rent space, charge at the door, don't sell liquor but encourage patrons to bring their own, and promote with ads, flyers, newsletters, and publicity.

Even when they move out of the field, **recreation leaders** often find second careers that sound like fun. A Red Cross and army recreation director became mayor of a little town in Maine, chairing council meetings, cutting ribbons, and presiding on ceremonial occasions. When the hospitality committee for the United Nations delegations' service and information was dissolved, its executive director went into the business of counseling and teaching on the basis of palm and tarot card readings.

NICHES FOR NEWCOMERS TO TRAVEL AND RECREATION

When people think about becoming a **travel agent** in their later years, they are thinking about the romance of sending people to exotic lands, the excitement of dealing with major airlines, steamship companies, and foreign governments, and the chance to get in some free trips abroad for themselves.

But it's not all beer and skittles. Pay is low and those flexible schedules are not geared to your convenience. A new or part-time travel agent may find she is busiest during the season she had hoped to go fishing or golfing or travel herself. During peak holiday season, everyone works overtime. During a slump the lowest-level people may be laid off, and the small agencies where newcomers get their chance may not survive even a short recession.

Starting a travel agency is no business for a beginner. You have to meet the tough requirements of the airlines: an office accessible to the public, not a private home; at least one employee with two years of travel experience; proof of financial stability. If you're really a beginner, you are going to have to work for an existing agency for a couple of years or go into business with somebody who has the experience. And since earnings will be low while you are starting, you'll need $50,000 of working capital to carry you through the first year. Yet so many people want to get into the business that travel schools and travel agency franchises flourish.

Marjorie Anesko used both, but it wasn't easy to move from real estate broker to travel agent. What she got out of the travel school was a clerical job with the school. She tried to buy a franchise but was turned down for lack of money and experience. Finally she was able to buy a franchise for Cruise Holidays by teaming up with a young man who shared the expenses. They've carved out a niche for themselves in selling cruises to groups that need special arrangements, such as Alcoholics Anonymous, which wants no liquor served. She travels more than before she owned the agency, but it's so successful she doesn't have the time to get away as much as she would like.

It's easier — but still no cinch — to get a job in a travel agency owned by somebody else. You may have to start by working for commissions only. Because he had no experience, Burley Carson was turned down for a travel agent job when he retired from the post office. Undaunted, he persuaded another agency to take him on as an outside agent and spent so much time helping out at the office that they eventually hired him to fill a clerical vacancy. He read up on travel, took courses offered by the airlines, and when the manager was indicted for arson he wound up running the agency.

Successful older newcomers are almost always people who have done enough traveling themselves to know how the business works. You might even apply to an agency that knows you as a customer. When he was an office manger at Marathon Oil, Duane Warren hired a big national agency to set up a travel department for the company. When he retired he went to work for them as an outside agent and eventually rose to regional manager.

If you really know nothing about the travel business, a travel school may help you get your foot in the door, but it may not be the job of your dreams. The administrative assistant to the president of a college went to a travel school when she retired and was placed with Thomas Cook Travel as a vacation counselor. She's paid on commission but guaranteed the minimum wage for a forty-hour week.

Do those free trips make it all worthwhile? For starters, none of them are really free — not even the "fam," or familiarization, trips the airlines, hotels, resorts, and national tourism offices used to offer as promotions. In the nineties, each travel agency gets discounts based on the number of full-time travel agents employed for at least a year. On airfares, the foreign and domestic airline conferences give each travel agency a number of "passes" (trips at 75 percent off list), based on the total business the agency does in their area. The passes belong to the agency, which doles them out to whomever the owner pleases.

There are all sorts of special arrangements. A retired social worker gets to the San Francisco airport at 6:00 A.M. two or three times a week to assist groups booked by Pleasant Hawaii Holidays. Each time she earns $45 in cash and a $20 discount on her own fare when she visits her son in Hawaii. She fell into the job when she was working at the airport helping distressed passengers for the nonprofit Travelers Aid Society.

Does all this mean that you can never get out of the country without paying? Well, never say never. But there's always a catch:

If you're what a **cruise line** calls "a congenial single gentleman" over 50, you may get to travel free as a "host" to dance, chat, play bridge, and squire the excess of single females on these tours. Hosts are explicitly instructed to mingle and show no favoritism to any one passenger. Retired businessmen and military officers are preferred.

If you're a celebrity, an entertainer, a golf or tennis pro, a professional football player, or an authority on something like the stock market, you may get your passage free for entertaining the passengers on a theme cruise. These jobs are booked by an outside entertainment agency in the city where the cruise line is based.

Contrary to what you may hope, cruise lines do not barter free passage for common skills such as bartending, but pay regular wages to help hired through employment services in the ship's home port. Concessions for services to passengers such as hairdressers may be awarded to the highest bidder.

Far simpler is to get a whopping reduction on airfare by traveling as a **courier** for an international delivery service. An air courier service will sell you a round-trip ticket to your overseas destination at a discount that may be as high as 85 percent off list in exchange for taking their suitcases of parcels as your checked baggage. If you are willing to go on short notice, you may get by without paying anything at all.

The trick is to find a service that has parcels to deliver where you want to go. There are directories of these services, but the firms doing it blink in and out of business so fast that you'd do better to call one of the firms listed in the yellow pages under "Air Courier." If they don't go where you're going, they'll know who does. Some are so big they operate like regular travel agencies with reservations departments, but usually you have to negotiate the date and the discount. You get the ticket and the bags to check from an agent who meets you at the airport with instructions about where to meet the agent who will take it from you at the airport on the other end. You don't even have to lift the bag. It may contain small parcels for many addressees — documents, film, product samples, machine parts, anything small and valuable that has to get there faster than air freight. Arrangements have been made with customs officials so you won't have any trouble. The only real problem is that you have to be able to get along with what you can carry on.

What are your chances of becoming a **tour guide**? It's a complicated industry. The tours you see advertised are set up by tour wholesalers who operate them with hired tour guides and sell them through tour retailers — usually travel agents — or directly to travelers. But travel agents, nontravel organizations such as professional associations with members interested in a particular kind of travel experience, and enterprising individuals may package and promote tours, too. And if you know enough about a local tourist attraction, you can "document" or explain it to visitors from around the world who come to see it. Free enterprise reigns in the sightseeing industry: the possibilities are infinite and so are the financial arrangements.

For an older newcomer who wants to lead groups out of town, there are three ways into this jungle. You can become a professional **escort**, paid by the day to lead tours planned and sold by a tour operator. You can sell enough tickets to a prepackaged, existing tour to get your own way paid as its leader. Or you can make all the arrangements, package, sell, operate, and lead a tour of your own. The last, of course, is the most fun but also the most difficult.

For a beginner, landing a job as a professional guide for a prepackaged international tour is a little easier than breaking into the somewhat similar world of acting; there are only ten applicants for every job instead of the dozens pursuing a stage part. You have an edge if you've been a teacher, supervisor, or organizer before, and are more interested in the welfare of other people than in the personal escape of travel. According to one tour operator, "the ideal candidate is a recent widow, completely vigorous, well-traveled, very caring and understanding."

The straightforward way to start is to go to one of the vocational schools for tour guides. They will teach you the nuts and bolts of leading a group — maps, airline schedules, what to do in an emergency. Then, to get comfortable with the microphone, volunteer to lead a few local tours. All you may have to do to lead a local bus tour is to be in the right place at the right time.

One right place to be is on a tour as a customer. Dick Yocham was recruited by the director of a domestic bus tour he and his wife were taking. He now takes his wife along and gets $50 a day in addition to all their expenses, which include "staying in the best hotels and eating in good restaurants." A former teacher was called years ago by a friend to pinch-hit for an escort who didn't show up and has been doing it ever since. A widow — presumably the ideal candidate — was recruited at a dinner for widows to escort and pay the bills on local tours by the hour at the minimum wage. And many older people organize and guide tours for senior citizens as volunteers.

Patricia Harris is a former secretary who went to tour guide school and was hired by Saga Travel, a big British-owned tour operator that has sent her everywhere in the world except Europe, which they handle out of England. She's been to Australia eleven times for them. Like all the big tour operators, Saga hires local guides to explain the sights in foreign countries, but on domestic tours Patricia has to provide the commentary, so when she's not actually leading a tour she's apt to be reading up for one.

She warns that it's harder work than it sounds. You're handed an itinerary and a list and cash for an emergency, and from there on out you're on duty around the clock. You may be outside in all kinds of weather, counting luggage. You have to maintain good relations with bus drivers, hotels, and restaurants. You have to keep thinking about where forty people are going to be able to go to the bathroom or buy stamps to send their postcards, and you never eat a meal without listening to complaints or answering questions.

And you don't get rich at it. Guides are usually independent contractors. In addition to whatever is provided for members of the tour, they are paid at rates that range from a high of $100 a day to zero for amateurs who volunteer to lead a special group, such as senior citizens. Pat Harris takes in $5,000 in fees for several dozen trips that keep her on the move for four and five months of the year.

The other way for a beginner to lead a tour is to sell it. If you want to go anywhere in the world and can persuade fifteen or twenty other people to go with you, a travel agent will find a tour for you and pay your expenses and perhaps a fee for each member you bring in. You can get literature from the travel agent, but the time and money you spend is on you. This works if you have a ready-made group of friends, colleagues, fellow tennis players or stamp collectors — any group of like-minded people who would like to go together.

Some people are such naturals at it that they keep doing it deep into their 70s. Beryl Grilley led her eighth tour to Kenya the year she was 81. A veteran traveler, she got started when the Ask Mr. Foster Travel Service asked her to take the place of a guide who couldn't go at the last minute. Over fifteen years of leading tours all over the world she has acquired a following of people who simply like to travel together. She gets her own expenses and $25 for each tour member she recruits. "Prepare for glitches," she advises. "Have a wonderful sense of humor. The first activity on the trip should be a cocktail party."

The hardest but also the most rewarding way is to package, sell, lead, and own the tour as its operator. This is something to consider if you have special knowledge about some attraction. Ken Wendel is a former history teacher who got into the business when he was asked to conduct a bicentennial tour of the site of the Battle of Brandywine. But any special interest will do if you know how to reach like-minded people with the time and money for travel. With a little imagination you can find a travel angle to anything. A gardener? Others, too, may dream of exploring the jungle flowers of the Amazon. An architect? Other architects may be as eager as you to visit the Palladian villas of northern Italy. A collector of Haviland china? Other collectors may want to visit the French village where it is made from local clay.

If you happen to be a natural-born promoter, a special purpose can serve as well as a special interest. Clergy lead tours to the Holy Land and branch out to lead their congregations to other places as well. Professors lead tours designed so that students can get college credit for going. Travel is so appealing that it can even be attached to fundraising. Symphonies and museums sponsor tours organized around music and art, which package a tax-deductible donation into the price tag.

There's a lot of paperwork and responsibility to operating a tour. In Pennsylvania, where Ken Wendel lives, tour directors have to be bonded and licensed. It helps to have experience in business or promotion and at least a few months of work with a travel agent before taking the plunge.

William Yocum had all these good things going for him when he set up Key Tours for seniors after he retired as industrial development manager for the Reading Railroad. Because of his experience in transportation, he took on the volunteer job of chairing a travel committee for the AARP. He set up a few bus trips for seniors as a hobby, and to learn about how the professionals did it he spent his spare time for a couple of months helping out with the clerical work of a travel agency. Key Tours now goes anywhere in the world he and his wife want to go. He makes all the arrangements himself and while he isn't making a lot of money he's obviously having a lot of fun.

But there is something in travel for everybody. If you're a stay-at-home you could become the tour guide who explains a local attraction to out-of-town visitors. If you're a former teacher, actor, or just a natural ham who knows a lot about your local history, you could try for a paying job as the **"step-on" guide**, taking over the commentary for a tour that brings in sightseers. You can get experience by volunteering to make the spiel for a locally owned attraction such as a boat ride, a historic house, gardens, or a natural wonder like caves. People who are good at this love the microphone so much that they are willing to wield it for little or nothing.

If you are retired from a winery, candy factory, or other enterprise that welcomes the public, your former employer may pay you a modest hourly wage for showing visitors around the place.

What about museums and historic sites managed by the National Park Service? Salaried professionals are being replaced by volunteer **docents** who commit a given number of hours in exchange for training that is valuable in itself. At the Boston Museum of Fine Arts, for instance, the docents who take children around the Egyptian collection are given a regular course in Egyptology. The way to get this work is to apply to the site directly and get on their waiting list. And since somebody has to teach these volunteers, if you qualify as an expert on the site, you might create a job for yourself setting up a docent program for them.

If local history is your hobby, you may want to volunteer or even set up a tour of your own. At 88, John P. Meynink was sharing his love for the history of Portland by volunteering to show school groups around a local museum and conducting walking tours. In 1988, his "Portland on Foot" brought in $4,586.

Recreation is another field where you can earn a little money while sharing in the fun. Older newcomers are the ideal candidates for work-play jobs in the growing number of recreational programs designed for people their age, and those who are willing to work part time for low pay have the satisfaction of bringing recreational opportunities to young people and cultural activities such as ballet, little theater, and concert programs to everyone in the community.

Recreation for seniors is a growth industry. In Los Angeles, a retired librarian earned $10,000 a year for five hours of work a week coordinating the program of classes for senior citizens offered by May department stores. It's called Older Adult Service and Information Systems (OASIS), and it's so smart a promotional move for the store that you might create a job for yourself by suggesting it to a local merchant interested in community service.

Retirement communities, nursing homes, and senior citizens' centers employ older people for a few hours a week at modest hourly pay to organize crafts, music, social events, discussion groups, or whatever entertainment works for their constituencies. A resident is preferred — particularly one who is willing to volunteer — but your local Office for the Aging may be able to steer you to a nearby paid opportunity.

If you're a resident of one of these communities, there are many opportunities to earn small fees at occasional chores that are fun to do. A 78-year-old man gets $25 a week for leading discussions in a senior housing project ("keeps me alert"). A 76-year-old man gets $50 a month from the Council for the Jewish Elderly coordinating Sabbath festivities for senior citizens ("so many senior citizens telling me what to do!").

If you are a senior willing to work with the young you may be a godsend to a hard-pressed local recreation program. A nun who formerly taught in a Catholic college likes directing the student center of her diocese, although it isolates her from her religious community. A pensioned high school counselor earns modest hourly pay from the state extension service for helping the 4-H clubs for rural youth.

The Scouts are always in desperate need of help. District executive for the Boy Scouts is a challenging full-time job for a newly retired navy man, but a life-preserving labor of love for a disabled college professor and his wife. The couple donates not only many hours of time mobilizing local citizens to support the Scouts, but over $500 of their own cash to the program. "If you work and don't get paid, you are a volunteer," he says. "If you pay to work, you are a scouter." But there are ways to get paid for what you'd be doing anyway. A retired policeman has switched from tracking crooks to tracking animals as an outfitter and guide to people who want to hunt, fish, or photograph in the wilds of Wyoming. A retired optometrist bought a sports fishing boat and goes along as captain when he charters it out to fishing parties. After depreciating the equipment, the business shows up as a loss on his income tax.

Have you ever thought of starting a **dating service**? It will take you two years to develop a clientele and cost you $10,000 in newspaper ads and yellow page listings, but you don't need any special training or license and you'll never again know a dull or lonely moment. When Rachel Levesque was divorced at 65 and a stranger in Salt Lake City she starting a dating service. Ten years later, with a thousand marriages to her credit, she was taking in $30,000 and could make much more if she wanted. She says that San Francisco dating services charge $1,000 per client per year.

There's even a way to be sure of bringing money home from a casino. Most of the courses in **dealing poker** are offered in Nevada and New Jersey but there are a few in other states. The school will place you in a job that is just as much fun and much more profitable than actually playing. Some dealers earn as much as $100 a day at it.

Sports-minded? You can stay with it longer by **coaching** or **teaching**. Tennis, horseback riding, skiing, skating, swimming, sailing — whatever your sport, there are people eager to learn it. Pay and auspices vary. A tennis coach charges $35 an hour for running the program of a private camp. A riding instructor who used to own her own training stable charges $15 an hour for riding lessons. A retired professor of physical education gets $6.50 an hour for running the aquatics program of a private athletic club.

Age is no bar if you've been doing it all along. At 73, a retired tool design engineer was teaching sailing and skippering chartered boats for a sailing company. Jim Lucas and his wife Joy taught skiing before Jim retired from building elevators, and they've never stopped. The winter he was 76 and she 71 they both worked five days a week training ski instructors at $12 an hour.

Some recreation jobs seem to seek out older people. One is **public**

address announcer. Another is **umpire**. At 70 a former sportswriter for the *San Francisco Chronicle* was earning $60 a game as a baseball scorer for the National and American Leagues and liking everything about it in spite of what he sedately calls "occasional disagreements with players."

Another occasional job that attracts older people is the **tee starter** or course marshal, who schedules players so that they keep out of each other's way on a golf course. It can be a full-time job with a big-city park department, but may be done for as little as $4 or $5 an hour by a veteran golfer who likes to spend time with people in the open air. Another way to work in golf is to help sell and rent equipment and collect greens fees in the pro shop.

If you are more interested in making the scene than in making money, remember that ski resorts need **lift operators**. Park departments hire older people as **campground attendants** and, if they are certified by the Red Cross, even as **lifeguards**. Theater companies, even the circus itself, may be hard up for a **wardrobe mistress** to keep all the costumes in order.

Jobs in recreation are sometimes advertised in the paper, but they tend to go to patrons of the activity who are on the ground when a vacancy occurs. This is particularly true of community programs. In Burlingame, California, evening volleyball games were led by a housewife in her 50s who had been playing in the program for years, but when her knee went bad, the $21-a-session fee went to another faithful participant, a man who happened also to be in his 50s. The simplest way to get occasional work of this kind is to go to the place where you'd like to work and ask for it.

Travel and recreation is a roller coaster industry that is often frustrating and never highly paid, but hanging around people who are having fun and helping them to enjoy themselves even more is a special form of having fun yourself.

☑ SALES AND MARKETING

Do you think you could never sell? Don't be so sure. Some of the happiest salespeople belie the stereotype of the brash, intrusive salesman everyone tries to avoid. Many of the most successful salespeople have been surprised to discover, late in life, that they are good at it and like it.

For all you know, you may have one of the many talents required to move clothes, machinery, equipment, food products, cars and parts, hardware, plumbing, electrical goods, and all manner of consumer products from manufacturers to the companies who use them or the wholesalers and retailers who distribute them to the ultimate consumers.

The marketing of a consumer product or service begins with market research that identifies potential customers, determines the best way to reach them, and tests its acceptance in a local market. If all signals are go, professionals in engineering, production, cost accounting, selling, advertising, sales promotion, public relations, and accounting work together to create a marketing plan.

When the product is ready to be launched, advertising has to be created, placed in the appropriate print or broadcast media, and monitored for effectiveness. Salesmen have to be hired, trained, and deployed to the various markets and territories. The sales have to be analyzed to monitor changes in demand and keep inventory in balance with demand.

Products and services for the military, the government, hospitals, schools, and other institutional users are bought rather than sold. The buyer invites selected vendors to bid on the requirement, and the lowest bidder with an acceptable proposal is normally awarded the contract. Relations with the buyer are managed by a team of specialists coordinated by a contract administrator who is responsible for fulfilling the contract. Smaller institutions increasingly buy in bulk through a service which contracts, say, with a drug company for all the aspirin needed by a dozen hospitals instead of just one (see Purchasing).

Keeping everyone concerned informed about products used by physicians, architects, and engineers is an industry in itself. Technical communications between buying and selling organizations are maintained through trade shows, conferences, technical literature, and personal visits.

Distribution systems vary with the product. Newspapers and publications have to be sold and distributed to readers in their places of business or homes. Print and broadcast media have to sell their space and time to advertisers who want to reach their audiences. Classified ads, furniture moving, warehouse space, shipping, mailing, trucking and freight, construction, commercial printing, telephone service, and printing are among the services sold to businesses.

Sales work is not for the fainthearted. It's for you if you are naturally self-confident and optimistic, like talking and listening to people and working on your own, and believe in what you are selling. Salesmen of products such as drugs, computer systems, insurance, real estate, securities, or travel may be quiet, thoughtful, even introverted.

Marketing managers responsible for the marketing plans of big national companies earn high pay. In 1990 median weekly earnings of salaried marketing, advertising, and public relations managers were $797.

Pay for manufacturers' representatives is by a combination of salary, commission, and bonus, varying with the company and product. In 1990 their median full-time weekly earnings were $596. Manufacturers' agents are paid by commission only and have to pay their own travel expenses. Median weekly earnings of sales representatives for business services in 1990 was $514; for sales representatives for advertising, $504.

SECOND CAREERS FOR EXPERIENCED SALESMEN AND MARKETERS

High pay, high stress, high turnover. During the eighties, sales careers ended abruptly: "Did not like new owners"; "Closed operation, replaced with an 800 number"; "Travel burnout. Covered all of hot Arizona"; "Company went broke due to deregulation"; "Jap import killed the market"; "Management changed, found better job." Established older salespeople were so afraid of being replaced by younger and cheaper people that one veteran sales manager had to be dissuaded by his wife from dyeing his silver hair.

Many were shortchanged. The **sales manager** for a packaging company was making more than $50,000 in salary, commission, and bonus until his company was acquired by a concern that didn't have a retirement plan. At 55, after thirty years of building up his territory, he was retired with a small lump sum. He's now clerking in the local hardware store.

But takeovers aren't always bad. Beverly Schroeder earns $67,000 selling Quality Books to New England libraries, more than she made when she did the same job for a smaller publisher.

What can you do if you're forced to retire before you want to quit sales work? Titles and companies change, but the work of selling is still flexible enough to offer opportunities for those who are looking for more money and challenge, as well as those who want less work and stress, or merely a different cast of characters. You can move up, down, or around. Change companies or product line. And if you are willing to take the risk you can write your own ticket.

Try to stay with the products and the people you know. If you're a good salesman you can probably sell anything, but good customers who know and trust you are worth money in the bank if you can find another way to work with them. You may have to go no further than your last employer. A wholesaler of tires didn't want to relocate with her company, so her boss helped her find a job with a competitor who wasn't moving.

Prime prospects are companies who know you as a competitor, particularly if they are newer or smaller. The sales manager of a pressure-sensitive tape company who disagreed with his boss walked right into the same job with another tape company. When he was reorganized out of his sales job selling paint for Sherwin-Williams, Ted Thormahlen took his knowledge of the paint distribution system to another paint company. A regional parts representative retired early from International Harvester earned almost as much calling on the same customers for a small company making a cooling system cleaner, conditioner, and sealant. It's a perfect match with what he used to do.

If you've worked on **contract proposals** for a prime contractor of the military or the federal government, you know your way around a world that thousands of smaller firms would like to enter. A specialist who had worked on the contract proposals for a manufacturer of helicopters found a job managing the administration of contracts for a company making satellite navigation receivers. Another contract administrator went into the business of helping small businesses locate opportunities to sell to the government. He gives seminars as a government contract specialist.

Network. Don't burn any bridges. Products are going to be sold one way or another, and you never know where an opportunity will open up. They may come through your competitors, your old bosses and coworkers — anyone who knows what you can do is a potential helper. In the topsy-turvy world of selling, you may find yourself working for the people who used to work for you. Since his retirement, a Chrysler branch manager of a group of dealers works full time selling them management advice, with no diminution in his earnings.

Customers who know firsthand the kind of sales job you do may want you to sell their product. After he was fired, the branch sales manager of an office machines manufacturer wound up grossing $20,000 a month selling on straight commission for a former customer.

Consider going into business for yourself. It's an easy transition, because whatever the terms or titles, sales people are ultimately compensated on the basis of what they produce. The manager of warehouse distributors for an instrument company found himself "over 40 and overqualified" when the new owners made life unbearable, so he started selling on commission for other companies serving the distributors he knew. His old customers helped him develop new markets, and while he spends a lot of time on the road and didn't earn as much right away, he enjoys the freedom to do as he pleases.

If you're willing to take the risk, the reward can be very high. When he was fired after thirty-six years, the marketing vice president of a manufacturer of construction equipment found a very small competitor and went to work selling its products on straight commission. He's grossing $80,000 a year and wouldn't consider any other arrangement.

Straight commission is the fast way to get your foot in the door. The trick is to find a market for a product you like and convince the manufacturer that you can cover it better than it's being done. On a straight commission of, say, 5 percent, you cost him nothing and may work harder because you're your own boss. You plan your time, pay your expenses, and do what you please, subject only to rules set down in the agreement.

If you can't get the agreement you want, you might begin by working for the **manufacturer's agent** who has it. A sales manager who retired from Armco rather than move is now earning more money selling similar steel products to the same customers through a manufacturer's agent that represented Armco in some markets. He learned about the agency through the grapevine.

A more ambitious but less risky way in is to buy an established manufacturer's agency. With one child still in college, a regional sales manager for electrical products who had always dreamed of being on his own bought out a manufacturer's agent who was about to retire. He grosses $100,000 a year, but puts forty-five thousand miles on his car doing it.

Supposing, however, that you don't want to work all that hard and make all that money. If you can find someone willing to pay for what you know you could become a consultant.

Advertising and **public relations** savvy is relatively fungible. Specialists like William Hogan, who created marketing videos for Exxon, can do the same for other companies when they retire. Former advertising managers of big companies can be useful to advertising agencies, or to the media they used to sell. Since his retirement, the former corporate advertising manager of a chain of grocery stores has been advising a group of weekly newspapers. The **marketing director** in charge of advertising for a brewery had no trouble doing the same thing for a network of psychiatric hospitals.

It's harder to cut down in the strenuous business of selling, but if you have a real following among your customers the company may invite you to work part time introducing your successors and putting out fires for a few years after your retirement. A **sales rep** for a pharmaceutical company continues calling part time on physicians and hospitals, and a veteran salesman for a supplier of aerospace companies agreed to work five hours a week for the highest amount of money he could earn a month without losing any of his Social Security benefits.

Planning for gradual retirement is easier if you own the business as a **manufacturer's agent**. You can keep on serving the old customers you like on your own schedule, and bring in younger salesmen to keep volume steady or growing. Some continue working this way well into their 70s.

But supposing you want to get out of sales. Before venturing further afield, look around to see if there's nonselling work in an industry you already know. Could you work buying what you used to sell? Joseph Stone was at loose ends after he sold his candy brokerage business, so he accepted the invitation of a former customer to work part time buying candy for his seven stores.

Is there anything you'd like to do in the production of what you used to sell? If you've been an **advertising manager**, you know enough about the media you've been using to switch sides and run a radio station, but there are more arcane possibilities. A district sales manager for the genetics division of the Carnation Company moved from selling semen for the artificial insemination of cows to supervising the re-covery and transfer of fertilized embryos for the Arizona Dairy Company.

Finally, if you're tired of the rat race, your skills in persuasion are a marvelous springboard to a second career in sales training, teaching, writing, real estate, or even coaching weight reduction or exercise programs. An IBM regional sales manager who took early retirement rather than move out of Seattle went to work at higher pay doing one-on-one coaching of eighty marketing managers for the Seattle Times Company. Eventually he'll have two private pensions.

NICHES FOR NEWCOMERS TO SALES

If you'd like a second career in sales, try to find a product or service you know and like. If you love to sail and talk about boats, you may have a second career ahead in brokering yachts. You may be just the right person to sell the product your company makes. A telephone operator made more money by getting transferred to the department selling public telephones.

If you've been a teacher, there may be a product on which you are an authority. Since his retirement as dean of culinary arts at Schoolcraft College in Michigan, Bob Breithaupt has been selling special beef certified by the Angus Association to restaurants, country clubs, and hotels. In Wisconsin a retired director of school bands visits schools for a firm that sells them music, instruments, and instrument repair, and in a suburb of New York City a retired director of physical education sells physical therapy equipment.

If you've been an engineer or technician, there may be products nobody else but you could even begin to sell. At 74, a technician for a manufacturer of opthalmic instruments was selling special diagnostic and laser treatment lenses to eye doctors. And even if the connection isn't close, a technical background is a good recommendation for many of the jobs selling technical products in the help-wanted ads.

You may not think of yourself as a salesman, but you may find it natural and easy to sell former colleagues the products you have used or bought in the course of your work. Siegfried Kohl is well fitted to sell new products to the engineers of utility companies because he was one himself. Jerry Adams was a field superintendent supervising the growing and harvesting of vegetables. When his canning company was sold, he walked into a better-paying job as corporate relations (read sales) manager for a company producing vegetable seeds. Richard Meier switched from buying truck transportation for a manufacturer to selling space in big flatbed trucks for a trucking company.

Switching sides goes on all over. Military procurement officers become salesmen for defense contractors. Grocery storekeepers do it. Billy Balch works part time for Campbell Soup "on the other end — to sell and not to buy as I did in store work." A former traffic manager sells trucking to traffic managers. A former school official sells school furniture. When you're thinking of a second career in sales, be sure to network all the people you know in the companies that used to sell to you.

Do you have access to any big community such as a hospital, a government agency, the military, or a school system? If so, you have a potential role in selling them a wide variety of goods and services.

Even professionals are willing to pay for people who can help them get new business. Architects and lawyers serving school systems employ retired school superintendents to talk with school superintendents in their area about their building plans or the problems they are having with legal service.

The Girl Scout cookies aren't the only products that are used in fundraising. Marketers of cookies, candies, pizza, Christmas cards, and magazine subscriptions are selling the scheme to other worthy causes in need of money. They pay substantial commissions to teachers or other school insiders who persuade a club or football team to sponsor a door-to-door fundraising drive or event that features their product. In Florida, a burned-out football coach was making $400 a week on these outside sales to schools.

Events range from the relatively elaborate enterprise of a carnival for which the fundraiser provides tents, bingo, chairs, and prizes for a share of the gate to the selling of cheeses, candles, candy bars, Christmas cards, and jewelry, among other products, either by door-to-door kids or at fundraising fairs. The practice is now so widespread that competition has reduced the return originally available to the promoters.

Selling **business services** is another natural niche for older newcomers who want to work from their homes. Local advertising space and time, advertising specialties such as calendars, specially imprinted pens or T-shirts, and storage space or haulage are among the services that are best sold locally by one-on-one discussions with the large number of small enterprises that could use them.

This local, personal selling is flexible enough to allow you to choose your hours and try out your own ideas. A retired secretary who likes to write enjoys selling ads for her town's newspaper. A retired director of nurses goes even further. She sometimes writes copy to persuade customers to buy time on the local radio station.

Another niche for gregarious newcomers is selling **advertising specialties** such as calendars to small businesses. In Wheat Ridge, Colorado, a mother and housewife earns up to $20 an hour for five hours a week as a "business counselor," helping local organizations get their message across. What she's really doing is thinking up ways they can put it on one of the fifty thousand give-away novelties in the Edward I. Plottle Company catalog, which she sells on commission. Caps, T-shirts, ballpoint pens, anything you can print a name or slogan on will do.

Advertising specialties are surprisingly big, both nationally and locally, and the variations are endless. If you're intrigued, you'll find a list of companies to call listed in the yellow pages of your phone book under "Advertising Specialties."

Finally, if you have special knowledge about the value of any kind of property you may get occasional work as an **appraiser**. When he retired, a senior appraisal engineer for the state of California did appraisals of natural resources for private companies owning them. And there's a steady demand from insurance companies and lawyers settling estates for people who know the value of art, antiques, or collectibles such as stamps and rare books. A retired teacher in Vermont adds $5,000 to her income appraising antiques and personal property and conducting estate sales.

Advice on the value of a business you know is worth money to a potential buyer. In San Francisco Rudolph Solomon, the retired owner of a chain of toy stores, earns $80 an hour as a **business appraiser**, putting a price on business enterprises for investors, estates, and divorce settlements. Customers come because he teaches a community college course and writes a newspaper column on small business.

Commission sales work attracts people who earn big money preparing bids for defense contractors and people on commission who may go for months without earning anything at all. But there are so many things to be sold on so many different terms that there's likely to be something in it even for people who have never considered selling.

☑ RETAILING

The customer is always right. Identifying *what* she wants is the problem. Big retailing chains study consumers through sophisticated research. Pilot programs test who wants to buy what by television, computer, telephone, mail order, or personal visits.

Retailing is the frontier of the free enterprise system, and big rewards go to those who recognize a new market or a new way of serving it. Good **storekeepers** look for opportunities in cultural trends, such as the rise in the employment of mothers. The two-paycheck family all but ended the retailing of dress fabrics, but sparked a boom in mail-order sales, night store hours, and rather unexpectedly, upscale maternity clothes for pregnant women who prided themselves on dashing directly from the office to the hospital.

Customers are increasingly diverse, even for the same product. If you want to buy a hammer, you could study a mail order catalog, order by phone, pay by credit card, and wait until the purchase is delivered to the house. You could spend hours going from store to store, hefting all the hammers in stock to find the one that feels most comfortable, or stop in at the local hardware store and chat with the owner about the project for which you need it.

Competition and sophisticated accounting ensure that you pay for personal service, delivery, or convenient location. But however a product is sold, people are needed to buy it and price it; physically transport, store, tag, and pack it; show it to customers; answer their questions, record sales, and take payment. In addition, books have to be kept, almost always by computer, the stock tracked and reordered, and statistics kept as a guide to future ordering.

Those who deal directly with customers work in "the front of the house" as **sales clerks, cashiers, or customer service representatives**. All retailers provide some nonselling services such as exchanges of defective merchandise, but upscale stores may offer others ranging from gift wrapping to events designed to attract people into the store.

Those who unload, inventory, keep stock, affix price tags, sweep, clean, and maintain a safe, attractive, and orderly environment work in the "back of the house" as **stock clerks**, **buyers**, and support staff such as bookkeepers, warehouse workers, and security guards.

An increasing proportion of retail sales are made in chain stores such as Sears or K-Mart, which purchase in bulk and maintain elaborate management structures and accounting systems to assess markets, set sales and profit goals, mount advertising campaigns, and move quickly to respond to changes in taste and profitability.

Not all merchandise is sold in stores. An increasing volume of goods is sold by mail or phone, and some by personal visits from commissioned retail sales solicitors. For these retailing operations, catalogs, mail-order procedures, mailing and phone lists, market research studies, telephone expenses and training, and a costly system of motivating door-to-door solicitors replace the expense of attracting customers to a store.

The decisionmakers who direct these activities lead a hectic life. **Store managers** and **merchandisers** are under constant stress to set and meet sales and profit goals. They have to be good numbers people, understand statistical analyses and computer systems, and be physically able to sustain long hours on the job. Pay for storekeepers and retail sales managers depends on the annual sales volume, and in big chains the store manager may get a percentage of this "handle" in addition to salary and benefits.

Front-of-the-house retailers have to be pleasant, neat, and responsive to customers. Sales clerks in big self-service stores requiring no persuasion of customers may be paid little more than the minimum wage. They usually get a discount on what they buy in the store. The median weekly pay of full-time cashiers was $215 in 1990, and sales clerks who have technical knowledge of such products as auto parts earned $320. But earnings may be substantial for commission-based door-to-door **solicitors** and salesmen of apparel and other big-ticket items such as automobiles, $464; appliances, $350; and furniture, $345.

Back-of-the-house stock people may need considerable physical stamina. **Stock handlers** and **baggers** averaged $228 a week.

SECOND CAREERS FOR EXPERIENCED RETAILERS

Retailing is a volatile game. In Shawnee, Oklahoma, the manager of a hardware store who was fired by its new owner one Saturday got a job offer from the owner of a lumberyard on Monday morning. Years later, at 76, he was working at the lumberyard part time and loving everything about it except the computer he had learned how to use.

Store managers who quit or are fired may have only to present themselves to the competition. When his company was sold off piecemeal for its real-estate value, a district manager of a chain of hardware stores walked into a part-time job helping customers with special orders in another hardware store.

If your store has been closed by a change of chain-store policy you may be able to take your experience elsewhere. A displaced Montgomery Ward manager maintained his income selling cars. When Singer Sewing closed its sewing centers, one of its redundant managers went to work dealing with the same kind of customers for a service that repaired sewing machines. A grocer who lost his store found a part-time job as field director, visiting other grocers for the Pennsylvania Food Merchants Association to sell the association's products.

Most people who work in retailing can think of things they could do better if the store were theirs, and some are in a position to take a shot at it. While he was in uniform, Jake Henry had managed millions of dollars of sales in post exchanges. After his retirement he worked for a while managing tire sales for Montgomery Ward. With all this experience under his belt, he was able to start a successful tire store with $3,000 cash, a good line of credit, and his service pension for groceries during the critical first year.

It's less risky to buy a store in which you have worked and have a personal following. After the owner died, Peggy Hernandez was able to buy, for a few thousand dollars, a little shop in Santa Barbara where she designed and sold ethnic clothes from Mexico, Greece, India, and Java. It flourished as long as the tour buses stopped nearby for lunch, but now she's filling in as a saleslady in another, better-located little tourist shop.

It's possible to better yourself in retailing by moving. A man who supervised 250 retail tire stores now works as a contract administrator for Goodyear, bidding for the business of municipalities. If you're going to solicit sales over the phone you can probably earn more money selling a big-ticket item like home remodeling or the replacement of windows than selling portraits of children for a photographic studio.

There are limited opportunities for better-paying but mainly more interesting jobs, which are easier on the feet than selling, in one of the big retail chains. In Park Forest outside Chicago, for instance, Ileana Bocek moved up from the sales floor to coordinating the installation services Sears offers to purchasers of its major appliances. She enjoys using her ingenuity to solve the problems that arise.

But most people who stay for years in retailing are less interested in higher pay or promotion than in an easier or nicer job with shorter hours. A Radio Shack store manager who resigned because she was working sixty hours a week without extra pay came back to help another Radio Shack manager part time, on her own schedule. She loves it although she admits it's sometimes hard to back off after fifteen years as the manager.

You may be willing to take what looks like a demotion to work part time in pleasant surroundings. A department manager at Bloomingdale's who quit to run a showroom for a wholesaler is happy checking stock, part time, at a discount liquor store in plush Palm Springs, California, at $9 an hour. In Las Vegas, a 71-year-old retired customer service representative for a cable television company was selling candy to visitors to the factory and showing them how it is made.

Former owners are in an especially good position to find nice part-time work. A man who sold his liquor store simply walked into another liquor store and went to work as a salesman. At 72, he was enjoying "the constant test of my knowledge and sales ability." A woman who sold her children's store likes waiting on people in a "beautiful department store" because it's "something to dress and get up for."

You may want to go part time when you take Social Security so you won't earn enough to lose any of it. A records clerk at J. C. Penney went to selling on the floor in the children's department when she turned 62. It means standing instead of sitting, but it's only eighteen hours a week. In California, a woman who was keeping the inventory for a pharmacist solved the problem by arranging to share her job with another widow so that neither of them earned enough to lose any Social Security.

If you're mechanically inclined, you may get part-time work at home, servicing the products you used to sell. It's a short step from selling vacuum cleaners to repairing them, or from renting recreational equipment to maintaining it.

NICHES FOR NEWCOMERS TO RETAILING

Personal selling of big-ticket items on commission is the way to make money in retailing, and some newcomers have the experience for it. A real-estate broker who wanted a change after her divorce had no trouble maintaining a respectable income selling furniture. If you've sold real estate or insurance you can sell replacement windows or automobiles.

The word skills of professionals transfer easily into jobs that require a lot of one-on-one persuasion. In San Francisco, for instance, a retired police captain does well selling Cadillacs. In Dallas, a former college teacher earns $30,000 selling the services of photographers through day-care centers.

Although most **direct sales solicitors** earn less, nurses, secretaries, and teachers are among those who report earning more than $10 an hour selling cosmetics to people in their homes. A nurse who quit the hospital to travel with her husband finds the time in a busy social schedule to sell cosmetics. She likes meeting people and seeing them "look so pretty." The main prerequisite for success seems to be genuine enthusiasm for the product. "Some might find commission sales to be a disadvantage," a Mary Kay beauty consultant admits. "I don't because the product sells itself and our commission is tops."

Buying standard merchandise is a career job in a buying service or big retailer and part of managing for smaller stores, but it's something you could do if there's a big-ticket item on which you can qualify as an expert. Kenneth Rose was an art teacher in Livonia, Michigan, who taught jewelry making at the high school and museum. He liked making sketches of how gemstones people brought him could be set. When he retired from the school system he went into the profitable one-man business of buying gemstones and selling them to jewelers.

Have you thought of starting your own **retailing business**? The door is wide open for anyone who gets aboard a new trend. When dollhouse furniture was becoming popular, Mac Willson started retailing museum-quality miniatures, made by craftsmen he met at trade shows, from his home. His whole family now participates in running the profitable store he has in Houston.

Every year thousands of newcomers start a retailing business, but it's a rough go. Even with the help of a franchise it takes sixty hours a week of your time, well over $50,000 in cash, and much more in bank credit to start up a video rental, tape and record, launderette, or sports attire store from scratch. Most retail businesses are much smaller ventures, started with no more than a few thousand dollars of capital and run part time in a low-rent location or even from home: gifts, antiques, books, greeting cards, souvenirs, yarn, sports specialties such as bait and tackle, secondhand goods, or used cars. A year later, most of these ventures are gone. Which ones make it? Those who find and serve the market for a specialty too small or labor-intensive for a big retailer. If you have a really good new idea you can go into business for yourself on a shoestring. (See Your Own Business.)

Paula Boswell was one of the pioneers in the school fundraising business (see page 231). She discovered the need when she was a teacher, and started rounding up and selling prizes and other material for fundraising carnivals to grade school teachers. She figured that a good-sized elementary school will buy $300 or $400 worth of prizes, enough to yield a modest commission. For six years she worked out of her home, getting business by writing letters and advertising in local throwaway papers and plowing her earnings back into the business. When other people got into school fundraising, she started selling supplies for parties. Her discount party store would now cost several hundred thousand dollars to start from scratch.

The new market can be small and odd if the demand it supplies is real. Betty Goldin sells tools by mail for people who are building sports aircraft at home from a kit. She discovered the need when she was married to a flyer. When she was divorced, she spent $250 compiling a typewritten list of sources, which she offered free through ads in sports aviation magazines. Later she added photographs of the tools, which she took herself, and when she couldn't find what the kit assemblers needed she sold tools she designed herself and had made at a local machine shop.

Some of the best ideas grow out of needs so familiar most people don't see them. Like everybody else, a woman who spent sixteen years selling *Parents' Magazine* to mothers in their homes was appalled at how quickly usable toys were cast aside. So she started a little store where she sells new and secondhand clothes, toys, furniture, and gear of every kind for children from newborns up to the age of six. She encourages mothers to bring in useable gear that their children no longer need, and pays them half what she sells it for.

It's a relaxed, pleasant business. All of her trade comes by word-of-mouth and she doesn't hesitate to close the store when she has something else she'd rather do, yet she nets $20,000 a year. To succeed in a consignment business like this, you need a visible location, preferably on a corner and with reasonable rent, and a habit of respecting customers however little they buy.

Whether or not you own the store, you are going to be happier selling something you know. A school choir director sells in a music store. A researcher, a librarian, a religious educator, a journalist, and a high school teacher sell in bookstores. A former school bus driver buys, sells, and repairs cars. A widow who once worked as a commercial artist sells kits and supplies for needlework and teaches it in a little store. She doesn't make any money but she likes the customers. Engineers sell tools. Shop foremen and mechanics who have maintained equipment in the armed services become parts salesmen. A helicopter technician earns $12.05 an hour taking in merchandise for repair and selling parts for Montgomery Ward.

Retailing is where the jobs are. Big stores are always in the market, and sometimes so desperate for clerks, cashiers, and stockers that they'll hire almost anyone who applies. And there's a good reason. Store work is very poorly paid. Clerks selling big-ticket items such as appliances, furniture, women's shoes, men's clothes, or home computers get a commission on their sales as well as a salary. Customer service people in credits and returns, gift wrapping, or customer information may get a dollar or two an hour more than the regular clerks. But the hourly wages of the regular clerks are seldom enough to keep a full-time worker above the poverty level. Most salespeople are women, many of them self-supporting and no longer young.

In addition to poor pay and awkward weekend and night work, older retail clerks complain about standing on their feet long hours, rude young colleagues and customers, and the constriction of rigid store rules such as dress codes. A former space salesman for a newspaper sells paint in a store, but in order to qualify for health insurance he has to work forty hours and lose some of his Social Security.

"Terribly low pay," complains a clerk who likes her coworkers and customers, "no benefits, being on my feet all the time for the first time in my life."

"Located on one of the busiest highways in New Jersey," complains a former librarian who loves her job in a bookstore.

If you must clerk in a retail store, avoid big, impersonal department stores unless you have special knowledge that qualifies you to sell a product that carries a commission. Clerks who love their jobs are more apt to be working in a small store that sells gifts, greeting cards, books, music, or a low-traffic specialty.

Many older people go into store work because they want to be with people or to handle a hobby or a product they like. A good example is the former teacher who helps women find extra-large-size clothing. She works from her home at hours she arranges, and doesn't mind netting very little because she's trying not to lose any of her Social Security. And she gets a kick out of really helping her customers.

If you like to get out of the house and see other people, you could be the "**people greeter**" who stands at the door of a big self-service store to welcome and direct incoming customers. Many of them are friendly older people.

Even more gregarious — you really have to be something of a

ham — is the strenuous work of attracting the attention of shoppers by demonstrating a food or product in a store or handing out leaflets. It doesn't pay very well and it's hard on the feet, but you get the work by the day from a service supplying demonstrators to stores, so you can turn it down on a day you don't want to do it.

Restocking the shelves of a big store is arduous physical work. For some brand name products, it is done by the manufacturers directly or through a service such as Powerforce, which retains people to call on retailers to restock, check on displays, and notify the retailer of upcoming promotions for several manufacturers. Although it pays only a little more than store clerking, restocking is an attractive job for a retiree who wants permanent part-time work that gets him into a number of stores in his neighborhood. Restocking greeting card racks is especially attractive to older people. A greeting car company will pay you $5 or $6 an hour for this work, and the hours are flexible. Most seniors get the job by hearing about an opening, so the thing to do is to find out who's doing it now in a store near you.

Hobbies are another attractive retail niche. You need little if any money to get into the business of buying and selling antiques, toy trains, dolls, art, or old books, and if you come out even you've had the joy of your hobby without it costing you anything.

In Texas, a former secretary earns $12,000 a year working eighty blissful hours a week buying, selling, bookkeeping for, mailing, and packing antique and collectible dolls. The only drawback is that she no longer has enough time for family, friends, and church. In Colorado, a former public relations director agrees that the pursuit of antiques can be all-consuming, but advises rationing yourself to a few hours each day or week. She earns $5,000 a year on the antiques she buys and sells, working mostly at home but one day a week in a shop maintained by a group of antique dealers.

You may enjoy retailing flowers, gifts, cards, music, books, yarn, souvenirs, or other products that are fun to handle and bring you in contact with people who are enjoying themselves. Or helping other older people with a very personal problem that takes a lot of one-on-one consultation, such as fitting a hearing aid or selecting a cemetery monument.

Telemarketing has a bad reputation. No one really likes to call strangers away from their dinner to ask them if they need to subscribe to a magazine or replace their windows, but it's a second career for older people who have learned how to fend off rejection selling insurance, advertising time, or some other product through cold canvassing.

Some telemarketing work is much more attractive. Taking phone orders for a good catalog house like L. L. Bean pays better than clerking in a store. The hours are flexible because it takes a lot of shifts to cover phones twenty-four hours a day, and the older people who do it like talking with the customers. Setting appointments with patients is another phone job where you aren't likely to be hung up on. Watch the ads for jobs and evaluate each opportunity on its own merits.

Business-to-business telemarketing can be more rewarding. In Massachusetts, a retired phone company executive has become a consultant, designing telemarketing systems that do a better job of targeting prospects. Callers work from lists of people who have expressed an interest in the product at a trade show, or who already buy a similar product. The purpose of the call might be to alert the prospect to an upcoming trade show or open house, or merely to collect market information. Business-to-business telemarketing can be a natural outgrowth of the work you have done all your life. You could earn $10 to $15 an hour talking to people in the business you know about a product that might help them. If you used to be a sheet metal worker, for instance, you might be given a list of sheet metal shops to call about how an automated cutting system could save them time and money. You might even suggest yourself to a company whose products you know and like.

Retailing has many disadvantages, especially for older people. Commission selling and store ownership may require long hours and high risk, while jobs in stores are low-paying and physically demanding. But retailing work is a front-row seat on the way people live their daily lives, and it is widely available on short notice everywhere on a variety of schedules.

☑ THE OUTDOORS

Technological advance has scored its most spectacular gains in the traditional work of extracting the basics of life from the land and the sea. Hunting, farming, fishing, lumbering, and mining now employ fewer than 5 percent of the work force. And though the work is concentrated in ever fewer and bigger firms, it still draws people who like to work on their own in the outdoors.

The tradition may be old, but the tasks foreshadow the twenty-first century. Decisions once left to chance or judgment have become professional specialties. Livestock are artificially inseminated. Some seafood is collected by divers, while other species can be grown in ponds and harvested like crops. Eggs are mass-produced in exquisitely air-conditioned factories designed to accommodate tens of thousands of laying hens at a time. In populated areas, tall trees are taken down a limb at a time by cutters raised to a comfortable level in the bucket of huge cherry picker machines. Rare flowers and shrubs are propagated in small greenhouses by horticultural specialists.

Protecting the outdoors itself has become one of the most important of these specialties. Government, university, and private conservation groups watch over threatened range lands, forests, and the wildlife of land and sea. Forests have to be watched for fire and disease, and renewed by long-term plans for planting and cutting.

And though it's less glamorous, perhaps, there's still plenty of satisfying, small-scale work to be done supplying and maintaining parks, yards, gardens, lawns, and grounds for governments, institutions, and individuals.

Outdoors people have to be risk takers. Mining and drilling for oil are hazardous occupations. Farmers are at the mercy not only of the weather but of the economic climate for their crops. In addition to learning outdoor skills that are ever more specific to each task, those who work for themselves need to understand accounting and machinery and be willing to try new methods as well as work long hours.

The financial rewards are commensurate with the risks. Large-scale wheat, cotton, and fruit growers and people who have struck it rich in oil are well represented among the million or more Americans who now enjoy an income of a million dollars a year. But at the other end of the income scale, occasional groundskeepers for homeowners commonly still earn less than the minimum wage, and some of our least-privileged workers are the hired hands who pick vegetables for canneries and freezeries.

Earnings statistics tell us little. Median weekly pay for salaried farm managers in 1990 was $363, but farm income depends on the size of the farm and its crop. In 1990, for instance, the average yearly income was over $100,000 for farms — some of which are very large — producing such horticultural specialties as vegetables and melons, cotton, and rice, but the median was less than $15,000 for farms producing tobacco, corn, cattle, and other livestock, many of which are small.

SECOND CAREERS FOR EXPERIENCED OUTDOOR WORKERS

If you've managed oil wells or mines you have a potential second career as a consultant, either checking and approving the kind of project you formerly supervised or training younger people coming up in the business. You may even be recruited by a rival company after your retirement.

If you've been a **forester** or **conservation manager** for a federal or state agency you have interesting opportunities. After thirty-two years with the U.S. Forest Service, James Perry earns $35 an hour making environmental studies for private enterprises and government agencies. In Wamic, Oregon, a former manager of a district for the Federal Bureau of Land Management manages the system of sealed bids through which trappers of beaver, muskrat, and coyote sell their furs to commercial buyers. Other foresters and land managers become farmers or land surveyors.

The highly paid managers of big multimillion-dollar food and fiber enterprises have the career options of manufacturing executives. A retired **resource manager** of a 325,000-acre tract of timber for Kimberly-Clark consults on the valuation of trees. In Tennessee, a **woodlands division manager** for the Packaging Corporation of America is a real-estate broker specializing in land sales. A **field superintendent** contracting for cannery crops switched sides to sell seeds.

Big food producers have so much money invested that their managers are often well equipped for second careers in finance. After he sold his farm in the Boston milkshed, Dick Scott used his understanding of the dairy business to buy and sell farm mortgages and counsel other farmers in New England. Andrew Griffiths superintended a cranberry bog for sixteen years, spent thirteen years in baking, and at

52 went back to farming as the $80,000-a-year **supervisor** and **field-man** for a cooperative cranberry-growing company.

If your first career has taught you a lot about farming and marketing you could do well as a **farm manager** for absentee owners, but to make a living you have to round up a lot of acreage. "Bud" Rogers learned by studying the growers he served when he was managing a fertilizer company in Oregon. He now earns $40,000 a year managing 2,500 acres of potatoes that supply a nearby processing plant.

The traditional family **farmer** who worked his own land retired gradually if at all, selling out slowly to more vigorous children or junior partners, and all over the country these men are still farming. Bill Jones sold his orchard to his children, but at 79 he was drawing $600 a month from the new owners of the ranch for twenty hours a week of planning and supervising the work from town. At 72, Alfred Russell was still working his vineyard part time — "a lifetime has not ended yet" — and wishing he had power steering in his truck.

Many older farmers find less physically demanding second careers in agribusiness enterprises that sell agricultural machinery, advanced technology, and services to farmers. In South Dakota, a retired **rancher** is a **fieldman**, visiting neighboring ranchers to encourage them to consign the animals they have for sale to the livestock exchange that employs him. One farm wife is now a **tester** of butterfat content for a milk company. Others find occasional work driving trucks (see Transportation), repairing farm machinery (see Production), or in grounds-keeping. In some rural communities, minimum-wage work is provided through Operation Green Thumb, a means-tested public employment service.

It's tragic when family farms go broke. "Never believe politicians," advises one South Dakota cash grain farmer who lost $500,000 in a downturn. "Times were supposed to improve!" Now divorced, he's lost his wife and 350 acres, but he likes being his own boss, so he still hangs on, netting $5,000 a year from the 150 acres he was able to keep. But every year there are fewer left. In Texas, for instance, an equally independent-minded farmer dissolved his twelve-thousand-laying-hen operation because he could no longer compete with larger operations and didn't want to get any bigger himself. He and his wife live happily on their savings and the $600 a month they can make at his lifetime hobby of repairing band instruments. Their only regret is that they didn't get out sooner.

NICHES FOR NEWCOMERS IN EXTRACTIVE INDUSTRIES

A second career in outdoor work sounds good to many restless, highly stressed city executives. The retired chief executive officer of an insurance company earns $20,000 as a **gold miner**, digging out ore and running a mill in Idaho, which is fine except when the water freezes in winter. Some go to work, if only seasonally, in a national or state park.

A few hardy souls make a second career of fishing. Rather than take a transfer, a 55-year-old Citicorp manager retired to the Florida Keys, where he adds a net of $2,000 a year to his pension **diving for lobster**. And in California, a retired automotive teacher makes more money than he would like the IRS to know "fighting the federal and state of California" fish and game authorities as a commercial fisherman.

But the compelling dream is an independent, wholesome, outdoor life on an **old-fashioned farm** you own and run with the help of your family. And for some it works. Disgusted with the bureaucratization of medicine, a doctor and his wife bought a sixty-acre, dilapidated, run-down farm. They lived in a trailer while remodeling the house and then the outbuildings. Later, when the doctor's health failed, they leased most of the acreage, built greenhouses, and learned the nursery business. "We really like our life here in the peace and quiet of the farm on a dead-end road," he writes at 77. "We can tailor our work to coincide with our state of health."

If you grew up on a farm, you may be happy retiring to it after a career in the city, especially if you have no illusions about making it pay. It depends on how hard you are willing to work at it. A retired sheriff's deputy who does all of the physical work and sells through a roadside stand makes $20,000 a year from the ten acres of avocado and orange trees he inherited, but one hundred avocado and citrus acres still don't yield a livelihood for a family that hires out for all of the work to be done and sells to a packer. Both farmers inherited the land and like the life, but the ten-acre owner talks about his aching body, the hundred-acre family about their lovely views.

If you want to move onto a large-scale, picture-postcard farm, you had better be prepared to put up a lot of money. In Iowa, for instance, farmland goes for from $500 to $2,000 an acre, to say nothing of the $40,000 tractors, $75,000 combines, $100,000 buildings, complex elevators, or feed-mixing systems you may want to add. It's something to consider only if you have retired with a wad of cash from a business you owned and don't really care if you make a lot of money at it.

Even if you have the cash, the right farm may be hard to find. Richard Gerhan hunted four years before he found the "little farm" in Ohio on which he and his son raise beef, corn, oats, hay, and rabbits. An avid backyard gardener during the years he spent as a professor of economics, he was in great shape when he retired. At 71 Gerhan lets his son do most of the heavier work, but he loves the sixty hours a week he invests in outdoor labor, and most of the $50,000 a year they gross goes right back into terracing the land, planting trees, building fences, and enlarging the herd.

It's smoother to ease into the new life gradually, starting on a small scale while working at something else. Marv Janzen started growing rhododendrons ten years ago, when he was still employed in the school system. He now nets more than $25,000 a year from sales to retail nurseries from four acres, with ten thousand plants to the acre. William Cole and his wife started while they were teaching, too. Now that they can give their ten acres of apples full-time attention they can hope to net $10,000 a year by doing all the work, including selling at a roadside stand as well as through a fruit growers exchange. When the work gets too heavy, they may subdivide their orchard and sell it to other retirees moving into the area.

A well-heeled "gentleman farmer" can afford to lose a little of the money that would otherwise go for income taxes. If you are lucky enough to be in a high tax bracket, you can indulge in the expensive hobby of raising livestock, making wine from grapes grown in your own vineyard, or breeding Arabian horses, and if you tire of the venture there are always others who are willing to take it off your hands, usually for more than you put into it.

Christmas-tree farming has been a popular retirement investment for people who want "just a little sideline that will pretty much take care of itself." And it works fine if you start it early and don't expect much money. A retired conservation officer who bought land in New Hampshire back in 1946 and started planting the trees as a hobby now figures he nets $1,800 a year for five hundred hours of work.

But tree farming is a long wait for people who aren't young to begin with. In New York State, a retired management consultant is waiting six years to realize on twenty thousand four-year-old trees, but since his wife owned the land, his major investment was $5,000 for clearing it. It's worse if you have to pay for the land. In Washington

State, a retired insurance claim supervisor may have to wait even longer for any return on the $300,000 he paid for twenty-seven acres.

Smaller-scale specialties make more affordable outdoor second careers. The horse breeders are the most enthusiastic of the hobbyists, and not all of them are rich. Bernice Kalland started with a stallion and two mares while she was still working as a postal clerk. Now that she's retired, she adds about $10,000 a year to her pension working full time, all year, at it. The hardest part is selling the foals because she loves them all.

If your hobby is gardening, you can always sell what you grow to a local farmer's market, but it's more fun to breed plants, like the widow who earns a little pocket money raising and selling rare iris plants. It's a flexible hobby you can start on your back porch and a corner of your backyard while you're working full time at something else, and you can get as sophisticated about it as you like. After cataracts ended his career in accounting, Charles Ullman worked with growers in the Caribbean to breed exotic tropical plants known as Heliconias, which have a colorful flower that looks like a crab claw.

Aquaculture is an undemanding sideline for people who have a pond on the place. When he was 77, former revenue agent Jim Gatewood spent $3,900 getting an acre and a half of water set up to raise catfish on the 120-acre farm to which he had retired. It's not much work, only an hour a day, but not a lot of revenue, either. You can get good advice, and perhaps a design and financial assistance, from your agricultural extension service.

There's no end of outdoor hobbies that can be made to pay. Vivian Nightingale likes raising birds, and she now has five hundred of them. After ten years, she makes as much as $1,000 a month selling them. Another woman earns about $750 a month breeding canaries at home. It's confining, but she has to stay at home anyway to care for her 86-year-old mother.

The least demanding way to earn some money working outdoors is to help maintain all the yards and grounds that have to be tended. Groundskeeping for tightly scheduled landscaping or lawn services is a young man's job, but in a small town you may enjoy working directly for a park, cemetery, golf course, or as an individual yard worker for homeowners. In Sequim, Washington, a 75-year-old supplements his small pension from Sears doing yard work at the minimum wage for seniors who can't do the work themselves. One ad in a weekly newspaper brought him all the work he wanted.

Finally, there's volunteer work. You may be able to help in a national park. If you love gardening and know a lot about it, you may qualify as a master gardener and work at an arboretum or botanical garden answering questions from the public. And at the very least, you can always spend some of your time outdoors growing flowers and vegetables for your own table.

A second career outdoors offers peace, freedom, and occasionally even a little money. It can be physically hard and dangerous, but it's good for the body and the soul.

☑ PRODUCTION

Everything man-made was fashioned by someone somewhere — even intangibles like electric current, broadcast signals, the warmth of a bath. Manufacturing involves so many stages that the simplest object may have passed through dozens of hands in as many countries since it began as raw material.

Most of these stages no longer depend on a big force of unskilled labor. Bales are no longer toted by a large number of strong backs, but by a few forklift operators who may even have to know how to consult a computer. Technology dims the line between blue-collar and white-collar, boss and worker. Instead of bossing armies of unskilled workers, production managers coordinate teams of specialists. Occupational titles change so fast that they mean different things from one decennial census to another.

Whether it's a dairy, garment factory, power plant, automobile assembly line, or small shop, every step of the work has to be planned and budgeted. Standards of quality have to be set up and plans made to monitor them. The tools, equipment, and materials have to be established and plans made to store them so that they will be at hand when they are needed. Plants and equipment have to be designed, installed, repaired, and maintained.

Workers have to be hired, trained, and ready to work when their skills are needed. Costs, quality, and inventories have to be constantly monitored to see that they are meeting expectations. Finished product has to be stored in a warehouse, packed, and shipped to customers.

In a small machine shop, a handful of people may do all the managing as well as the manual labor. By contrast, a big manufacturer with many products and plants may divide the same functions among hundreds of specialists responsible for managing operations, materials, purchasing, cost control, quality control, inventory control, machinery maintenance, labor relations, training, warehousing, traffic, and shipping. Each product and plant may have its own functional managers reporting through many levels of authority.

More machinery in homes and offices means more work for installers and repairers outside the regimented factory setting. The more sophisticated the equipment, the harder to keep it repaired. Service organizations have to keep mechanics on hand to fix all the washing machines that break down in homes and all the outside automated teller machines that balk at dispensing cash after-hours when you most need it. There are still a lot of locks, pianos, clocks, furniture, and sewing machines around to be repaired.

Finally, not everyone is in love with modern technology. Millions of Americans are willing to pay for furniture, clothes, dishes, jewelry, and a long list of everyday products that are made the old-fashioned way by hand.

Industrial production managers and foremen need to be able to write and speak well, supervise people of all educational backgrounds and experience, deal with emergencies, and comply with company policies. Production workers have to know or be capable of learning specific skills and following explicit instructions.

Pay is highest in big operations and highly technical industries such as aerospace. Plant and production managers of sizeable operations earn more than $50,000, but it's not impossible for a mechanic or repairer in a highly technical industry such as nuclear power to earn that much. Unionized workers get higher wages than their nonunionized counterparts. In 1990, the median weekly salary for supervisors of mechanics and repairers was $586; for automobile mechanics, $393; and for inspectors, testers, and graders, $504. Median weekly earnings for production, craft, and repair workers depended on the trade: of those reported by the Labor Department, the highest in 1990 were $626 for telephone installers, the lowest $296 for textile machine workers.

SECOND CAREERS FOR EXPERIENCED PRODUCTION PEOPLE

Some experienced production people move up to more money and responsibility the second time around. If you've had any kind of experience managing production for a big manufacturer, you may get promoted to the top job of **production manager** for a smaller one. In addition to more freedom and even more earnings, you'll have the satisfaction of passing your skill and knowledge on to the next generation. Rather than move south with his plant, a shop supervisor for a big agricultural equipment maker took charge of the plant of a nearby manufacturer of automated material handling systems. Ads and employment agencies work well for experienced job changers.

Robert Eldridge lucked into the ideal second career for a telephone man. He was glad to retire after thirty-three years of working by the rules of the Bell system, the last fifteen as district plant manager. Now he's the general manager of an independent telephone company in a growing suburb outside of Knoxville. If he sees a way to serve the customers better he doesn't have to get the permission of a dozen people. His company served two thousand subscribers on antiquated equipment when the former owner asked him to overhaul the plant and then hired him to run the whole system. Now it serves twelve thousand. He earns more than the people who do his old job and at 73 has no plans to retire.

One way to do better is to switch sides. A troubleshooter for an elevator manufacturer went to work for the state as a safety **inspector** of passenger elevators. A retired Federal Aviation Administration (FAA) technician specializing in microwave communications has a challenging and freer second career with the base station of a mobile radio telephone service.

Skilled **mechanics** sometimes do better moving to an industry or company that is growing. When the navy bought out the shop, a machinist who had been making parts for offshore oil-drilling machinery for twenty-six years answered a Boeing ad and went to work machining parts for airplane fittings. "Nothing is permanent," he says, "but I would prefer the day shift."

Meanwhile, in New Jersey, when an aircraft plant closed, a maintenance welder with thirty-two years seniority answered an ad for a similar job in a chemical plant. The pay is better on the new job and "they don't throw old-timers out," but he doesn't like the toxic fumes he has to inhale.

Your craft skill could lead to stabler and better-paid white-collar work. One route is education. In Albany, a mechanic laid off by a trucking company helps set up exhibits for the Albany Institute of History and Art. In New York City, a former sheet metal mechanic enjoys working with students as a technician in the laboratory of a technical college. The ad he answered led to a job that pays more than he made on the bench in a shop.

Another route is liaison between the shop and the front office. When a dragline assembly plant went out of business, the pattern maker who had informally worked with the plant manager, the engineers, and the purchasing agent got a job as the salaried purchasing agent for a small assembler of big fifty-ton hauling vehicles.

Selling products like the ones you've made is still another way out and up. When the lead operator in a petrochemical plant was laid off, he went to work as a sales rep for another chemical company. If you've been a printer, you could sell classified ads. And anyone who has been a mechanic can use that knowledge selling parts as a counter clerk.

But plants close. Technologies change. Except in very big companies, production people don't stay in the same job with the same company to normal retirement, and as they get older, they are often looking for less work rather than more pay and responsibility. When Roy Griffith retired as an electrical **foreman** for Shell Oil he had no problem working when he wanted to as an electrical superintendent on construction jobs.

It sometimes makes personal sense to move down to work you formerly supervised. Milton Davis missed the citrus-packing house he used to run, so at 70 he went back to work full time maintaining it at $6 an hour, even though it meant taking orders where he had formerly given them.

When his children needed more help than he could afford on his retirement pay, a former manager of a glass and metal plant got a job estimating the glass entrances and metal work on a skyscraper for the company supplying it. He likes seeing the building go up, but he keeps his hours down so he doesn't lose any of his Social Security.

Troubleshooting and special projects are natural assignments for experienced older hands. After his retirement, the shop **foreman** of a management service for car dealers was asked to stay on, part time, to do unusual repair and modification jobs. At 77 the former superintendent of a manufacturer of the universal joints used in automobiles and other machines was helping the president of a manufacturer of automobile replacement parts develop new machines and processes.

Retired **factory managers** can often get part-time or temporary work that keeps them within the Social Security limitation in warehousing, quality control, repair work, estimating, or troubleshooting. At 67, the former owner of an electronics repair facility earned as much as he was allowed doing television repairs by the hour part time for Sears.

One way to continue the work you've done is to go into business for yourself. An assembler laid off after twenty-six years with a manufacturer customizing golf clubs now does it for the customers directly. Wesley Waite likes wood veneers, so he went into selling them as a manufacturer's agent when the plywood plant he managed was sold. James Sneller left his job managing the manufacture of test equipment to start up a little business, manufacturing, selling, renting, and repairing roller skates.

Finally, retired mechanics may turn their hands to lower-key, pleasanter, and more flexible work outside of a big factory setting. A mold maker works part time, at his own pace, making molds for a company that manufactures model trains. Skill with your hands makes you a natural to repair the recreational gear of other people who share your hobby. Skiers gladly pay $20 an hour to someone who can tune up their skis. In Houston, a retired tool and die maker works part time at home repairing fishing tackle. His main problem is that he spends so much time getting others ready to go that he doesn't have enough time to go fishing himself.

The most exciting second career for production people is lending your American know-how to fledgling operations in emerging nations overseas. Frank Neal thought he would be selling real estate and playing golf when he retired as manager of a General Electric plant. Instead, GE tapped him to advise their plants and licensees on every continent. He works less than twenty weeks a year at $30 an hour.

In third world countries without a trained labor force, an American foreman can do more good than a high-flown "consultant." If you know how to operate a commercial sewing or shoe machine, you may be able to help an underdeveloped community build its first industry. If you are willing to volunteer, talk to the International Executive Service Corps in Stamford, Connecticut, a volunteer organization that matches retired American managers and technicians with requests for help. In the eighties they sent a lot of volunteers to Africa. They expect to be sending more to former Communist countries in the nineties.

But you don't have to travel that far to pass on your skill. There's a younger generation that needs to learn it right here at home. As a nation, we've looked down on people who teach blue-collar work as well as those who stay in it, and with a few exceptions, such as the telephone company, American companies have taken a short-term view of training their workers.

These shortcomings create opportunities for older craftspeople to be of real service. In Pennsylvania, a retired maintenance foreman for a steel company who came back to manage an apprenticeship program found it hard to get craftspeople to teach in it. "They don't know that they know it," he says, "but they're better teachers than the engineers and college professors who try to teach craftspeople at community colleges."

If you're a skilled craftsman, you can be part of the solution to this problem. Ask about a second career as a teacher at your union, major employers of your skill, high schools, trade schools, and community colleges. You may find that a former employer has an employer-union apprenticeship program or a company training program. You might find a job teaching your craft in one of the special training schools maintained by the armed forces.

Training has always been a high priority in Japanese industry, so you might even get a job teaching in one of the factories they are "transplanting" to the United States. After his early retirement from Union Carbide, a quality-assurance **inspector** has been teaching basic electricity and the "right attitude toward maintenance" at the Toyota plant in Lexington, Kentucky.

If you don't want a second career as a teacher, you can help to raise respect for your craft by talking it up to younger people. Governor Mario Cuomo of New York State regards this role as so important that he has created a Skilled Worker Emeritus Program under which exemplary workers from trades such as sheet metal working are invited to talk about their work to schoolchildren, adults searching for careers, teachers, guidance counselors, and civic associations.

NICHES FOR NEWCOMERS TO PRODUCTION

Retired military officers sometimes become **factory managers**. Some civil servants and professionals have had enough administrative experience to run the second shift of a small factory or a routine operation such as the printing and binding of Bibles. With few exceptions, however, factories are run by people who have had long experience in their particular type of industrial production. The exceptions are usually newcomers with experience in a related profession.

One niche for professionals is the management of **quality control**. The new emphasis on quality has made it an attractive second career for scientists, engineers, and technicians laid off or forced into early retirement. In Minnesota, for instance, a former senior programmer has become what he calls a "flunkie" operating a computer-controlled testing machine for an air and hydraulics filter company. He got the $7-an-hour job through an instructor at a local technical institute and finds it somewhat boring except for the associated computer programming.

Working for an international inspection service is more varied. In Lubbock, Texas, a chief chemist forced into early retirement checks the quality, quantity, and packaging of shipments to overseas purchasers. Working from a list of what to look for, he has visited producers of fire-fighting sprinklers, steer hides, carbon black, and grain, among diverse other products. He gets only $9 an hour, but he likes the job because it gets him out of the retirement community to which he has moved and into the "real" world.

Pat Jetton was looking for something to do after she sold her airport flying school in Colorado, so she inteviewed for the job of part-time typesetter on a little biweekly newspaper, with no experience to recommend her beyond typing. As production supervisor, she now runs the whole show — composing, typesetting, camera, ad design and pasteup, pressroom, contract printing, and special sections. Her advice: "If you're honest about your limitations as well as your talents your employer may see something you didn't know you had."

What about starting **your own factory**? If you want to start manufacturing something late in life you'd better think small, be willing to get your own hands dirty, and find a product that's very special, like making sausages according to a family recipe or building concrete burial vaults (see page 180).

Gerald Hazen is a retired airline pilot who runs his own little winery in the Napa Valley above San Francisco, but he bought the ten acres for a song back when it was a goat farm and started planting it while he was still flying. It took five or six years before he got a crop worth using, and another year and a half to get the bond from the state required for selling the wine — plenty of time for him to learn all about the process at the University of California at Davis.

Think twice before you plunge into manufacturing an invention you have made. Even if the item is small, it can be a risky business. Boutiques could sell the magnetic earring fastener a retired nurse developed to help older women manage getting their earrings on and off, but she gave it up when she discovered that it would cost thousands of dollars to gear up for producing enough to sell through a mail-order catalogue.

You're on sounder ground with a **handicraft**, something you can enjoy making at home with your own hands. There's a world of things to choose from: furniture; birdhouses, birdfeeders, clothes trees; stained glass; metalworking; stuffed animals; paper toys; dolls, doll clothes, dollhouses, dollhouse furniture; quilts, rugs, children's clothes, knitted hats, and sweaters.

The more special your **hobby**, the better. A former printer produces switches and crossings for model street cars and sells them to model railroad hobbyists all over the world. A retired teacher designs and makes clothes for square dancers all over the United States, Canada, and Australia. Another former teacher makes campaign buttons for candidates and reunions. A third paints and sells wooden storybook characters. A former bookkeeper makes arrowhead jewelry from flint.

You may be able to find a paying hobby that grows out of the work you used to do. At 75, a stunt man retired by a couple of freak accidents makes special-effects models for Hollywood film studios. Usually, however, there's no connection at all. A former Central Intelligence Agency employee who says she was really only a secretary spins and knits angora garments from her own pet rabbits. An engineer retired from the Environmental Protection Agency makes and sells grandparent dolls, which he hopes will help bridge the gap between generations.

In the Bay Area of California, a woman retired from forty years of selling newspaper ads makes hats, veils, and corsages for a wedding shop. Further south, in El Monte, a woman who used to run a sewing machine for a manufacturer of horse blankets, saddles, and haystack covers makes baby quilts or whatever she pleases and often sells them to people in her senior citizens' group. She's 77.

What do they get out of it? "It's creative," says a cabinetmaker who makes copies of classical furniture by hand. "I can pick and choose the furniture I want to build for a client."

Control. People. "The freedom of my time is better than all the pay in the world" says a home economics teacher who makes miniatures for dollhouses. "I love the people who enjoy little things," she adds. "Mean, cruel people don't spend time with dollhouses, so all I see are smiling faces."

The downside is finding customers, long hours, and a low return for time spent on handwork, which has to compete with cheap, factory-made foreign imports. "My work is always new and beautiful," says the lady with the angora rabbits, "but $5 an hour is excessive compared with 22 cents an hour for Chinese factory workers who operate machines."

A few earn almost enough to live on from their work. The dollhouse furniture maker started selling her miniatures retail and through shows, but now grosses more than $20,000 a year through wholesalers. In Alaska, a former insurance broker adds about $20,000 a year to his retirement income building furniture, clock cases, bowls, and other items out of fine hardwoods, which he hopes will one day become cherished heirlooms. But in Arkansas, a retired public relations director who makes Shaker-style furniture is content to earn $5,000 a year for fifteen hours a week in his home workshop.

Most expect only to supplement a retirement income. A former salesman, now a blacksmith "when I want to be," has a wife who is a seamstress when she wants to be. They use the extra money to take trips they couldn't afford on his Social Security, veteran's benefits, and investments. A few years ago, a woman who used to work for Kodak in Rochester was selling little dolls that took twenty hours to make for $6.

Marketing is a problem. You can sell your homemade wares through fairs, local boutiques, mail order, networks of hobbyists, and satisfied customers, but it's hard to keep loaded with just the amount of work you want to do. Unlike mass producers, you can't do much to increase production. "Two years behind in my orders," a wood-carver reports cheerfully. "I could earn much more if necessary."

About a third of the people who think of their craft hobby as a second career don't even try to make money out of it. Some hope only to break even. A former teacher who makes toys "when, as, and if the spirit moves me" complains about the money he has to spend on materials and equipment. But so many gladly spend on their hobby that home craftwork supports a far-flung community of suppliers, teachers, publications, distributors, and associations. If you want to get into it, you can usually find an organization or a publication for the craft you are considering.

Of course, you don't have to manufacture something new to work with your hands. Factories depend on a corps of mechanics, installers, and repairers to keep their machinery up and running. Homes and businesses have a harder time keeping all their miscellaneous gear in repair. If you like to tinker, you can find a rewarding second career in fixing the growing number of things that are always getting broke.

You don't have to stick to **repairing** a product you used to make or sell. If you're mechanically inclined and starved for work with your hands, you can join the community of retired people who make a little extra money setting up locks, tuning pianos, altering clothes, cleaning carpets, or sharpening saws and knives.

Locksmithing work grows with crime. It appeals to retired or disabled military, police, and fire fighters, but there are trade schools and correspondence courses through which anyone with the patience can become a certified locksmith. Thomas DeMaria had learned to pick locks when he was a federal law enforcement agent, so he took the locksmithing course before retiring from the navy and was able to earn $90 a week for fifteen to twenty hours of work at home and in the van he set up for his shop.

Piano tuning is a service that appeals to people who like music and meeting other people with the same interest. An air force fighter pilot learned piano tuning through a correspondence course when he found out how much it would cost to have his wife's four pianos tuned. Now he tunes pianos for stores, churches, and colleges all over Georgia. A retired school psychologist has been able to add $10,000 a year to his income tuning pianos in an upscale suburb of Washington, but many earn much less. As a tuner in Springhill, Louisiana, complains, it's a nonessential service.

Locksmiths and piano tuners get a lot of their business through listings in the yellow pages and ads in neighborhood papers. Cleaning carpets, altering clothes, and fixing home appliances are among the many other repair services that are hard for homeowners to find. If you want this work, try ads in neighborhood papers or notices on the community bulletin boards maintained by supermarkets or shopping centers.

Repairing is especially attractive if the things repaired are connected with recreation or a hobby. If you're interested in antique **clocks** you may enjoy repairing them and taking courses in horology to prepare for this work. If you like to tinker, you've probably taught yourself how to fix the things you commonly use. It could be golf carts, boats, or jewelry, books that need to be rebound, furniture that needs to be repaired or refinished, or projectors and videotape equipment.

The best way to make a little money out of repairing things is to buy them when they're broken and sell them after you've fixed them, like the former service manager for the Ginsberg Music Company who makes a second career of "refinishing all the rich people's old junk." Restoring antique automobiles takes a little more space and capital. You have to pay something for the old junkers and you'll need equipment that is expensive because the special wrenches and other tools can't be used on modern cars. But once you've fixed them, you can sell them at fancy prices to wealthy collectors.

Buying, fixing, and reselling wheelchairs is a second career that will give you the satisfaction of helping disabled and elderly people cope with a disgraceful glitch in our health care system. Richard Daley was shocked at the price of the wheelchair he had to buy for his aged mother. As a retired mechanical engineer, he knew that the medical aid companies were making outrageous profits that keep Medicare costs high. He now buys up wheelchairs, potty chairs, walkers, and canes, and fixes them in a shop he's built in his backyard. He gets customers by selling this secondhand equipment for less than the 20 percent of the price that Medicare doesn't reimburse. He isn't getting rich, but he earns $10 an hour and the undying gratitude of the families he's helped.

Is production work for you? Psychologists like to divide people into those primarily interested in words, people, or things. If you're a thing person, you have a choice of many careers that deal with objects. The trick is to find something that you really enjoy doing, even if the pay is disappointingly low.

☑ TRANSPORTATION

We love our wheels. Every year we clock more miles per person per year. Some of this travel is by plane, train, bus, limousine, and taxi, but most of it is in private cars. Moving people is something we do for ourselves.

The big money is in moving *things,* and there's a lot to move. Fresh bread, the morning paper, the book we ordered over the phone, the gasoline in the service station, the soft drink in the vending machine, the medicine the doctor prescribed — some of the things we expect to find everywhere still move by train, and occasionally by air or sea, but most of our standard of living comes to us on wheels.

The trucking system that delivers it all was created by the free market competition of thousands of relatively small trucking lines of various sizes, lengths, rates, and capacities, some of them single trucks owned by their operators. Heavy goods move long distances over the road in trailers drawn by semis that keep going night and day, with drivers taking turns driving and sleeping. Even prefabricated houses arrive on a trailer, ready to be assembled.

Commodities move in big tank trucks designed to hold oil, gasoline, milk, and even water. There are trucks designed to transport cars, lumber, cement, produce, mail, soft drinks, household goods, and parcels. Huge cranes, bulldozers, loaders, scoops, shovels, graders, ditchers, and other heavy equipment move earth and materials for construction, mining, and manufacturing. Models of these specialized trucks and material-movers are favorite toys for children.

Delivery trucks of various sizes and shapes run regular trips delivering daily necessities to every hamlet where people buy them. We haul most of what we buy home in our own cars, but some local merchants still maintain trucks to deliver flowers, drugs, and dry cleaning, and messenger services operate fleets of cars for moving small items like documents, X rays, blueprints, or spare parts that can't wait for the mail.

Driving all these vehicles is one of the few well-paid occupations open to people with less than a high school education. All drivers need to be healthy, strong, tactful, careful people who can be trusted to follow regulations without supervision. They have to keep cool in heavy traffic, obey safety rules, and learn the varying regulations of the jurisdictions in which they operate.

Taxi drivers have to be licensed by the municipality, which usually requires a clean police record and a knowledge of locations in the area. **City bus drivers, school bus drivers, and heavy truck drivers** have to qualify for a state commercial driver's license, which requires them to pass a physical examination and written and road tests. Training is usually provided by the bus line or the school board.

Taxi drivers are in partnership with the cab company. They pay the company a "gate" amount for the use of the cab during the shift, reimburse them for the gas they burn, and keep the rest, including the tips. The driver of a limousine chartered by the hour gets 20 percent of the charter price, normally $6 or $7 an hour plus tips.

Pay of city bus drivers depends on unionization and city size. In Minneapolis, where the bus drivers are unionized, pay is over $13 an hour, but in a small place like Cottonwood, California, it may be as little as $6.

The highest-paid drivers are the operators of material-moving equipment covered by unions. Long-distance truck drivers are paid by the mile, local drivers by the hour, and **route drivers**, who also sell to stores, may be paid in part by commission. Median weekly pay for driver sales workers in 1990 was $438. **Heavy truck drivers** earned $430 and **light truck drivers** earned $321. Weekly earnings for **bus drivers** was $354, for **chauffeurs** $308, and for **messengers** $315.

SECOND CAREERS FOR EXPERIENCED TRANSPORTATION WORKERS

What happens to railroad men when they retire? Most take their pensions and scatter to other occupations. A few drive heavy equipment or a limousine. But one female railroad clerk achieved in retirement the post that railroads had long denied to women. She became a **yardmaster**, coordinating the movement of railcars for Dow Chemical.

Meanwhile, at 75, a retired male yardmaster was running the engine and punching tickets on the little Nut Tree Railway, a tourist attraction in Vacaville, California. Another recruited to tourism is a conductor retired from the Pennsylvania Railroad who looked for and landed a job driving a bus for the Gettysburg Tour Center. He adds $650 a month to his railroad pension and gets a chance to continue kidding with passengers.

Victor Murray wanted to "keep my hands and mind in a business I grew up in." When Gulf Oil closed its Philadelphia barge operations, he took early retirement from his job as **coordinator of marine**

operations and went to work dispatching barges for a bulk petroleum-moving service.

Pilots don't like to stay put. At 70, a retired airline pilot was feeding his habit of travel by writing for travel magazines. He likes everything about his second career except the "poor coffee in Turkey."

Air force and airline pilots can legally be grounded because of age, but you can continue flying freight, charters, or unscheduled or foreign airlines as long as you can pass the tough physical examination you have to take to renew your commercial license every year (20/20 vision with or without glasses, good hearing, and no heart disease, diabetes, or epilepsy).

Flying occasional charters pays about $125 a day. You can ferry businessmen and sightseers on short hops, spray herbicides on vegetable crops, or fly an airwatch helicopter reporting traffic conditions in a metropolitan area. And you can always give flying lessons.

Some pilots will do anything to stay flying. Fritz Fulton survived two mandatory retirements. After twenty-three years in the air force, he got a job testing planes for NASA. But NASA won't let a pilot fly alone after he's 61, so Fulton retired again and went to work testing prototypes of experimental planes for a small private company. He admits his reflexes aren't as fast as they were when he was flying bomber missions in Korea, but he's better at staying out of sticky situations.

Driving is almost as addictive. There's an interesting gender difference in the second careers of experienced drivers: women, most of them school bus drivers, tend to move to other work, but a majority of men stay in the driver's seat of some kind of vehicle. If you want to continue you can get less strenuous part-time work driving a school bus, a charter bus, a taxi, or a van delivering mail, drugs, airline tickets, flowers, spare parts, or pizza.

Over-the-road truckers and intercity bus drivers continue driving beyond normal retirement age, often moving to smaller vehicles. At 74, a freight handler who used to load and unload the freight he drove was driving a school bus at $6 an hour and loving everything about it except the weather. At 73, a retired long-distance trucker supplemented his small teamster's pension as a **courier** driving for a mechanical contractor, where they "treat me like a king." At 72, a former milk **delivery man** was transporting special education students in a small van.

One 70-year-old who used to drive one of those big soft-drink trucks was delivering flowers ("weddings must go on in all kinds of weather"). Another who used to drive a tractor-trailer was delivering machine parts in a van. A former long-distance driver continued to do local hauling ("anything to do in trucking") at the age of 82. All worked part time except the courier who was treated like a king.

Money has something to do with this love affair. For those with limited education, truck driving is the best-paying job they can get, so ill health doesn't stop them. An owner-operator who lost his truck after a heart attack ("it does not pay to own a truck") was back working for a truck line on an over-the-road team and hating it only because his teammate smoked and he wasn't driving his own semi.

Accidents don't stop them. A driver who wrecked three grocery trucks the year he was 64 was driving for the Safety Cab Company when he was 72.

Unruly teenagers don't stop them. A retired Greyhound driver finds some of the children on his school bus hard to handle, and he's getting only $5 an hour, but he still says "I love driving a bus."

A trucker who "retired" by moving down to a smaller truck works as an owner-operator for a "drive-away" company, which transports RVs (recreational vehicles) over the road. Drive-away companies hire drivers who transport cars and trucks by driving them as well as by towing them, and pay can be based either on weight or on miles.

If you've been a truck or bus driver, a tour bus is easier to drive and the passengers more fun to haul than heavy freight or the patrons of bus lines. A former line driver who drives a tour bus loves getting to see all the sights himself, although the hours on the road sometimes get to be long. He is 72. To explore the possibilities, apply to the big tour operators (see page 330).

Or you could find work driving people your own age. One former bus driver earns $5 an hour transporting residents of a senior citizens' community, another drives the van that takes seniors to the doctor, while others volunteer with social agencies to drive shut-ins to stores.

Pilots and drivers who are willing to sit still may do administrative work in their field. One air traffic controller is doing research leading to better handling of airspace. If you're an experienced driver with a good safety record, for instance, you might get work training or checking the safety performance of drivers of a large bus or truck company, or investigating damaged freight. If you've been in construction, oil extraction, the phone business, or some other industry with vehicles of its own, you may find a physically easier second career in dispatching them.

There's a lot of work to be done in training (see Education).

Experienced **air traffic controllers** are in demand to train the new ones we badly need. And a great many people could use a little more instruction in driving a car, including a lot of people who are already driving (see page 158).

NICHES FOR NEWCOMERS TO TRANSPORTATION

Do you dream of flying? A few lucky people make a second career of it. A former housewife and math teacher in Tulsa got into it by slow, easy stages. She began by learning to fly for fun, moved on to advanced ratings, and as a former teacher, to flight instruction. Teaching led to flying charters for a contract pilot service, where she made the acquaintance of a small businessman who now retains her at $1,400 a month to fly his corporate plane wherever he needs to go on short notice. She has a lot of time to herself while waiting, but she has to stay close to the phone and some of the trips are long.

Do you dream of driving a big tractor-trailer, bowling over the road from your high perch with everything but your boss in sight? If you've never done it, there are trade schools where you can learn how to drive these monsters. All kinds of people have had a go at it for a while, including a 66-year-old minister of a metaphysical church in California. In Arizona, a woman took early retirement from marketing telephone systems for the phone company to buy a semi and hustle loads for it. In Texas, a dental technician retired from the air force earned more per hour than ever before driving a tractor-trailer between Dallas and Abilene every night for a food company. The only thing about it that bothers him is the wind.

Driving through big-city traffic at the wheel of a **public service bus** is confining and often unionized work that discourages older newcomers, but it can be a nicer job (and less money) in a smaller city. When Gene Fischer retired from Los Angeles to Reno he had no trouble getting hired. At 62 he works only two or three days a week, a break for the company which would otherwise have to pay time-and-a-half to drivers called in as substitutes.

More attractive to older newcomers is the job of driving the **school bus**. The hours are good not only for the mothers of schoolchildren who hold many of the jobs, but for anyone who likes free time at home during the middle of the day. Routes are usually assigned to drivers on the basis of seniority. For special education routes, you are assisted by an aide and have to know how to operate the lifts that accommodate wheelchairs.

Some older people like the occasional work of outings. In Ogden, Utah, a former school janitor who happened to have the required license when a driver didn't show up prefers to drive the football and basketball teams so he can root for the team at the game. You get better benefits if you work directly for the school board instead of for a school bus operator. The school board trains you, and you have to get a commercial driver's license and pass other tests before you start driving.

In addition to passing the tests, you have to be able to get along with kids. "If you enjoy your grandchildren and like driving you'll love it," says a man who used to own a wholesale ice-cream business. "You have to remember your route and the time you can afford at each stop." He has a bad back, but he passed the physical examination because his back doesn't interfere with his driving.

Kids are what's both good and bad about the job. If they get on your nerves, school bus driving isn't for you, but there are other driving jobs you might want to consider. You might look into driving for a ground transportation service that picks up and delivers airline passengers to airports. Your yellow pages or, better yet, a local travel agent will guide you to services that might employ you.

Less stressful than school bus driving are the many niches for newcomers in low-key, small-scale jobs driving people and things outside the regularly scheduled transportation systems. Most fun and most pay is the job of private **chauffeur**, driving an individual in his or her own car. One retired office manager drove a blind business owner to his various offices at $10 an hour for two years, but lost the job when he took time off for a vacation of his own. Openings are few and far between — about one ad every week or so in a big metropolitan center under the listing "chauffeur," "driver," or "part-time driver," so you have to be one of the first to answer.

The luxury **limousine** services listed in your yellow pages always need drivers and they like to keep stable retired people on call so that they can supply a car on short notice. You get to meet interesting people and participate in occasions such as weddings, funerals, and parties, and you can turn down assignments you don't like. One senior who likes the work refuses to pick up anyone who sounds like a drug dealer, saving his own luxury limousine from confiscation in the event of trouble with the police. He's especially leery of calls to pick up people living at an address that he knows is a welfare hotel.

Driving a **taxi** is a second career that appeals to older people in many different circumstances. Don Hennerman took a job as a cab driver in order to learn the streets of the beautiful little mountain town of Sedona, Arizona, when he moved there after retiring from his main career as an accountant. Two years later he was working as Sedona's finance director.

One of San Francisco's most successful **cab drivers** is the former owner of an employment service who wanted a complete change of occupation while recovering from an assault with intent to rape. "It's a different kind of stress," she says. "You can walk away from it when you walk away from your cab. The hours are long, but you are always meeting interesting new people and you're really your own boss."

On a good day, a San Francisco cab driver who knows where to be at each hour can take home as much as $150 a day. But it's not unknown to cruise all day without bringing home anything at all. The best part of the job is meeting interesting people; the worst, picking up drunks late at night from bars.

But people who need a ride are not always able to pay. To make our services work, drivers have to be found for people too young, too old, too sick, or too poor to have wheels of their own. Teenagers who get into trouble with the law have to be transported to courts. Senior or disabled citizens need some way of getting to shopping, concerts, meals, the doctor, the senior citizens' center, or club meetings.

All this driving is organized by churches or public and private social agencies, and seniors love to do it. In Chicopee, Massachusetts, a housewife who went to work as a driver for a special-needs bus service maintained by the state and school board has a full-time, $8.43-an-hour job routing and dispatching them. In Spokane, Washington, a former railroad engineer who takes the elderly shopping puts the $100 check he gets every month from Catholic Charities into the church collection basket. He says he likes getting away from the house to where he's appreciated.

Some drivers are paid as much as $5 an hour and drive a van or car provided by the agency, some are volunteers driving their own cars who may be reimbursed for gas and tolls. Relatives of cancer victims often volunteer to drive cancer patients to their treatments through a program organized by the American Cancer Society. The local hospital, United Way, or other social service clearinghouse can tell you where your driving is needed.

If you really want to be appreciated, volunteer to drive hot meals to shut-ins who may be so far off the beaten track that you have to use your sixth sense to find the address on the map. You can earn modest hourly pay from the social agency that provides this service in your area, or you can volunteer to do it. In Joplin, Missouri, a former college secretary has committed herself to drive five hundred hours for Meals on Wheels a year in addition to the volunteer work she does at the information desk of the hospital that sponsors the service. For opportunities in your area, call your local Office for the Aging or the United Way.

There's also a world of occasional driving at modest pay for private businesses. You can **deliver** for a local druggist, florist, or dry cleaner, but remember that cars have to be delivered, too. If you love driving all the new models, you may find work delivering them, moving them from dealer to dealer, driving them to and from car auctions, relocating the cars of an auto rental service, or even moving the "dirties" returned to the service area. Most of it is minimum-wage, part-time work you can get through a newspaper or a friend in the business.

You might enjoy running errands as a **courier, messenger,** or "gofer." Traditionally, the person retained to "go for" something forgotten or needed was a youngster learning the business. Now the "gopher," "go-fer," or "go-for" may be an oldster who likes being close to the action without taking the heat. In Rochester, New York, for instance, a retired instrument engineer for Eastman Kodak is a part-time, $5-an-hour processor of black-and-white films who is happy to "gofer things" for the local Bureau of Cooperative Educational Services (BOCES). He doesn't need the money, but he likes being around educated people.

In Sarasota, a retired navy chief picks up and delivers payroll data for a bookkeeping firm that does the payrolls of small merchants. Although it interferes with his golf, a retired elementary school teacher in Waukegan, Illinois, spends fifteen hours a week running interoffice mail for a bank. Stay tuned to the ads in the paper for part-time work at modest hourly pay delivering flowers for florists, prescriptions for drug stores, dry cleaning, auto parts for wholesalers, office supplies, or documents for lawyers.

Can you make money driving your own car? If you love big gobby vehicles but don't want to drive them yourself, you can earn $13 to $15 an hour piloting loads wider than eight feet. Apply directly to the permit companies that handle the legal arrangements for wide-load truckers in your area. If they hire you, they'll lend you the flashing lights and flags and tell you how to conform to the regulations of the jurisdictions the load will pass through. In Sunnyvale, California, a retired technician earns about $1,000 a month doing overnight as well as local hauls.

Most regular courier and light delivery services provide a company car, but you may be ahead of the game using your own wheels for work involving short local hauls. In Massachusetts, a retired lawyer figures he and his Escort wagon earn $10 an hour delivering local weekly papers to stores, gas stations, and banks along Route 128. It's ten hours of work he can do any time within a day or two of the deadline, and he likes the exercise of handling the bundles as well as the beer money it brings him. He knows he could develop it into a business if that's what he wanted.

The advantage of using your own car on a regular run is that you can pick up extra business as people come to know you. Dry ice is hard to transport because it evaporates in a matter of hours. A navy chief whose run goes by a dry ice factory every day picks up this volatile commodity and delivers it to hospitals, shippers, and even gas stations, who use it to freeze out every vestige of gasoline in a tank condemned for leakage by the Environmental Protection Agency.

Courier work is one of the very few profitable businesses you can start with no more capital than your automobile. In Louisiana, a door-to-door salesman sold his business and contracted with a courier service to run some of their routes for 60 percent of its proceeds. He earns $32,000 a year.

If you like to be on the move and are happiest driving a vehicle, there's a second career you are going to like in transportation.

5. FINDING THE JOB

You've thought through what you want from a job. You have some clues about work that you are fitted to do. You've looked at the second careers of people with your experience and interests.

How do you go from here to an actual job?

STEP ONE: CAREER ADVICE

Jobs change so fast that no published book can hope to keep up with the opportunities. Talk with your friends and relatives and watch the newspapers to see what kind of jobs are being filled in your community.

Once you have a general idea of the kind of work you want, try browsing in the wealth of career information available at your library. Begin by looking in the card catalog or at the computer listings under "vocations" or "careers" and then under the specific field in which you'd like to work. In addition to these listings, the reference librarian may direct you to a "vertical file" or pamphlets and brochures about a field, trade and professional magazines covering it, and the annual reports of companies.

Not all of this material will be of equal value. Question career advice that sounds as if it were glamorizing the work, overstating the earnings, or exaggerating the opportunities to recruit you. Discount material more than two years old.

If you tell the reference librarian the kind of work you want, she may find additional information for you on videocassettes or in kits and computerized information systems. She will also have information for you on upcoming local programs that you may want to attend. Community colleges may offer low-cost seminars, short courses, and workshops where you can get individual counseling and advice on every aspect of the job search. Many local organizations put on job fairs, some of them for senior citizens, at which employers can meet job applicants.

Even if your plans are beginning to jell, it's a good idea to check them out with a career counselor who can help you clarify your goals, recommend tests, direct you to institutions where you can get the training you will need for the occupation you want, and suggest occupations that might suit you even better.

Career counseling is available free to everyone at the local office of your state job service or the career planning office of your local community college. Counseling services may also be offered by nonprofit community organizations such as the Y. Consult the community pages of your phone book for organizations to query.

You may also get counseling through a service provided by your church or synagogue, your professional association, labor union, or college, or a former employer that maintains an outplacement department for relocating separated employees. If you are disabled, you may get specialized help from a vocational rehabilitation agency.

Special counseling for older people may help you get the right job for you. For general information about their programs, consult the American Association of Retired Persons, Worker Equity Department (601 E St., NW, Washington, DC 20049; 1-202-434-2277) or the National Association of Older Workers Employment Services, c/o National Council on Aging (600 Maryland Ave., SW, Washington, DC 20049; 1-202-479-1200). For opportunities near you offered by all agencies, call the hot line of the Office for the Aging listed under state government numbers in the blue or government pages of your phone book.

Career advice for women is available in the literature and programs sponsored by the Women's Bureau of the U.S. Department of Labor (200 Constitution Ave., NW, Washington, DC 20210; 1-202-523-6611); Catalyst (250 Park Ave. S., New York, NY 10003; 1-212-777-8900); Wider Opportunities for Women (1325 G St., NW, Washington, DC 20005; 1-202-638-3143), or the Older Women's League (OWL) (730 11th St., NW, Washington, DC 20001; 1-202-783-6686).

Your community organization hot line or local Office for the Aging can tell you about employment advice available in your area. The kind of help these nonprofit social agencies provide may be limited to brochures sent on request, but some have programs of counseling, testing, advice on job searches, and occasionally job placement.

More elaborate but not necessarily more effective advice is available at a fee from private counseling services. Reputable private counseling services will be listed in the *Directory of Counseling Services,* available at your library or by sending a self-addressed, stamped envelope to the International Association of Counseling Services (IACS), 5999 Stevenson Ave., 3d Floor, Alexandria, VA 22304.

Wherever you are counseled, bring to the session a draft of your resume listing your job experience and schooling and the decisions you have made about what you want from a job at this stage of your life (see Chapter 2). You should come away with a better idea of the kind of work you would like, your marketable skills, an expanded list of target jobs, the cost-effectiveness of further training each requires, and some idea of how to go about locating training and jobs in your area.

STEP TWO: ADDITIONAL TRAINING

Is it worth your time and money to go back to school before you go hunting for a job for which you have no previous experience? If you don't have experience with computers, it's well worth your while to take one of the courses available for a modest fee through the adult education program of your local high school or community college. There will be few office jobs available for applicants who do not know the computer keyboard and how to use at least one software package.

For many semiskilled office and factory jobs your employer will train you during your first few days or weeks on the payroll. But even for these jobs, the level of your formal schooling is a credential because it shows that you can read, write, figure, and absorb further training.

If you do not have a high school diploma, by all means get one by taking the General Education Development (GED) examination. In most places it's free, and so are the special courses you may need to prepare for it. You can take them at night classes or at home. Someone at the office of your local public school system can tell you all about it.

But the jobs you have targeted may not be so simple. If you've been a salesman, you may have to go back to college to become a social worker. If you're a housewife with a bachelor of arts degree, you may have to go to a real estate school to become a licensed broker. If you've been a bookkeeper you may want to take the training that leads to work as a computer programmer.

If you possibly can, get more schooling or training. Even if specific training in the field isn't required for the job you want, it may give you an advantage over younger applicants whose training is older and improve your chances of being hired.

You'll get more than money out of going back to college. It's more fun the second time around, and some of the students will be your age. And don't let the money stop you. You may be eligible for financial aid. Laws prohibiting age discrimination apply to scholarships and student loans as well as to employment, but there are many programs and eligibility rules are complicated.

For a general view of financial aid through federal programs, consult the *Student Guide to Federal Financial Aid Programs,* updated annually, available by calling 1-800-333-4636 or writing to Federal Student Aid Programs, P.O. Box 84, Washington, DC 20044. For aid available under state programs, write or phone the State Department of Education in your state capital.

The best plan is to determine the school you wish to attend first, and then find out from their counselors what kind of financial aid is available to you. Appendix C tells you some of the places where you can find out about the training you'll need, but you may have to get the specifics from a career counselor. Occupations requiring a license, such as real estate broker or nurse, usually require prescribed courses or college credits plus supervised internship, which often leads to job offers.

Education and training is offered in many settings. There are different kinds of public and private degree-granting colleges, an even greater variety of public and private vocational and technical schools, and a trackless jungle of special-purpose, occasional short courses, seminars, and workshops offered under private and public auspices. It's better to start shopping for training at your local community college. If they don't offer what you need, they can tell you where to go for it, and they usually have the catalogs of other institutions from which you can check a description of the courses, admission requirements, schedules, and tuition costs.

Four-year and two-year colleges offer professional and business training as well as academic degrees. If you are interested in qualifying for a license, such as for nursing, the career adviser may have a computer program that will pull up information on the institutions near you that offer it. If all you want to do is brush up on a skill you already possess, ask your adviser whether there is a short course, seminar, workshop, or continuing education course coming up that is just what you need.

Be sure that the course you take leads to the job you want. Delightful as they may be, courses older people are allowed to audit without credit, charge, or transcript usually have no vocational value. This is also generally true of the college programs specially designed for older people that are offered at a small fee on most college campuses through an association called Elderhostel.

Public vocational education schools offer specific job training in subjects such as word processing, clerical skills, nursing, and culinary arts. They may be sponsored cooperatively with employers under programs such as the federally funded, state-run regional vocational training centers, which give you a chance for hands-on experience leading to employment.

There are also proprietary business and trade schools. Some are worth the expense, but others may train for nonexistent jobs, give inadequate training, or merely duplicate the training an employer would give you after you were hired.

Private business schools offer programs in secretarial science, business administration, accounting, data processing, court reporting, paralegal studies, fashion merchandising, travel/tourism, culinary arts, drafting, and electronics, among other subjects. For approved institutions near you, call the Career College Association (P.O. Box 2006, Annapolis Junction, MD 20007-2006; 1-203-333-1021), successor to the Association of Independent Colleges and Schools (AICS), for listings in the new directory it is preparing.

Private trade and technical schools tend to be small, confined to a single trade such as cosmetology, office skills, flight training, real estate, auto worker, commercial art, or heavy truck driving. Tuition has to be high enough to yield the school a profit, so find out how many of their graduates they actually place in jobs and if possible talk to some former students before enrolling. Before laying out your money, check to be sure that the training is not available cheaper elsewhere, such as from an employer. To check on a trade school, call your state education department or the Career College Association (see above), successor to the National Association of Trade and Technical Schools, which is updating the *Handbook of Accredited Private Trade and Technical Schools*, formerly issued by NATTS.

Home study programs offer training by correspondence, augmented by videotapes, cassettes, and in some cases computer networks. For those in special circumstances, such as the housebound, the geographically isolated, or those whose activities preclude regular attendance, there are proprietary for-profit home study courses. Without leaving home or attending school, you can train for specific skills such as firearms or motorcycle repair, or licensed occupations such as travel agent. If this is a convenient way for you to learn, consult the *Directory of Accredited Home Study Schools* (National Home Study Council, 1601 18th St., NW, Washington, DC 20009; 1-202-234-5100). Call your state's education department to check the bona fides of any particular home study or proprietary trade school about which you have doubts.

In addition to established institutions, there are private, for-profit organizations which travel from community to community offering short courses, workshops, and one- or two-day seminars on specific topics such as sales training or tips on business writing. Prices are very high for the content delivered and the courses are aimed at employers who are willing to pay the tab for people already on the payroll.

STEP THREE: FINDING A JOB

When you are what the state employment people call "job ready" to look for an employer, the first thing you should do is to create a **resume** summarizing your qualifications, education, and employment history. There are books and even courses devoted to the resume, but start by getting all the relevant facts on a single page.

Your one-page basic resume should contain:

- Name, address, phone number

- Employment goal, in a phrase or sentence; e.g., "part-time work in bookkeeping"

- Skills listed under appropriate categories, stating under each your employers and what you accomplished on the job. If you've been a sales manager but also a sales clerk, lump the two jobs together under the skill heading "Sales." If you've been a bookkeeper on one job but a secretary on another, list the two employers under the heading "Office Skills." List what you did — your skill — rather than your title. Try to use the terminology of the field in which you are seeking employment to show that you are up-to-date. The idea is to spotlight your accomplishments rather than produce a chronological listing of jobs that focuses attention on dates. Include military service and volunteer jobs under their appropriate headings

- Special skills, licenses, honors, organizations

- Education, beginning with most recent or highest degree, giving school name, address, and dates of attendance

- References available on request

This basic resume contains the information you will need for filling out most employment applications, and it can be left with an employer on whom you call in person. You can organize your experience around a specific job opening in a personal letter of application.

Now you are ready to go looking for an employer. "Job Search" has become the title of courses in community colleges as well as of an industry. **Private job search counselors and outplacers** paid by former employers charge several thousand dollars to teach you how to look for a job, how to write a resume, and how to behave on an interview, and hold your hand while you do it, but they do not themselves locate an employer (see Human Resources).

This self-directed job search is taught to classes in community colleges and in short courses offered by the AARP and other agencies serving job seekers. The techniques are relatively straightforward, and while many people need support through the process, the actual work is something you can do for yourself with the help of books on the subject. The classic, now an annual, is *What Color Is Your Parachute?* by Richard Nelson Bolles.

Wherever you're counseled, the place to begin your search for an actual job should be with your friends and relatives. That's the way most jobs are filled. If you haven't looked for a job for years you may think you don't know anyone who could help you, but you are wrong. Everyone who knows your name and face knows scores of other names and faces, each of whom has still another set of acquaintances. Your **network** can be a powerful grapevine that sooner or later leads to someone who can lead you to what you want.

Networking is particularly important for older people. To begin with, your potential network is wider because you know more people, many of them people who know what you can do because they've worked with you on a job. Even more important, networking may be the only way to get exactly what you want. The plum jobs for older people seldom become advertised vacancies because they are snapped up by someone who hears about them before they get into the want ads or employment agencies.

If you're looking for more freedom and flexible hours in your own field, or a foothold in an occupation for which you have no direct experience, you have to look to small-scale, new, specialized, occasional work that doesn't go through the regular channels. The job you want may have no name, let alone a job description. You may even have to create it yourself. There are examples in the "Niches for Newcomers" sections of almost every job cluster described in chapter 4.

Books and seminars undertake to teach you how to network, but the principle is simple. Let everyone know what you want. Ask them about the jobs their own employers are trying to fill, or what they hear about the jobs available in places where their friends work. You aren't asking for a favor, you are asking for information people like to give and sharing information about yourself that people like to know and pass on.

Keep what you are looking for simple enough to say in a sentence: "I'm looking for a part-time bookkeeping job."

"I'm looking for an office job that will use my ability to speak and write Spanish."

"I'm going to give piano lessons to adults as well as children."

"We're selling the house and looking for a job managing an apartment building."

"I've been a surveyor and would like to go back to it."

Don't rule anybody out. Begin, of course, with the people in your union or professional association and your former employers. Then go on to people in your address book, the tradespeole who know you, the people in your church, synagogue, or club. Make a list of the places you'd like to work and share it with people on your list who may have friends who work there.

Mention your plan to everyone you see in person. Call up people you haven't seen for a while to say hello. And don't forget people who've worked for you in the past. A retired head nurse spent eleven happy years working as a bookkeeper for the head of a stitchery supply house who had once worked for her in the hospital.

Watch the **want ads**. Even if there's nothing interesting in them, you need to keep up with what employers need and what they are paying for skills comparable to yours. When you go to the library, the reference librarian can suggest professional and trade journals or newsletters and newspapers in neighboring towns that have ads, too. And don't neglect the local shopping paper that comes to your mailbox free. They often have just the occasional, part-time work for a small employer near your home that you are looking for. Their rates are so low that they are a good place for you to advertise through a situations-wanted ad of your own.

Look not only at the help-wanted ads, but the situations-wanted ads placed by people looking for a job. Would advertising for the job you want make sense for you? Remember that not all want ads are in publications. When you go to a church, shopping mall, supermarket, post office, or government office, glance at the help-wanted notices on their bulletin boards. These local sources are especially good for occasional, part-time work. If you want to work for the government, watch the bulletin boards of government offices for civil service announcements of openings or examinations for jobs for which you might qualify.

But don't pin your hopes on the ads. Some are deliberately vague about the work, the working conditions, the employer, or the pay. "No experience necessary" ads may be for low-paying commission work, or work undesirable in some other way. Watch out for want ads that demand money for information about the job, such as ads that ask you to send $10 to learn about the opportunity to stuff envelopes. Glowing descriptions may be for jobs placed by private employment agencies that expect to be paid for recruiting you. But if you find something interesting, answer it promptly. It may be filled before the ad stops running.

Private employment agencies are designed for people with specific skills and recent job experience. These agencies work for money; they charge the employer and/or the employee a percentage of the salary of jobs they fill. The law forbids them to discriminate on the basis of age, but the employers they serve are usually large-scale enterprises looking for promotable young people with scarce, highly paid technical or financial skills. Find out their fees and who pays them before you register. If you are the one who will have to pay, decide whether they really have access to jobs you couldn't locate on your own.

Executive searchers or **head hunters** find very highly paid executive or professional people for employers who may be hiring them to approach people already working for someone else. They have no time for talking with general job seekers. Unless you just happen to fill the order of a client they may not give you the time of day.

A **temporary employment service** is a private agency that acts as a labor contractor for employers. The national services such as Manpower and Kelly supply office, factory, and technical workers of every kind to employers who need extra help for a few days or weeks, but there are also many regional and national agencies specializing in professional skills such as drafting and accounting. Those near you will be listed in the yellow pages of your phone book under "Employment Contractors — Temporary Help." If you have a scarce skill such as computer-aided design (CAD) drafting or a marketable skill such as word processing, they may be able to place you with an employer right away.

Temp jobs have many advantages. For starters, they may pay better than the jobs you get for yourself, and if you work enough hours, they may even give you benefits. The system works against age, sex, or race discrimination because you get a chance to show what you can do before the employer decides he doesn't like your looks.

Finally, a good temp agency may be able to find or create exactly the schedule you want and you can always accept or reject each assignment. If there's a part of town you don't like, you can just say no to an assignment there. This is so attractive to older people who like new faces and places that retired office managers who used to contract for temps sometimes choose to work as temps themselves. And it's increasingly attractive to employers because they don't have to pay for employees when they don't actually need them.

If you are looking for a permanent part-time job, a series of temp assignments can serve as a guided tour of the local possibilities. When the fit is good on both sides, a temporary job can lead to a custom-tailored schedule. One retired supervisor gets all the office work for a little New England calendar company done in twenty-one hours a week and takes four months off every summer.

By far the best — and most underused — resource is your local **state job service**. Older people tend to shy away from their local job service because it makes them think of out-of-work people standing in line to collect unemployment insurance. But the state employment services offer a full range of services, from counseling and testing to actual placement, at no cost to you. Look for your office in the state government telephone listings under "Job Service," "Employment," or "Labor Dept."

When you register, an interviewer will determine whether you need counseling, testing, or further training. If you are ready for a job, you get to look at the Job Bank, a computerized listing of public and private sector job openings that is updated daily. From this roster, you can select openings that interest you, and get more details about them from a staff member who will set up an interview for you.

If the job service doesn't have the job you want, they can often tell you where to find it. Their staff people will know whether you are eligible for a government assistance program, such as those available under the Job Training Partnership Act to aid economically disadvantaged people facing barriers to employment. They will also alert you to public and private job-finding programs for seniors for which you may be eligible.

This sounds ponderous, and none of it may be necessary. Nothing beats applying in person. It's worth deciding where you'd like to work and then stopping by to let them know that you are interested. One new widow who went into a bank to open a savings account was recruited on the spot and went out with a job in the bank.

Routine jobs in government and big organizations are often filled from applications left by people who have come in looking for employment. If you apply at a hospital or store that is always short of help you may get hired almost immediately. Lengthen your list of places you'd like to work by scanning the yellow pages of your phone book and watching the business page of your local newspaper for word of new or expanding concerns that sound as if they would be hiring.

Direct application is the only way to create a job that does not exist. Don't just talk to your family about what you think you could do for some firm in town if only they had the sense to hire you. Tell that company about it. If you don't already know who could authorize your project, network through your acquaintance for the name of the person to see and get an appointment to discuss it. If necessary write a one-page letter stating in no more than one sentence what you'd like to discuss, and enclose your one-page resume.

If you apply cold to a big enterprise, you will be referred to a personnel office for an impersonal screening by people who have the authority only to prevent your application from reaching the person who could hire you. One way to get around them is to phone or write the department for which you would like to work and offer your skill on a contract or consulting basis. That's how a housewife created a job in community relations for a bank. Another way to get started is to volunteer your services for a special project.

You're in the driver's seat if you are looking for a job as a **volunteer**. Instead of allowing yourself to be recruited, decide what you want from a volunteer job and go hunting for it. You can find what your local community *needs* through the hot line of your United Way or similiar community organization, but there are organizations (see page 63) that match you with the kind of volunteer work that *you* want.

Before you sign up, find out exactly what you will be doing, what training you will get, and whether your expenses will be reimbursed. See the occupational cluster that you are interested in for examples of some of the volunteer work available.

STEP 4: NEGOTIATING ACCEPTANCE

Once you've secured an interview you are ready for the final step — deciding whether you want the job and negotiating it if the employer wants you. You may have been through this process many times and need only to use your common sense. If you haven't, look at the suggestions on page 175 for homemakers who have never worked for money before.

The interview is the most important step in getting the job. Prepare in advance by learning about the organization. If it's a big organization, the reference librarian at your local library may have an annual report or other data about it worth scanning. She may also be able to direct you to data on the pay ranges for the work you are seeking. Think about jobs in the organization you could do.

When you go to the interview, take along your Social Security number, your driver's license (or its number), and your resume. Arrive a little ahead of time and think about what you can say about yourself that applies to the job you will be discussing. Shake hands firmly, speak up and look the interviewer straight in the eye, and project an image of health and self-confidence.

You should be ready to answer questions about your resume, especially questions about how your previous jobs ended, and to elaborate on the duties of your past jobs, especially duties that illustrate that you are cooperative and conscientious. Respond to probes for the gaps in your employment truthfully, but accentuate the positive. This is no time to beef about how badly a former employer treated you.

Now is your chance to demonstrate the qualities that make your years a plus instead of a minus. Tell what you learned from a previous job. It may have been patience in a trying situation. The job — or some other event you may be willing to share — may have taught you to get along with all kinds of people. A prospective employer wants to know what experience you have had in giving and taking instructions and in managing time and money, and you can convey these qualities best in anecdotes about previous jobs.

Answer questions promptly, truthfully, and concisely or politely refuse questions you don't want to answer that have no bearing on the job. You aren't required to give your age, race, color, religion, or marital status, or answer questions about your health that do not relate directly to your ability to do the job in question. But there's no law against volunteering personal information that may help you.

You don't have to give your age, but you can always mention an active sport in which you participate. You don't have to give your marital status, but you can mention that you intend to remain in the area because you own a house or your grown children live nearby. And don't forget to talk about special interests and hobbies that demonstrate a quality that may be relevant to the job. Stamp collectors have to be good at detail. Genealogists have to know something about libraries. Leaders in church work have to know how to get along with people. Play it by ear as the conversation proceeds.

Ask questions that show that you are informed about the organization and your field and take a responsible interest in what you are getting into. If pay has to be negotiated, try to get the interviewer to state a range, or give a range yourself if asked for the minimum you will accept. And whatever the outcome, write a short letter thanking the interviewer for her time as soon as you get home.

Don't be discouraged when you're turned down. Job hunting is a job in itself, and you may have to work at it every day for a couple of months to get just what you want. Getting a job takes more time when the economy is slow, and outplacers who track the time it takes to relocate older executives and professionals document that it takes them longer than younger jobseekers.

Does this mean that your age is going to be a problem in finding a job? About 13 percent of all the respondents to our survey thought so, and the percentage was higher for technical specialists in their 50s forced into a second career by early retirement. But not all the problems of age discrimination are within the meaning of laws prohibiting it.

The Age Discrimination in Employment Act (ADEA) does not cover workers over 70 or employers with fewer than twenty workers. It generally prohibits hiring, firing, compensation, fringe benefits, and job advertising on the basis of age, but not criteria that may be age-related. An employer can't advertise for a "recent college grad" but there are many gray areas, such as requiring specific training that few older applicants will actually have. A court would have to decide whether the requirement was intended to get around the law.

If you think you have a case, is it worth pursuing? The quick answer is you're probably better off forgetting the damages you could win and getting another job. But if you have good documentation of a violation and you are mad as hell about it, talk to the Equal Employment Opportunity Commission (1801 L St., NW, Washington, DC 20507-0001; 1-800-872-3362); the AARP Worker Equity Department (601 E St., NW, Washington, DC 20049; 1-202-434-2040); or the National Senior Citizens Law Center (2025 M St., NW, Washington, DC 20036; 1-202-887-5280) for the nearest office to discuss your case. While waiting for them to respond, try to find a lawyer supplied free by a local legal services agency you can find in the white pages of your phone book or by asking someone at the local bar association.

If you are thinking of suing a large, national corporation, you may get quicker relief by addressing the equal employment officer in its corporate human resources department, especially if you can cite a provision in the company's own employee handbook that you think has been violated. Write a one-page letter addressed to "Equal Opportunity Officer" describing the injury in one sentence, and listing the kind of evidence you have in no more than two or three sentences.

To sum up, think of your job hunt as an adventure in learning about future possibilities. It can be as much fun as window shopping or house hunting. The second time around, you are in a better position to anticipate those futures. That's the advantage of life experience.

AVOIDING AGE DISCRIMINATION

In job hunting:

Seek employers who are

    small or new
    recruiting seniors
    selling/serving seniors
    using temporaries/part timers

On resumes:

    Omit age/irrelevant dates
    Omit photographs
    Omit earliest jobs
    List recent training/jobs

On job interviews:

Don't talk about

    why you were retired early
    why you are "overqualified"
    faults of young people
    age, pro or con

Do talk about

    recent training
    hobbies/active sports
    your specific experience
    what you've done
    concerns of interviewer

On the job:

Don't talk about age

Do volunteer

    for further training
    for challenging tasks
    to mentor newcomers

Prevent age discrimination by

    knowing your rights
    refusing to waive them
    asking how performance is judged
    recording your job performance
    volunteering for training
    seeking challenging tasks

APPENDIX A

THE RESULTS OF CAROLINE BIRD'S QUESTIONNAIRE IN *MODERN MATURITY* MAGAZINE

WHAT'S YOUR SECOND CAREER? (6347)

1. Why do you continue to work?
2. Which is the MOST important reason? (6152)

Like working (1089)	18%
Like to be with people (647)	11%
Keep busy (1064)	17%
Help others (473)	8%
Money (2312)	38%
Other (566)	9%

3. Have you had problems in continuing to work? (6320)

1. No (4385)	69%
2. Yes (1935)	31%

   (circle all that apply)*

a. Finding work (734)	38%
b. Discrimination (807)	42%
c. Social Security income limitation (539)	28%
d. Schedule (154)	8%
e. Pay (480)	25%
f. Other (357)	18%
g. Health, self (193)	10%
h. Health, others (8)	<1%

(Number of people who responded to the question is in parentheses.)
*Some respondents checked more than one answer so percentages total more than 100%.

4. At what age do you plan to quit working? (6147)

Never/Until death	15%
Don't know	30%
As long as health permits	8%
73 or more	11%
66 to 72	13%
63 to 65	12%
56 to 62	9%
55 or under	<1%

5. What is your present job? (6346)

The Money Business (757)	12%
Public Policy (85)	1%
Military Service (1)	0%
Public Service (222)	3%
Social Work (127)	2%
Religion (79)	1%
Science, Engineering, and Technology (174)	3%
Library and Research Work (57)	1%
The Word Business (257)	4%
The Visual and Performing Arts (142)	2%
Real Estate and Insurance (342)	5%
Law and Enforcement (85)	1%
The Health Business (204)	3%
Housing and Construction (94)%	1%
Education (393)	6%
Personal Caregiving (179)	3%
Homemaking (0)	0%
Your Own Business (25)	<1%
Human Resources (59)	1%
Purchasing (8)	<1%
Business Services (825)	13%
Hospitality (210)	3%
Travel and Recreation (175)	3%
Sales and Marketing (300)	5%
Retailing (538)	8%
The Outdoors (161)	3%
Production (70)	1%
Transportation (291)	5%

6. Do you like this job? (circle one) (6316)

1. Yes, love it	64%
2. Yes, well enough	31%
3. No, not much	4%
4. No, hate it	1%

7. How long have you had this job? (circle one) (6336)
   1. Less than six months   10%
   2. Six months to a year   12%
   3. Over a year   79%
8. Is your job (circle one number) (6343)
   1. Full time   41%
   2. Part time   47%
   3. Part year   11%
9. Do you work at home? (6296)
   1. No   73%
   2. Yes   27%
10. How much do you now earn? (4933)
   1. Under $9,999   46%
   2. $10,000–$19,999   25%
   3. $20,000–$34,999   17%
   4. $35,000–$49,999   6%
   5. $50,000 +   6%
11. How did you get your present job? (circle one) (6320)
   1. Newspaper ad (1473)   23%
   2. Employment agency (316)   5%
   3. Friend or relative (1488)   23%
   4. Former employer (464)   7%
   5. Started own business (1169)   18%
   6. Other (370)   6%
   7. Applied or went in and asked (732)   12%
   8. Was recruited (273)   4%
   9. Went back to school (75)   1%
   10. Began as volunteer (115)   2%
   11. Natural outgrowth (354)   6%
12. What, if anything, do you like about your job*
   People, friends   32%
   The work itself   25%
   Challenge, use talents   21%
   Helping others   18%
   Freedom, little supervision, own boss   13%
   Like being in labor force   7%
   Keep busy   9%
   Money, benefits   8%
   Like hours or flexibility   8%
   Like place of work   6%
   Recognition, status   4%
   Like management   3%
   Low stress, little responsibility   3%

Work is outdoors	2%
Like nothing	1%

13. Every job has its drawbacks. What are the disadvantages of yours? (5821)*

The work itself	19%
Schedule, not enough time off	18%
Low pay, too few benefits	16%
No disadvantages	13%
Overworked, too stressful	10%
Getting to work, transportation	7%
Management	7%
Don't like the people	6%
Too little work	5%
Physical problems, too much standing or lifting	5%
Environment, place of work	4%
Boring	2%
Lack of recognition, challenge	2%
Age discrimination	1%
Lack of freedom, too much supervision	1%

14. What was your longest job? (6347)

The Money Business (1044)	16%
Public Policy (83)	1%
Military Service (306)	5%
Public Service (227)	4%
Social Work (71)	1%
Religion (55)	1%
Science, Engineering, and Technology (329)	5%
Library and Research Work (40)	1%
The Word Business (133)	2%
The Visual and Performing Arts (85)	1%
Real Estate and Insurance (209)	3%
Law and Enforcement (62)	1%
The Health Business (256)	4%
Housing and Construciton (107)	2%
Education (664)	10%
Personal Caregiving (39)	1%
Homemaking (151)	2%
Your Own Business (78)	1%
Human Resources (86)	1%
Purchasing (18)	<1%
Business Services (804)	13%
Hospitality (148)	2%
Travel and Recreation (45)	1%

Sales and Marketing (433)	7%
Retailing (394)	6%
The Outdoors (88)	1%
Production (275)	4%
Transportation (103)	2%

15. How did this job end? (6302)
    1. Retired voluntarily (2653) — 42%
    2. Company closed, merged, reorganized (670) — 11%
    3. Quit, moved, got pregnant or married (1618) — 26%
    4. Involuntary, forced retirement (173) — 3%
    5. Fired, laid off (304) — 5%
    6. Sold business of your own (254) — 4%
    7. Medical — self (284) — 5%
    8. Medical — others (75) — 1%
    9. Other (271) — 4%

16. If you left it voluntarily, would you do so again? (5321)
    1. Yes, at the same time — 66%
    2. No, I should have left sooner — 15%
    3. No, I should have stayed longer — 19%

17. Do you, or will you when you are old enough, receive a private pension in addition to Social Security? (6282)
    1. No — 37%
    2. Yes — 63%

18. Did you learn anything on your longest job that helps you on your job now? (6280)
    No (1032) — 16%
    Yes (5248) — 84%*
        People skills — 41%
        Techniques or Procedures — 31%
        Body of knowledge — 15%
        Computers — 10%
        Skills — 5%
        Other — 7%

19. Did you have to learn anything new for your present work? (6303)
    No (1851) — 29%
    Yes (4452) — 71%*
        Techniques or Procedures — 40%
        Body of knowledge — 21%
        Computers — 13%
        Skills — 12%
        People skills — 7%
        Other — 14%

20. Your sex (6341)
    1. Male   52%
    2. Female   48%

21. Your marital status (6330)
    1. Never married   3%
    2. Married or living with a partner   62%
    3. Divorced or separated   16%
    4. Widowed   18%

22. Your present work status (6347) (circle all that apply)*
    1. Employed   87%
    2. Unemployed   2%
    3. Retired   47%
    4. Looking for work   6%

23. Your present age _____years
    <50 (22)   <1%
    50–54 (403)   6%
    55–59 (1418)   22%
    60–64 (1661)   26%
    65–69 (1537)   24%
    70–74 (817)   13%
    75–79 (299)   5%
    80–84 (106)   2%
    85–89 (29)   <1%
    90–94 (5)   <1%

24. Your education (circle highest level completed) (6320)
    1. Less than high school   4%
    2. High school   26%
    3. More than high school   70%

25. What year did you earn the most money from your work? 19 _____

26. How much did you earn that year? (circle one) (6141)
    1. Under $9,999   11%
    2. $10,000–$19,999   24%
    3. $20,000–$34,999   31%
    4. $35,000–$49,999   17%
    5. $50,000 +   17%

If you are willing to talk to us on the phone:
Name _____
Address _____
Phone _____

APPENDIX B

A TECHNICAL NOTE ON THE CHAPTER 3 QUIZZES

The quizzes in chapter 3 were expressly constructed for use with mature persons. They were conceptualized by dividing the occupational clusters into "People" and "Not-People"–oriented activities, in accord with the frequently found first factor in the interest domain. Each pole of this first factor was divided into three categories of "doing," reflected in the scales of the second quiz.

In general, items were stated in terms of the habits and behaviors that represent preferences as they would be observed in individuals over the age of 50.

Items for Quiz One were developed by recasting the content of several measures of introversion-extroversion. A pool of forty-three pair-comparison items was submitted to a nationally distributed sample of one hundred retirees from a major insurance company. The final scale was developed from items that exhibited relatively equal gender balance and nonextreme frequencies of endorsement. Cronbach's alpha for the final eleven-item set was .58.

Items for the second set of six quizzes were generated in a focus group of individuals aged 55+ in response to general descriptions of the types. Item statistics were generated from the responses of a pool of 143 retired university faculty and staff and participants in a health care program for age 60+. The items in the final version of each quiz were selected for the best combination of high intrascale correlations and low correlations with items in other scales, as well as nonextreme frequencies of endorsement.

Donald G. Zytowski, Ed. D.

APPENDIX C

RESOURCES

THE MONEY BUSINESS

Financial Manager, Credit Analyst, Loan Officer, Credit Manager

Contact the American Bankers Association, Reference Librarian, 1120 Connecticut Ave., NW, Washington, DC 20036, for information about the workshops and adult education courses they sponsor through their education, policy, and development division, or call the Banker Education network at 1-202-663-5430.

Apply directly to financial institutions found in *Moody's Bank and Finance Manual* (annual; Moody's Investors Service).

Financial Planner

For a list of schools, write to the International Board of Standards and Practices for Certified Financial Planners, 5445 DTC Pkwy., Suite P-1, Englewood, CO 80111.

The College for Financial Planning in Denver offers a certified financial planner's degree that can be taken as a six-month correspondence course. For information about becoming certified, write to the College for Financial Planning, 9725 E. Hampden Ave., Denver, CO 80231-4993, or call the Institute of Certified Financial Planning at 1-303-751-7600.

Budget Analyst

Apply directly to organizations listed in the *Corporate Finance Bluebook* (annual; National Register Publishing Company).

Federal, state, and local governments are the largest employers of budget analysts. For application instructions see Public Service, page 295.

Accountant

In most states, a certificate and license or permit are required only for certified public accountants. Contact your state board of accountancy for information on licensing requirements for accountants.

Apply directly to local employers found in the yellow pages under "Accounting & Bookkeeping" and "Tax Return Preparation."

Certified Public Accountant

Information about CPA requirements is available from the American Institute of Certified Public Accountants, 1211 Avenue of the Americas, New York, NY 10036; 1-800-242-7269 or 1-212-575-5696 in New York State. A sample CPA examination, including questions, answers, and references, is available for $6.

CPA examination eligibility requirements and addresses of state boards of accountancy are also published in the *Accountants Digest* (quarterly; School of Accounting, College of Business and Public Administration, Florida Atlantic University, Boca Raton, FL 33431; $20), which is available in many college libraries.

Auditor

The Institute of Internal Auditors, Inc., 249 Maitland Ave., Altamone Springs, FL 32701-4201, confers the designation of certified internal auditor after graduation from an accredited college, two years of experience, and a four-part examination.

Enrolled Agent

Enrolled agents are former IRS employees or have passed an examination given by the IRS. For information, contact the IRS or write to the National Association of Enrolled Agents, 6000 Executive Blvd., Suite 205, Rockville, MD 20852.

Tax Preparer

H & R Block's tax preparation school is listed in local telephone directories, or call 1-800-782-9529 for information. Training begins in September. Textbooks and supplies are included in the fee. Graduates receive certificates of achievement and may be offered job interviews with H & R Block.

For information about becoming an IRS taxpayer service representative, or other tax preparation training, call IRS Taxpayer Education Coordination at 1-800-424-1040 in August.

Volunteer

AARP volunteers staff the Tax Aid Program, working with retired people during tax season. Locate the program in your area through the IRS at 1-800-424-1040.

PUBLIC POLICY

Urban Planning, Communications, Transportation, or Utility Management

For information on careers and salaries, lists of schools that offer training, and job referrals, contact the American Planning Association, 1776 Massachusetts Ave., NW, Washington, DC 20036.

For job opportunities near you, find the name of the personnel director in all counties in the United States, and city officials for cities over 2,500 in population, in the *Municipal Year Book* (International City Management Association). For more information on public employment, see Public Service, page 295.

Utility Manager

For job opportunities near you, apply directly to companies listed in the *Electrical World Directory of Electric Utilities,* available at larger public and industrial libraries.

Public Member of a State Board

Contact the secretary of state in your state capital for a list of public boards and their addresses, which the state is required to keep.

Emergency Disaster Service Coordinator

Ask the governor's office in your state for a list of municipalities that employ someone to coordinate disaster services, and consult the *Municipal Year Book* to locate personnel officers in those cities.

Lobbyist or Activist

Apply directly to organizations listed in the *North American Human Rights Directory*, a guide to seven hundred organizations in the U.S. and Canada concerned with human rights and social justice.

For a list of causes represented in Washington, consult *Washington Representatives* (annual; Columbia Books), which has a helpful subject index.

Contact the American League of Lobbyists, P.O. Box 20450, Alexandria, VA 22320; 1-703-960-3011, for information about their seminars. They also publish a monthly magazine, *ALL News*.

To contact the organizations mentioned in the text, write to the American Association of Retired Persons (601 E St. NW, Washington, DC 20049), the American Civil Liberties Union (22 E. 40th St., New York, NY 10016), and the American Society for the Prevention of Cruelty to Animals (441 E. 92nd St., New York, NY 10128).

The largest employer of public information officers is the U.S. Government. For application instructions see Public Service, page 295.

MILITARY SERVICE

Transferring Military Skills to the Civilian Job Market

See William G. Fitzpatrick and C. Edward Good, *Does Your Resume Wear Combat Boots? Successful Transition from Military to Civilian Life, a Job-Seeker's Guide* (1990; Blue Jeans Press, P.O. Box 5628, Charlottesville, VA 22905).

Job Services for Veterans

For information, see Robert L. Berko, *Complete Guide to Federal and State Benefits for Veterans, Their Families, and Survivors* (annual; Consumer Education Research Center, P.O. Box 336, South Orange, NJ 07079; write for price of the latest edition) and Ralph Roberts, *The Veteran's Guide to Benefits* (annual; NAL, 1633 Broadway, New York, NY 10019), or call the U.S. Department of Labor (1-202-523-9110) or the Veterans Administration (1-800-442-5882).

Employment assistance to veterans is provided primarily through state job service local offices. Each of these offices has a staff member assigned as a local veterans employment representative (LVER). The LVERs are state employees who supervise job counseling, testing, and employment-placement services provided to veterans. Information is available from your nearest state job service office, in the state government listings in the blue pages of your telephone book.

Job Training Partnership Act

This is a national job training program for disabled, Vietnam-era, and recently separated vets; information should be available through state job service offices.

Disabled Veterans Outreach Program

Contact your local VA office for services offered in your area. Under the Vocational Rehabilitation program all veterans awarded VA pensions during the period February 1, 1985, through January 31, 1989, may be eligible for up to twenty-four months of vocational training to prepare for and enter employment counseling, job search, and work adjustment services. Pension recipients awarded pensions prior to February 1, 1985, are not eligible for this program.

Under this program, every veteran under age 50 must submit to an evaluation of his ability to benefit from vocational services. Veterans over 50 may elect to be evaluated amd apply for the program. Pension may be reduced any time work or training income exceeds the person's annual pension limit. Contact your local VA office for information.

Veterans' Preference

The Veterans' Preference Act of 1944, as amended, provides for preferential treatment of veterans and certain dependents in federal employment. Additional points can be added to passing scores of veterans, certain dependents, and survivors, who are known as "preference-eligibles," in examinations for federal government appointments. A five-point preference is given to any veteran who was separated from active military duty under other than dishonorable conditions from any branch of the armed forces, and who served in wartime (including the period April 28, 1952 through July 1, 1955, in peacetime campaigns or expeditions for which campaign badges or service medals have been authorized, or for more than 180 consecutive days (other than an initial period of active duty for training) during the period January 31, 1955, through October 15, 1976.

Effective October 1, 1980, veterans' preference was eliminated for nondisabled military persons who retired at or above the rank of major or equivalent.

A ten-point preference is given to those veterans separated under other than dishonorable conditions who served on active duty in any branch of the armed forces and have a service-connected disability or are receiving compensation, disability retirement benefits, or a pension under public laws administered by the Veterans Administration, army, navy, air force, coast guard, or Public Health Service. If you hold the Purple Heart and want to get the full ten points, you need to find a service officer and file a claim with the VA to get a disability rating. The Purple Heart in itself gives the veteran who received it a service-connected disability rating but no compensation, or a rating of 0 percent. But a disability rating, even one of 0 percent, is required to obtain the ten-point preference.

Veterans with a 30 percent or greater disability rating receive additional benefits, including appointment without competitive examination, the right to be converted to career appointments, and restoration rights over other preference-eligibles in lay-offs.

Under certain circumstances, the spouse or mother of a veteran may be eligible for veterans' preference (see *The Veteran's Guide to Benefits*, above). More information about veterans' benefits in federal employment is available from any federal job information center of the U.S. Office of Personnel Management; see Public Service, page 296.

PUBLIC SERVICE

State and Local Government Agencies

Visit your local state job service office.

Contact the personnel departments of agencies that interest you and ask if they have any job openings, where job announcements are posted, and whether there is a special telephone number that plays a recorded list of their current job openings even when the office is closed.

For local job openings in a part of the country in which you are interested, monitor classified ads in local newspapers, and ads in commercial publications. One of these is the *City-County Recruiter and the State Recruiter* (biweekly, by subscription; P.O. Box 2400, Station B, Lincoln, NE 68502), a national listing of city, county, and state employment opportunities.

Human Service Worker

Apply directly to agencies that interest you, listed in the *Directory of State and Local Consumer Organizations* (Consumer Federation of America, 1992).

Work in the U.S. Postal Service

Apply at the post office where you wish to work. A civil service examination is required for most positions, and veterans' preference applies (see Military Service, page 294). Applicants for some positions may be asked to show that they can lift sacks of mail.

Seasonal Employment with the IRS

Call the Internal Revenue Service at 1-800-424-1040 in August for information.

Seasonal Employment with the National Park Service

Write to the Department of the Interior, National Park Service, Seasonal Employment Unit, P.O. Box 37127, Washington, DC 20013, for an application form in December.

Work in Federal Government Agencies

Visit your local state job service office and take advantage of their services. Federal job openings are posted there.

For job openings and application form SF-171, call or write the nearest U.S. Office of Personnel Management's federal job information center.

Two helpful pamphlets, *Working for the U.S.A.* and *Current Federal Examination Announcements*, are available from the federal job information centers.

Consult a job search guide at your library. David E. Waelde, *How to Get a Federal Job* (Fedhelp Publications, 1989), and Ronald L. and Caryl Rae Krannich, *The Com-*

plete Guide to Public Employment, (Impact, VA, 1990), are two good places to start.

Monitor classified ads. In addition to your local paper, check the ads in the *Washington Post*, the *Federal Times*, *Federal Career Opportunities*, or the *Federal Jobs Digest*, at your library or job service office.

Some agencies have special numbers for recordings of job openings. These numbers are listed in the directories above. For example, the number for the Census is 1-301-763-5537; the Environmental Protection Agency, 1-202-755-5055; the Patent and Trademark Office, 1-800-368-3064; the NOAA/Weather Service, 1-301-443-8274; and the National Park Service, 1-202-343-2154.

Federal Job Qualifications

To find out whether you are qualified for a federal job, consult the *X-118 Handbook: Qualification Standards for White-Collar Positions under the General Schedule* and the *X-188A Handbook: Qualification Standards for Blue-Collar Positions under the General Schedule*, available at federal job information centers and most federal depository libraries.

Federal Job Information Centers

Alabama: Building 600, 3322 Memorial Pkwy. S., Suite 341, Huntsville, AL 35801-5311; 1-205-544-5802

Alaska: 222 W. Seventh Ave., Box 22, Anchorage, AK 99513

Arizona: U.S. Postal Service Bldg., 522 N. Central Ave., Room 120, Phoenix, AZ 85004; 1-602-261-4736

Arkansas: See Oklahoma listing

California: Linder Bldg., 845 S. Figueroa, 3d Floor, Los Angeles, CA 90017; 1-213-894-3360

   1029 J St., 2d Floor, Sacramento, CA 95814; 1-916-551-1464

   Federal Bldg., 880 Front St., Rm. 4-S-9, San Diego, CA 92188; 1-619-557-6165

   P.O. Box 7405, San Francisco, CA 94120; office located at 211 Main St., 2d Floor, Rm. 235; 1-415-974-9725

Colorado: P.O. Box 25167, Denver, CO 80225; office is located at 12345 W. Alameda Pkwy., Lakewood, CO; 1-303-236-4160

Connecticut: Federal Bldg., 450 Main St., Rm. 613, Hartford, CT 06103; 1-203-240-3263

Delaware: See Philadelphia listing

District of Columbia: 1900 E St., NW, Rm. 1416, Washington, DC 20415; 1-202-653-8468

Florida: Commodore Bldg., 3444 McCrory Pl., Suite 150, Orlando, FL 32803-3701; 1-407-648-6148

Georgia: Richard B. Russell Federal Bldg., 75 Spring St., SW, Rm. 960, Atlanta, GA 30303; 1-404-331-4315

Guam: Pacific Daily News Bldg., Rm. 902, Agana, GU 96910; 1-671-472-7451

Hawaii: Federal Bldg., 300 Ala Moana Blvd., Rm. 5316, Honolulu, HI 96850; 1-808-541-2791; overseas jobs, 1-808-541-2784

Idaho: See Washington listing

Illinois: 175 W. Jackson Blvd., Rm. 530, Chicago, IL 60604; 1-312-353-6192

Indiana: Minton-Capehart Federal Bldg., 575 N. Pennsylvania St., Indianapolis, IN 46204; 1-317-226-7161

Iowa: See Missouri listing; 1-816-426-7757

Kansas: One-Twenty Bldg., 120 S. Market St., Rm. 101, Wichita, KS 67202; 1-316-269-6794

   In Johnson, Leavenworth, and Wyandotte Counties, dial 1-816-426-5702

Kentucky: See Ohio listing

Louisiana: 1515 Poydras St., Suite 608, New Orleans, LA 70112; 1-504-589-2764

Maine: See New Hampshire listing

Maryland: Garmatz Federal Bldg., 101 W. Lombard St., Baltimore, MD 21201; 1-301-962-3822

Massachusetts: Thos. P. O'Neill Federal Bldg., 10 Causeway St., Boston, MA 02222-1031; 1-617-565-5900

Michigan: 477 Michigan Ave., Rm. 565, Detroit, MI 48226; 1-313-226-6950

Minnesota: Federal Bldg., Fort Snelling, Twin Cities, MN 55111

Mississippi: See Huntsville, AL, listing

Missouri: Federal Bldg., 601 E. 12th St., Rm. 134, Kansas City, MO 64106; 1-816-426-5702

   Old Post Office Bldg., 815 Olive Street., Rm. 400, Saint Louis, MO 63101; 1-314-539-2285

Montana: See Colorado listing; 24-hr. info, 1-303-236-4162; forms, 1-303-236-4159

Nebraska: See Kansas listing

Nevada: See Sacramento, CA, listing

New Hampshire: Thomas J. McIntyre Federal Bldg., 80 Daniel St., Rm. 104, Portsmouth, NH 03801-3879; 1-603-431-7115

New Jersey: Peter W. Rodino Jr. Federal Bldg., 970 Broad St., Newark, NJ 07102; 1-201-645-3673. In Camden, dial 1-215-597-7440

New Mexico: Federal Bldg., 421 Gold Ave., SW, Albuquerque, NM 87102; 1-505-766-5583. In Dona Ana, Otero, and El Paso Counties, dial 1-505-766-1893

New York: Jacob K. Javits Federal Bldg., 26 Federal Plaza, New York, NY 10278; 1-212-264-0422

   James M. Hanley Federal Bldg., 100 S. Clinton St., Syracuse, NY 13260; 1-315-423-5660

North Carolina: P.O. Box 25069, 4565 Falls of the Neuse Rd., Suite 4445, Raleigh, NC 27609; 1-919-856-4361

North Dakota: See Minnesota listing

Ohio: Federal Bldg., 200 W. 2d St., Rm. 506, Dayton, OH 45402; 1-513-225-2720

Oklahoma: (mail or phone only) 200 N.W. 5th St., 2d floor, Oklahoma City, OK 73102; 1-405-231-4948

Oregon: Federal Bldg., 1220 S.W. Third Ave., Rm. 376, Portland, OR 97204; 1-503-221-3141

Pennsylvania: Federal Bldg., Rm. 168, P.O. Box 761, Harrisburg, PA 17108; 1-717-782-4494

Puerto Rico: Frederico Degetau Federal Bldg., Carlos E. Chardon St., Hato Rey, PR 00918; 1-809-766-5242

Rhode Island: John O. Pastore Federal Bldg., Kennedy Plaza, Rm. 310, Providence, RI 02903; 1-401-528-5251

South Carolina: See North Carolina listing

South Dakota: See Minnesota listing

Tennessee: 200 Jefferson Ave., Suite 1312, Memphis, TN 38103-2335; 1-901-521-3956

Texas: (mail or phone only) 1100 Commerce St., Rm. 6B12, Dallas, 75242; 1-214-767-8035

   (Mail or phone only) 8610 Broadway, Rm. 305, San Antonio, TX 78217; 1-512-229-6611 or 1-512-229-6600

   (Recording) 1-713-226-2375

Utah: See Colorado listing; 24-hr. info, 1-303-236-4165; forms, 1-303-236-4159

Vermont: See New Hampshire listing

Virginia: Federal Bldg., Granby St., Rm. 220, Norfolk, VA 23510-1886; 1-804-441-3355

Washington: Federal Bldg., 915 Second Ave., Seattle, WA 98174; 1-206-442-4365

West Virginia: (phone only) 1-513-225-2866

Wisconsin: Residents in counties of Grant, Iowa, Lafayette, Dane, Green, Rock, Jefferson, Walworth, Waukesha, Racine, Kenosha, and Milwaukee should dial 1-312-353-6189 for job information. All other Wisconsin residents should refer to the Minnesota listing.

Wyoming: See Colorado listing; 24-hr. info, 1-303-236-4166; forms, 1-303-236-4159

SOCIAL WORK

Social Worker

For information on education and licensing requirements, contact the National Association of Social Workers (NASW), toll-free, at 1-800-638-8799. Over half the states require social workers to be licensed. The NASW will give you the address and telephone number of the board that oversees social workers in your state.

Apply directly to organizations listed under "Social & Human Services" in the yellow pages of your telephone book.

Rehabilitation Counselor

Apply directly to organizations listed under "Rehabilitation Services" in the yellow pages of your telephone book.

Contact your local department of mental hygiene for job openings in your area.

Manager of Volunteers

For paid work managing volunteers, apply directly to community service organizations. Contact your local United Way agency to locate a directory of community service organizations in your area.

Contact ACTION, Personnel Management Division (Washington, DC 20525;

1-202-606-5263). ACTION is an umbrella organization under which several federal agencies, staffed primarily by volunteers, are gathered. ACTION also employs paid workers in a variety of supervisory positions.

RELIGION

The Clergy

For information about requirements for the Protestant ministry, write to the National Council of Churches, Professional Church Leadership, 475 Riverside Dr., Rm. 770, New York, NY 10115.

For similar information for the Jewish faith, write to Beth Medrash Govoha Seminary, 626 7th St., Lakewood, NJ 08701 (Orthodox); the Jewish Theological Seminary of America, 3080 Broadway, New York, NY 10027 (Conservative); or the Hebrew Union College/Jewish Institute of Religion, Director of Admissions, 3101 Clifton Ave., Cincinnati, OH 45220 (Reform).

For information regarding requirements for the different religious orders of the Roman Catholic Church, contact the director of vocations in your own diocese or write to the National Conference of Diocesan Vocation Directors, 1307 S. Wabash Ave., Chicago, IL 60605.

For career counseling services, contact one of the following interdenominational career development centers accredited by the Career Development Council:

The Career and Personal Counseling Service
St. Andrews Presbyterian College
Laurinburg, NC 28352; 1-919-276-3162

The Career and Personal Counseling Service
4108 Park Rd., Suite 200
Charlotte, NC 28209; 1-704-523-7751

The Career and Personal Counseling Center
Eckerd College
St. Petersburg, FL 33733; 1-813-864-8356, Ext. 356

The Center for Ministry
7804 Capwell Dr.
Oakland, CA 94621; 1-415-635-4246

Lancaster Career Development Center
561 College Ave.
Lancaster, PA 17603; 1-717-397-7451

North Central Career Development Center
3000 5th St., NW
New Brighton, MN 55112; 1-612-636-5120

Northeast Career Center
83 Princeton Ave., Suite 2D
Hopewell, NJ 08525; 1-609-466-0774

Career Development Center of the Southeast
531 Kirk Rd.
Decatur, CA 30030; 1-404-371-0336

Midwest Career Development Service
Box 7249
Westchester, IL 60153; 1-312-343-6268

Southwest Career Development Service
Box 5923
Arlington, TX 76011; 1-817-265-5541

Center for Career Development and Ministry
70 Chase St.
Newton Centre, MA 02159; 1-617-969-7750

Deacon or Elder
Contact the pastor of your church; or Catholics may contact the office of the permanent deaconate of their archdiocese.

Nonliturgical Work in Churches and Church-Related Agencies
Apply directly to agencies listed under "Churches" in the yellow pages of your telephone book with a resume of your particular skills; musical, secretarial, janitorial, etc.

For names, addresses, and activities of possible employers, consult the *Yearbook of American and Canadian Churches* or the *Directory of Religious Organizations in the United States*. These employers include parochial schools; colleges supported by religious groups; religious book, magazine, and newspaper publishers; religious radio and television stations; domestic or foreign missionary programs; clubs that support the spiritual life of their members; and church-sponsored organizations addressing social problems.

SCIENCE, ENGINEERING, AND TECHNOLOGY

Licensing
To find out if a license is required in your state for the job you want, if your old license is still valid, or if licenses from other states are transferable to your state, contact the board of examiners or licensing board for your profession in your state. If you need help locating the correct board, write to the Federation of State Licensing Boards, 501 E. California Ave., Glendale, CA 91206.

Professional Organizations
Look for help from the professional organization serving your particular field, asking if it has a discount for retirees. It may notify you of job openings, operate a job hot line, or run help-wanted ads in its publications. Find your association by checking

the lists in the *Directory of Engineering Societies and Related Organizations,* and *National Trade and Professional Associations of the U.S.*

Employers

For a list of organizations that employ research scientists and engineers in your field, with complete information about how and where to apply, consult *Peterson's Engineering, Science and Computer Jobs* (annual; Peterson's Guides).

If you are interested in working in a very specific area of research, these directories may help in locating employers who may be hiring in your field: the *Directory of American Research and Technology, the Research Centers Directory,* and the *American Council of Independent Laboratories Directory.*

Full-time and seasonal positions for physical scientists are listed each month in *Environmental Opportunities* (P.O. Box 969, Stowe, VT 05672; 1-802-253-9336).

To enter your resume in the Professional Engineering Employment Registry you must be a member of a participating professional society. Contact your professional society directly to find out if they offer this membership service.

For information on locating and applying for jobs with federal, state, and local government agencies, see Public Service, page 295.

LIBRARY AND RESEARCH WORK

Librarian

For a job as a professional librarian in your hometown, find and keep watching the newsletters of local library associations, which usually advertise local openings before they appear in *American Libraries* (American Library Association, 50 Huron St., Chicago, IL 60611; 1-800-545-2433; in Illinois only 1-800-545-2444; Telecommunications Device for the Deaf (TDD), 1-312-944-7298), *Library Journal* (P.O. Box 1977, Marion, OH 43306; 1-800-842-1669; in Ohio 1-614-382-3322), or *Library Hotline* (Box 445, Mount Morris, IL 10011; 1-800-435-0715).

Names, addresses, and full descriptions of public, college, and special libraries, arranged geographically, are available in the *American Library Directory.* Apply directly to possible employers in your area of interest.

College Librarian

In addition to the publications listed above, consult the classified advertising in the weekly *Chronicle of Higher Education* (1255 23d Street, NW, Suite 700, Washington, DC 20037; 1-202-466-1000).

Positions in Federal Libraries

See Public Service, page 295, for the nearest federal job information center or call the Washington, DC, office at 1-202-653-8468 and ask for the application forms for librarian positions.

Information Scientist

Apply directly to businesses listed in the *Encyclopedia of Information Systems and Services.* (annual; Gale Research Company), which is indexed by both subject and by state.

For information about starting your own business, consult John Everett and

Elizabeth Powell Crowe, *Information for Sale: How to Start Your Own Data Research Service* (TAB Books, 1988).

Another book on starting your own business is Alice Sizer Warner, *Mind Your Own Business: A Guide for the Information Entrepreneur* (Neal-Schuman Publications, 1987).

Job openings are listed in *Jobline,* the monthly newsletter of the American Society for Information Science, 1424 16th St., NW, Suite 404, Washington, DC 20036; 1-202-462-1000. Write or call for brochure and membership application form.

Genealogical Researcher

Courses are offered by local genealogical and historical societies, community colleges, or high school adult evening programs. See *The Independent Study Catalog* (annual; Peterson's Guides) for study by mail. To combine vacation with genealogy courses, write Elderhostel, 80 Boylston St., Boston, MA 02116, for their free catalog.

For information about certification, write to the Board for Certification of Genealogists, P.O. Box 19165, Washington, DC 20036. The four levels of certification are certified genealogical record searcher, certified American lineage specialist, certified genealogical lecturer, and certified genealogical instructor.

Visit the librarian in charge of genealogy or local history in the biggest public library near you to find out how to get on the list of researchers they recommend to out-of-town inquirers. Use the *American Library Directory* to locate other libraries in your area that maintain lists of researchers.

Use the *Genealogical Helper* (Everton Publishers, P.O. Box 368, Logan, Utah 84321; 1-800-443-6325) to locate customers or advertise your services in the classified advertising.

Curator or Archivist

A comprehensive list of degree programs, courses, internships, fellowships, and workshops in museum studies is available in *Museum Studies International* (annual; Smithsonian Institution, Office of Museum Programs, P.O. Box 37481-OMP, Washington, DC 20013).

Apply directly to possible employers listed in the *Official Museum Directory,* (annual; American Association of Museums, 1225 I St., NW, Washington, DC 20005; 1-202-289-1818; available from the National Register Publishing Company, 3004 Glenview Rd., Wilmette, IL 60091; 1-312-441-2211). The directory is available for use in college libraries and many historical societies and art galleries.

Apply directly to organizations listed in the *Directory of Historical Agencies in the U.S. and Canada* (AASLH Press, 1990).

Request a free catalog of products and services from the American Association for State and Local History, 172 Second Ave. N., Suite 102, Nashville, TN 37201; 1-615-255-2971. They sell a careers information kit and their bimonthly magazine, *History News,* contains information on job opportunities for curators, archivists, and others in the field of history.

Research Expeditions

For information, write to Earthwatch, 680 Mount Auburn St., P.O. Box 403, Watertown, MA 02272; 1-617-926-8200. Descriptions of expeditions and application forms are part of *Earthwatch Magazine.*

For their expedition brochures, contact the Smithsonian National Associate Program, Washington, DC 20560; 1-202-357-1350.

For a free catalog of expeditions, contact the University Research Expeditions Program, University of California, Berkeley, CA 94720; 1-415-642-6586.

THE WORD BUSINESS

Writer

Employers are listed in *Working Press of the Nation* (annual; National Research Bureau).

Publishers who purchase articles, short stories, and book-length manuscripts are listed in *Writer's Market* (annual; Writer's Digest Books).

Publishers and contests are listed in the periodicals *Writer's Digest* and *The Writer*.

Publishers of book-length manuscripts are listed in Jeff Herman, *The Insider's Guide to Book Editors and Publishers, 1990–1991* (Prima).

Broadcaster

To find employers in your area, see the *Gale Directory of Publications and Broadcast Media* (annual; Gale Research Company) or *Working Press of the Nation* (annual; National Research Bureau).

Public Relations Specialist

Apply to companies listed in *O'Dwyer's Directory of Public Relations Firms* (annual; J. R. O'Dwyer) or in the *Literary Market Place* (annual; R. R. Bowker).

Public Speaker

To locate organizations that may be looking for speakers, consult the *Encyclopedia of Associations: Regional, State, and Local Organizations* (annual; Gale Research Company).

For information and opportunities to speak contact the International Platform Association (P.O. Box 250, Winnetka, IL 60093; 1-312-446-4321); the National Speakers Association (4747 N. 7th St., Suite 310, Phoenix, AZ 85014; 1-602-265-1001), or Toastmasters International (P.O. Box 10400, 2200 N. Grand Ave., Santa Ana, CA 92711, 1-714-542-6793), which has 6,200 local chapters across the country.

Newsletter Publisher

For information about their services to newsletter publishers, contact the Newsletter Clearing House, 44 W. Market St., Rhinebeck, NY 12572; 1-914-876-2081.

For information on publishing your own newsletter, consult Fred Goss, *Success in Newsletter Publishing: A Practical Guide* (1985; Newsletter Association, 1401 Wilson Blvd., Suite 403, Arlington, VA 22209; 1-703-527-2333) or Mark Beach, *Editing Your Newsletter: How to Produce an Effective Publication Using Traditional Tools and Computers* (Writer's Digest Books, 1988).

Self-Publisher

Some sources of information are Robert Holt, *How to Publish, Promote and Sell Your Own Book* (St. Martin's Press, 1986); Dan Poynter, *The Self-Publishing Manual* (Para

Publishing, 1988); Tomm and Marilyn Ross, *The Complete Guide to Self-Publishing* (Writer's Digest Books, 1989); Judith Appelbaum, *How to Get Happily Published* (Writer's Digest Books, 1988); and John Kremer, *The Directory of Book, Catalog, and Magazine Printers* (Ad-Lib Publications, 1988).

Desktop Publisher

Check your library or bookstore for *The Desktop Publishing Bible* (Howard Sams Company, 1987).

Two current monthly magazines with the latest information for desktop publishers are *Personal Publishing* and *Publish!*

For membership information contact the National Association of Desktop Publishers, P.O. Box 508, Kenmore Station, Boston, MA 02215; 1-617-437-6472.

Translator or Interpreter

Apply to translation services listed in the *Literary Market Place* (annual; R. R. Bowker).

For information on becoming a certified court interpreter, contact the National Association of Judicial Interpreters and Translators (P.O. Box 506, Albuquerque, NM 87109; 1-505-242-8085) or the American Society of Interpreters (P.O. Box 9603, Washington, DC 20016; 1-301-657-3337).

For a free information kit send a stamped, self-addressed No. 10 envelope to the American Translators Association, 109 Croton Avenue, Ossining, NY 10562.

THE VISUAL AND PERFORMING ARTS

Artist

To find buyers, consult the *Artist's Market* (annual; Writer's Digest Books; 1-800-289-0963).

For information about the services they offer, contact the National Arts Jobbank, Western States Arts Foundation (207 Shelby St., Suite 200, Sante Fe, NM 87501) and the National Network for Artist Placement and Career Development, California Institute for the Arts (2400 McBean Pkwy., Valencia, CA 91355).

To locate art organizations, arts councils, and art magazines, consult the annual *American Art Directory* (R. R. Bowker Company).

For information on selling your art see Caroll Michels, *How to Survive and Prosper as an Artist* (Henry Holt and Company, 1988), which also has an excellent appendix of resources in the back.

Illustrators

For information about working as a medical illustrator, send for *Medical Illustration*, a free pamphlet from the Association of Medical Illustrators, 2692 Huguenot Springs Road, Midlothian, VA 23113.

To locate publishers who buy art for children's books and magazines, consult *Children's Writers' and Illustrators' Market* (annual; Writer's Digest Books).

Calligrapher

Talk to the owners of print shops, bridal shops, and party stores. Ask to post a notice that your services are available to hand-letter envelopes for a fee. Leave an example of your work. Be sure to thank the store owners when jobs result from their referrals. See *How to Survive and Prosper as an Artist,* listed above.

Cartoonist

For publishers who buy jokes and cartoons, consult *Humor and Cartoon Markets* (annual; Writer's Digest Books).

To locate employers of animators, storyboard artists, directors, puppet makers, and voice artists, see the *Animation Industry Directory* (annual; Expanded Entertainment, P.O. Box 25547, Los Angeles, CA 90025).

Photographer

To find buyers for your photographs, see *Photographer's Market* (annual; Writer's Digest Books).

For information on selling your photographs, see Barbara and Elliott Gordon, *How to Sell Your Photographs and Illustrations* (Allworth Press, 1990).

Theater Technician

Apply directly to employers listed in *Theater Profiles* (annual; Theatre Communications Group, Inc.).

Actor

To locate courses in acting and agents who find employment for actors, consult the *International Directory of Model and Talent Agencies/Schools* (Peter Glenn Publications, Ltd., 17 E. 48th St., New York, NY 10017; 1-800-223-1254 or 1-212-688-7940 in New York). This publication is usually owned by libraries that have a special performing arts collection or schools that offer instruction in the performing arts.

For advice from an actress and a casting director, consult Mari L. Henry and Lynne Rogers, *How to be a Working Actor: The Insider's Guide to Finding Jobs in Theater, Film, and Television* (1989; National Book Network, 4720 Boston Way, Lanhan, MD 20706).

Musician, Dancer, Director, Producer, or Composer

To locate employers, see *Stern's Performing Arts Directory* (annual; DM, Inc., 33 W. 60th St., 10th Floor, New York, NY 10023; 1-800-458-2845). This book also includes listings of unions, competitions, government agencies, income tax services, and service and professional organizations for artists and is found in large libraries or schools that teach performing arts.

To locate employers who supply products and services for audio, video, and film producers, see *AV Market Place* (annual; R. R. Bowker).

Clown, Magician, Comic, or Santa

Post a notice at toy stores, party stores, and free bulletin boards that your services are available for children's birthday parties, retirement parties, or whatever is appropriate.

Monitor classified ads in your local newspaper in October for positions as Santa or Santa's helper during the holidays in department stores, shopping malls, and with children's photographers.

Consult Bruce Fife, *Creative Clowning* (1988; Java Publishing, 6510 Lehman Dr., Colorado Springs, CO 80918; 1-719-548-1844).

Interior Designer

For a free pamphlet, *Interior Design Career Guide,* send a stamped, self-addressed envelope to Interior Design Educators Council, 14252 Culver Dr., Suite A331, Irvine, CA 92714.

Model

For work as a model acting in commercials, see Georgette Baker, *You Too Can Be in TV Commercials* (1988; Talented, 23612 Maple Springs, Diamond Bar, CA 91765; 1-714-860-3891) or Squire Fridell, *Acting in Television Commercials for Fun and Profit* (Crown, 1987).

For work as a fashion model, see Retailing, page 333.

REAL ESTATE AND INSURANCE

Insurance Salesperson, Underwriter, or Claims Worker

Information about licensing requirements for insurance workers in your area may be obtained from the department of insurance in your state capital, from the Independent Insurance Agents Association in your state, or by calling any large insurance agency listed in your telephone book.

For a free pamphlet, *Career Opportunities for You in Life and Health Insurance,* write to the American Council of Life Insurance, 1001 Pennsylvania Ave., NW, Washington, DC 20004.

Apply directly to employers listed in the *Insurance Almanac* (annual; Underwriting Printing and Publishing Co.), or *Best's Agents Guide to Life Insurance Companies* (annual; A. M. Best).

Insurance Clerk

Apply directly to companies listed under "Insurance" in the yellow pages of your telephone directory and in the *Insurance Almanac* or other insurance directory.

Property Manager

For information about becoming a certified property manager (CPM), training courses, and publications, request a free catalog from the Institute of Real Estate Management, National Association of Realtors, P.O. Box 109025, Chicago, IL 60611; 1-312-661-0004.

For information about becoming a registered apartment manager, contact the National Association of Home Builders, 15th and M Sts., NW, Washington, DC 20005.

For information about the requirements for becoming a real property administrator, contact the Building Owners and Managers Institute International, 1521 Ritchie Hwy., Arnold, MD 21012.

For work as a property manager, apply directly to companies listed in the yellow pages of your telephone book under "Warehouses — Self-Storage" and "Real Estate Management."

Real Estate Sales

Real estate sales brokers and agents are licensed in all states. For a pamphlet on how to get started in real estate, write Career Pamphlet, National Association of Realtors, 430 N. Michigan Ave., Chicago, IL 60611-4087.

State licensing requirements for real estate agents and brokers in your state may be obtained from the board of realtors in your area or from your state real estate commission. Boards of realtors are usually listed in the telephone book under the name of the county that they cover.

Real estate licensing examination requirements for every state are published by the National Association of Real Estate, License Law Officials, Commercial Security Bank Powers, 50 S. Main St., Suite 600, Salt Lake City, UT 84144; 1-801-531-8202.

For work in real estate, apply directly to agencies listed in the yellow pages of your telephone directory under "Real Estate." Some real estate agencies are willing to hire trainees and coach them for the licensing examination.

For information about renovating and selling old houses, consult Suzanne Brangham, *Housewise: The Smart Woman's Guide to Buying and Renovating Real Estate for Profit* (Harper & Row, 1988).

Real Estate Appraiser

Real estate appraisers often begin as trainees in real estate offices, government agencies, or banks. The Institutions Reform, Recovery and Enforcement Act of 1989 requires all appraisers working for federally chartered or insured lending institutions after July 1, 1991, to be licensed or certified.

For information on certification, contact the American Association of Certified Appraisers, 800 Compton Rd., Suite 10, Cincinnati, OH 45231; 1-800-543-2222. They also publish a newsletter for their members, which lists job opportunities.

For a free pamphlet, *Should You Consider an Appraisal Career?* send a stamped, self-addressed envelope to the National Association of Independent Fee Appraisers, Inc., 7501 Murdoch Ave., Saint Louis, MO 63119.

For information about their services and publications, contact the American Institute of Real Estate Appraisers (430 N. Michigan Ave., Chicago, IL 60601); the Society of Real Estate Appraisers (225 N. Michigan Ave., Suite 724, Chicago, IL 60601; 1-312-819-2400) or the National Association of Real Estate Appraisers (838 E. Evans, Scottsdale, AZ 85260; 1-800-537-2069).

LAW AND ENFORCEMENT

Employers

For all occupations in law, see the *Directory of Legal Employers* (annual; National Association for Law Placement, 440 1st St., NW, Suite 302, Washington, DC 20001; 1-202-783-5171) or apply directly to law firms listed in the annual *Martindale Hubbell Law Directory*, in larger libraries or at most courthouses.

Lawyer

For current licensing requirements contact the bar examiner in your state or the appellate court listed in the state government pages of your telephone directory. Most states require a J.D. or LL.B. degree from a law school approved by the American Bar Association and that you pass the bar exam. For more information, contact Information Services, American Bar Association, 750 N. Lake Shore Dr., Chicago, IL 60611.

Paralegal

For free information on certification and training in your state, write to the National Association of Legal Assistants, Inc. (1420 S. Utica, P.O. Box 7587, Tulsa, OK 74105) or the National Paralegal Association (P.O. Box 629, Doylestown, PA 18901).

For a free list of approved paralegal training programs, write to the American Bar Association Standing Committee on Legal Assistants, 1155 E. 60th St., Chicago, IL 60637.

Legal Secretary

For information about the one-week, forty-hour course at the Career Legal Secretarial Training Institute and professional legal secretary certification, contact the National Association of Legal Secretaries, 22 E. 73d St., Suite 550, Tulsa, OK 74136.

Referee or Arbiter

Inquire at court offices listed in *Want's Federal-State Court Directory* (annual; Want Publishing Co., 1500 K St., NW Washington, DC 20005) and local, state, or county personnel offices in your area for openings. For how to find and apply for government jobs, see Public Service, page 295.

Arbitrator

For a free brochure, *Commercial Arbitration: How You Can Volunteer Your Services,* contact the American Arbitration Association, 140 W. 51st St., New York, NY 10020; 1-212-484-4000. Ask for a list of other available arbitration brochures.

Clerk of the Court

Contact courts in your area for job requirements. Clerks in some areas may be elected rather than appointed. A few states require a law degree but this is usually a paralegal position.

To locate employers, consult *Want's Federal-State Court Directory* (see Referee/ Arbiter, above). The Supreme Court Information Office, 1-202-479-3211, also has information on court and court-support groups in your area to whom you can apply directly.

Title Searcher

For entry-level positions, apply directly to companies listed in the yellow pages under "Title Companies & Agents."

Notary Public

For the test required by your state see Jack Rudman, *Notary Public* (1991; C-531 of the Career Examination Series; National Learning, 212 Michael Dr., Syosset, NY 11791; 1-800-645-6337).

If you are working from your home and will depend on drop-in business, advertise your services to banks, copy shops, and office-supply stores in your area. You might consider a small sign or "Notary Public" after your name on the mailbox.

Law Enforcement Officer

For work as a state trooper, contact your local state Job Service office. Most positions require both written and physical fitness tests and most have a maximum starting age of 29.

For full-time work as a police officer, apply directly to employers listed in the *Municipal Year Book*, (International City Management Association), which contains a list of municipalities that employ their own police forces, the hours they work, and their salaries. Check with the police department for their requirements.

For part-time, temporary employment or clerical positions contact your local state job service office or your local police department for openings and apply according to their instructions.

Special Agent

Contact the state job service office and the U.S. Office of Personnel Management's federal job information center near you for job openings. For complete information on locating and applying for federal jobs see Public Service, p. 295. Many positions in federal law enforcement have a maximum starting age of 29.

For some job openings in the federal government call the job vacancies recording for the Department of Justice at 1-202-633-3121, or for the Department of the Treasury at 1-202-566-2540.

Crossing Guard

Contact your local police department to find out who hires crossing guards in your area. Apply directly to the hiring office well in advance of the start of the new school year.

THE HEALTH BUSINESS

Licensing

To find out if a license is required in your state for the job you want, if your old license is still valid, or if licenses from other states are transferable to your state, contact the board of examiners or licensing board for your specialty. If you need help locating the correct board, write to the Federation of State Licensing Boards, 501 East California Ave., Glendale, CA 91206.

General Information on Health Care Opportunities

Call the National Health Careers Information Hotline toll-free at 1-800-999-4248.

For job opportunities in health care in your community, apply directly to health care agencies listed in the yellow pages of your telephone book under "Hospitals," "Health Related Facilities," "Health Maintenance Organizations," or "Home Health Svcs."

Apply directly to health care agencies listed in one of the major health care directories, including the annual *Consumers' Guide to Hospitals, Directory of Nursing*

Homes, Hospital Phonebook, or *Health and Medical Care Directory,* a list of 70,000 physical and mental health care facilities and suppliers, 400 medical libraries, 360 poison control centers, and 350 overseas medical assistance centers for travelers. If your public library does not own these reference books, it is usually possible to see them at a hospital or university library.

Apply directly to agencies with job openings advertised in professional journals such as *American Family Physician,* the *Annals of Internal Medicine,* the *New England Journal of Medicine,* and the *Journal of the American Medical Association.* These journals, available in hospital, college, and larger public libraries, advertise full-time and part-time jobs.

Apply directly to help-wanted ads in local newspapers. In April and May watch for seasonal employment at summer camps and resorts.

For job openings in nonprofit nursing homes, life care communities, and housing for the elderly, write to Job Mart, American Association of Homes for the Aging, 1129 20th St., NW, Suite 400, Washington, DC 20036.

For employment in a Veterans Administration medical center, contact the Veteran's Administration medical center near you or write to Recruitment and Placement Service, Veterans Administration, 810 N. Lake Shore Dr., Chicago, IL 60611.

Ambulance Driver or Attendant

State requirements vary. Contact local ambulance companies under "Ambulance Svce." in your yellow pages. Some may require their drivers to be emergency medical technicians (see below), or have other first aid training.

Cardiology Technologist

No license is required at this time. Training is available on the job or at hospitals and community colleges. For information about certification write to Cardiovascular Credentialing International, P.O. Box 611, Wright Brothers Sta., Dayton, OH 45419.

Chiropractor

A license is required in all states. For information contact the American Chiropractic Association, 1701 Clarendon Blvd., Arlington, VA 22209; 1-202-276-8800. The *Journal of Chiropractic* advertises job openings.

Clinical Psychologist

A license or certification is required in all states for private practice. More information is available from the American Association of State Psychology Boards, P.O. Box 4389, Montgomery, AL 36103.

Clinical Medical Laboratory Technician

A license is required in a few states and New York City. There are several agencies that issue certificates. For information, contact the Board of Registry, American Society of Clinical Pathologists (P.O. Box 12270, Chicago, IL 60612), American Medical Technologists (710 Higgins Rd., Park Ridge, IL 60068), the National Certification Agency for Medical Laboratory Personnel (1725 DeSales St., NW, Suite 403, Washington, DC 20036) or the International Society for Clinical Laboratory Technology (818 Olive, Saint Louis, MO 63101).

Dental Hygienist
A license is required in all states. A dental hygienist must graduate from an accredited dental hygiene school and pass both a written and a clinical examination. Few states recognize a license issued by another state. A bachelor's degree is required to work in public or school health programs. For information, contact the Commission on Dental Accreditation, American Dental Association, 211 E. Chicago Ave., Suite 1814, Chicago, IL 60611.

Dental assistants are usually trained by the dentist who hires them but may attend an accredited program at a vocational school or community college. For information, contact the American Dental Assistants Association, 919 N. Michigan Ave., Suite 3400, Chicago, IL 60611.

Apply to offices listed in the yellow pages of your telephone directory under "Dentists."

Dentist
A license is required in all states. For information, contact the board of dental examiners in your state, or the American Dental Association, 211 E. Chicago Ave., Chicago, IL 60611; 1-312-440-2500.

Dietitian or Nutritionist
A license is required in some states. A registered dietitian usually has a bachelor's degree, has served an American Dietetic Association–accredited internship, and has passed an examination. Seventy-five hours of continuing education are required every five years to continue registration. For information contact the American Dietetic Association, 216 W. Jackson Blvd., Suite 800, Chicago, IL 60606.

For information about their employment opportunity program, write to the American Society of Medical Technology, 2021 L Street, NW, Suite 900, Washington, DC 20036.

Electroencephalograph Technologist or Technician
No license is required at this time. Voluntary registration is based on one year of training and an exam. For information, contact the American Board of Registry for Electroencephalographic Technology, California/Davis Medical Center, EEG Lab, Rm. 5203, Sacramento, CA 95817.

Emergency Medical Technician
A license is required in some states. Certification is required in all states. For information contact the National Registry of Emergency Medical Technicians, P.O. Box 29233, Columbus, OH 43229. Training and job placement are offered by fire departments, police departments, hospitals, and some community colleges.

Health Service Manager
Write to the American College of Healthcare Executives, 840 N. Lake Shore Dr., Chicago, IL 60611, for information about their services for members.

Home Health Aide
Sixty hours of training and a fifteen-hour practicum are required by many states and for Medicare reimbursement of services. Training is offered by adult education pro-

grams, state programs for the aging, and private agencies. For information write to the National Home Caring Council, 519 C Street, NE, Washington, DC 20002.

Hospital Volunteer
Contact the volunteer coordinators at hospitals near you. Contact the American Red Cross or other agencies listed in the yellow pages of your local telephone directory under "Blood Banks & Centers."

Hypnotherapist
A license may be required in your state. For more information contact the American Society of Clinical Hypnosis, 2250 E. Devon Ave., Suite 336, Des Plaines, IL 60018; 1-312-297-3317.

For information about nontraditional health care, contact the American Foundation for Alternative Health Care, 25 Landfield Ave., Monticello, NY 12701; 1-914-794-8181.

Licensed Practical Nurse
A license is required in all states. In California and Texas the job title is Licensed Vocational Nurse.

For a free career information packet write the National Federation of Licensed Practical Nurses, P.O. Box 18088, Raleigh, NC 27619.

For part-time employment and private duty for home health aides and nurses, apply to agencies listed in the yellow pages under "Nurses" and "Home Health Care."

Massage Therapist
A license is required in many states. For informational brochures and referrals to certified schools, contact the American Massage Therapy Association, 1130 W. Lake Shore Ave., Chicago, IL 60626; 1-312-761-2682.

Medical Records Technician
The accredited record technician and registered record administrator exams are voluntary but enhance employability. For information, contact the American Medical Record Association, 875 N. Michigan Avenue, Suite 1850, Chicago, IL 60611.

Medical Secretary
No license or certification is required. Training courses are offered at vocational schools and community colleges. Apply at health care facilities listed in the yellow pages and watch local classified ads for job openings.

Nursing Aide, Orderly, or Attendant
There are no licensing requirements at this time but some states require training, often on the job. Contact health care agencies in your area for their requirements.

Occupational Therapist
A license is required in many states. It can be obtained by graduates of accredited occupational therapy educational programs who pass the certification examination of

the American Occupational Therapy Association, 1383 Piccard Dr., Rockville, MD 20850.

Occupational Therapy Aide
Graduates of a one-year vocational program or two-year community college program may take the exam to qualify as a certified occupational therapy assistant. For information contact the American Occupational Therapy Association, 1383 Piccard Dr., Rockville, MD 20850.

Optometrist
A license is required in all states. For requirements and career possibilities, write to the American Optometric Association, 243 N. Lindbergh, Saint Louis, MO 63141.

For a free pamphlet describing volunteer opportunities, contact Volunteer Optometric Services to Humanity International, 243 N. Lindbergh Blvd., Saint Louis, MO 63141; 1-314-991-4100. Members travel to the Caribbean, Africa, and other locations on eyecare missions.

Pharmacist
A license is required in all states. Most states will accept a license issued in other states. For information, contact the American Association of Colleges of Pharmacy, 1426 Prince St., Alexandria, VA 22314.

Physical Therapist
A license is required in all states. It can be obtained by graduates of accredited physical therapy educational programs with a passing score on the state licensure examination. For information, write to the American Physical Therapy Association, 1111 N. Fairfax St., Alexandria, VA 22304.

For information on careers in exercise physiology, write to the American College of Sports Medicine, P.O. Box 1440, Indianapolis, IN 46206. Their newsletter lists job openings.

Physical/Corrective Therapy Aide
A license and completion of a two-year accredited degree program may be required in your state. For information contact the American Physical Therapy Association, 1111 N. Fairfax St., Alexandria, VA 22304.

Psychiatric Aide
See Nursing Aid, above.

Physician or Surgeon
A license is required in all states. Board certification in a specialty may require three to five years additional residency and an examination by the appropriate board. For information contact the American Medical Association, 535 N. Dearborn St., Chicago, IL 60610; 1-312-645-5000.

Radiology Technician
A license may be required in your state. Requirements are satisfied by a two-year accredited education program, usually offered by hospitals, and certification by the

American Registry of Radiologic Technologists, 2600 Wayzata Blvd, Minneapolis, MN 55405.

Recreation Therapist

Some states require certification for employment. A bachelor's degree, eighteen hours of graduate credit, and five years of experience are required to become a certified therapeutic recreation specialist. An associate's degree and one year of experience are required for certified therapeutic recreation assistants. For information contact the National Therapeutic Recreation Society, 3101 Park Center Dr., Alexandria, VA 22302, or the National Council for Therapeutic Recreation Certification, 49 S. Main St., Suite 5, Spring Valley, NY 10977.

Registered Nurse

A license is required in all states. For more information, contact the American Nurses' Association, 2420 Pershing Rd., Kansas City, MO 64105; 1-816-474-5720.

Respiratory Therapist

A license may be required in your state. For information, contact the National Board for Respiratory Care, Inc., 11015 W. 75th Terr., Shawnee Mission, KS 66214. For a list of accredited educational programs, write to the Joint Review Committee for Respiratory Therapy Education, 1701 W. Euless Blvd., Suite 200, Euless, TX 76040.

Speech Pathologist or Audiologist

A license is required in many states. A master's degree and internship are required for the certificate of clinical competence (CCC) needed for Medicare reimbursement and a state-issued practice certificate to work in public schools. For information write to the American Speech-Language-Hearing Association, 10801 Rockville Pike, Rockville, MD 20852.

Veterinarian

A license is required in all states. For information write to the American Veterinary Medical Association, 930 N. Meacham Rd., Schaumburg, IL 60196.

Apply directly to member hospitals listed in the annual directory of the American Animal Hospital Association, P.O. Box 150899, Denver, CO 80215; 1-303-279-2500; $44.50 to nonmembers.

For volunteer opportunities, contact the American Humane Association (9725 E. Hampden, Denver, CO 80231; 1-303-695-0811) and the American Society for the Prevention of Cruelty to Animals (441 E. 92nd St., New York, NY 10128; 1-212-876-7700).

For information on veterinary acupuncture contact the National Association for Veterinary Acupuncture, 1905 Sunnycrest, Fullerton, CA 92635; 1-714-871-3000.

HOUSING AND CONSTRUCTION

Trade Schools for Construction Workers

To locate an accredited vocational school near you that teaches the trade that interests you, consult the *Handbook of Accredited Private Trade and Technical Schools* at your library, or write to the publisher, The Career College Association, P.O. Box 2006, Annapolis Junction, MD 20007-2006 (1-202-333-1021) for information.

Apprenticeships in the Construction Trades

For information about entry-level work opportunities and apprenticeships, contact local contractors listed in the yellow pages of your telephone directory and the nearest state job service office or state apprenticeship agency, listed in the government pages of your telephone directory.

Free brochures, *Apprenticeship Information* and *The National Apprenticeship Program,* are available from the Bureau of Apprenticeship and Training, U.S. Dept. of Labor, 200 Constitution Ave., NW, Washington, DC 20210; 1-202-535-0545.

Licenses

Many municipalities require electricians, plumbers, or independent contractors to be licensed to work in that locality. For requirements in your community, contact your city or town government offices or a local contractor.

Employers of Construction Workers

For job opportunities in construction, apply directly to employers listed under "Contractors — General," as well as headings cross-referenced under "Contractors," in the yellow pages of your telephone book. Check listings for your specialty under "Insulation Contractors — Cold & Heat," "Glass — Automobile, Plate, Window, etc.," "Plumbers," "Painting Contractors," "Mason Contractors," "Carpenters," and "Electric Contractors."

For a list of builders who employ construction help, consult *Builder and Contractor,* the membership directory of Associated Builders and Contractors, 444 N. Capitol St., Washington, DC 20001; 1-202-637-8800. This book is not usually available in libraries; you might be able to use it at a local builder's office or a large builders' supply store.

For a list of construction contractors who employ skilled, semiskilled, and professional personnel, and a list of employment agencies specializing in construction openings, consult the *Construction Employment Guide in the National and International Field* (1986; World Trade Academy Press, 50 E. 42nd St., Suite 509, New York, NY 10017; for $20.00, postage paid).

Other Opportunities for Experienced Construction Workers

Certification is required by some states and municipalities for employment as a building inspector. For a free brochure, *Building Inspection as a Career,* and information about certification, send 25¢ to the International Conference of Building Officials, 5360 S. Workman Mill Rd., Whittier, CA 90601.

Contact Building Officials and Code Administrators International, Inc., 4051 W. Flossmoor Rd., Country Club Hills, IL 60477, for information about their certification program for building inspectors.

For information about certification and training as a construction cost estimator, write to the National Estimating Society (1001 Connecticut Ave., NW, Suite 800, Washington, DC 20036) or the American Society of Professional Estimators (6911 Richmond Hwy, Suite 230, Alexandria, VA 22306).

EDUCATION

Licenses

To find out if a license is required in your state for the particular job you want, if your old license is still valid, or if licenses from other states are transferable to your state, contact your state education department or department of public instruction. The address is available from any school, library, or from the Federation of State Licensing Boards, 501 E. California Ave., Glendale, CA 91206.

For training and licensing requirements for work in elementary and secondary schools, consult John Tryneski, *Requirements for Certification of Teachers, Counselors, Librarians, Administrators for Elementary and Secondary Schools* (annual; University of Chicago), which also contains a list of addresses and phone numbers for state offices of certification, arranged alphabetically by state.

College and University Teacher

Certification and licensing are not required. Colleges and universities usually require that their teachers obtain a doctorate, but community colleges often hire teachers with only a master's degree.

For work as a teacher or counselor in colleges, apply directly to colleges and universities listed in *Peterson's Guide to Four Year Colleges, Peterson's Guide to Two Year Colleges,* and the regional *Peterson's* Guides for New England, the Southeast, the Southwest, New York, the West, and the Mid-Atlantic states. Colleges are also listed in *Paterson's American Education* (1986; Educational Directories, Inc.).

For employment, respond to advertised openings in the *Academic Journal* (monthly; P.O. Box 392, Newton, CT 06470), the *Affirmative Action Register* (monthly; Affirmative Action, Inc., 8356 Olive Blvd., Saint Louis, MO 63132), or the *Chronicle of Higher Education* (weekly; 1255 23rd St., NW, Suite 700, Washington, DC 20037).

Preschool Teacher

Requirements vary. Many preschool programs may require their teachers to hold an associate's degree in early childhood education, and teachers' aides to have a high school diploma.

For information about working with disadvantaged children, contact the Head Start Program, Administration for Children, Youth, and Families, P.O. Box 1182, Washington, DC 20013.

For information about job opportunities and requirements in private nursery schools and day-care centers, contact the National Association for the Education of Young Children (1834 Connecticut Ave., NW, Washington, DC 20009), the North American Montessori Teacher's Association (2859 Scarsborough Rd., Cleveland Heights, OH 44118), or the American Montessori Society (150 Fifth Ave., Suite 203, New York, NY 10011).

Kindergarten, Elementary, and Secondary School Teacher

The minimum requirement for a license to teach full time in public elementary and seondary schools is a bachelor's degree, including certain courses and the period of supervised practice teaching specified by your state. Many states have alternative programs to help older students obtain their teaching certificates. Some requirements may be waived for substitute teachers, teachers in private and parochial schools, or teachers in areas where there are shortages.

For job opportunities, request application forms from the personnel offices of local schools and apply according to their instructions. Locate private schools and public school districts under "Schools" in the yellow pages of telephone directories, area directories produced by chambers of commerce, and other local directories such as the *New York City Education Bluebook*.

For additional job opportunities, apply to schools listed in *Patterson's American Education* (annual; Educational Directories, Inc.), which lists 19,000 high schools, 11,000 junior high schools, 2,000 parochial schools, and 9,000 colleges, trade, technical, private, and prep schools in the United States, arranged by category of school and with an alphabetical index.

For job opportunities in boarding schools, apply directly to schools listed in *Boarding School Guide: Facts and Figures on 231 Leading Schools Throughout the United States* (Agee Publishers, Inc., 1989).

To find out if your state offers free employment services for teachers, contact your state education department or department of public instruction (see Licenses, above). One example is New York's Teacher Career Recruitment Clearinghouse. Applicants who submit the required information to the clearinghouse receive vacancy lists so that they may apply directly to the school districts indicated on the list. School districts with listed vacancies may also request information about qualified applicants registered with the clearinghouse.

Teachers' Aide

Requirements vary but a license is not required.

For job opportunities, apply directly to school districts (see resources listed for Kindergarten, Elementary, and Secondary School Teacher, above).

Tutor

Requirements vary but a license is generally not required.

For job opportunities, apply directly to school districts (see resources listed for Kindergarten, Elementary, and Secondary School Teacher, above).

For information about going into private practice and starting your own business as a home tutor, see Your Own Business, page 322.

For local jobs with national tutoring services that prepare students for tests such as the SAT (Scholastic Aptitude Test) and GRE (Graduate Record Examination), monitor classified ads in your newspaper. The major qualifications are having scored high yourself on the relevant examination and the ability to communicate with a group of teenagers.

Counselor

Most states require that counselors have a state license in counseling to work in private practice. Requirements vary but generally a master's degree in counseling is required. For more information, write to the National Board for Certified Counselors, 5999 Stevenson Ave., Alexandria, VA 22304.

To work in a public school, most states require counselors to have both counseling and teaching certification. Depending on the state, a master's degree in counseling and two to five years of teaching experience may be required (see Licenses, above).

Individuals with a bachelor's degree in psychology, counseling, or a related field and work experience in personnel or job placement may qualify for certain positions, but not those requiring a state license.

For job opportunities, use the resources listed above for jobs in elementary and secondary schools and colleges.

Trainer

For information about jobs as a trainer, write to the American Society for Training and Development (ASTD), 1630 Duke St., Box 1443, Alexandria, VA 22313.

Adult Education

The requirements for teachers of adult and continuing education are varied. If the continuing education is in a particular profession, the teacher must at least be fully qualified in that profession. Requirements may include a degree and certification or license in that profession. In the case of artisans and craftspeople, practical experience may be qualification enough. The emphasis may be on experience and skill rather that on formal credentials. There is, however, a move to tighten qualifications for adult educators in some states.

To locate organizations offering adult education, contact local high schools, community colleges, the Board of Cooperative Educational Services, and the YMCA and YWCA. If they offer adult education classes, request a copy of their catalog of courses. Ask their coordinator of adult education how they choose the classes that they will offer each semester. Most offer certain basic classes every semester and choose the teachers from applications. In other cases, a person who wishes to teach a course will be asked to submit a written proposal describing the content of the course that she would like to teach. If the school feels that the person is qualified and that the course is worthwhile and interesting, the teacher is hired.

Driving Instructor

Generally, a driving instructor will be a high school graduate, be over 21, and have a valid driver's license and a good driving record. There may be other requirements in your state.

For more information about teaching traffic school or defensive driving classes, contact the local traffic safety board in the government pages of your telephone directory or write to the American Driver and Traffic Safety Education Association, 123 North Pitt St., Alexandria, VA 22314.

For other job opportunities in drivers' education, contact your local board of education and the offices of commercial driving schools regarding possible openings in your area.

County Extension Agent

For information on locating and applying for public service jobs, see Public Service, page 295.

Volunteer

To teach basic reading skills or English as a second language on a volunteer basis, contact Literacy Volunteers of America. They will train you and pair you with a student. For help locating your local chapter, write Literacy Volunteers of America, 5795 Widewaters Pkwy., Syracuse, NY 13214.

For a free booklet about the Peace Corps, contact them at 1990 K Street, NW, Room 8500, Washington, DC 20526; 1-800-424-8580.

PERSONAL CAREGIVING

Funeral Director or Mortician

Some states license funeral directors. Those who do embalming are licensed in all states. For the address of your state examining board and list of accredited mortuary schools, send a stamped, self-addressed envelope to the American Board of Funeral Service Education, 14 Crestwood Rd., Cumberland, ME 04021.

Funeral Attendant

For work as a funeral attendant, apply directly to businesses listed in the yellow pages of your telephone directory under "Funeral Homes."

Weight Loss or Fitness Coach

Education and certification requirements for weight loss and fitness coaches vary according to the services offered. Some employers may require on-the-job training under an experienced coach. Fitness coaches may be required to have first aid training and supervisors of aquarobics to hold Red Cross certification in lifesaving.

For coaching in schools, see Education, page 316. For work as a dietitian or nutritionist see The Health Business, page 309.

Hairdresser, Barber, or Cosmetologist

Hairdressers, barbers, and cosmetologists are licensed in all states. A list of accredited schools and licensing requirements can be obtained from your state board of cosmetology or from the National Accrediting Commission of Cosmetology Arts and Sciences, 1333 H St., NW, Suite 710, Washington, DC 20005, or the National Association of Accredited Cosmetology Schools, Inc., 5201 Leesburg Pike, Falls Church, VA 22041.

For a free booklet, *Cosmetology as a Career,* send a stamped, self-addressed envelope to the National Cosmetology Association, 3510 Olive St., Saint Louis, MO 63103.

Housekeeper, Maid, or Cleaner

For work as a cleaner or housekeeper, monitor classified ads in your local newspapers or apply directly to housecleaning services listed in the yellow pages of your telephone book under "Cleaning Service."

Handyman

Find jobs as a handyman by advertising your services by word of mouth, posting small printed advertisements on bulletin boards in grocery or hardware stores, or advertising in small local newspapers.

Child Care in the Child's Home

For job openings in child care, monitor classified ads in local newspapers.

Contact your local fire department, hospital, or rescue squad to find out if they offer a Safe Sitter Certificate program. While the program may be aimed at beginners, it offers an update of skills and an added credential when applying for positions.

For information about working as a nanny and special nanny employment agencies, contact the International Nanny Association, 976 W. Foothill Blvd., Suite 591, Claremont, CA 91711; 1-800-274-6462.

To locate nanny placement services, check the yellow pages of your telephone directory under both "Employment Agencies" and "Day Nurseries & Child Care."

For the location of accredited nanny certificate programs near you, contact the American Council of Nanny Schools, Delta College, University Center, MI 48710. The Council sponsors a nationwide registry for graduates of these programs.

Child Care Outside the Child's Home

For the telephone number of the licensing agency in your area, and information about child care center standards, contact the Child Care Division, Children's Defense Fund (122 C St., NW, Washington, DC 20001; 1-202-424-2460) or Information Services, National Association for the Education of Young Children (1834 Connecticut Ave., NW, Washington, DC 20009; 1-800-424-2460). For their book, *Setting Up for Infant Care; Guidelines for Centers and Family Day Care Homes* by Annabelle Godwin, send $5.00 to the National Association for the Education of Young Children.

For information about applying for the Child Development Associate Credential (CDA), write to CDA National Credentialing Program, 1718 Connecticut Ave., NW, Suite 500, Washington, DC 20009.

For job oportunities, apply to businesses listed in the yellow pages of your telephone directory under "Day Nurseries & Child Care."

For complete information on starting your own day-care business, see Helen and Dolores McCrory, *The Business of Family Day Care* (1988; Roundtable Publishing, 933 W. Pico Blvd., Santa Monica, CA 90405; 1-800-222-5322 or 1-800-826-7611 in California) or Patricia C. Gallagher, *Start Your Own At-Home Child Care Business* (1989; Doubleday, Customer Service Dept., 30 E. Oakton Ave., Des Plaines, IL 60016; 1-800-223-6384).

For more information on starting a new day-care business see Your Own Business, page 322.

Respite or Adult Day Care

To locate programs in your community that may hire adult caregivers, call the Office for the Aging in the government pages of your telephone directory or your local office of the United Way. Programs are often sponsored by hospitals, churches, YMCAs or YWCAs, or other community service organizations. Daily home care may be provided by agencies listed in the yellow pages of your telephone directory under "Home Health Care." Contact these organizations directly for information about applying for job openings.

Animal Attendant, Veterinary Assistant, or Dog Groomer

To find the nearest accredited school for becoming an Animal Health Technician (AHT), a two-year college-level program, contact the American Veterinary Medical Association, 930 North Meacham Rd., Schaumberg, IL 60196.

For job opportunities, apply to businesses listed in the yellow pages of your telephone directory under "Pet & Dog Training," "Kennels," "Pet Washing & Grooming," and "Pet Shops."

For information on becoming a pet sitter, send a stamped, self-addressed envelope to the National Association of Pet Sitters, 1020 Brookstone Ave., Suite 3, Winston-Salem, NC 27101.

More information about starting your own business as a pet sitter is available in Patti J. Moran, *Pet Sitting for Profit* (1988; New Beginnings, 540 High Bridge Rd., Pinnacle, NC 27043; $12.45, postage paid).

For information on buying a pet-sitting franchise, contact Pets Are Inn (27 N. 4th St., Suite 500, Minneapolis, MN 55401; 1-800-248-PETS) or Pet Nanny of America Inc. (1000 Long Blvd., Suite 9, Lansing, MI 48911). Also see Your Own Business, page 323.

If you wish to volunteer in animal care there are many opportunities at local animal shelters and other agencies. To volunteer to raise a puppy until it is old enough for formal training, contact the Guide Dog Foundation for the Blind (371 E. Jericho Turnpike, Smithtown, NY 11787; 1-800-548-4337) or Canine Companions for Independence (P.O. Box 446, Santa Rosa, CA 95402; 1-707-528-0830).

House Sitter

Advertise your services by word of mouth or with a classified ad in a local newspaper. Much of the information in *Pet Sitting for Profit* (see above) applies to house sitters and plant sitters as well.

HOMEMAKING

Vocational Guidance

Contact your local community college for information about their services. They may offer free job counseling, job-hunting tips, and inexpensive classes to update your skills.

For information about their activities and services, contact the Displaced Homemakers Network (1411 K St., NW, Suite 930, Washington, DC 20005; 1-202-628-6767) and the American Association of Retired Persons, Worker Equity (601 E St., NW, Washington, DC 20049; 1-202-434-2277). They can put you in touch with local chapters and workshops that may be scheduled to be held in your area.

A free pamphlet called *Career Development Resources* is available from Catalyst, 250 Park Ave. S., New York, NY 10003; 1-212-777-8900.

For career ideas, see Beatryce Nivens, *Careers for Women Without College Degrees* (1988; McGraw-Hill Publishing Co., Princeton Rd., Hightstown, NJ 08520; 1-800-262-4729).

For information about working at home, see Patricia McConnel, *Woman's Work-at-Home Handbook* (Bantam, 1986) and Lynie Arden, *The Work-at-Home Sourcebook* (Live Oak Publications, 1990).

Books for Job Hunters

Ask your library or bookstore to find you both Richard Nelson Bolles, *What Color Is Your Parachute?* (annual; Ten Speed Press) and Samuel N. Ray, *Job Hunting After 50* (Wiley, 1991). Not just for women, these books contain practical job-hunting information for anyone.

Locating Employers

For information about working for temporary agencies see Business Services, page 325.

Monitor help-wanted ads in local newspapers for job openings in companies that offer to train new employees.

Apply directly to companies listed in Baila Zeitz and Lorraine Dusky, *The Best Companies for Women* (1988; Pocket Books, 200 Old Tappen Rd., Old Tappen, NJ 07675; 1-800-223-2348).

Specialty Modeling

For jobs in specialty modeling see Retailing, page 333. Specialty modeling includes theme modeling at shopping malls, parts modeling (hands, etc.), and character modeling.

Nanny

For information about becoming a nanny, contact the International Nanny Association toll-free at 1-800-274-6462. Also see Personal Caregiving, page 319.

Teaching

Request a list of the adult education classes offered by your local community college. Mail the college a proposal for a new class that you could teach, based on your hobby or volunteer experience. For more information see Education, page 318.

Starting Your Own Business

See Your Own Business, below, and the resource sections of occupations of interest to you, but also ask your reference librarian to recommend books about your interest.

YOUR OWN BUSINESS

Small Business Ideas

Entrepreneur, Inc., Success, Income Opportunities, New Business Opportunities, and *Income Plus,* periodicals available at libraries or at your newsstand, run articles about new businesses and small business ideas.

Starting Your Own Business

For information on starting your own business, consult *Running a One-Person Business* (1988; Ten Speed Press, P.O. Box 7123, Berkeley, CA 94707; 1-800-841-2665; $12.00 plus $1.50 handling).

Two books for starting your own business after fifty are Nancy Olsen, *Starting a Mini-Business: A Guidebook for Seniors* (1988; Fair Oaks Publishing Co., 941 Populus

Pl., Sunnyvale, CA 94086; 1-408-732-1078; $8.95) and Ina Lee Selden, *Going Into Business For Yourself: New Beginnings After 50* (AARP Books, 1988. For information call AARP at 1-202-434-2277).

For information about starting a new business according to the laws in your state, see the *Starting and Operating a Business of Your Own* state-by-state series (Publishers Group West, 4065 Hollis St., Emeryville, CA 94608; 1-800-982-8319). Current handbooks for most states are $29.95 each.

For *Starting and Managing a Business from Your Home,* send $2 to the Small Business Administration, P.O. Box 15434, Fort Worth, TX 76119. Ask for form 115A, which lists their other publications with prices.

For information about setting fees and marketing your service, see Herman Holtz, *The Consultants Guide to Winning Clients* (1988) and Howard L. Shenson, *The Contract and Fee-Setting Guide for Consultants and Professionals* (1990), both from John Wiley, 605 Third Ave., New York, NY 10158-0012.

For expert advice when starting your own business, consult the Service Corps of Retired Executives (SCORE), sponsored by the Small Business Administration. Call 1-800-368-5855 for help in locating your local SCORE volunteers.

For information about Small Business Administration (SBA) loans, contact the Small Business Administration office in your region. If you can't locate one in your telephone directory, call the SBA's Washington office at 1-202-653-7562 and they will locate it for you. Ask your district office for the SBA guaranteed loan pamphlet and application form. Contact SCORE (see above) for help filling out and submitting the application form correctly.

For information about selling to the federal government, consult Barry L. McVay, *Proposals That Win Federal Contracts* (1989; Panoptic Enterprises, P.O. Box 1099, Woodbridge, VA 22193-0099; 1-703-670-2812).

Franchises

Franchise Opportunities Handbook (Superintendent of Documents, U.S. Government Printing Office, Washington, DC 20402; 1-202-783-3238).

Raymond J. Munna, *Franchise Selection: Separating Fact From Fiction* (1988; Granite Publications, P.O. Box 31, Abinton, PA 19001; 1-215-659-6279).

Tim Redden, *Franchise Buyers Handbook* (1989; Scott Foresman & Co., 1900 E. Lake Ave., Glenview, IL 60025; 1-800-982-4377).

Franchising World, a periodical available at your newsstand or by mail (International Franchising Association, 1350 New York Ave., NW, Suite 900, Washington, DC 20005; 1-202-628-8000; $2.50 each, six issues for $13.95). Write for a free catalog of their publications for franchisees.

HUMAN RESOURCES

Career Counselor

For employment as a career counselor, apply directly to career counseling offices at local colleges.

Contact the American Association for Counseling and Development, 5999 Stevenson Ave., Alexandria, VA 22304; 1-703-823-9800, for information about their programs and services.

Executive Recruiter or Outplacement Counselor

Apply directly to offices listed in *The Directory of Executive Recruiters,* (annual; Consultants News), available at larger libraries.

A list of reputable outplacement firms is available from the Association of Outplacement Consulting Firms, Inc., 364 Parsippany Rd., Parsippany, NJ 07054. Letters of application may be sent directly to the firms.

For a free brochure, contact the Association of Executive Search Consultants, 17 Sherwood Pl., Greenwich, CT 06830; 1-203-661-6606. The association's services for its members include a newsletter.

Equal Opportunity or Affirmative Action Officer

For futher information about training, contact the American Association for Affirmative Action, 11 E. Hubbard St., Suite 200, Chicago, IL 60611; 1-312-329-2512.

Retirement Counselor

For information about train-the-trainer workshops on preretirement planning, contact the International Society of Pre-Retirement Planners, c/o L. Malcolm Rodman, 11312 Old Club Rd., Rockville, MD 20852; 1-800-327-4777.

For job opportunities, apply directly to agencies listed in the yellow pages of your telephone directory under "Retirement Planning Services."

PURCHASING

Purchasing Manager

For information and the requirements for certified purchasing managers, contact the National Association of Purchasing Management, Inc., P.O. Box 22160, Tempe, AZ 85285.

Apply directly to employers listed in the "Marketing and Sales" section of *Peterson's Business and Management Jobs* (annnual; Peterson's Guides). The guide also contains instructions on how to submit applications to these employers.

To locate possible employers of purchasing managers in the construction industry, see Housing and Construction, page 315.

Contract Administrator

For information and the requirements for certified associate contract managers (CACMs) and certified professional contract managers (CPCMs), contact the National Contract Management Association, 1912 Woodford Rd., Vienna, VA 22182.

For job application forms and application instructions for work in the General Services Administration, contact the Federal Acquisition Institute, GSA, 18th and F Sts., NW, Washington, DC 20405.

For instructions for applying for jobs with other government agencies, see Public Service, page 295.

Purchasing Agent

For information and the requirements for certified public purchasing officers (CPPOs), contact the National Institute of Governmental Purchasing, Inc., 115 Hillwood Ave., Falls Church, VA 22046.

Apply directly to companies listed in the yellow pages of your telephone directory under "Purchasing Svce."

For other potential employers of purchasing agents, see Sales and Marketing, page 331.

BUSINESS SERVICES

All Business Services
Contact the state job service office or the senior community service employment program listed in the government pages of your local telephone directory.

Part-Time and Seasonal Jobs
For interesting seasonal and part-time jobs, see Jeffrey Maltzman, *Jobs in Paradise: The Definitive Guide to Exotic Jobs Everywhere* (1990; Harper & Row, Keystone Industrial Park, Scranton, PA 18512; 1-800-242-7737 or 1-800-982-4377 in Pennsylvania).

Temporary Employment
For advice about finding temporary jobs and the rights of temporary employees, see William Lewis and Nancy Schuman, *The Temp Worker's Handbook* (1988; AMACOM, 135 W. 50th St., New York, NY 10020; $13.95).

For a list of employment services in your area that are members of the National Association of Temporary Services Firms, send a stamped, self-addressed envelope to NATS, 119 S. Saint Asaph St., Alexandria, VA 22314; 1-703-549-6287.

Temporary help services vary, so you should visit more than one of the companies listed under "Employment Contractors — Temporary Help" in your yellow pages. Ask whether they offer 1) free training in word processing and personal computers, 2) fringe benefits, and 3) special services to workers over 55. Look for companies like Reflex Services, Inc., who have built their business around retirees.

Secretary
Apply directly to agencies listed in the yellow pages of your telephone directory under "Secretarial Services."

For information about becoming a certified professional secretary, contact Professional Secretaries International, 301 E. Armour Blvd., Kansas City, MO 64111; 1-816-531-7010.

For employment as a medical secretary, see The Health Business, page 312.

Typist or Stenographer
Apply directly to agencies listed in the yellow pages of your telephone directory under "Typing Svce." and "Copying & Duplicating Svce."

Survey Interviewer
Apply directly to agencies listed in the yellow pages of your telephone directory under "Market Research & Analysis."

For information about survey jobs and companies that employ interviewers, see

Lynie Arden, *The Work-At-Home Sourcebook* (1990; Live Oak Publications, P.O. Box 2193, Boulder, CO 80306; $14.95).

Apply to companies listed in *Agencies and Organizations Represented in AAPOR Membership* (annual; American Association for Public Opinion Research, P.O. Box 17, Princeton, NJ), which can be found in the libraries of large colleges or those that sponsor public opinion research.

Private Investigator or Detective

A license is required in most states. For information, contact the National Association of Legal Investigators (Box 210, 303 N. Shamrock, East Alton, IL 62024) or the Society of Professional Investigators (1120 E. 31st St., Brooklyn, NY 11210).

For a free job information packet, write to the Office of Publications, National Employment Listing Services, Criminal Justice Center, Sam Houston State University, Huntsville, TX 77341.

For a free catalog, write the Nick Harris Detective Academy, 6740 Kester Ave., Van Nuys, CA 91405.

Security Guard

Apply for job openings advertised in the *National Employment Listing Service Bulletin* (monthly; National Employment Listing Services [address above]; subscription, $30.00).

Apply to companies listed in the yellow pages of your telephone directory under "Guard & Patrol Svce." and to large stores or shopping malls in your area.

For work as a federal security guard you must have a valid driver's license, and military service is desirable. For information on applying for federal jobs, see Public Service, page 295.

Custodian or Cleaner

Apply directly to employers listed under "Cleaning Svce. — Industrial" in the yellow pages of your telephone directory, and monitor the classified advertisements in local newspapers.

Your Own Cleaning Business

Read Vikki C. Wachuku-Stokes, *How to Start Your Own Cleaning Business with as Little as Five Dollars* (1989; Vikki's Creative Communications, 119 E. Grand River, Suite 6, East Lansing, MI 48823; 1-517-336-9100; $19.95).

For more information on starting your own business, see Your Own Business, page 322.

HOSPITALITY

Information and Educational Opportunities in Hospitality

For free informational pamphlets, *Chef and Cook, Waiter/Waitress, Bartender,* or *Restaurant/Food Service Manager* contact the Educational Foundation of the National Restaurant Association, 20 N. Wacker Dr., Suite 2620, Chicago, IL 60606; 1-800-424-5156.

For a free copy of the *Independent Learning Course Catalog for Hotel, Motel, and*

Food Service Management, write to the Educational Institute of the American Culinary Federation, P.O. Box 1240, East Lansing, MI 48826.

Food Service Worker

For job opportunities as a food service manager, apply directly to employers listed in the yellow pages of your telephone directory under "Food Svce. Management."

For job opportunities as a waiter, waitress, or other food service worker, apply directly to businesses listed in the yellow pages under "Restaurants," "Caterers," "Foods — Carry Out," "Gourmet Shops," "Taverns," and "Banquet Facilities." "Inns," "Clubs," and "Golf Courses — Private" may also employ food service workers.

Baker

For job openings in a bakery, apply directly to businesses listed in the yellow pages under "Bakers — Retail" and "Bakers — Wholesale."

Bartender

For information about schools that offer courses in bartending and bar management, consult the *College Blue Book,* vol. 5, *Occupational Education* (annual; Macmillan). The Career College Association, P.O. Box 2006, Annapolis Junction, MD 20007-2006, will tell you which bartending schools are accredited. Most of these schools offer placement services to their graduates; see Chapter 5.

Chef or Cook

For free brochures, *National Certification Program for Chefs and Cooks* and *National Apprenticeship Training Program for Cooks,* contact the Educational Institute of the American Culinary Federation, P.O. Box 3466, Saint Augustine, FL 32084; 1-904-824-4468.

For a comprehensive guide to cooking schools and culinary travel programs worldwide, see *The Guide to Cooking Schools* (annual; Shaw Associates Educational Publishers, 625 Biltmore Way, Suite 1406, Coral Gables, FL 33134; $14.95).

Shoppers' Service Worker

For jobs in shoppers' service, monitor the help-wanted ads in your newspaper. If a distant shopping service is checking a business in your area, they do advertise in local papers for help. They may ask you to mail a resume and be interviewed by telephone or at a rented location in a shopping mall or large hotel.

Shopping services are usually members of the national organizations for the industries that they monitor. Services that check restaurants, for example, would be members of the National Restaurant Association, 1200 7th St., NW, Washington, DC 20036. National organizations for other businesses can be found listed in the annual *Encyclopedia of Associations.*

For other jobs in shoppers' services, see Lynie Arden, *The Work-at-Home Source-book* (Live Oak Publications, 1990).

Bed-and-Breakfast Manager

For complete information on opening your own bed-and-breakfast business, consult Mary E. Davies, *So You Want To Be an Innkeeper* (1989; Professional Association of

Innkeepers International, Box 90710, Santa Barbara, CA 93190; 1-805-965-0707; $12.95 plus $2 postage). On request, the association will send a free kit, including "Ten Questions to Ask Yourself in Considering Innkeeping as a Profession," a list of classes and consultants on inns, and information about membership in the association.

For advice on running a bed-and-breakfast business from a bed-and-breakfast owner, consult Jan Stankus, *How To Own and Operate a Bed and Breakfast* (1989; Globe Pequot, 138 W. Main St., Chester, CT 06412; 1-800-243-0495; $13.95) or Barbara Notarious and Gail Brewer, *Open Your Own Bed and Breakfast* (1991; J. Wiley, Eastern Distribution Center, 1 Wiley Dr., Somerset, NJ 08873; 1-201-469-4400). Barbara Notarious offers a seminar on setting up a bed-and-breakfast at her local board of cooperative educational services. Watch for similar adult education courses in your area.

For reports on popular inns and a place to advertise your new business, see *Country Inns Bed and Breakfast* (P.O. Box 182, South Orange, NJ 07079; write for current subscription price).

Other Lodging Jobs

For job opportunities as a bellhop, concierge, or hotel clerk, apply directly to businesses listed in the yellow pages of your telephone directory under "Motels & Hotels" and "Inns."

TRAVEL AND RECREATION

Employers

For information about thousands of seasonal jobs at resorts, camps, amusement parks, hotels, summer theater, ranches, and national parks, see the *Summer Employment Directory of the United States* (annual; Writer's Digest Books, 1507 Dana Ave., Cincinnati, OH 45207; 1-800-543-4644 or 1-800-551-0884 in Ohio). Many of the employers listed here also offer year-round employment.

For a list of employers and instructions on how to apply for many jobs in travel and recreation, consult Jeffrey Maltzman, *Jobs in Paradise: The Definitive Guide to Exotic Jobs Everywhere* (1990; Harper & Row, Keystone Industrial Park, Scranton, PA 18512; 1-800-242-7737 or 1-800-982-4377 in Pennsylvania).

For information about job opportunities in travel, consult Karen Rubin, *Flying High in Travel: A Complete Guide to Careers in the Travel Industry* (1986; J. Wiley, 1 Wiley Dr., Somerset, NJ 08875; 1-201-469-4400).

For leads to employers hiring temporary help for special and seasonal events, request any brochures that are offered by your local or state tourist office. Apply directly to the operators of the events.

Card Dealer or Croupier

Croupiers in Las Vegas must meet the requirements of the casino where they wish to work. This may include courses at one of the dealers' schools. For exact requirements, contact the casino where you wish to work.

In Atlantic City, beginners must attend a state-approved school. Blackjack and craps are primary games and involve 160 to 240 hours of training. Secondary games, such as roulette and baccarat, require 80 to 120 hours of training. Graduates must then be approved by the New Jersey Casino Control Commission. Anyone convicted of a felony is automatically rejected. For more information contact the Casino Employment Licensing Assistance Center, 177 S. Ocean Ave., Atlantic City, NJ 08401; 1-609-348-5770.

For a list of schools that offer casino training, consult *The College Blue Book*, vol. 5, *Occupational Education* (annual; Macmillan), under "Dealers, Dice and Blackjack" and "Card Dealing, Professional." For a list of accredited schools, contact the Career College Association, P.O. Box 2006, Annapolis Junction, MD 20007-2006.

For information about their program and services contact the Atlantic County Community College, 1535 Bacharach Blvd., Atlantic City, NJ 08401; 1-609-343-4848.

Crew Staff

Cruise ships usually hire in the country of ownership or registry. Americans seeking a staff position as a cook, nurse, steward, or deckhand on a cruise ship should apply directly to personnel directors of the cruise lines. Locate companies that own ships of United States registry in the current *OHRG Cruise Directory* or other cruise directory, available at your library or travel agency. Singers, actors, or comedians for entertainment and athletes, writers, or lecturers for theme cruises are hired through entertainment agencies (see The Visual and Performing Arts, page 305). Bramson Entertainment Agency, 1440 Broadway, New York, NY 10018, is probably the largest agency that hires for cruise ships. To get started working the cruise ship circuit they suggest that an experienced entertainer write to the agency, describe his skills, and request an audition.

For tips on finding crew positions, see Alison Muir-Bennett, *The Hitchhiker's Guide to the Oceans: Crewing around the World* (1990; Seven Seas Press, P.O. Box 220, Camden, ME 04843; 1-800-822-8158; $10.95).

Amusement or Recreation Attendant

Apply directly to "Recreation Centers" listed in the yellow pages of your telephone directory. For employment in municipal recreation departments see Public Service, page 295.

Ski Instructor

For information about certification, contact the Professional Ski Instructors of America, 133 Vinegordon #240, Lakewood, CO 80228; 1-303-447-0842.

Apply directly to "Skiing Centers & Resorts" listed in the yellow pages of your telephone directory, or to ski areas where you have skied.

Boat Captain

For information about licensing and commercial use of a boat, contact the U.S. Coast Guard, Captain of the Port Office, Customhouse, New Orleans, LA 70130; 1-800-336-2628.

Golf Starter, Course Marshal, or Ranger

Knowledge of the game is required. Apply directly to courses listed in the yellow pages of your telephone directory under "Golf Courses — Private," "Golf Courses — Public," and "Golf Practice Ranges."

Travel Agent

Consult *How to Become a Spare Time Travel Agent* (1987; Stan Volin, Box 571-B, Hicksville, NY 11802).

For information about correspondence courses, contact the American Society of Travel Agents (4400 McArthur Blvd., NW, Washington, DC 20007; 1-202-965-7520) and Trans World Travel College (11500 Ambassador Dr., P.O. Box 20127, Kansas City, MO 64195; 1-800-821-7373).

Apply directly to businesses listed in the yellow pages of your telephone directory under "Travel Agencies & Bureaus" and to agencies listed in *Travel Weekly's World Travel Directory* or one of the other industry directories, available in larger libraries and at travel agencies.

Tour Guide

For information about certification as a tour manager, contact the International Association of Tour Managers, 1646 Chapel St., New Haven, CT 06511; 1-203-777-5994. Courses in tour management are offered through New York University and Metropolitan State College in Denver. The association has a job bank and placement service for members.

The American Tour Managers Association, 8909 Dorrington Ave., West Hollywood, CA 90048, publishes a newsletter with job news and runs a job network for members.

For information about their training programs for tour guides, write the American Tour Management Institute (271 Madison Ave., New York, NY 10016) and the International Tour Management Institute (625 Market St., San Francisco, CA 94105).

For more information on becoming a tour guide, consult *How You Can Travel Free as a Group Tour Organizer* (1987; Pilot Books, 103 Cooper St., Babylon, NY 11702; 1-516-422-2225).

Apply directly to tour operators lited in the yellow pages of your telephone directory under "Tours — Operators & Promoters" and "Travel Agencies & Bureaus" or listed in *Travel Weekly's World Travel Directory*.

Docent

Applications for summer employment in the position of park ranger (interpretation), who explains park rules, safety, plants, and wildlife to park visitors, are available from the National Park Service site where you wish to work or from the U.S. Department of the Interior, National Park Service, Seasonal Employment Unit, P.O. Box 37127, Washington, DC 20012-7127. For permanent, full-time employment see Public Service, page 294.

For job openings as a docent, apply directly to employers listed in museum directories. See employers of curators in Library and Research Work, page 302.

Ticket Agent

Apply directly to airlines listed in *The Official Airline Directory* or contact the Air Transport Association of America, 1709 New York Ave., NW, Washington, DC 20006, for a list of airlines with sales outlets in your area.

Flight Attendant

There is very stiff competition for positions with major airlines and very good looks are an important factor. To locate small regional airlines, who are more likely to need applicants, check with the nearest airport and in the yellow pages of your telephone directory under "Airline Companies."

To locate airlines see Ticket Agent, above.

Air Courier

For work as an air courier, see Jesse L. Riddle, *A Simple Guide to Courier Travel* (1989; Carriage Group, P.O. Box 2394, Lake Oswego, OR 97033; 1-800-344-9375; $12.45, postage paid).

Theater Wardrobe Keeper

Apply directly to performing arts groups and theater companies in your area. Use *Stern's Performing Arts Directory* (annual; D.M., Inc.) to locate them. You may find both movie theaters and drama companies listed together under "Theatres" in the yellow pages of your telephone directory. Look for names like Community Experimental Repertory Theatre Company or County Players, and apply directly to them.

SALES AND MARKETING

For job opportunities in all areas of sales and marketing, apply directly to employers listed in the "Marketing and Sales" section of the latest edition of *Peterson's Business and Management Jobs* (annual; Peterson's Guides; 1-800-338-3232).

Marketing, Advertising, or Public Relations Manager

To locate job openings, monitor trade magazines such as *Sales and Marketing Management* (633 Third Ave., New York, NY 10017; 1-212-986-4800) or *Marketing Times* (Sales and Marketing Executives International, 330 W. 42nd St., New York, NY 10017; 1-212-239-1919).

Market Research Analyst

For information about careers and salaries in market research, write to the American Marketing Association (250 S. Wacker Dr., Chicago, IL 60601) or the Marketing Research Association (111 E. Wacker Dr., Suite 600, Chicago, IL 60601).

For information about finding and applying for jobs with the federal government, see Public Service, page 295.

Sales Manager

Contact the National Network of Women in Sales (P.O. Box 95269, Schaumburg, IL 60195; 1-312-577-1944) or Professional Salespersons of America (100 Marie Circle, NW, Albuquerque, NM 87114; 1-505-898-9511) for information about their services to members.

For information about the growing business of automotive recycling, contact the Automotive Dismantlers and Recyclers of America, 1000 Vermont Ave., NW #1200, Washington, DC 20005.

Sales Representatives/Agents

For information on sales and marketing educational programs, contact Distributive Education Clubs of America, 1908 Association Dr., Reston, VA 22091.

For job opportunites, monitor trade magazines such as *Agency Sales Magazine* (Manufacturers' Agents National Association, P.O. Box 3467, Laguna Hills, CA 92654; 1-714-859-4040) and *The Marketing News* (American Marketing Association, 250 S. Wacker Dr., Chicago, IL 60606; 1-312-993-9504).

For information about companies that employ sales representatives and agents in your area, see the Job Bank publications available from Bob Adams, Inc., 840 Summer St., Boston, MA 02127; 1-800-USA-JOBS or 1-617-268-9570 in Massachusetts. Each volume covers the employers in one metropolitan area and sells for $12.95.

For job opportunities selling promotional items, apply directly to companies listed under "Advertising Specialties" in the yellow pages of your telephone directory. A job placement service is available to members of the Promotion Industry Club, P.O. Box 5243, Palatine, IL 60078; 1-312-666-1178.

For detailed information about a few top employers, see Michael David Harkavy, *The One Hundred Best Companies to Sell For* (John Wiley, 605 Third Ave., New York, NY 10158-0012; $19.95), which is available in larger or business-oriented libraries.

To locate companies that employ manufacturers' representatives where you can apply for work, see the current *MacRaes' Blue Book, Moody's Industrial Manual,* the *Thomas Register of American Manufacturers,* or the *U.S. Directory of Manufacturers.*

For more information, see Leigh and Sureleigh Silliphant, *Making $70,000 a Year as a Self-Employed Manufacturers Representative* (1988; Ten Speed Press, P.O. Box 7123, Berkeley, CA 94707; 1-800-841-2665).

Appraiser

For information about work as an appraiser of personal property and a free catalog of training courses, contact the American Society of Appraisers, P.O. Box 17265, Washington, DC 20041; 1-800-278-8258.

For information and training to be a business appraiser, contact the Institute of Business Appraisers, Inc., P.O. Box 1447, Boynton Beach, FL 33425; 1-407-732-3202.

For information about work as a real estate appraiser, see Real Estate and Insurance, page 307.

RETAILING

Retail Sales and Customer Service

For any job in retailing, monitor classified advertising in your local newspapers. Visit the state job service office in your area and apply directly to local businesses.

To locate retail stores in a new area consult the *Directory of Consumer Electronics, Photography, and Major Appliance Retailers and Distributors,* the *Directory of Department Stores,* and the *Directory of General Merchandise/Variety Chains and Specialty Stores* and apply directly to the stores listed there. These books are used by wholesalers in their businesses but are usually available for use in libraries of colleges that teach business and merchandising courses.

Sales Merchandiser

For work preparing stores for manfuacturers' promotions, setting up displays, and restocking them in your area, monitor classified advertising in your local newspaper for openings or apply to Powerforce, 79 Fifth Ave., New York, NY; 1-800-443-7239 or 1-800-521-2142 in New York.

Retail Sales Solicitor

For job opportunities, monitor the classified advertising in your local newspaper.

For more information, see Shirley Hutton and Constance Deswann, *Pay Yourself What You're Worth: How to Make Terrific Money in Direct Sales* (Bantam, 1988). Hutton is national sales director for Mary Kay Cosmetics.

Storekeeper

For job opportunities as a store manager or department manager, monitor classified advertising in local newspapers and apply directly to stores in your area.

For information about opening and running a store, see Ruth Pittman, *Small Store Success* (Bob Adams, Inc., 1990).

For information about going into the antiques business, see William C. Ketchum, *How to Make a Living in Antiques* (Henry Holt & Co., 1990).

Many books are available to help those who wish to buy and sell dolls. Free catalogs or price lists are available from Hobby House Press, Inc. (900 Frederick St., Cumberland, MD 21502; 1-301-759-3770), Wallace-Homestead (201 King of Prussia Road, Radnor, PA 19089; 1-800-345-1214), and R. Shoemaker (1141 Orange Ave., Menlo Park, CA 94025; 1-415-854-5768).

For information about their services to members, contact the American Stamp Dealers Association, 3 School St., Suite 201, Glen Cove, NY 11542; 1-516-759-7000.

Write to the American Philatelic Society Summer Seminar, P.O. Box 8000, State College, PA 16803, for information about their courses.

For information about correspondence courses for coin dealers, contact the American Numismatic Association, 818 N. Cascade Ave., Colorado Springs, CO 80903; 1-719-632-2646. For more information, see Q. David Bowers, *How to be a Successful Coin Dealer* (1988; Bowers & Merena, Box 1224, Wolfeboro, NH 03894; 1-603-569-5095).

For information about bookselling, see A. G. Gersdorf, *Selling Used Books by Mail* (1990; Spoon River Press, 2319-C West Rohmann, Peoria, IL 61604-5072; 1-309-672-2665; $9.50 plus $1.75 postage). Also ask for a free catalog of other books for book dealers from the Spoon River Press.

For information about starting and running a mail-order business, see William Bond, *Home Based Mail Order: A Successful Guide for Entrepreneurs* (1989; TAB Books, Inc., Blue Ridge Summit, PA 17214), or John Kramer, *Mail Order Selling Made Easier* (Ad-Lib, P.O. Box 1102, Fairfield, IA 52556; 1-800-669-0773).

For information about starting your own business or buying a franchise, see Your Own Business, page 322.

Modeling

Write to the World Modeling Association, P.O. Box 100, Croton-on-Hudson, NY 10520, for information about their services to members and the new magazine *World of Modeling Publication.* Past articles have included information on large-size and petite modeling as well as the job of modeling for clothing manufacturers as a size model.

Consult Vik Orenstein, *How to Break into Modeling* (Writers Digest Books, 1987).

For information about training, agents, and acting in commercials, see The Visual and Performing Arts, page 305.

THE OUTDOORS

Petroleum Careers

For advertisements of job openings, consult *Butane Propane News, LP-Gas News, National Petroleum News,* and the *Oil and Gas Journal.* If your library does not subscribe to any of these, perhaps you could ask to see issues at the office of your nearest gas or oil distributor.

A good source of job openings is the local chapter of a trade organization or professional society. For information, contact the Association of Oil Pipe Lines (1725 K St., NW, Washington, DC 20006), the American Petroleum Institute (1220 L St., NW, Washington, DC 20005), or the American Gas Association (1515 Wilson Blvd., Arlington, VA 22209).

Forester or Conservation Worker

The Forest Service, an agency of the Department of Agriculture, runs the Forestry Products Research Laboratory at Madison, Wisconsin, and eight regional centers where research is done on problems associated with forestry. For information on applying for jobs with the Forest Service, see Public Service, page 296.

For information about applying for jobs with the National Park Service, see Public Service, page 295.

Work in Agriculture

For information about certification as an accredited farm manager, write to the American Society of Farm Managers and Rural Appraisers, 950 S. Cherry St., Suite 106, Denver, CO 80222.

For information about becoming a master gardener, contact the Cooperative Extension Service in your area. The fifty hours of training are developed by the local extension agent in response to local needs and may be good preparation for employment at nurseries, in grounds maintenance, or landscaping. After training, the individual is expected to give back some hours of volunteer service to the community. The organization that has been formed to link the master gardeners in all states is MaGIC, 2904 Cameron Mills Rd., Alexandria, VA 22302.

For work in a plant nursery, apply directly to businesses listed under "Nurserymen" in the yellow pages of your telephone directory.

For job opportunities in agriculture, apply directly to businesses listed under "Farms" in the yellow pages of your telephone directory. Other employers of agricultural workers may be listed under "Fruit & Vegetable Growers & Shippers," "Fruits & Vegetables — Whol.," or "Orchards." Monitor classified ads in your local newspapers for seasonal employment.

There are organized groups of hobbyists and professional growers for many specialty plants; roses, day lilies, rhododendrons, and many others. To locate a society that specializes in the plant that interests you, consult the annual *Encyclopedia of Associations* in the reference section of your library.

Christmas Tree Farm Owner

For advice on starting a tree farm in your area, sources for seedlings, and information about services, call the U.S. Department of Agriculture's Cooperative Extension Service office, in the government pages of your local telephone directory. If you wish to buy an established tree farm, they will be able to help you locate the farms in your area if they are not listed under "Christmas Trees" in the yellow pages of your telephone directory.

For more information, consult Lewis Hill, *Christmas Trees: Growing and Selling Trees, Wreaths, and Greens* (1989; Storey Communications Inc., available from Harper & Row, Keystone Industrial Park, Scranton, PA 18512; 1-800-242-7737).

Volunteer

For information about finding a volunteer job that gets you outdoors, see "Shopping for a Volunteer Job," page 63.

PRODUCTION

People new to production work may locate schools teaching the needed skills by using the *American Trade Schools Directory,* the *Chronicle Vocational School Manual,* the *Technical, Trade and Business School Data Handbook,* or another trade school directory.

The Career College Association (P.O. Box 2006, Annapolis Junction, MD 20007-2006; 1-202-333-1021) is preparing a new directory of approved private career colleges and schools similar to those issued by its predecessor organizations, the National Association of Trade and Technical Schools (NATTS) and the Association of Independent Colleges and Schools (AICS). Write for its pamphlets, *College Plus* and *Career Short Cuts.*

For information about apprenticeships see Housing and Construction, page 315.

Industrial Production Manager or Foreman

For volunteer work giving technical assistance to small businesses in developing countries, contact the International Executive Service Corps (IESC), 8 Stamford Forum, P.O. Box 10005, Stamford, CT 06904-2005; 1-203-967-6000. When a match is made between a business and a volunteer the overseas assignment lasts two to three months. Travel and living expenses are paid by IESC.

Motor Vehicle Repair

For information about becoming an Automotive Service Excellence (ASE) certified mechanic, write to the National Institute for Automotive Service Excellence, 13505 Dulles Technology Dr., Herndon, VA 22071-3415. To find out if a school in your area has been certified by the National Institute for Automotive Technicians Education Foundation, write to them at the same address.

For more information on starting your own business in auto repair, customizing, or bodywork on current or classic cars, see Your Own Business, page 322.

Home Appliance and Power Tool Repair

For information about training and work repairing appliances and power tools, contact the Appliance Service News, P.O. Box 789, Lombard, IL 60148.

Heating, Air Conditioning, and Refrigeration Mechanic

For information about career opportunities and training, write to the National Association of Plumbing, Heating, and Cooling Contractors, P.O. Box 6808, Falls Church, VA 22046.

Make, Sell, or Teach a Handicraft

If you feel that you are interested in a craft career but are still not sure which craft to pursue, take some time to look through the craft books at your library, visit a craft supply store, and visit a craft show to see finished work.

For complete information on setting up any kind of craft business, read Barbara Brabec, *Creative Cash* (1991; Aames-Allen Publishing Company, 1106 Main St., Huntington Beach, CA 92648; 1-714-536-4926; $12.95).

A number of schools now offer marketing, management, and finance courses that are specifically directed toward professional craftspeople who plan to market their own work. Some of these schools are listed in *The College Blue Book* (annual; Macmillan) under "Crafts," and in the trade school directories listed on page 335.

For opportunities to teach a craft, begin making personal contact with craft shops, community organizations, tourist attractions that offer demonstrations, and school systems that offer adult education. It is also possible to offer private lessons or to write instruction books (see The Word Business, page 303).

To identify craft shows where you can sell your crafts, subscribe to one or more craft magazines that are related to your particular field. The American Craft Council prints a list of shows that are running throughout the country in their magazine. For membership information, contact the American Craft Council, 401 Park Ave. S., New York, NY 10016; 1-212-696-0710. For markets in the far west, see *West Coast Craft Fair Guide* (by subscription; Box 5508, Mill Valley, CA 94942; 1-415-924-3259).

To find a craft guild that supports your hobby, see the annual *Encyclopedia of Associations* at your local library.

Watchmaker

For information about their home study course, contact the American Watchmakers Institute, 3700 Harrison Ave., Cincinnati, OH 45211; 1-513-661-3838. They offer certification for master watch- and clockmakers and have a placement service for their members.

Musical Instrument Repairer and Tuner

Piano tuners may apprentice with an experienced piano tuner, take a correspondence course, or buy a tuning meter and instruction book and study on their own, or a combination of all three. For information, contact the Piano Technicians Guild, 4510 Belleview, Suite 100, Kansas City, MO 64111; 1-816-753-7747.

Locksmith

For names of schools for locksmiths and information about services to members, contact the Associated Locksmiths of America, 3003 Live Oak St., Dallas, TX 75204; 1-214-827-1701.

Jeweler or Silversmith

For information about job opportunities and training programs, contact Jewelers of America, Time-Life Building, 1271 Avenue of the Americas, Suite 650, New York, NY 10020.

To start your own small jewelry business, see one of the many jewelry-making books available at libraries; one is Stefany Tomalin, *Make Your Own Unique Jewelry* (1989; Sterling, 387 Park Ave., New York, NY 10016-8810; 1-800-367-9692). Also see Your Own Business, page 322.

Woodworker

For job opportunities in woodworking, contact local furniture manufacturing or cabinetmaking firms, lumber dealers, and the state job service office in your area.

To start your own woodworking business, see *Woodworkers Thirty-Nine Sure-Fire Projects* (TAB Books, 1989) or *Weekend Wood Projects* (Goodheart, 1989). See Your Own Business, page 322.

Bookbinder

For information about doing custom bookbinding at home, see Pauline Johnson, *Creative Bookbinding* (1990; Dover Books, 31 E. 2nd St., Mineola, NY 11501; 1-516-294-7000). Ask your librarian for other books and for information about courses in bookbinding and paper conservation offered by colleges or library associations.

Quilt Maker

If you are interested in quilting, contact the National Quilting Association, P.O. Box 393, Ellicott City, MD 21043; 1-301-461-5733, for information on the educational seminars, teacher certification, and other special services they offer to members.

Golf Club Repair

For complete instructions on golf club repair and manufacturing, see *The Hobby of Golf Clubmaking* (Golfsmith Custom Golf Clubs, Inc., 10206 N. IH-35, Austin, TX 78753-9982; 1-800-456-3344; they also sell kits and parts for making golf clubs).

Doll Making and Repair

For instructions and patterns for making dolls, doll clothes, or teddy bears, contact Hobby House Press, Inc., 900 Frederick Street, Cumberland, MD 21502; 1-301-759-3770 for their free catalog of books, including Jodie Davis, *Easy to Make Cloth Dolls and All the Trimmings* (Williamson, 1990), and Sheila Lile, *Dressing the All-American Teddy Bear* (Hobby House, 1987).

TRANSPORTATION

Licenses

Licensing requirements for chauffeurs, truck drivers and bus operators vary by state. For information about driver's licenses in all states for all vehicles, consult current *Driver License Administration Requirements and Fees* (U.S. Department of Transportation), at your library or local department of motor vehicles.

To meet federal standards, as of April 1, 1992, each state must carry out the new Commerical Driver License (CDL) program. This includes tests of knowledge and driving skills. The CDL program will apply to all drivers of large trucks, drivers who transport hazardous materials, and drivers of vehicles carrying fifteen or more persons. Qualification include good health, good hearing, vision of at least 20/40, and normal use of arms and legs. For more information call 1-800-CDL-INFO.

Dispatcher

For job opportunities as a disptcher, apply directly to businesses listed in the yellow pages of your telephone directory under "Messenger Svce.," "Taxicab Svce.," and "Trucking," and check with companies in your area that have radio trucks for emergency services, such as plumbing companies, towing services, and tree removal businesses.

For work as a medical dispatcher for a hospital or ambulance company, see The Health Business, page 309.

Heavy Truck Driver

For informational booklets, *Careers in Truckdriving, What to Look for in a Truck Driver Training School,* and *The Commercial Driver License Program,* write to the Office of Public Affairs, American Trucking Association, Inc., 2200 Mill Rd., Alexandria, VA 22314.

For the *Checklist of Quality Programs in Tractor Trailer Driver Training* ($4.00) and a free list of certified tractor-trailer driver training programs, write to the Professional Truck Driver Institute of America, 8788 Elk Grove Blvd., Suite M, Elk Grove, CA 95624.

Light Truck Driver

For work as a light truck driver, apply directly to businesses listed under "Delivery Svce.," "Messenger Svce.," or "Trucking" in the yellow pages of your telephone directory and monitor classified ads in your local newspaper.

For more information about light trucking, see Don Lilly, *How to Earn Fifteen Dollars to Fifty Dollars and More with a Pick-Up or Van* (1987; Darian Books, P.O. Box 3091, Glendale, AZ 85311; 1-602-843-8212).

Charter or City Bus Driver

For work as a charter or local transit bus driver, apply directly to companies listed under "Buses — Charter & Rental" in the yellow pages of your telephone directory. Transit systems may be listed under "Bus Lines."

School Bus Driver

Contact your local school districts to find out if school bus drivers in your area are employed by the school district itself or by a company under contract to the school district. These companies are listed under "Bus Lines" in the yellow pages of the telephone directory.

Taxi Driver

Contact companies listed under "Taxicab Svce." in your telephone directory for information about job opportunities in your area.

Chauffeur

Apply to companies listed under "Limousine Svce." in the yellow pages of your telephone directory. There may also be job opportunities with funeral homes, public relations firms, other businesses, and individuals.

Automobile Transporter

Contact companies listed in the yellow pages of your telephone directory under "Automobile Transporters & Driveaway Companies." Very few use drivers to deliver single cars. The basic requirements of A-1 Auto Movers (1-800-876-1166 or 1-800-879-0099) are typical: drivers must be responsible, over 21, and have a valid driver's license. Drivers fill out an application, have their fingerprints taken, and put down a security deposit that is returned to them after the car is safely delivered. The driver pays for gas, food, and lodging on the trip. The procedure at All America Auto Transport (1-800-227-7447) is basically the same, but they require references.

Route Salesman

Apply to companies listed under "Vending Machines" in the yellow pages of your telephone directory and monitor classified ads in your local newspapers.

Water Vessel Pilot

Write to U.S. Coast Guard, Captain of the Port Office, Customhouse, New Orleans, LA 70130, for license requirements on oceangoing, coastwise, and river vessels.

Aircraft Pilot

There are four basic license ratings for aircraft pilots: student, private, commercial, and air transport. For information about the requirements for each, contact the Federal Aviation Administration, Public Information Center, APA-200, 800 Independence Ave., SW, Washington, DC 20591.

The major airlines require their pilots to have a commercial license with instrument rating and to get and keep an FAA first-class physical certificate from an aviation medical examiner. These airlines currently require aircraft captains to hold an air transport license, and all have set retirement ages.

For a free brochure containing descriptions of airline jobs and a list of employers, request *The People of the Airlines* from the Air Transport Association of America, 1709 New York Ave., NW, Washington, DC 20006-5206.

Consult Alexander C. Morton, *Official Guide to Airline Careers* (Simon & Schuster; call 1-800-223-2348 for information).

Anyone can pay dues and become an associate member of the Air Line Employees Association, 5600 S. Central Ave., Chicago, IL 60638-3797. Members receive job bulletins, information on training schools, travel discounts, a magazine, and a newsletter. Write for details.

Companies other than the major airlines generally do not have as strict requirements. However, a commerical pilot's license is required, and companies prefer applicants with experience in the type of plane they would be flying.

For a job as a commercial pilot, monitor employment ads in aviation trade magazines such as *Air Jobs Digest, Airport Press, Airport Services Magazine,* or *Air Transport World*. If the libraries in your area do not subscribe to any of these magazines, you might ask to see them at an airport.

For information about working as an aerial spray applicator and a list of certified pilot schools, write to the National Agricultural Aviation Association, 115 D St., SE, Suite 103, Washington, DC 20003.

Air Traffic Controller

Most control towers at small airports (under 110,000 combined landings and takeoffs annually) are run by private companies. Contact the airport for information.

Request the Air Traffic Controller Announcement from the U.S. Office of Personnel Management Job Information Center, Washington, DC 20415, or from the office that serves your state (See Public Service, page 294). At this time applicants over thirty years of age are eligible for positions at flight service stations but not for airport tower and enroute center positions.

Railroad Worker

Engineers are required to have at least one year of railroad experience and to pass tests on train handling and service rules. Engineer's assistants (firemen) ride with the engineer and help him perform his duties. Conductors are usually promoted from the entry-level positions of brake operator or switch operator.

For job opportunities, apply directly to local railroad companies or at the state job service office in your area.

For a free pamphlet about railroad careers, write to the Association of American Railroads, Office of Information and Public Affairs, 50 F St., NW, Washington, DC 20001.

BIBLIOGRAPHY

ADEA Guidebook (AARP, Worker Equity Department, 1987).

Banning, Kent, and Ardelle Friday, *How to Change Your Career* (VGM Career Horizons, 1990).

Birsner, E. Patricia, *The 40 + Job Hunting Guide* (Simon & Schuster, 1987).

Bolles, Richard N., *The Three Boxes of Life and How to Get Out of Them* (Ten Speed Press, 1978).

———. *What Color Is Your Parachute? A Practical Manual for Job-Hunters & Career Changers* (Ten Speed Press, 1991).

——— and J. Crystal, *Where Do I Go From Here With My Life?* (Ten Speed Press, 1974).

Hyatt, Carol, *Shifting Gears: How to Master Career Change and Find the Work That's Right for You* (Simon & Schuster, 1990).

Lathrop, Richard, *Who's Hiring Who?* (Ten Speed Press, 1989).

McWhirter, Darien A., *Your Rights at Work* (J. Wiley, 1989).

Occupational Outlook Handbook (U.S. Department of Labor, 1990).

Palder, Edward L., *The Retirement Sourcebook* (Woodbine House, 1989).

Parker, Yana, *The Damn Good Resume Guide* (Ten Speed Press, 1989).

Ray, Samuel M., *Job Hunting After 50: Strategies For Success* (J. Wiley, 1991).

INDEX